THE TREASURY OF

FLOWERS AND PLANTS

IN COLOUR

Two of the most popular books on the recognition, selection and cultivation of flowers are here offered bound in one volume. They are Flowers in Colour *and* Garden Plants in Colour—*both with text by A. G. L. Hellyer and reproductions from water colours by Cynthia Newsome-Taylor plus a wealth of line drawings*

SPRING BOOKS

FIRST PUBLISHED IN GREAT BRITAIN IN ONE VOLUME IN 1961 BY

W.H. & L. Collingridge Limited
This edition published in 1989 by Spring Books
An imprint of Octopus Publishing Group PLC
Michelin House
81 Fulham Road
London SW3 6RB
© *A.G.L. Hellyer 1955*
ISBN 0 600 56284 0
Printed in Yugoslavia

FLOWERS
IN COLOUR

an Amateur Gardening encyclopaedia

BY A. G. L. HELLYER, F.L.S

illustrated from watercolour drawings

BY CYNTHIA NEWSOME-TAYLOR

and from wood engravings

BY J.D.C.SOWERBY, F.L.S

FOREWORD

This book differs from many gardening encyclopaedias in that I have made no attempt to cover all the plants that are known in gardens. Instead I have chosen only those that are the best and most commonly grown in this country in the hope that this will enable many gardeners to acquire a better knowledge of more familiar and important plants. What has guided me throughout in its preparation is the belief that illustration is often more helpful than description when trying to familiarize gardeners with the varied and beautiful flowers that are now available to them. For this reason I have included one coloured picture of a typical species (kind) of each genus (group) I have mentioned and at least one illustration in line. In achieving this I have made use of the work of two artists, one living and the other long dead. Miss Cynthia Newsome-Taylor, who has prepared all the original paintings from which the coloured illustrations have been made, has worked in the closest association with me over a period of two years. Every painting has been done from living material. First she prepared hundreds of sketches in which she set down all the essential characteristics of the plant while it was still fresh, and then from these she made the final composite paintings in which all this miscellaneous material was assembled alphabetically. Both the artist and I have had a great deal of invaluable collaboration from other people, notably from Mr W. M. Campbell, the Curator of the Royal Botanic Gardens, Kew, from which most of the specimens were obtained.

For most of the line illustrations I went to a source which many people have forgotten, J. C. Loudon's *Encyclopaedia of Plants*, first published in 1829 and enlarged by supplements in 1841 and 1855. For this over 20,000 drawings were made by James de Carle Sowerby (1787-1871) the eldest son of James Sowerby (1757-1822) whose beautifully hand-coloured *Botany of British Plants* is still eagerly sought by collectors. Never before had so many species of garden plants been illustrated in a single volume. As Loudon stated in his preface of 1829, J. D. C. Sowerby, assisted by Mr David Don (librarian to the Linnean Society) and Messrs Loddiges, sought out the figures, dried specimens, or living plants, necessary for illustration, and made drawings of them on the blocks to be engraved, in that accurate and scientific manner and that appropriate taste for which his late father was so distinguished. One of the most expert wood-engravers of the day, Robert Branston, then cut the blocks. Their preparation occupied Sowerby for upwards of seven years. Loudon, an economical Scot, crammed his encyclopaedia almost indigestibly with information and Sowerby had to make his figures as small as possible so that from four to twenty could be fitted on to the same page as the corresponding text. For my book they have been enlarged about one and a half times, but such was the skill of both artist and engraver in preparing the minute originals that they actually gain by this enlargement.

Of course, in this book I have only used a very small proportion of the illustrations in Loudon's encyclopaedia. In making a selection I have taken those that seemed to me to be most typical of the genus they represent or to add most useful pictorial information to Miss Newsome-Taylor's paintings. They do not always depict the precise species I have described in my text, for here I have been guided rather by what is most readily available today or most

5

likely to be seen in gardens, but each of the plants illustrated is a desirable kind which is in cultivation, though not necessarily commercially popular.

The cultural notes I have prepared are inevitably very brief, but not more so than in most encyclopaedic books. For more detailed information the reader is referred to specialist works and this is particularly necessary with highly developed garden plants with rather complicated cultural requirements such as the rose, chrysanthemum and dahlia.

The nomenclature is botanical, but I have also included popular names wherever possible, including some which are not, perhaps, very familiar in this country but in my view might well be used. The American name Silk Tassel Bush for *Garrya elliptica* is an example, for it is most descriptive of the long, greenish-yellow winter catkins of that beautiful evergreen shrub. Most of the botanical names are those used in *Sanders' Encyclopaedia of Gardening* which I revised a few years ago, but sometimes I have kept to what I call the 'popular' botanical names to avoid confusion. Montbretia instead of Crocosmia, and Gloxinia instead of Sinningia are examples. I hope that even purists will agree that this is a sensible departure from strictly scientific nomenclature in what, after all, is meant to be a popular book with a particular appeal to the beginner and the unlearned.

For the benefit of readers who know the popular but not the botanical name of a particular plant I have included a comprehensive index of popular names with the appropriate cross-references. In this index I have also included some outdated botanical names which are still commonly used in nursery catalogues and are often the only reference to the plant which the gardener possesses. I hope that this system of arrangement will make the book easy to use by both the beginner and the expert.

In closing I want to thank a number of people for their help; Mr W. T. Stearn for detailed notes about Loudon and the Sowerbys from which I have quoted in this foreword; all the Assistant Curators at Kew for the generous way in which they have assisted me in finding suitable specimens, and Dr H. R. Fletcher, lately Director of the Royal Horticultural Society's gardens, Wisley, for making the great resources of that garden equally available. Without this help it would have been quite impossible to complete this book in so comparatively short a time.

Rowfant, 1955   A.G.L.HELLYER

THE PLATES

PLATE EIGHT
facing page 45

Dahlia (medium decorative) — Daphne Burkwoodii — Delphinium elatum (garden form) — Deutzia scabra — Dianthus plumarius (garden form) — Dianthus barbatus — Dicentra formosa — Dictamnus albus — Digitalis purpurea — Dimorphotheca aurantiaca — Dodecatheon Meadia — Doronicum plantagineum

PLATE NINE
facing page 48

Eccremocarpus scaber — Echinacea purpurea — Echinops bannaticus — Epimedium versicolor sulphureum — Eremurus himalaicus — Erica carnea — Erodium Manescavii — Eryngium planum — Erysimum Allionii — Escallonia langleyensis — Eschscholtzia californica — Euonymus europaeus — Felicia tenella

PLATE TEN
facing page 49

Forsythia intermedia spectabilis — Freesia refracta (garden form) — Fritillaria gracilis — Fuchsia 'Royal Purple' — Gaillardia aristata (garden form) — Galanthus nivalis — Galega officinalis — Gardenia jasminoides — Garrya elliptica — Gazania (garden forms) — Genista aethnensis — Gentiana septemfida — Geranium grandiflorum

PLATE ELEVEN
facing page 64

Gerbera Jamesonii — Geum coccineum (garden form) — Gladiolus (garden form) — Globularia cordifolia — Gloxinia (garden form) — Godetia amoena Schaminii — Gypsophila elegans — Hamamelis mollis — Helenium autumnale (garden form) — Helianthemum nummularium — Helianthus decapetalus multiflorus — Helichrysum bracteatum — Heliopsis scabra

PLATE TWELVE
facing page 65

Heliotropium arborescens — Helleborus niger — Hemerocallis (garden form) — Heuchera sanguinea (garden form) — Hibiscus syriacus — Hippeastrum (garden form) — Hosta lancifolia — Hoya carnosa — Hyacinthus orientalis — Hydrangea macrophylla Hortensia — Hypericum calycinum — Iberis sempervirens — Impatiens Sultanii

PLATE THIRTEEN
facing page 68

Incarvillea Delavayi — Ipomoea Leari — Iris siberica — Ixia hybrida — Jasminum nudiflorum — Kalanchoë Blossfeldiana — Kalmia latifolia — Kerria japonica — Kniphofia Uvaria nobilis — Laburnum vulgare — Lamium maculatum — Lantana Camara — Lapageria rosea

PLATE FOURTEEN
facing page 69

Lathyrus odoratus — Lavandula Spica — Lavatera trimestris — Leontopodium alpinum — Leptosyne maritima — Leucojum autumnale — Lewisia Tweedyi — Leycesteria formosa — Liatris spicata — Lilium candidum — Lilium speciosum rubrum — Limonium sinuatum

PLATE FIFTEEN
facing page 76

Linaria purpurea (garden form) — Linum narbonense — Lithospermum prostratum — Lobelia cardinalis — Lobelia tenuior — Lonicera Periclymenum — Lupinus polyphyllus (garden form) — Lychnis chalcedonica — Lysimachia vulgaris — Lythrum Salicaria — Magnolia Soulangeana — Mahonia Aquifolium — Malcolmia maritima

*Abutilon
venosum*

*Abutilon
integerrimum*

*Acacia armata
angustifolia*

*Acacia
verticillata*

FLOWERS IN COLOUR

ABUTILON *(Chinese Bellflower, Flowering Maple)*

All the important garden abutilons are shrubs, and all are either definitely tender, requiring protection in winter from all frost, or else are on the border-line of hardiness, thriving outdoors in sheltered places but liable to be destroyed by unusually severe weather. Some kinds are popular pot plants and some are much used for bedding out in summer, especially in the more elaborate schemes found in some public parks. All can be grown in any well-drained soil and can be increased by cuttings of firm shoots rooted in sandy soil in a close frame at practically any time, preferably in early autumn. Plants can be pruned to shape in spring.

The hardiest species is *A. vitifolium*, a big loose bush with grey-green leaves and soft mauve flowers in May. It makes a beautiful specimen in a warm sheltered place outdoors. Very striking is the sprawling *A. megapotamicum* with drooping red and yellow flowers in summer. It may be trained against a sunny wall outdoors or be grown as a cool greenhouse plant. The abutilons used for summer beddings are mostly hybrids with drooping bell shaped flowers and handsome lobed leaves. Very popular is *A. striatum Thompsonii*, with green leaves heavily mottled with yellow.

ACACIA *(Mimosa, Wattle)*

These are the shrubs or trees commonly known as mimosas though botanically that name belongs to quite a different plant. The common 'mimosa' of florist's shops with its fernlike leaves and fluffy yellow pompon flowers is *A. dealbata* which is just hardy enough to grow outdoors in some very mild parts of the country but must normally be treated as a greenhouse shrub. It will eventually make a fairly large tree if permitted to do so but can be kept far smaller by judicious pruning after flowering. There are a great many other species, mostly, like *A. dealbata*, natives of Australia where they are popularly known as wattles. The most popular as garden plants are *A. armata* with rounded phyllodes (flattened stems) instead of leaves and the typical yellow pompon flowers carried along the length of the branches; *A. decurrens* which is very like *A. dealbata* except that its foliage is green instead of grey; *A. Drummondii* with the yellow flowers crowded together in cylindrical spikes, and *A. longifolia* with loose spikes of yellow flowers and long narrow phyllodes.

All thrive in warm sunny places and rather light, well-drained soils. In greenhouses they may be grown in large pots but are really happier planted in a border. The most satisfactory way of increasing them is by seed sown in a warm greenhouse as soon as ripe (usually in late spring). Cuttings of half ripe shoots will root in summer in a close frame.

ACANTHUS *(Bear's Breech)*

Herbaceous plants with very handsome, thistle-like leaves and stiff, erect spikes of broadly tube shaped flowers which are

10

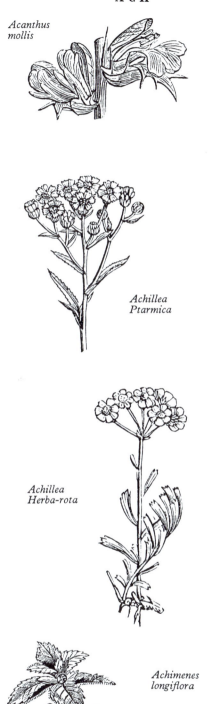

Acanthus
mollis

Achillea
Ptarmica

Achillea
Herba-rota

Achimenes
longiflora

usually dull rose or purple and white. The effect is subdued but distinctive and the cut flower stems keep their colour for a long time and make good winter decorations. All flower in summer. These attractive plants are not in the least fussy about soil and will thrive in full sun or partial shade. They can be increased from seed sown in a frame in spring but usually sufficient plants for all requirements can be obtained by carefully dividing old roots in spring. The two best species are *A. mollis* with 3-foot flower spikes and broad lobed leaves, and *A. spinosus*, similar in height, but with much more deeply and finely cut leaves, which are spiny.

ACHILLEA *(Milfoil, Yarrow)*

A big family of hardy perennials very easily grown in practically any kind of soil and reasonably open situation. They can be increased by dividing the roots in spring or autumn and can also be raised from seed sown in a frame or greenhouse in spring.

Achilleas may be roughly divided into two groups, the taller kinds, most suitable for herbaceous borders, and the dwarf and spreading kinds for rock gardens or walls. Of the former one of the best is *Achillea filipendulina* (sometimes known as *A. Eupatorium*). Four or five feet tall, it produces in July and August, nearly flat, plate-like heads of yellow flowers. Not unlike this but much smaller is *A. taygetea* with finely divided silvery leaves and lemon yellow flower heads on 2-foot stems in June and July. Another good border plant is *A. Ptarmica*, best known in its double flowered form, The Pearl, a fine plant for cutting. About 2 feet high, it bears small, almost globular pure white flowers, in small clusters, from June to August.

A fourth herbaceous species is *A. millefolium* in either of its brightly carmine coloured varieties, *Kelwayi* or Cerise Queen.

Perhaps the best of the dwarf kinds is the hybrid King Edward VII, with small heads of sulphur yellow flowers produced continuously from June to September. *A. tomentosa* is a little coarser and bright yellow rather than sulphur. A refined hybrid of this, with grey leaves and pale yellow flowers, is *A. Lewisii*. Others worth consideration are *A. argentea* and *A. Clavennae*, two similar plants, with white flowers and silvery leaves, and *A. ageratifolia*, also white and silver but more dwarf in habit.

ACHIMENES *(Hot Water Plant)*

These showy greenhouse plants are sometimes known as hot water plants because Victorian gardeners thought that they liked to be watered with hot water. They produce small tubers and it is by new tubers produced as offshoots from the old ones that they can most readily be propagated. Seed may be used but needs a temperature of around 70° to germinate it. Cuttings of the firm young growths may be taken in spring, but a fairly high temperature is needed to ensure root formation.

Tubers are started into growth in sandy soil in shallow seed boxes from January to May. They should be just covered with similar soil and made slightly moist, and afterwards placed in a

11

Achimenes
grandiflora

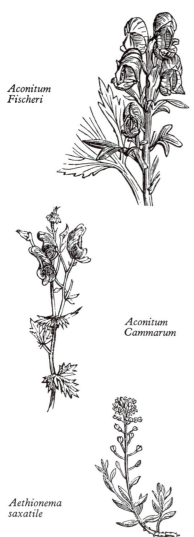

Aconitum
Fischeri

Aconitum
Cammarum

Aethionema
saxatile

temperature of 60–65°. When the young shoots are an inch or so high, the tubers should be transferred to pots in John Innes compost. They may be grown either singly in 3½ or 4–inch pots or several together in larger pots, and as they are trailing in habit, they may be placed in baskets suspended from the greenhouse roof or in their pots at the edge of the greenhouse staging. They will need plenty of water while growing and flowering, which they will do from June to September if batches of tubers are started successionally. After flowering, watering must be decreased until growth dies right down, when the tubers can be shaken out and stored in a dry, frost-proof place until it is time to start them once more.

All the achimenes grown in gardens to-day are unnamed hybrids in a variety of rich colours including blue, purple and red.

ACONITUM (Monkshood, Aconite, but not the Winter Aconite which is Eranthis Hyemalis)

Hardy herbaceous perennials, related to the delphiniums and having a faint resemblance to them when bearing their erect spikes of mainly blue or purple flowers. The individual flowers, however, are hooded and not open as in the delphinium. All like cool, moist soils and thrive in the edges of woods or on shady borders. They can be increased by division of their roots in spring or autumn and can also be raised from seed sown in a greenhouse or frame in the spring.

One of the best species is *A. Napellus* an uncommon British wild plant, well worth a place in the garden. Its 3–foot spikes of bluish-purple flowers are produced in June and July. It has several useful varieties including Sparke's variety a very deep purple. *A. Cammarum bicolor* is white edged with blue. Other worthwhile species are *A. Fischeri*, a good medium blue which flowers in September, and *A. Wilsoni*, said to be a form of *A. Carmichaelii*, a taller plant.

All are poisonous and all resent being transplanted and may take some little time to recover.

AETHIONEMA (Stone Cress)

These are tiny shrubs or half-woody plants for the rock garden or dry wall. They have narrow leaves closely set all along the stems which are terminated by small heads of pink flowers like those of a very neat candytuft. They love sun and good drainage and, though usually seen as quite small plants, perhaps 1 foot high and as much through, will double those dimensions under favourable conditions. All can be most readily raised from seed sown in a frame or unheated greenhouse in spring, but cuttings of firm young shoots will also root readily in sandy soil in a close frame or propagating box in July.

The best kinds are *A. grandiflorum*, light rose pink, *A. pulchellum*, usually rather paler in colour, and *A. warleyense* (Warley Rose), neater and bushier in habit than either of the foregoing and brighter in colour.

AGAPANTHUS *(African Lily)*

The popular African lily, most familiar as a pot or tub plant, bears bright blue, lily-like flowers all the summer. This is *A. umbellatus* which is not quite hardy except in the very mildest parts of Britain, and must, therefore, be given greenhouse protection from October to May. However, a fine form of this plant, named *Mooreanus*, not only has darker blue flowers, but is considerably hardier and can be grown in the open in many parts of the country.

All kinds can be increased by division of the roots in March or by seeds sown in spring in a greenhouse or frame. Under glass very little water should be given in winter, when the plants may be allowed to become almost completely dormant. Outdoors the agapanthus should be given a sunny, well-drained position and watered well in summer if dry.

Agapanthus umbellatus

AGERATUM *(Floss Flower)*

A very attractive little plant with fluffy heads of soft blue flowers. A favourite bedding plant for use as a groundwork beneath taller plants or as an edging, it is almost always treated as a half-hardy annual though it is a perennial and can be kept from year to year provided it is protected from frost. The easiest way of growing ageratum, however, is to sow seed thinly in a warm greenhouse in February or March, prick off the seedlings $1\frac{1}{2}$ inch apart and then harden them off in a frame ready for planting out about 6 inches apart in May when the spring bedding has been cleared away. Ageratum will grow in full sun or partial shade and is not fussy about soil.

Ageratum Houstonianum

ALLIUM *(Onion, Garlic)*

There are several onion species sufficiently decorative in flower to be worth a place in the flower garden. The most familiar is *Allium Moly*, a cheerful plant with heads of buttercup yellow flowers carried on stiff, foot high stems in May. It will grow anywhere, indeed it can become a bit of a weed. Less invasive and far more imposing is *A. Rosenbachianum* with great, globular heads of reddish purple flowers on 4-foot stems in May. *A. Ostrowskianum* has equally large and spherical heads of bloom, much paler in colour and carried on rather stumpy stems. *A. albo-pilosum* has lilac flowers and is otherwise similar to the last, but completely different is *A. descendens* with quite small, compact, egg shaped heads of deep maroon flowers produced in July at the tips of slender stems. *A. pulchellum* is a dainty species with heads of lilac flowers. All can be grown in almost any kind of soil provided they have plenty of sun. They are best increased by dividing the clusters of bulbs in late summer.

Allium descendens

ALSTROEMERIA *(Peruvian Lily)*

Best known of the Peruvian lilies is *A. aurantiaca*, which has small orange flowers, flecked or speckled with black, very freely produced in July and August on 3-foot stems. Its white, ropy

Allium Moly

13

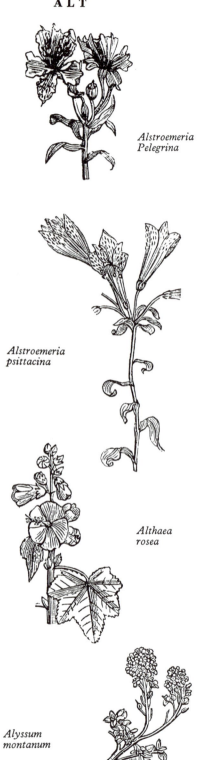

Alstroemeria
Pelegrina

Alstroemeria
psittacina

Althaea
rosea

Alyssum
montanum

roots are sometimes slow to recover after being moved, but once established they spread rapidly. The flowers last well when cut and are much grown for market. Choicer but more difficult is *A. Ligtu*, with large heads of pink flowers in July. Hybrids have been raised from this in many shades of pink, salmon, apricot and flame and these are the best of all to grow. They are very readily raised from seed sown either as soon as ripe in late summer, or in spring, but the seedlings must be handled with care if they are to be established successfully. I find it best to sow thinly in rather deep seed boxes and leave the seedlings undisturbed the first year. In March the fleshy, almost transparent roots can be carefully shaken out and planted 5 inches deep and 3 to 4 feet apart in fairly rich well-drained soil, in a sunny position. They may do little the first year but will spread underground and should come up with increasing vigour each succeeding spring.

A. aurantiaca can be increased from seed, but it is easier to lift and divide the roots in spring, replanting them at least 5 inches deep.

ALTHAEA (Hollyhock)

The hollyhock is so familiar that it needs no introduction. There are few better tall plants for the back of the border and none that will thrive better in poor soil, though they will also respond to more generous culture, particularly the fine double-flowered forms. Though a short-lived perennial like the lupin, it is often more convenient to treat the hollyhock as a biennial, sowing seed outdoors in May to flower the following year. Seedlings should be removed to a nursery bed in July and planted about 6 inches apart to grow into sturdy plants ready for removal in October to their flowering quarters. There are also strains which can be treated as annuals, being sown in a greenhouse in February, hardened off and planted out in May, to flower in summer. Specially desirable forms of the ordinary hollyhock can be increased by root cuttings inserted in sandy soil in winter, thus keeping them true to type.

ALYSSUM (Madwort, Gold Dust)

Two principal kinds of alyssum are grown in gardens, one an annual and the other a perennial. The annual is *A. maritimum*, often known as sweet alyssum because of the honey-like fragrance of its clusters of small white or purple flowers. A dwarf plant very suitable for carpeting beneath taller plants or for use as an edging, it will flower for weeks on end, in early summer if sown in September or March, and in later summer if sown in April or May. Seed should be sown thinly where the plants are to flower and the seedlings thinned to 6 inches apart.

The common perennial species is *A. saxatile*, often known as gold dust because of the abundance of its small golden yellow flowers. A taller and bushier plant than the annual alyssum, with coarser, greyish leaves, it is most suitable for rock gardens or dry walls. It is readily raised from seed which may be sown in a greenhouse or frame in March or outdoors in April or May,

*Amaryllis
Belladonna*

to flower the following year. The variety *citrinum* has lemon yellow flowers, and another named *flore pleno*, with double flowers, is best increased by cuttings struck in a close frame in spring or early summer.

Smaller, neater but less showy are *A. spinosum* with white flowers in early summer and *A. montanum* with yellow flowers. They should be grown in the same way as *A. saxatile*. All like sunny places and well-drained soils but are not difficult.

AMARYLLIS *(Belladonna Lily, Jersey Lily)*

Amaryllis Belladonna is a choice plant which produces its intensely fragrant, rose pink, trumpet shaped flowers in the autumn before the leaves appear. Hardy in a sunny sheltered position, it does very well in most of the southern counties, particularly if planted near the foot of a wall facing south. The bulbs should be planted 4 or 5 inches deep in early autumn and thereafter should be left undisturbed for as long as possible as they re-establish themselves rather slowly. Though it likes light, well-drained soils, it does not appreciate being starved and can be fed from time to time with top dressings of well rotted manure or compost. It can be increased by splitting up the bulb clusters at planting time.

*Amelanchier
vulgaris*

AMELANCHIER *(Snowy Mespilus)*

These are graceful flowering trees of small to medium size, which deserve to be better known. Their small but abundant white flowers are produced in April and May and in the autumn their dying foliage turns a brilliant crimson. The best species, *A. canadensis*, may eventually reach a height of about 25 feet. *A. oblongifolia*, which is very similar, rather smaller but still a tree. By contrast *A. ovalis* (syn. *A. vulgaris*,), seldom exceeds 8 feet in height and is a shrub rather than a tree. None of these requires pruning. They can be increased rather slowly by seed sown in greenhouse or frame in spring, but nurserymen, to save time, often bud or graft them on to mountain ash. Some kinds produce suckers freely and these can be dug up in autumn and planted separately. November is the best planting month. Amelanchiers are not particular about soil.

*Amelanchier
oblongifolia*

ANCHUSA *(Alkanet)*

The most popular of the alkanets, *Anchusa italica*, a hardy perennial, might be described as a very stiff forget-me-not on a vastly increased scale. It grows 4 or 5 feet in height and the individual, bright blue flowers, produced in June, may be an inch in diameter. The garden varieties of this fine plant, differ mainly in the precise shade of their blue. Opal is a light blue, whereas Morning Glory and Dropmore are a deeper blue. All can be increased by root cuttings inserted in winter in sandy soil or by careful division of the roots in March. Seed sown in a frame in March or outdoors in May also germinates readily but there may be some slight variation in the colour of the flowers produced by the seedlings. The perennial alkanets dislike excessively damp soil in

*Anchusa
capensis*

15

Androsace Chamaejasme

Androsace lanuginosa

Anemone coronaria

Anemone apennina

winter and may prove short lived under such conditions.

Another useful species is *A. capensis*, a biennial about 18 inches high with smaller blue flowers. Seed should be sown outdoors in May to produce plants to flower the following year.

ANDROSACE *(Rock Jasmine)*

The androsaces have no resemblance to or connexion with the climbing jasmines. They are tussock-forming or trailing plants suitable for rock gardens and dry walls. Some come from high altitudes and prove difficult in cultivation, only thriving when given the sharpest possible drainage in soil containing an abundant quantity of stone chippings. *A. Chamaejasme*, *A. helvetica* and *A. imbricata* belong to this class. By contrast there are quite easy androsaces such as *A. lanuginosa* and *A. sarmentosa*, which can be grown in any ordinary soil provided it is reasonably well drained. Both have grey-green leaves and small, round pink flowers, but whereas *A. sarmentosa* is compact, forms rosettes and flowers in May, June, *A. lanuginosa* is more trailing and flowers several weeks later. All these can be increased by careful division in spring or by seed sown in spring in very sandy compost in greenhouse or frame.

ANEMONE *(Windflower)*

There are a great many anemones differing so much from one another in appearance that it may seem strange that they should all be grouped in one genus. From the garden standpoint one may broadly distinguish three principal groups; the dwarf, woodland windflowers with small, fragile flowers; the poppy anemones, all sun lovers and excellent for cutting, with cup shaped flowers in brilliant colours and stems a foot to 18 inches in length; and the herbaceous border anemones 2 to 4 feet in height, all good perennials, with a tendency to ramble.

The most familiar woodland kind is the native *A. nemorosa*, a common plant in woods, very pretty with its dainty white flowers on slender stems, but not worth cultivation except in the wild garden. It has, however, a number of good varieties of which *Robinsoniana* with pale blue flowers, is worth using as a carpeting plant beneath shrubs. More popular and more showy are *A. apennina* and *A. blanda*, very similar plants making rapidly spreading clumps of deeply cut, almost ferny leaves from which spring, in March and April, a profusion of delightful blue flowers. There are also white and pink coloured forms but not so beautiful as the common blue. All these will spread rapidly given a reasonably good, leafy soil and a position sheltered from hot sunshine but not too densely shady. They can be propagated by division immediately after flowering.

The poppy anemones are derived from *A. coronaria*, but *A. fulgens*, with scarlet flowers, is a very similar plant which should be grown in the same way. They like a sunny place in fairly good, well drained, but firm soil. Often planted in straight rows in large beds specially for cutting, they may also be grown in the rock garden or towards the front of the herbaceous border. They

Achillea
filipendulina

Aconitum
Cammarum
bicolor

Acacia
armata

Althaea rosea

Allium
descendens

Agapanthus
umbellatus

Achimenes
[garden form]

Acanthus
spinosus

Aethionema
grandiflorum

Istroemeria
aurantiaca

Abutilon
megapotamicum

Ageratum
Houstonianum

Anthemis tinctoria

Arctotis stoechadifolia grandis

Anemone japonica

Anchusa italica

Anthericum Liliago

Amaryllis Belladonna

Armeria maritima

Amelanchier canadensis

Alyssum saxatile

Aquilegia [long-spurred hybrid]

Androsace sarmentosa

Arabis albida flore pleno

Antirrhinum majus

make quite sizeable tubers which may be lifted in late summer and stored in a dry, frost-proof place until the following February or March. This is advisable in very cold or damp places. Propagation is either by dividing the clusters of tubers when they are lifted or by sowing seed outdoors in late May or early June. There are a number of fine strains of the poppy anemone of which St Brigid with double flowers in various shades from purple to scarlet and Du Caen with single flowers in similar colours are the best.

The most familiar herbaceous species is *A. japonica* in its white and pink flowered forms, flowering in August and September. The flowers are 2 to 3 inches across, saucer shaped and carried well above the vine-like leaves. Once established it is capable of taking complete charge of quite a lot of ground, but it dislikes root disturbance and is sometimes slow to start. Roots can be divided or transplanted in spring.

*Anemone
japonica*

ANTHEMIS *(Chamomile, Golden Marguerite)*

The most useful anthemis for the garden is the so-called golden marguerite, *A. tinctoria,* a first rate border plant and a very useful cut flower. It makes a big, bushy plant 2 or 3 feet in height and even more through, with deeply cut, rather ferny leaves and masses of bright yellow daisy flowers carried on long stems during July and August. The varieties differ mainly in the size and precise shade of their flowers. All should be planted in a sunny place in March or April and should not be disturbed in autumn. Propagate by cuttings of firm young shoots inserted during spring or early summer in sandy soil in a frame.

*Anthemis
montana*

ANTHERICUM *(St Bernard's Lily)*

The true St Bernard's Lily, *Anthericum Liliago,* is an attractive hardy herbaceous plant making neat clumps of narrow grassy foliage from which spring in June, foot high stems carrying white, lily like flowers. Nearly allied is the St Bruno's Lily, which used to be known as *A. Liliastrum* (and still is in most gardens) but has now been renamed *Paradisea Liliastrum.* It is very similar to the St Bernard's Lily but about twice as tall. Both have garden varieties, distinguished by such names as 'major' and 'grandiflorum', which have larger flowers. All grow in any ordinary soil and open place and are readily increased by dividing the roots in spring.

*Anthericum
ramosum*

ANTIRRHINUM *(Snapdragon)*

Though almost always grown as a half hardy annual, the antirrhinum is, in fact, a nearly hardy perennial. In warm, sheltered places, particularly in poor and sharply drained soil, plants several years old are often to be seen. Nevertheless, the most satisfactory method of growing antirrhinums is to sow seed each January or February in a warm greenhouse or frame, prick out the seedlings as soon as they can be handled and then harden off in a frame for planting outdoors in May.

Antirrhinums like sunshine and good drainage but in very

*Antirrhinum
majus*

*Aquilegia
alpina*

*Aquilegia
glauca*

*Arctotis
acaulis*

*Arctotis
stoechadifolia*

hot, dry places are apt to suffer badly from rust disease. This is far less likely to be troublesome where the climate is cool and rather damp. Rust resistant varieties are available and should be used where the disease is prevalent.

Antirrhinums are available in a wide range of colours including yellow, apricot, orange, pink, scarlet and crimson, and in varying heights ranging from 'Tom Thumb' varieties about 1 foot high, to 'Tall' varieties, 3 feet high. All are useful for filling beds and borders with a mass of colour.

AQUILEGIA (Columbine)

The long-spurred columbines with their very graceful flowers, carried like butterflies on stiff but slender stems are among the best loved flowers of early summer. The colours are mostly delicate shades of yellow, pink, lavender, blue and mauve but there are also quite bright shades of red and crimson. All can be raised from seed sown outdoors in May or early June. Selected colour forms may be increased by careful division of the roots in March or April. Aquilegias will thrive equally well in full sunshine or in light shade and in any soil but are apt to be short lived in heavy and wet clay soils. There are smaller species which are delightful rock garden plants. Among the best are *A. caerulea*, pale blue and white flowers on 15 to 18-inch stems, and *A. glandulosa*, lilac blue and white flowers on foot high stems. Both are spring flowering. *Aquilegia alpina* with blue flowers borne on 6 to 18-inch stems is more difficult.

ARABIS (Rock Cress)

A grand trailing plant that will soon cover a square yard or more of wall or rock garden with its carpets of grey-green leaves which completely disappear in April beneath the smother of its pure white flowers. *Arabis albida* has single flowers whereas in *A. albida flore pleno* each bloom is double, like a little white pompon. For some reason the double form, which is the better plant, has become quite scarce. Both will grow easily in any sunny position and any soil. They are seen to best advantage if planted at the top of a wall to cascade down its face. They can be increased by cuttings of young shoots taken a few weeks after flowering, inserted in sandy soil in a frame. The single arabis can also be raised from seed sown in a frame in March or outdoors in May.

ARCTOTIS

These South African half-hardy annuals are attractive plants for a sunny position. All are large summer-flowering daisies, some with long slender stems, some stemless, and many with stems of intermediate length. *Arctotis stoechadifolia grandis* is most unusual in colour, a silvery white with pale blue reverse and these elegant flowers are carried on long slender stems. There are also hybrids with shorter and stouter stems and large flowers in various shades of orange, red, yellow and wine, often with a darker central zone of colour. All can be raised from seed sown in February or March in warmth under glass, the seedlings being pricked off at least 2 inches apart and hardened off for planting out 1 foot apart in late May where they are to flower.

ARMERIA *(Thrift)*

The smaller thrifts, such as our native *Armeria maritima*, with its globular heads of pink or rose flowers on 6-inch stems, and the stemless and paler pink *A. caespitosa*, are excellent for the rock garden or dry wall. The taller kinds, of which *A. pseudo-armeria* (*cephalotes*) and its improved variety 'Bees Ruby' are the best, can also be grown in the rock garden but are really more at home towards the front of the herbaceous border. All flower in May or June. The small kinds make tussocks of rather narrow, grassy leaves, but *A. pseudo-armeria* has rather broader, heavier leaves. They like sunny places and well-drained soils and will grow in the poorest of sandy soils. They can be increased by careful division of the roots in spring or autumn.

ARTEMISIA *(Wormwood, Southernwood)*

It must be confessed that most artemisias are too coarse or unattractive to be of much use in the garden. Nevertheless there are some excellent silver-leaved plants for the front of the herbaceous border. *A. gnaphalodes* is typical of these, a hardy perennial 2 feet high, with inconspicuous flowers but very handsome grey-white leaves. *A. frigida* is even more decorative because its silvery leaves are deeply and finely divided. *A. argentea*, *A. Ludoviciana* and *A. Stelleriana* are three more of the same persuasion but their names tend to be confused and it is desirable to see them in growth before purchasing them. A taller plant with green leaves and fine sprays of small cream coloured flowers in August is *A. lactiflora*, a fine plant for the middle or back of the herbaceous border and one that does not mind a certain amount of shade. The silver-leaved kinds prefer sun and are seen to best advantage in rather poor soils. All these can be increased by division, in the spring. There are, in addition, some sub-shrubby kinds of which the Southernwood or Old Man, *A. Abrotanum* is the most familiar example, which cannot be divided but can be increased by cuttings of firm young shoots inserted in sandy soil in a frame in early summer. The Southernwood makes a big bush 4 or 5 feet in height and as much through, with finely divided, fragrant grey-green leaves. Another sub-shrubby kind is the true Wormwood, *A. Absinthium*, with silky white leaves.

ARUM

The familiar white arum lily of florists' shops, once known botanically as arum or richardia, is now *Zantedeschia aethiopica*. It is a greenhouse plant which can only be grown outdoors in a few of the mildest parts of the country, as in Cornwall or the Channel Islands. The 'flowers' are, in fact, spathes surrounding a central yellow spadix which carries the true flowers.

All arums have fleshy roots and can be increased by careful division of these roots in August or early September. This is

19

Armeria maritima

Armeria pseudo-armeria

Artemisia spicata

Arum (Zantedeschia aethiopica)

*Aster
Amellus*

*Aster
grandiflorus*

*Aster
alpinus*

*Aster
novae-angliae*

also the time to pot or re-pot the plants. Single roots may be placed in 6 or 7–inch pots or two or three roots can be accommodated in a 10–inch pot. The crown of the root should be just at soil level. John Innes compost will suit these plants well but it may be an advantage to add just a little well-rotted stable or cow manure, particularly if the loam is not very rich. After potting, the arums should be kept quite cool in a frame or unheated greenhouse for a month, and watered moderately, but as growth increases, more water can be given and the temperature can be gradually increased if early flowers are required. However, if flowers are not needed until the normal time in May, no heat need be used except to exclude frost. In June the plants can be knocked out of their pots and planted outdoors without further root disturbance but they should not be allowed to get dry at any time for they like abundant moisture while in growth.

ASTER *(Michaelmas Daisy)*

This is a family in which botanical and popular names are muddled. The plants which the botanist calls aster are all herbaceous perennials and the most familiar of them are the michaelmas daisies. The half-hardy annuals which are popularly known as 'asters' in gardens, are called callistephus. However, for simplicity I am treating them all together here.

The perennial asters are all very hardy and will thrive in practically any soil and situation. The michaelmas daisies may be considered in three groups; those with smooth leaves derived from *Aster novi-belgii*, the downy-leaved varieties derived from *A. novae-angliae*, and the much more bushy and branching varieties derived from *A. Amellus* and *A. Frikartii*. These are usually known simply as 'Amellus varieties'. They differ from the others not only in their habit but also in their rather earlier flowering season (they are at their best in August and early September) and by their dislike of being transplanted at any time except the spring. Most are between 2 and 3 feet in height and have large, single flowers in shades of blue, lilac or mauve.

The *novae-angliae* varieties all tend to close their flowers at night, which is a disadvantage. They are rather tall plants, increasing rapidly in size, and their flowers are either a deep rose or else purple. One of the best known is Barr's Pink.

The most highly developed race of michaelmas daisies has been derived from *A. novi-belgii*. Heights range from about a foot to at least 6 feet, colours from white and palest pink or mauve to deepest rose, carmine and purple. There are varieties with semi-double flowers as well as singles and the flowering season is September and October.

All these asters, and also such species as *A. ericoides* with small white flowers, *A. cordifolius* with arching sprays of mauve flowers, and the alpine species *A. alpinus, A. Farreri* and *A. subcaeruleus*, can be readily increased by division of the roots in autumn or spring (but only spring for *A. Amellus* and its varieties).

The annual asters derived from *Callistephus chinensis* are

totally different plants. They have much larger flowers borne singly on stems seldom above 2 feet in length. There are fully double as well as single flowered varieties and the doubles vary greatly in form, some having narrow curled petals building up a rather shaggy looking bloom and others being broader, stiffer and more formal in character. The ostrich plume asters are an example of the shaggy type, whereas the comets have straight petals. Colours include blue, mauve, pink, red and white.

All these can be raised from seed sown in a greenhouse or frame in March or April or outdoors in early May. Seedlings raised under glass must be pricked off and then hardened off for planting outdoors in May. All flower in late summer and early autumn. They are ideal for late bedding and the long stemmed varieties make good cut flowers.

ASTILBE *(False Goatsbeard)*

There is some confusion between the astilbes and the spiraeas. The latter are mainly shrubs whereas the astilbes are herbaceous perennials bearing graceful plumes of flowers. Plants for moist places, they will stand a certain amount of shade as well. They are, perhaps, happiest near the water side but can also be grown in the ordinary border provided the soil does not dry out too severely. Though perfectly hardy and quite happy if left out of doors all the year, they also make good pot plants for the unheated or slightly heated greenhouse or conservatory. For this strong roots should be lifted in October or November, placed in pots that will contain their roots comfortably and, after a month or so in a frame, removed to the greenhouse. No attempt should be made to force them unduly and they must be kept well watered throughout the time that they are growing and flowering.

There are many garden varieties, from $1\frac{1}{2}$ to 5 feet high, ranging in colour from white and palest pink to a deep wine red. All flower in June or early July but may be had in flower at least two months earlier under glass. Propagation is by careful division of the clumps in spring or autumn.

AUBRIETA *(Coloured Rock Cress)*

This will soon make fine sheets and curtains of its neat bright green leaves which will be completely covered in April and May by the mauve, purple, pink or crimson flowers. Aubrietas thrive in chalky soils but will grow anywhere if the drainage is good and there are stones to ramble over or walls to hang down. They can be raised from seed sown in spring in a frame, or in early summer outdoors. Seedlings always vary a little in colour and selected forms must be propagated by cuttings taken in late June or early July. It is a good plan to trim over the plants lightly with scissors or shears after flowering. The first young shoots that appear after this trimming make the best cuttings. They should be inserted in sandy soil in a frame.

AZALEA

Botanically all azaleas are rhododendrons but from the garden standpoint it is convenient to consider them separately. They

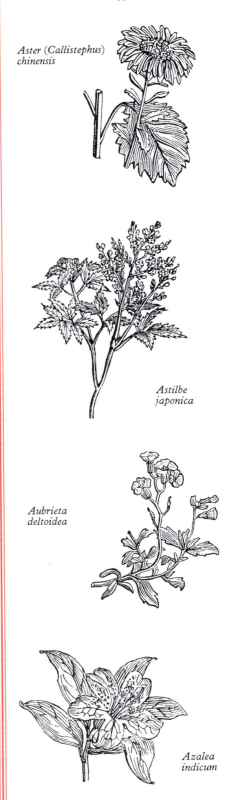

Aster (Callistephus) chinensis

Astilbe japonica

Aubrieta deltoidea

Azalea indicum

*Azalea
luteum*

*Azalea
obtusa*

*Begonia
nitida*

*Begonia
Evansiana*

may be divided into two main groups, the evergreen azaleas, compact bushes with neat foliage and comparatively small, but often very brilliantly coloured flowers, and the deciduous azaleas which make larger and looser bushes with flowers which are also much bigger individually though they do not, on that account, necessarily make a better display.

Very popular examples of the evergreen azaleas are the Kurume varieties. These are comparatively dwarf plants though they may eventually grow into quite big bushes 4 or 5 feet high and even more through. They are related to the vividly magenta flowered *Azalea obtusum amoenum* but are generally in colours a little less barbaric and difficult to associate. All flower in late April or early May and are grand for a large rock garden, for the front of shrub borders or for fairly open places in woodland. They like cool soils, well supplied with humus and they dislike lime. The varieties of *A. indica*, which have fine double flowers are a little tender and are grown as greenhouse plants.

The deciduous azaleas succeed very well in full sun but also thrive in thin woodland. They make big bushes 6 to 8 feet high and as much through and have flowers in many bright colours, particularly shades of yellow, apricot, orange, flame, pink, rose and crimson. There are several different races distinguished by such names as Mollis hybrids, Ghent hybrids, etc. There is also a beautiful race with semi-double or 'hose-in-hose' flowers known as *rustica flore pleno*. All are at their best in the latter half of April and throughout May.

All single-flowered azaleas can be increased from seed sown very thinly in spring and barely covered with fine soil containing plenty of peat and sand. Selected varieties and doubles must be propagated by cuttings prepared from firm young shoots in July and rooted in sandy peat in a close frame, preferably with a little bottom heat.

BEGONIA

Begonias are popular greenhouse plants and some can also be used for bedding out displays in summer, though all are too tender to survive frost. There are many different kinds, but for ordinary purposes it will be sufficient to consider five principal types. There are the summer-flowering tuberous rooted kinds, mostly with very large double blooms, though there are also single-flowered varieties; the nearly allied pendulous begonias also with tuberous roots; the small-flowered summer begonias, readily raised from seed and, for that reason, often treated as half-hardy annuals; the small-flowered winter flowering begonias of which the famous variety Gloire de Lorraine is the type; and the Rex begonias which are grown for the beauty of their large, multi-coloured leaves.

Taking these in order, both the large-flowered, tuberous-rooted and the smaller-flowered pendulous varieties may be stored in winter in some dry peat or sand in a frost proof place, such as a cupboard indoors. In January, February or March, according to the artificial heat available, the tubers are laid in seed boxes filled with damp peat or leaf mould and placed in a temperature of around 60°. Leaves will soon appear and then the tubers can be potted singly in 4–, 5– or 6– inch pots.

The small-flowered summer begonias, with pink, red or white flowers, popular for bedding, are derived from *B. semperflorens*, and are usually raised from seed sown in February or March in a temperature of 60° to 65°. The seedlings are pricked out into small pots or fairly deep seed boxes in which they can be hardened off for planting outdoors in early June. They will grow and flower perfectly well in full sun provided plenty of peat, leaf mould or old compost is first mixed with the soil to hold moisture. After flowering the plants are usually thrown away.

Winter flowering begonias of the Gloire de Lorraine type with their loose sprays of small pink or white flowers, are very pretty plants to have around Christmas, but they need temperatures of about 65° to 70° to be flowered successfully. They are usually raised from cuttings of firm, young basal shoots rooted in a propagating frame, with bottom heat, from January to March.

The Rex begonias also need warmth throughout the winter as they are tender and have no resting season. Otherwise their treatment is much the same as for the tuberous rooted begonias and they will certainly survive in lower temperatures than the winter flowering begonias.

BELLIS *(Daisy)*

The common daisy of lawns and meadows (*Bellis perennis*) has given rise to a number of varieties with larger double flowers, useful plants for spring displays, particularly beneath taller plants such as tulips. Some are white, some pink and some red, and they also differ in the size of their flowers. They are perennials and can be kept from year to year but it is usual to treat them as biennials, sowing the seed outdoors each year in May, or early June, pricking the seedlings out about 6 inches apart in a nursery bed in July, and transferring them to their flowering quarters in September or October. They are then thrown away after flowering. The choice varieties, of which the most notable is the small pink Dresden China, should be increased by division in spring.

BERBERIS *(Barberry)*

The barberries are shrubs, some evergreen and some deciduous, producing yellow or orange flowers some time in spring or early summer, followed by berries, usually deep purple or black in the evergreens and red in the deciduous kinds. Generally it is the flowers which make the best display in the evergreens and the berries which are the principal attraction in the deciduous species. All are very hardy, not fussy about soil, preferring fairly sunny and open places. They do not need pruning. Most are quite easy to transplant in autumn or early spring, but one or two, notably *Berberis Darwinii*, are a little difficult as they resent root disturbance. It is best to raise this fine species in pots so that it

Begonia
semperflorens

Begonia
coccinea

Begonia
Meyeri

Berberis
Darwinii

23

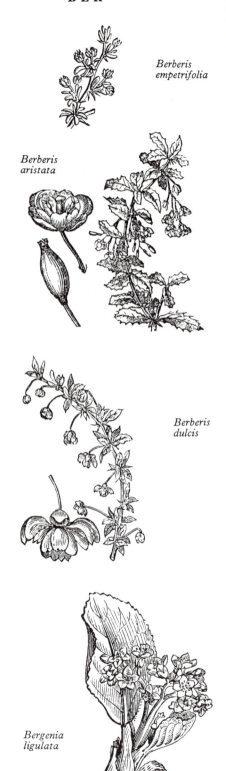

Berberis
empetrifolia

Berberis
aristata

Berberis
dulcis

Bergenia
ligulata

can be planted with its roots more or less intact. Propagation is very easily effected by sowing seed in pots or boxes, or direct in the open ground in March. Seedlings usually begin to flower and fruit in about their third or fourth year. Alternatively cuttings of well-ripened young shoots may be struck in a frame or in a sheltered spot outdoors in autumn.

There are so many fine barberries that it is difficult to make a reasonably small selection. Among the evergreens *B. Darwinii* should certainly be grown. It makes a big bush with small, shining green, prickly leaves like holly leaves on a tiny scale, and it bears hanging clusters of orange flowers in April and early May. I regard it as among the best dozen evergreens for the garden.

Equally good is *B. stenophylla*, rather looser and more arching in habit than *B. Darwinii*, with much narrower leaves and yellow flowers, produced a week or so later. Unlike *B. Darwinii* it is easy to transplant. *B. buxifolia*, in the same group is less effective.

Then there is *B. lologensis*, with apricot yellow flowers and *B. linearifolia*, like an even more free flowering and brilliantly red-orange *B. Darwinii*, but slow in growth and not always satisfactory. It is a grand shrub where it succeeds.

To this brief list I would add *B. Gagnepainii* for its very handsome clusters of lance-shaped leaves and *B. verruculosa* for its extremely dense habit and leaves like those of *B. Darwinii*.

Of the deciduous kinds *B. Jamesiana* is notable for its very long, grape-like clusters of berries, pale green in summer, changing to coral in autumn. It is a tall shrub with long, arching branches. I would also select *B. Wilsonae* for its dense yet graceful growth and magnificent crops of coral red berries. Often it does not exceed 3 feet in height.

B. aggregata Prattii and *B. polyantha* have extra large clusters of fruit, while *B. rubrostilla* has very large, long berries and *B. Thunbergii* has brilliantly coloured leaves in autumn. *B. vulgaris*, the British barberry, has a dangerous addiction to rust disease.

BERGENIA *(Large-leaved Saxifrage)*

These plants were at one time united with the saxifrage by botanists. Nevertheless they are very different in appearance, with their large, thick usually round or oval leaves, and their short, rather clumsily formed spikes of pink flowers produced early in the year. Their very early flowering season and the handsome, almost evergreen, character of their foliage makes the bergenias good garden plants. They will thrive in full sun or partial shade and in any soil, in fact they make very good town garden plants. All are readily increased by division after flowering.

The best kinds are *B. cordifolia* and *B. crassifolia*, both about 18 inches in height, and *B. ligulata* and *B. Stracheyi*, nearer one foot.

BOUGAINVILLEA

Unfortunately *Bougainvillea glabra*, a brilliant climber from Brazil, is too tender to be grown outdoors in this country. In

Mediterranean countries it has established itself so firmly that it is one of the commonest climbers. There are also numerous garden varieties of this and of *B. spectabilis*, some, like Mrs. Butt, with pink flowers, and some, like Louie Wathin, orange. All are lovely but none exceeds the species in brilliance.

Bougainvilleas should be grown in greenhouses or conservatories with a minimum winter temperature of 45°. They may be grown in pots but are happier in a border of good soil, where their abundant stems can be trained, without too much restriction or pruning, to the rafters. If they must be kept to a limited space, prune them each February by cutting back all the previous year's growth to within an inch or so of the main vines, in the same way as grape vines under glass.

They appreciate plenty of water in summer. The temperature then should average 65° and it does not matter if it runs up much higher sometimes. Propagation is by cuttings of firm young shoots pulled off in spring with a heel of older wood, and rooted in sandy soil in a close frame with bottom heat in temperature of around 70° until roots are formed.

BRACHYCOME *(Swan River Daisy)*

Brachycome iberidifolia, a pretty South African annual, produces blue, pink or white daisy-like flowers freely in summer on a dwarf bushy plant, usually little over a foot high. It is raised from seed sown in a greenhouse or frame in March or early April, the seedlings being pricked off and later hardened in a frame for planting outdoors in June. It is also possible to sow in early May direct in the beds in which the plants are to flower. It likes warm sunny places and open, well-drained soils.

BUDDLEIA *(Butterfly Bush)*

The purple buddleia is one of the commonest and best of summer flowering shrubs. It has naturalized itself in many places, filling waste areas with its loosely-formed bushes covered in July and August by the long, tapering spikes of mauve or purple flowers. This is *Buddleia Davidii*, a grand shrub which used to be known as *B. variabilis*. Numerous garden varieties have been raised of which two of the best are Ile de France and Royal Red, both with very deep purple flowers. There are also white flowered forms but these are not so decorative. Another useful variety is *nanhoensis*, only about half the height of the common buddleia, with elegant flower spikes.

All delight in sun and good drainage and thrive in the poorest of soils, even finding roothold in walls. They need not be pruned, but for the finest spikes of bloom the previous year's stems should be cut back each March to within a few inches of the older wood.

Two very different species are *B. alternifolia* and *B. globosa*. The former makes a big bush, with long slender arching stems wreathed with small purple flowers in June. It is more graceful but not as spectacular as *B. Davidii*.

B. globosa has much the same open habit as *B. Davidii*

Bougainvillea spectabilis

Brachycome iberidifolia

Buddleia madagascariensis

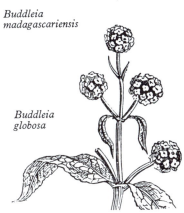

Buddleia globosa

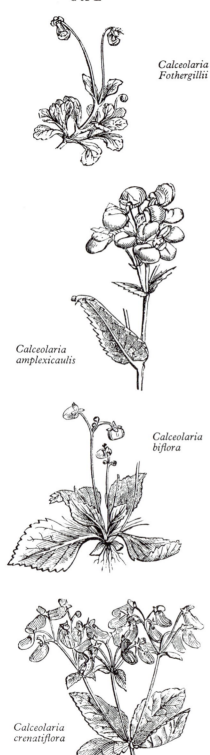

*Calceolaria
Fothergillii*

*Calceolaria
amplexicaulis*

*Calceolaria
biflora*

*Calceolaria
crenatiflora*

(both are apt to get somewhat gaunt if left unpruned) but instead of purple spikes it has orange coloured balls, rather less than an inch in diameter, in June. It is not as good a shrub as either of the other species, but is unusual and worth growing.

All these can be increased by cuttings of well-ripened young stems inserted in a frame or a sheltered place outdoors in the autumn.

CALCEOLARIA *(Slipper Flower)*

Calceolarias need to be considered in two quite distinct groups, the half-shrubby and nearly hardy kinds used for summer bedding, and the soft-stemmed (herbaceous) kinds grown in greenhouses. All have the curious, pouch-like flowers characteristic of the genus, which are quite small in the bedding calceolarias, but often very large and showy in the greenhouse varieties.

Because of their very different growth the two groups need quite different treatment. The bedding calceolarias are raised from cuttings, usually taken in early autumn and rooted in an unheated frame, whereas the greenhouse varieties are treated as annuals and raised from seed every year. The seed is sown in June or July in pots, pans or boxes in an unheated greenhouse. The seedlings are pricked off as soon as they can be handled and a few weeks later potted singly in small pots. All this time they are happier in a frame than a greenhouse as they like a cool moist atmosphere. But in October, as soon as sharp frost threatens, they must be removed to a greenhouse and grown on steadily in a temperature of 45° to 55° to flower the following spring. They will need 5 to 8-inch pots in which to flower, according to the size of the plants, and they may have their last potting in early March. For all these pottings John Innes compost may be used. Avoid hot, dry atmospheres, shade the plants from strong sunshine, and water fairly freely, without allowing water to collect at the bases of the leaves.

There are many varieties or strains all with handsomely blotched flowers in shades of yellow and red.

Bedding calceolarias only need frost protection in a frame from October to early May when they can be planted out where they are to flower. There are two principal varieties, one with yellow and the other with chestnut red flowers.

CALENDULA *(Pot Marigold)*

This is one of the easiest flowers to grow, a showy hardy annual which, once in the garden, will keep itself going for years by self-sown seed. But the many fine modern varieties tend to deteriorate rapidly when grown in this way. After a few years the flowers will probably be nearly single and little different from those of the wild pot marigold. Good seed should be purchased each year and sown in March, April, May or September where the plants are to bloom the following summer. Thin to about a foot apart and thereafter leave them to themselves except for removing weeds and faded flowers.

Varieties differ in colour from yellow to deep orange. All have double flowers of varying form, some having flat petals and some quilled.

CALTHA *(Marsh Marigold, Kingcup)*

Caltha palustris, one of the loveliest of British bog plants, may be seen in many damp meadows or at streamsides in spring. The flowers are like very large buttercups carried on stout stems 1 to 2 feet in height. The leaves are broad and shining. It is well worth a place in the garden in very damp soil. The double-flowered form is interesting and showy but not as beautiful as the single-flowered wild form. There are also other species of which the best is *C. polypetala*, similar to the marsh marigold but with even larger flowers. Both can be increased by dividing their roots immediately after flowering, and this is also the best time at which to plant them.

CAMELLIA

This is a big family of evergreen shrubs and from *Camellia japonica* a great number of garden varieties has been produced, some with single flowers, some semi-double or anemone centred, and some fully double. They vary in colour from white and palest pink to scarlet and crimson and many are handsomely blotched with white on pink or red. All will make large shrubs, perhaps 15 feet or more in height and nearly as much through, but are usually seen as much smaller specimens and were once extensively cultivated as pot plants for the cool greenhouse or conservatory. Indeed it is only of recent years that the full hardiness of *C. japonica* has been realized and that it has begun to be planted outdoors at all extensively. Growth seldom gets cut by frost, even in very cold places, but the flowers are sensitive to frost and as they are produced very early in the spring (sometimes even in winter) the plants should be given a fairly sheltered position if possible. They will thrive in full sun or in partial shade and they like slightly acid soils such as those that suit rhododendrons and azaleas. They need no pruning and, once established, may be left entirely alone except for an occasional mulch of grass mowings or compost to keep them well fed.

In addition to *C. japonica* and its varieties, there are some other good kinds but these are not all so hardy. *C. saluenensis*, one of the most reliable, is a lovely shrub with evergreen leaves smaller than those of *C. japonica* and more fragile single pink flowers, rather like single roses. It has produced a grand race of hybrids with *C. japonica*, the lilac pink J. C. Williams being one of the best. One advantage of all these kinds is that these single flowers fall when they fade instead of remaining on the bush as a disfigurement as so often happens with the double-flowered forms of *C. japonica*.

Another magnificent species is *C. reticulata* which has very large, usually semi-double, rose-pink flowers. It makes a very big shrub, looser and more sprawling in habit than *C. japonica*,

Caltha palustris

Camellia reticulata

Camellia Sosanqua plena

Camellia japonica

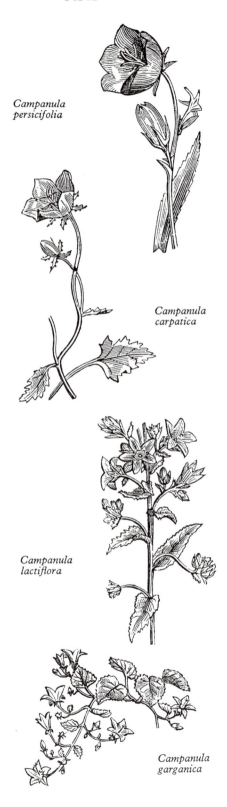

Campanula
persicifolia

Campanula
carpatica

Campanula
lactiflora

Campanula
garganica

but it is tender and really a shrub for the mild counties such as Devon and Cornwall.

Varieties of *C. japonica* can be increased by cuttings of firm young growth taken in July and rooted in a close frame. Varieties of *C. reticulata* and some other camellias must be grafted in spring on to seedlings of *C. japonica*.

CAMPANULA *(Bellflower)*

Another big family, which spreads itself into rock garden and herbaceous border as well as providing in the familiar Canterbury bell an excellent plant for bedding.

It is difficult to generalize about campanulas because they are so numerous and so different, but most of them are easy plants to grow in ordinary soil and open position. Many will even tolerate a measure of shade. Almost all can be readily increased by dividing their roots in spring or autumn and most can also be raised from seed sown in spring in frame or greenhouse. A slightly different method is required for the Canterbury bell (*Campanula Medium*) a biennial, seed of which should be sown in a frame or in a sheltered place outdoors in May or early June. The seedlings are pricked out, about 6 inches apart, in a nursery bed where they can grow on into fine clumps for removal in September or October to their flowering quarters.

One of the best of the herbaceous bellflowers is *C. persicifolia*. It spreads fairly fast making low clumps of narrow leaves above which stand, each June and July, the 2 to 3–foot high slender stems bearing numerous large nodding bell shaped usually lavender blue flowers. There are deeper coloured and white forms and some with double flowers.

Another good plant, which does well in shady places, is *C. lactiflora*. This is 5 feet in height and produces, in July and August, large, loose sprays of small, widely opened bells, either pale blue or near-white.

C. latiloba, also known as *C. grandis*, is a much stiffer and less elegant plant with 2 to 3–foot spikes of blue flowers in June and July. It will grow well in practically any place.

The two finest rock garden bellflowers are *C. Portenschlagiana* (*C. muralis*), and *C. cochleariflora* (*C. pusilla*). The first makes great sheets of small shining green leaves down any retaining wall on which it is planted, completely covering these in May and June with its widely opened purple flowers. I regard it as one of the twelve best rock plants. *C. cochlearifolia*, a more fragile plant with thread-like stems 3 or 4 inches high, bears nodding bells of blue or white.

CANNA *(Indian Shot)*

These are tropical plants with large, handsome, upstanding leaves usually either rich green or purplish in colour, and bold spikes of gaudily coloured flowers, usually red or yellow variously splashed and spotted with one colour on the other. They are not difficult to grow as they have fleshy roots which can be stored in a frost-proof greenhouse during the winter and re-started into growth in spring in a temperature around 60°. It is best to pot the roots individually in pots large enough to accommodate them comfortably. They can, if preferred, be grown in pots throughout and used for greenhouse or conservatory decoration or, alternatively, they can be bedded out in June as soon as all danger of frost is past. They should have a sunny position, a fairly rich soil and abundant water. Directly frost threatens, outdoor plants should be lifted, boxed or potted and returned to the greenhouse where they can be gradually dried off ready for storing again. It is best to keep them in soil all the time even when they are completely without water. Propagation is by division of the roots in spring or by seeds sown in spring, but seeds are hard and need thorough soaking and a fairly high temperature to germinate them.

CARYOPTERIS   (Blue Spiraea)

The popular name is not inappropriate in that it gives some idea of the appearance of this attractive shrub with its rather fluffy looking clusters of blue flowers in early autumn.

The best kind for the garden is *C. clandonensis*, a hybrid with blue flowers, and a fine vigorous habit which makes it more generally reliable than the better known of its parents, *C. Mastacanthus*. Unpruned it will make a loose bush, 3 or 4 feet high, but it can be cut back quite severely each April when it will branch freely and make a much more compact plant perhaps 2½ feet in height. It is easily increased by cuttings of firm young growth, taken at practically any time in summer and rooted in a frame.

CATANANCHE   (Cupid's Dart)

The only species grown in gardens is *Catananche caerulea*, a hardy herbaceous plant that might be mistaken at first for some kind of cornflower. It has similar lavender-blue flowers but they are silvery underneath and the petals feel dry and chaffy. It grows about 2 feet high and flowers in late summer. It is quite hardy but does not like winter wet and is most permanent in rather poor, well-drained soils. The flowers are useful for cutting and, with care, will last some time though they are not true 'everlastings'. Propagation is by division of the roots in spring or autumn.

CEANOTHUS   (Californian Lilac)

These are very beautiful shrubs mostly with blue flowers, though there are pink and white kinds. The individual flowers, usually quite small, are carried in clusters neat and thimble-like in the evergreen kinds such as *Ceanothus Burkwoodii*, *C. dentatus*, *C. rigidus*, *C. thyrsiflorus* and *C. Veitchianus*, or larger, looser and more cone-shaped in the deciduous *C. azureus* and its numerous garden forms or hybrids. The evergreen kinds mostly flower in spring, though *C. Burkwoodii* blooms continuously all the summer. *C. azureus* and the varieties associated with it, are all late summer flowering. While most of the evergreen kinds are happiest against a sunny wall, the deciduous kinds are seen to

29

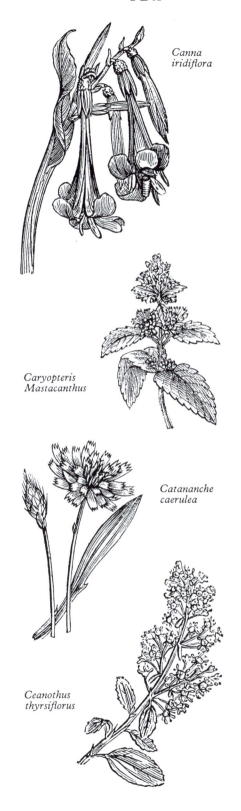

Canna iridiflora

Caryopteris Mastacanthus

Catananche caerulea

Ceanothus thyrsiflorus

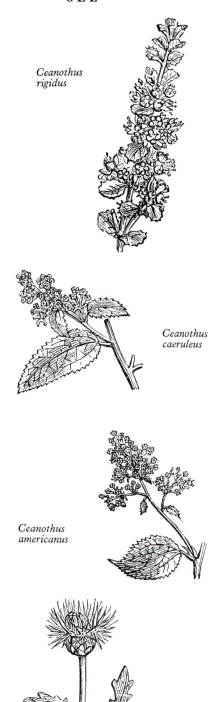

Ceanothus
rigidus

Ceanothus
caeruleus

Ceanothus
americanus

Centaurea
moschata

better advantage in a bed or border in which they have room to expand. Once again *C. Burkwoodii* occupies a midway position, for though it can be grown against a wall, it is equally happy in the shrub border.

Sharp frost may injure many species but usually the hybrids of *C. azureus* and *C. americanus* are unharmed and this is also true of *C. thyrsiflorus*. Among the best of the *C. azureus* varieties and hybrids are Gloire de Versailles, light blue; Indigo and Topaz, both deep blue; and Perle Rose, pink.

All like well-drained soils. The evergreen kinds may be cut back a little after flowering to keep them in shape, and the deciduous kinds can be pruned back quite severely each March if desired. They will then make strong, cane-like growths carrying flower trusses of extra size. *C. Burkwoodii* is best pruned in April.

Propagation is by cuttings of firm young growth taken in July or August and rooted in a close frame.

CELOSIA   *(Cockscomb, Prince of Wales's Feather)*

The most popular varieties are derived from *C. argentea* and carry feathery plumes of yellow, scarlet or crimson flowers on stems 12 to 18 inches in height. In the curious cockscomb (*C. argentea cristata*) the crimson flowers are huddled together to form a compact, twisted mass not unlike the comb of a cock.

All are half-hardy annuals flowering throughout the latter half of the summer. They need a fair amount of warmth in the early stages and seed should be sown in January or February in a temperature of 65° to 70°, the seedlings being grown on singly in small pots in rich soil, and potted on to 4-inch pots as they need more room. They must be carefully hardened off for planting outdoors in June. They should be given as sunny and sheltered a position as possible. Alternatively celosias may be grown as pot plants for summer flowering in the greenhouse.

CENTAUREA   *(Cornflower, Sweet Sultan)*

The centaureas may be considered in three distinct groups; the hardy annual varieties, the hardy herbaceous perennials and the slightly tender grey-leaved perennials, popular in summer bedding schemes.

Best known of the annuals is the common cornflower, *Centaurea Cyanus*. It grows 3 or 4 feet in height and has bright blue flowers, but there are also pink, lilac, pale blue and white varieties as well as dwarf varieties not exceeding 1 foot in height. All can be raised from seed, sown in March, April, May or September, where the plants are to flower. They like open sunny places but are not fussy about soil. They will need thinning to about 9 inches apart and supporting with some hazel branches or similar brushy material. The dwarf varieties need only be thinned to 6 inches and will not require support. The tall varieties are admirable for cutting.

Another useful annual is the sweet sultan, *Centaurea moschata*, averaging 18 inches in height, with fragrant flowers individually larger than those of the cornflower and in a wider range of colours, including yellow, mauve, various shades of purple, wine red and white. It is a little more difficult to grow as although it may be sown outdoors in March, April or September, where the plants are to flower the following summer, a little more care must be taken to prepare a good, crumbly, easily worked seed bed. Thin the seedlings to about 9 inches. They will not need any support. The sweet sultan likes sun and warmth and is not so robustly hardy as the cornflower.

The hardy perennial centaureas are not on the whole so well known, though *C. montana*, with its starry blue cornflowers produced on 18-inch stems in May, is seen fairly frequently. It also has a white form.

Another good perennial species is *C. dealbata*, about 2 feet in height, with rosy-pink flowers in June and July. *C. macrocephala*, 4 feet in height, has yellow flowers 4 inches in diameter, and *C. ruthenica*, a smaller yellow flowered kind, has handsome, deeply cut leaves.

All these hardy perennials will grow in any ordinary soil and fairly open position and can be increased by division in either spring or autumn.

In the grey-leaved bedding centaureas, *C. Cineraria*, *C. gymnocarpa*, and *C. ragusina*, the flowers are unimportant as they are grown for the beauty of their deeply cut, grey or nearly white leaves. They are often used as a foil for the bright colours of 'geraniums', scarlet salvias and similar flowers. They can be increased by cuttings in spring or early autumn, and should be given frame or greenhouse protection in winter.

CENTRANTHUS *(Red Valerian)*

The common red valerian, *Centranthus ruber*, one of the best plants for dry walls, cliff faces and other stony places provided there is plenty of room for it, may be seen growing wild in many parts of the country. It is a hardy perennial, about two feet in height, producing its small rosy-pink flowers in fine heads throughout June and July with some odd spikes appearing later in the summer. It is so trouble-free and decorative that it is well worth planting wherever there is a suitable spot for it. Good drainage is essential and it really does not matter how poor and stony the soil may be.

There is a white flowered variety and another with much brighter, nearly crimson, flowers, which is usually named '*coccineus*'. All can be increased by careful division in spring or autumn, or by cuttings of firm young shoots rooted in a frame in early spring or summer.

CERATOSTIGMA

These are very closely related to the leadworts (plumbago), indeed at one time they were known as plumbago. Of the two kinds commonly grown *Ceratostigma plumbaginoides* (*Larpentae*) is a herbaceous perennial and *C. Willmottianum* is a shrub which is often killed to ground level in winter but shoots up again from

Centaurea montana

Centaurea Cineraria

Centaurea ragusina

Centranthus macrosiphon

31

Ceratostigma plumbaginoides

Chaenomeles japonica

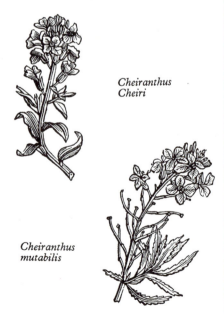

Cheiranthus Cheiri

Cheiranthus mutabilis

basal buds like a herbaceous plant. Both are valued for their blue flowers, shaped like those of a phlox and extremely pure and bright in colour. *C. plumbaginoides*, about 1 foot in height and spreading in habit, flowers in late summer. *C. Willmottianum* may reach 3 or 4 feet in a sheltered place where it does not get cut by frost. More often it is seen as a spreading bush about $1\frac{1}{2}$ to 2 feet in height. It will flower from July to November in a favourable season and is worthy of a good situation, in a sheltered, sunny border with good but well-drained soil. Both can usually be increased by careful division in the spring and *C. Willmottianum* also by cuttings taken in July and rooted in a frame.

CHAENOMELES *(Japanese Quince)*

Many gardeners simply know this as 'japonica'. It has suffered from having too many different names, and even to-day is frequently listed as *Cydonia japonica* though its correct name is *Chaenomeles lagenaria*. It flowers in early spring and the commonest variety has brilliant scarlet flowers, though there are also white, pink, and crimson forms. Though perfectly hardy and capable of making a densely branched bush in the shrub border, it is most frequently seen trained against walls where it certainly looks well as the flowers benefit from the protection. Grown in this way it will want a little careful pruning after flowering, to get rid of surplus growth, and training to spread it out fanwise on the wall. It will grow to 10 feet under favourable conditions.

A similar species, often called *Cydonia Maulei* but which should really be *Chaenomeles japonica*, is dwarfer in habit, rarely exceeding 3 feet in height, with orange-scarlet flowers. A very fine form named *Simonii* has rich crimson flowers.

The Japanese Quinces are shrubs for sunny places but are not at all fussy about soil. All can be increased by layering in spring or early summer. All flower in May.

CHEIRANTHUS *(Wallflower)*

Our old friend the wallflower looks a little strange under its botanical title, *Cheiranthus Cheiri*. Everyone loves it for its showy and richly scented flowers in spring, and it is a universal favourite for spring bedding. For this it is grown as a biennial, though in fact it is a herbaceous perennial and old clumps of it are to be seen on many walls or in rocky places. But in the richer and less well drained soil of the garden it is apt to get soft and be badly damaged by frost in winter and for bedding it is more convenient to throw the plants away when they have finished flowering and raise a fresh batch for next year. This is done by sowing seed outdoors in May, pricking the seedlings out at least 6 inches apart into a nursery bed, finally transferring them in October to their flowering quarters.

There are many varieties varying in the colour of their flowers, through shades of yellow, chestnut red, crimson and a rather curious purplish-mauve. In addition there are other species such as *C. mutabilis*, purple and cream.

Bergenia cordifolia

Artemisia
luctiflora

Azalea
[Ghent hybrid]

Bougainvillea
Louie Wathin

Aubrieta [garden form]

Aster Frikartii

Begonia Rex [leaf]

Bellis perennis
[garden form]

Astilbe
Arendsii

Arum
[Zantedeschia
aethiopica]

Berberis
Darwinii

Berberis
polyantha

Begonia
[double flowered
garden form]

CN-T

Camellia japonica

Campanula
cochleariifolia

Calceolaria
integrifolia

Caryopteri
clandonensi

Buddleia Davidii

Canna indica

Catananche
caerulea

Brachycome
iberidifolia

Ceanothi
Burkwoo

Campanula
Medium

Calendula
officinalis

Caltha
palustris

Celosia
plumosa

CNF

CHIMONANTHUS *(Winter Sweet)*

This is a deciduous shrub often heard of but seldom seen, no doubt because, though its fragrant flowers are produced in mid-winter, they are not at all showy and may even pass unnoticed until one is attracted to them by their scent. Moreover though *Chimonanthus fragrans* is itself reasonably hardy, its flowers are readily damaged by frost and it is best against a wall except in the mildest parts of the country. Unpruned it makes a big, open bush but with a little judicious pruning each year after flowering, it can easily be trained as a wall shrub. The flowers are pale yellow and semi-transparent and they have purplish-maroon centres. A variety, *luteus*, has primrose yellow flowers lacking the purple centre. Both will grow in ordinary soil and can be increased by seed sown in spring or by layers in late summer.

CHIONODOXA *(Glory of the Snow)*

Very attractive small bulbous-rooted spring flowering plants. Two of the best are *Chionodoxa Luciliae* and *C. sardensis*, both with starry flowers in loose clusters on 8–inch stems but whereas the flowers of *C. Luciliae* are bright blue with a white centre, those of *C. sardensis* are a deeper blue throughout. The bulbs should be planted 3 inches deep in September or October, in ordinary soil either in full sun or partial shade and thereafter left undisturbed for years. They will gradually increase in number and become progressively more lovely. If bulbs are required elsewhere one or two clumps may be lifted in July or August, divided into single bulbs, and replanted. These are excellent plants for the rock garden.

CHOISYA *(Mexican Orange)*

Choisya ternata is a first-class evergreen shrub but it will not stand a great deal of frost. In milder parts and near the coast it is usually quite safe, but in colder places it may need the protection of a wall. With that one exception it has all the virtues; attractive, glossy foliage, an excellent rounded habit, fine clusters of white flowers very like orange blossom, fragrance, and a long flowering season. It is at its best in May but may carry some flowers from April to September. It is not fussy about soil and, though it likes sun, will grow in partial shade. It can be easily increased by cuttings of firm young growth inserted in a frame between July and September inclusive.

CHRYSANTHEMUM

This is one of the great families of the flower garden, so rich in its diversity that many books have been devoted to it alone.

Broadly speaking chrysanthemums may be considered under four main headings, annual varieties flowering in summer and readily raised from seed sown in spring where the plants are to bloom, hardy border perennials, Japanese chrysanthemums derived from *C. morifolium* which may themselves be divided into two sections, one for outdoor and the other for greenhouse

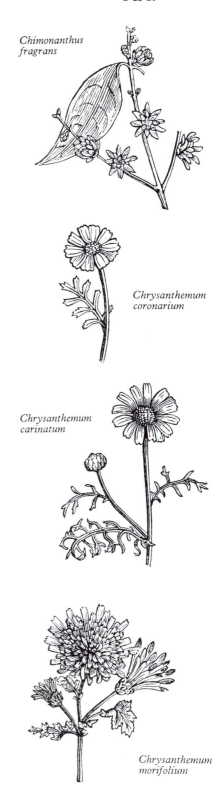

Chimonanthus fragrans

Chrysanthemum coronarium

Chrysanthemum carinatum

Chrysanthemum morifolium

C

Chrysanthemum
(reflexed)

Chrysanthemum
(incurving)

Chrysanthemum
(anemone-centred)

Chrysanthemum
(pompon)

cultivation, and the half-hardy, semi-shrubby varieties of which the common marguerite (*Chrysanthemum frutescens*) is the best-known example.

The annuals, *C. carinatum* and *C. coronarium*, will grow freely in any soil and reasonably open situation. All have daisy-like flowers on good stems, heights varying from $1\frac{1}{2}$ to 3 feet. Some are single, some double-flowered and the ground colour is usually white or yellow though often this is banded with crimson or maroon. Among the best hardy annuals for summer flowering in the garden, they make excellent cut flowers. For an extra early display seed should be sown in September where the plants are to flower the following year. Seedlings should be thinned to 1 foot apart.

The hardy herbaceous chrysanthemums are familiarly known as moon daisies (or ox-eye daisies) and shasta daisies, the former being varieties of our own native *Chrysanthemum Leucanthemum*, a beautiful weed in meadows, and the latter varieties of the Pyrenean *C. maximum*. Here again there are double as well as single-flowered forms but all are white or at most no more than cream and all flower in June and July. Heights vary between 2 and 3 feet. Propagation is by division in spring.

The Japanese chrysanthemums are the most varied of all and thousands of varieties have been raised. Every year sees scores of new ones added to the list. In addition to the two great divisions already noted, into outdoor and indoor kinds, chrysanthemums are also classified according to the shape and size of their flowers. There are single-flowered varieties, doubles which may be reflexed (that is the petals curling outwards and downwards) or incurving (that is the petals curling inwards). The most perfect of the latter, which form almost completely globular flowers, are known as incurved. Intermediate between the singles and doubles are anemone-centred varieties which have an outer ring of single petals and a pincushion-like centre of fluted or tubular petals.

A further division is made according to size, decoratives being of intermediate size suitable for garden display or arranging in the house and exhibition varieties being larger. Smallest of all are the pompons, often with flowers little over an inch in diameter.

For details of cultivation the reader is referred to specialist books on the subject.

Finally there is the marguerite of which there is a primrose yellow variety as well as the familiar white. These are the popular 'daisies' used for summer bedding. They make fine bushy plants and will flower continuously all through the summer. They can be increased by cuttings rooted in a frame or greenhouse at almost any time of the year except winter.

CINERARIA

There are no more showy plants for the cool greenhouse than the cinerarias (*Senecio cruentus*). All have single daisy flowers carried in big, loose clusters, the colour range embracing all shades of blue and purple, pink and crimson, some with broad white bands of white which make the colour seem even more brilliant. There are two principal groups, one the large-flowered cinerarias in which the individual blooms are 3 or 4 inches in diameter, and the other the star-flowered or stellata varieties in which the individual flowers are much smaller though there are more of them in every cluster. Both are useful, the stellata varieties perhaps being better for decorative arrangements because of their lightness, the large-flowered varieties being superior where a mass of colour is required.

All are treated as annuals, seed being sown under glass some time between April and early July according to the time the plants are to flower. From the earliest sowings November flowers will be obtained and from the latest plants that will bloom in April or May. Very little heat is required, and throughout the plants should be grown as though they were nearly hardy. The seedlings must be pricked off and later potted singly, first in small pots, later in 4– or 5–inch pots and finally into the 6–, 7– or 8–inch pots in which they will flower. From June to early October the plants will be happier in a frame and will need little protection. When they are returned to the greenhouse in the autumn they should be ventilated freely whenever the weather is favourable, and be watered carefully. Leaf mining maggots sometimes disfigure the leaves badly but can be kept in check by occasional spraying with nicotine.

CISTUS (Rock Rose)

Rock rose, although officially the popular name of the cistuses, is used frequently for the helianthemums, which causes a good deal of confusion. The two genera are very closely allied, the most obvious difference from the garden standpoint being that whereas almost all the helianthemums are sprawling plants most suitable for rock garden or dry wall, the cistuses are far more definitely shrubs, with strong woody stems which often form big bushes 5 or 6 feet in height and even more in diameter. All have rather fragile saucer-shaped flowers and though the individual blooms do not last long, they are so freely replaced by opening buds that the display continues for several weeks in June and July with some stragglers appearing right on into the autumn.

The cistuses are evergreen and would be in the very front rank of shrubs if they were a little hardier. Few kinds are completely reliable in the colder parts of the country. They will survive mild winters but will be killed in a really hard winter. Nevertheless they are so readily and rapidly renewable, either from seed sown in spring or by cuttings taken in summer, that they are worth a slight risk. All like well-drained soils and seem not to mind how poor it may be. They are ideal for hot stony or gravelly places in full sun. No pruning is required.

The hardiest kind is probably *Cistus laurifolius* with pure white flowers but even more showy is *C. cyprius* a fine hybrid with large white, purple-blotched flowers. *C. ladaniferus*, often known as the gum cistus because of its sticky leaves, is one of the parents

Cistus ladaniferus

Cistus purpureus

Cistus cyprius

Cistus laurifolius

35

*Clarkia
elegans*

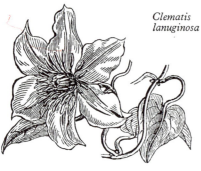

*Clematis
lanuginosa*

*Clematis
indivisa*

*Clematis
heracleifolia*

of *C. cyprius* and equally beautiful but not so hardy. Its flowers are white either with or without a purple blotch.

Handsome but rather tender is *C. purpureus* with very large rosy-purple flowers with a maroon blotch. Where it succeeds it will make a big bush in time. Smaller and more delicate in colouring, and also, I think, rather more hardy, is the lovely hybrid *C. Silver Pink. C. crispus* and *C. albidus* have deeper magenta flowers.

CLARKIA

One of the best and hardiest of annuals, clarkias can be sown outdoors in March, April, May or September where they will flower from May to September according to the time at which they were sown. They will need a little thinning out and weeding. They do not seem to mind what soil they are grown in and they will even flower tolerably well in shady places.

Clarkias produce long, slender spikes of double flowers, pink, brick red or white, individually rather shapeless, but attractive in the mass. Heights vary from $1\frac{1}{2}$ to 3 feet and seedlings should be thinned accordingly, the shorter varieties to 9 inches the taller to 1 foot or thereabouts.

CLEMATIS *(Virgin's Bower)*

The purple *Clematis Jackmanii*, with its tangled but slender growths and great masses of large rich purple flowers in July and August, is justly one of the most popular of hardy climbers.

There are many other kinds differing in the size of their flowers, their colour and their time of flowering. One of the earliest is the evergreen *C. Armandii*, with masses of small white flowers in March or April.

A little later, in May, comes *C. montana*, another small-flowered kind, typically white though there are also pink forms.

Later still, flowering from June to October, come a great many beautiful hybrids, mostly with rather large single or double flowers, from white and palest lavender or pink, to intense purple and carmine. A few good varieties are Comtesse de Bouchaud, double pale pink; Ernest Markham, petunia red; Henryi, white; Lady Northcliffe, lavender and blue; Lasurstern, purplish-blue; Nelly Moser, mauve and red; Perle d'Azur, double light blue; Ville de Lyon, carmine, and Duchess of Edinburgh double white. These come from such species as *CC. florida, Jackmanii, lanuginosa, patens* and *viticella*.

An uncommon but beautiful clematis is *C. tangutica* with small lantern-shaped yellow flowers followed by silvery seed heads.

All these thrive in rich soils that hold moisture without becoming waterlogged. That may explain their fondness for chalk soils for these usually possess such characteristics. Another peculiarity is that although they like to have their roots in the shade they prefer to have their heads in the sun. This can often be arranged either by screening them with a shrub which will shade their roots, or by planting them in the shady side of a building but training their shoots round to the sunny side.

The very vigorous kinds do not need regular pruning but some

Chrysanthemum maximum

Cistus laurifolius

Chrysanthemun [decorative]

Chaenomeles lagenaria

Cheiranthus Cheiri

Centranthus ruber

Centaurea Cyanus

Ceratostigma Willmottianum

Clarkia elegans

Chionodoxa Luciliae

Choisya ternata

Cineraria [Senecio cruentus]

Chimonanthus fragrans

Clianthus
Dampieri

Convolvulus
minor

Clematis
[garden form]

Cobaea
scandens

Clerodendrum
trichotomum

Clivia
miniata

Clerodendrum
Fargesii

Collinsia
bicolor

Cleome
spinosa

Coreopsis
lanceolata

Convallaria
majalis

Colchicum
autumnale

Coleus Blumei

Cornus Kousa

of the weaker varieties should be pruned annually in February. The previous year's growth may then be shortened quite severely, even as much as to within a few inches of the main vines. Care should be taken to make each cut just above a bud that is just starting into growth.

All these clematis can be increased by layering in early summer and the species, such as *C. Armandii*, *C. montana* and *C. tangutica*, can also be increased readily from seed sown in a greenhouse or frame in spring.

There are also herbaceous species such as *C. heracleifolia* and *C. recta* which are increased by careful division.

CLEOME *(Spider Flower)*

An uncommon but beautiful half-hardy annual which makes a big plant about 4 feet in height carrying loose spikes of pink flowers with very narrow petals and long stamens which give them a curiously spidery appearance. A fine plant for the centre of a large bed or for a back position in borders devoted to annuals or summer bedding plants, it may also be used effectively to fill gaps in the herbaceous border. It flowers in July or August.

Seed should be sown in a greenhouse or frame in February or March and the seedlings pricked off and then hardened off in a frame in readiness for planting out in May. *C. spinosa*, the kind usually grown, likes sun but is not particular about soil.

CLERODENDRUM *(Glory Tree)*

Clerodendrums may be conveniently divided into two groups, the tender kinds only suitable for warm greenhouses, and the hardy or nearly hardy shrubs which can be grown outdoors. In the former group are *C. Thomsoniae* (syn. *C. Balfouri*) and *C. fallax*; in the latter group are *C. Bungei* (syn. *C. foetidum*) and *C. trichotomum*.

C. Thomsoniae, an evergreen climber bearing loose sprays of fine crimson and white flowers in summer, can be grown in a tub or large pot but is really happier planted in a greenhouse border of moderately rich soil. Given plenty of room to be trained under the greenhouse rafters, it will soon make a fine specimen and require little pruning. Alternatively it can be trained over a crinoline-like frame and kept to this restricted size by being pruned immediately after flowering. All young shoots should be shortened to about 3 inches.

C. fallax, a shrubby plant, is most commonly raised from seed and discarded after flowering as if it were an annual. Seed sown in warmth in February will give plants that will produce their vivid orange-red flowers the following autumn. A second sowing can be made in August and the seedlings from this will flower from June to August the following year. But as these plants like a temperature that never falls below 50°, a good deal of artificial heat will be required.

C. Bungei and *C. trichotomum* are both shrubs. *C. Bungei* with clusters of rosy-red flowers in late summer is less hardy than *C. trichotomum* which has loose sprays of white and reddish-

Clematis
patens

Clematis
florida

Cleome
gigantea

Clerodendrum
splendens

37

*Clianthus
puniceus*

*Clianthus
Dampieri*

*Clivia
nobilis*

*Cobaea
scandens*

brown flowers in late summer, followed in a favourable season by blue berries. These shrubs like warm sheltered places. They can be increased by cuttings of firm young growth in July.

CLIANTHUS *(Glory Pea, Parrot's Bill, Lobster Claw)*

This always excites comment when in flower because of the extraordinary shape of its flower. Two of its popular names, parrot's bill and lobster claw are based on fancied resemblances and I think of the two the second comes nearest the mark. The hanging flowers are long, pointed and curved, not unlike a claw, crimson in the most familiar species, *Clianthus puniceus*, and scarlet with a nearly black blotch in the more difficult and weakly *C. Dampieri*.

Semi-trailing shrubs, of doubtful hardiness in most parts of the country, they may survive if trained against sunny, sheltered walls. Alternatively they can be grown in slightly heated green-houses or conservatories, in large pots or tubs or planted in a border of good soil. Their rather weak stems should be given some support. Both flower in summer. They can be increased by seeds sown in a warm greenhouse.

CLIVIA *(Kaffir Lily)*

Clivia miniata, a showy and easily grown plant for the green-house, should be better known. Though not a true bulb, its fleshy roots are bulb-like and it can be increased by the removal of offsets in February. Alternatively it can be raised from seed sown in a cool greenhouse in spring but seedlings take several years to attain flowering size.

Clivias produce clusters of lily-like flowers on stout 2–foot stems in spring. Typically they are scarlet outside and yellow within, but there are many variations, some of the loveliest varieties being in shades of yellow or orange throughout. All need winter rest and should be kept nearly dry in a frost-proof greenhouse from November to January. Then they can be re-potted, if necessary, and watered more freely. In a temperature of 55° to 60° they will soon come into flower. From June to Sep-tember they are happy in a frame, but should be returned to the greenhouse when frost threatens.

COBAEA *(Cups and Saucers)*

C. scandens, a vigorous climber usually treated as an annual, has green and purple bell shaped flowers not unlike Canterbury bells, though not so showy. They are produced freely in summer (usually in August and September outdoors). Seed is sown in a warm greenhouse in February or March, the seedlings are potted singly and hardened off in time for planting out in early June in a sunny place. They should be allowed to climb up a trellis or fence or over an archway or arbour which they will soon cover with their thin, clinging growths. After flowering the plants are left to be destroyed by frost. But they are, in fact, perennials and if grown in a frost-proof greenhouse will live for many years and eventually cover a considerable area.

COLCHICUM (*Autumn Crocus, Meadow Saffron*)

The common name, autumn crocus, is misleading as colchicums have no connexion with the true crocuses of which there are also autumn-flowering varieties. But the confusion is understandable as there is a strong superficial resemblance between the two flowers.

The bulbs of colchicum are very large but they do not, on that account, need to be planted very deep. It is sufficient to cover them with about 2 inches of soil. They should be planted in July or as early in August as the bulbs can be obtained, and thereafter, should be left undisturbed until over-crowding commences to impair their flowering. Ideal for naturalizing in grass, they may also be planted in large rock gardens, in borders, or at the front of shrubberies. They are mainly in shades of mauve pink but there are also fine white varieties and some that approach purple. Propagation is by division of the bulb clusters at planting time.

COLEUS

The coleus is an excellent greenhouse foliage plant for the beginner because it is so easily grown and has such variety. The hybrids commonly grown make soft-stemmed, bushy plants, with nettle-like leaves in a great diversity of colours and markings. They ask only for a frost-proof greenhouse and may even be kept in living rooms for considerable periods without harm. The John Innes compost suits them to perfection. Cuttings taken in spring or summer rarely fail to root in a close frame, or alternatively, they can be easily grown from seed sown in spring.

Two rather different species are *Coleus thyrsoideus* and *C. Frederici* which are cultivated for their long, slender spikes of purplish-blue flowers produced in winter. Cultivation is, on the whole, the same as for the ornamental-leaved varieties but in winter a temperature of about 55° will be needed to encourage flowering.

COLLINSIA

The collinsia commonly seen in gardens is *C. bicolor* a pretty hardy annual with neat parti-coloured flowers in shades of purple and white. It grows 9 to 12 inches high, flowers in summer and is a useful plant for the front or middle of annual borders. Sow seed from March to May for a succession of flowers, thinning the seedlings to about 9 inches and thereafter leaving them to grow undisturbed. A further sowing can be made in early September for May or June flowering the following year.

CONVALLARIA (*Lily of the Valley*)

The lily of the valley (*Convallaria majalis*) is so familiar to everyone that it can need no introduction or description, and I need only say that there is a pale pink flowered variety not nearly so beautiful as the common white.

It is a lover of cool, partially shady places and fairly rich, moist

Colchicum
variegatum

Colchicum
autumnale

Collinsia
bicolor

Convallaria
majalis

*Convolvulus
Cneorum*

*Convolvulus
althaeoides*

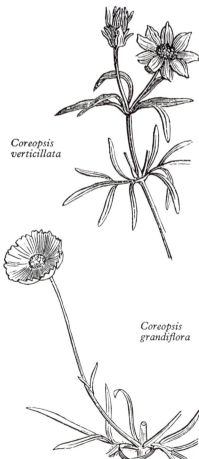

*Coreopsis
verticillata*

*Coreopsis
grandiflora*

(but not boggy) soils. It will often naturalize itself in thin wood-land, provided it has not too much competition from weeds and grass. In the garden a bed on the shady side of a wall suits it well and it is a good thing to work in some well-rotted manure and leaf mould before planting.

The best time for planting is in October or March. The roots should be spread out thinly in drills and covered with about an inch of soil. Propagation is by division of the roots at planting time, but it is unwise to disturb the plants frequently. Leave them to spread and make a solid carpet of foliage and only lift when starvation through overcrowding brings about a falling off in flower production.

CONVOLVULUS *(Bindweed, Dwarf Morning Glory)*

One of the garden flowers listed as convolvulus, *C. major* (often called morning glory) will be found under Ipomoea on page 74.

C. minor (*tricolor*) is a beautiful hardy annual making a foot high, sprawling plant, bearing funnel-shaped blue, purple, pink or white flowers in summer. Seeds can be sown thinly in the open in March, April or September, where they are to bloom.

C. Cneorum is a 2 foot shrub with silvery leaves and white flowers in summer. It likes a warm sunny place and can be increased by summer cuttings inserted in a frame.

COREOPSIS *(Calliopsis, Tickseed)*

The different kinds of coreopsis may be considered in two groups, the hardy perennials and the hardy annuals.

The four best perennials are *C. lanceolata*, *C. auriculata*, *C. grandiflora* and *C. verticillata*. The first three have large, flat yellow flowers carried on slender 2–foot stems during most of the summer, but *C. grandiflora* has larger flowers than the others and also has some double or semi-double varieties (Perry's variety is a fine example of the last named), while *C. auriculata* differs in having a small crimson blotch at the base of each petal. All are inclined to flower themselves to death but *C. grandiflora* is the worst offender, for which reason it has sometimes been referred to as a biennial. But it is a true perennial and will live for many years in a soil that is well drained and not too rich.

C. verticillata, quite a different plant and less well known, is extremely decorative. It grows about 2 feet high and has very small narrow almost fern-like leaves. The yellow flowers are also quite small but very freely produced in midsummer.

All these can be increased by division in the spring and also by seed sown in spring, though seedlings may prove a little variable.

The annual coreopsis are mostly hybrids and are often listed as calliopsis which, botanically, is an obsolete name. They vary in height from 1 to 3 feet and have flowers similar to those of *C. lanceolata* but in a variety of combinations of yellow and crimson. They are exceedingly showy plants both for the border and for cutting. Seed should be sown, in March, April, May or September, where the plants are to flower and the seedlings thinned to at least 9 inches apart.

CORNUS (Dogwood)

This is a big family of shrubs or small trees some of which are among the most beautiful and the most exclusive that can be cultivated in the open in this country, while others are little better than weeds. One needs, therefore, to be careful when making a selection of dogwoods.

The finest of the small trees are to be found among the American and Asiatic species such as *C. florida, C. Kousa, C. Nuttallii* and *C. capitata*. The last is tender and only suitable for the mildest places. The other three are also slightly suspect but are really much hardier and I have seen them thriving in quite cold gardens. Their young spring growth is apt to be cut by late frosts and this retards their growth and their flowering. Their true flowers are quite insignificant but they are surrounded by large and very showy petal-like bracts, usually **white** or ivory but a delightfully soft pink in *C. florida rubra*. All flower in spring.

Much easier to grow and a very useful garden shrub is *Cornus alba Spaethii*, a form of a wild British dogwood which is, therefore, perfectly hardy. A big bush with reddish stems and handsomely yellow-variegated leaves, I regard it as one of the ten or twelve best variegated shrubs and it has the added advantage that it will grow almost anywhere.

All these can be increased by cuttings of firm young wood in the autumn or by layering in early summer. The species (but not *C. alba Spaethii*) can also be raised from seed sown in a greenhouse or frame in spring.

CORYDALIS (Yellow Fumitory)

The most familiar corydalis is *C. lutea*, a pretty perennial with pale green, fern-like leaves and sprays of small yellow flowers carried most of the summer. Growing about a foot high, it is often to be seen on the crumbling walls of old cottages and is a useful plant for such stony places, though rather a menace in the rock garden because of its tendency to seed itself everywhere. It is perfectly hardy and likes dry, well-drained places and poor soils. It can be increased in the spring, either by division or by seed. There are also other and choicer (but more difficult) kinds of which one of the best is *C. cheilanthifolia*, also with yellow flowers but a far less invasive habit.

COSMOS (Purple Mexican Aster)

The cosmos commonly grown in gardens is *C. bipinnatus*, a familiar plant in late summer and early autumn, when its flat, broad-petalled daisy-flowers in various shades of pink, rose and wine red, as well as white, are at their best. Its tall masses of ferny foliage are also decorative but care must be taken not to grow this plant in too rich and moist a soil or it may be all foliage and no flowers.

It is a half-hardy annual, seed of which should be germinated in a warm greenhouse in February or early March. Prick off the seedlings and harden them off for planting out in late May or

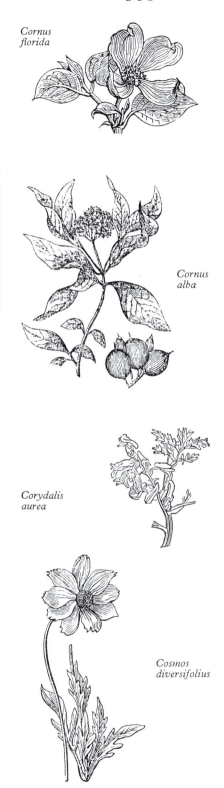

Cornus florida

Cornus alba

Corydalis aurea

Cosmos diversifolius

Cotinus
Coggygria

Cotoneaster
microphylla

Cotoneaster
thymifolia

Cotoneaster
frigida

early June in a sunny place. Seed should be purchased from a reliable source as some strains do not flower at all well or start to flower so late that they are of little use.

COTINUS *(Wig Tree or Smoke Plant)*

Closely related to the sumach (rhus), *Cotinus Coggygria* is an excellent small tree or bush, up to 10 or 15 feet tall. It is often known as *Rhus Cotinus*. In July and August it is covered with curious 'flowers' made up of a large number of silk-like hairs in a tangled mass, at first a pale pinkish brown in colour, later turning grey (hence the popular names). The leaves take on magnificent autumn colourings before they fall in November. The variety *purpureus* (or *atropurpureus*) has purple leaves and purplish hairs. Another species, *C. americanus*, grows eventually to 20 feet and is worth having for its intense autumn colouring.

All these shrubs grow readily in any ordinary soil and open position and can be increased by cuttings of well ripened shoots inserted in sandy soil in autumn.

COTONEASTER

One of the great families of berry bearing shrubs and small trees, rivalling berberis in its importance for garden decoration. There are so many excellent species that it is difficult to confine selection to a mere eight or ten, but the following are, in my view, as good as any for general planting.

C. horizontalis is indispensable and unique because its rigid, fishbone-like branches will mould themselves to any surface against which they are planted. Placed alongside a rock they will throw themselves over it, near a wall they will ascend it without either clinging to it or requiring any support. The small neat leaves fall off in winter, when the scarlet berries set closely to the branches make a splendid display.

Closely allied to this but more rounded in habit and with narrower, evergreen leaves and deeper coloured, almost crimson berries, is *C. microphylla*. It is a grand shrub which is never seen to better advantage than when ascending (or descending) a wall.

Like miniature versions of the last, but deciduous, are *C. adpressa* and *C. congesta*, excellent dwarf shrubs for the rock garden.

C. conspicua decora has stiff spreading horizontal branches rather like *C. horizontalis*, but producing larger and more showy white flowers in May and crops of larger, scarlet berries in autumn. It is in the first rank of berry bearing shrubs.

Of the taller species the best appear to me to be *C. Franchetii*, *C. frigida*, *C. Dielsiana*, *C. Henryana*, *C. salicifolia*, *C. Simonsii* and *C. Wardii*. If I had to reduce this list to two they would be *C. frigida*, because it will make a small and shapely tree carrying great crops of crimson berries with unfailing regularity, and *C. Wardii* because it is a most elegant evergreen shrub eventually 8 or 10 feet in height with neat clusters of orange-red berries which are usually held well into the winter.

All are completely hardy and will thrive in any ordinary soil and open position. They can all be raised from seed sown in spring and most can also be raised from cuttings of firm young shoots in a frame in July.

CRATAEGUS (Thorn, Quick)

Another big family of shrubs or small trees (mostly the latter), many notable for their fruits. The common thorn or quick, *C. monogyna*, used for farm hedges, is hardly worth planting in the garden except in its double-flowered forms, one of which has pink and the other crimson flowers. These make shapely small trees suitable for gardens of moderate size, and flower very freely in May, but as their flowers are sterile, they are never followed by berries. They must therefore be increased by grafting in spring on to stocks of common thorn.

The famous Glastonbury thorn, another variety of the common thorn, has ordinary single white flowers. It is remarkable for the fact that it often produces some leaves and flowers in midwinter. Its name is *C. monogyna biflora*.

The cockspur thorn, *C. Crus-galli*, notable for its very long and rigid thorns, is a good small tree with plentiful white flowers in May, good autumn foliage colour and handsome, deep red fruits.

Two other useful kinds are *C. Carrierei* and *C. prunifolia*, both small trees with handsome foliage and typical scarlet fruits. Those of *C. Carrierei* remain for a long time untouched by birds.

All are completely hardy and unfastidious. The species can be raised from seed sown outdoors in March. The varieties must be grafted on to seedling stocks.

CRINUM

These beautiful, lily-like plants suffer from the drawback of being on the border-line of tenderness. In warm and sheltered places they can be grown outdoors but an unusually severe winter may kill them. Probably the two hardiest kinds, and certainly the two most commonly seen, are *Crinum longifolium* (also known as *C. capense*) and *C. Powellii*. The first has white or pale pink trumpet shaped flowers, carried in crowded clusters on stout, 3–foot stems in August. *C. Powellii*, otherwise similar, has even larger flowers of a warmer pink.

They make very large bulbs which should be planted so that their necks are just out of the ground, in fairly rich but well-drained soils and warm sunny places. The foot of a south wall suits them well provided they are well watered in summer. They should be covered with a little dry straw or bracken in winter. Planting time is October and old clusters of bulbs can then be divided.

CROCUS

In addition to the well-known spring flowering crocuses in shades of mauve, lilac, purple and yellow, as well as white, there

43

Cotoneaster
rotundifolia

Crataegus
Crus-galli

Crataegus
prunifolia

Crinum
amabile

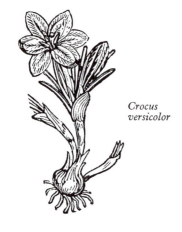

*Crocus
versicolor*

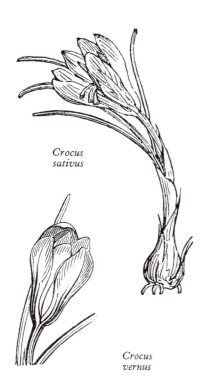

*Crocus
sativus*

*Crocus
vernus*

*Cyclamen
coum*

are a number of beautiful autumn and winter-flowering kinds which need a little more care in cultivation. These include *Crocus speciosus* with large violet-blue or white flowers in October or November; *C. zonatus* with lilac and yellow flowers at the same season; *C. chrysanthus*, which produces its yellow flowers in January or February; *C. Imperati*, usually January flowering and a very fine species, fawn without and violet within; *C. Sieberi*, pale-lilac, February flowering; *C. susianus*, golden yellow, either February or early March flowering; *C. versicolor*, which is variously striped purple on white; and *C. Tomasinianus*, with clear lavender flowers in February. The common, large flowered spring crocuses, hybrids sometimes referred to as Dutch crocuses, are available in mixed colours or in separate colours, sometimes under fancy names such as King of the Purples, Striped Beauty, etc.

The species, especially those that flower in autumn or winter, are really most at home in the rock garden though they can be grown in ordinary beds and borders provided the soil is fairly gritty and well drained. The common hybrids thrive in practically any soil. All like sunny places though they will also grow in the shade provided it is not too dense.

Planting time for autumn-flowering species is July or early August, for winter and spring kinds, September or October. The corms should be covered with 2 or 3 inches of soil and thereafter will require little attention beyond weeding. They should not be disturbed until they become so overcrowded that there is a falling off in the number and quality of their flowers. Then they can be lifted in July, divided into single corms and replanted.

CYCLAMEN *(Sowbread)*

These can conveniently be considered in two groups, for the varieties of *Cyclamen persicum* are greenhouse plants whereas most of the others are hardy plants to be grown outdoors. All make rather large tubers which have the peculiarity of growing either on the surface of the soil or just beneath it.

The greenhouse cyclamen are usually raised from seed sown in August in an unheated greenhouse. Germination is rather irregular and the seedlings are pricked off, a few at a time, into boxes of John Innes compost. When they begin to fill these comfortably they are potted singly, first into 3-inch pots, later into 4-inch, and finally into 5- or 6-inch pots, in which they will flower. John Innes potting compost can be used throughout.

The seedlings should be given greenhouse treatment until May or June of their second year. In winter they will need an average temperature of about 50°. In summer no artificial heat will be needed, but the glass should be lightly shaded and ventilation given freely. The seedlings should reach their flowering pots about 10 months after sowing. They will start flowering about November and continue most of the winter. After flowering the water supply can be gradually reduced to allow foliage to die down and the plants to rest. From the end of May until August they are best removed to a shady frame where they will

Cymbidium Pauwelsii
citrina

Crinum Powellii

Cytisus scoparius

Crocus vernus
[garden form]

Cyclamen persicun
[garden form]

Cotinus
Coggygria

Cynoglossum
amabile

Cypripedium insigne
[garden form]

Cosmos
bipinnatu

otoneaster

Corydalis lutea

Crataegus Oxyacantha 'Paul's Double Scarlet'

Delphinium
elatum
[garden form]

Dicentra formosa

Dictamnus
albus

Digitalis
purpurea

Daphne
Burkwoodii

Dimorphotheca
aurantiaca

Dahlia
[medium
decorative]

Doronicum
plantagineum

Dianthus
barbatus

Dodecatheon
Meadia

Deutzia scabra

Dianthus plumarius
[garden form]

need little attention. In mid-August they can be repotted and watered more freely, and about a month later should be returned to the greenhouse where they will flower again in the winter. The circular tubers should be kept sitting just on top of the soil and must never be buried when repotting.

The hardy cyclamen have smaller flowers and vary in their time of flowering. *Cyclamen coum* produces small crimson flowers in February and March; *C. europaeum*, deep red blooms in August; *C. neapolitanum*, bright pink or white flowers in September.

All like cool, leafy soils in the rock garden, at the edge of shrubberies or in shady beds and borders. They like a certain amount of shade and resent root disturbance. Once established they should be left severely alone except for hand weeding. Start with small plants in pots, which can be put in at practically any time of the year, though spring is probably best. The tubers should be just covered with soil.

All hardy cyclamen can be raised from seed sown in a frame or cool greenhouse in spring.

CYMBIDIUM

These fine orchids are beautiful and comparatively easy to grow. They produce their long arching sprays of butterfly-like flowers in winter in a great variety of unusual colours including shades of green, amber, honey, bronze, buff, crimson and maroon. They last a very long time when cut and are invaluable for decoration. Cymbidiums are epiphytes which means that they obtain much of their food from the air. They are grown in a mixture of loam, sphagnum moss, osmunda fibre and decaying leaves, one recommended mixture being 3 parts of good fibrous loam, 1 part of sphagnum moss, 2 parts of osmunda fibre and 1 part of old, partly decayed oak or beech leaves. Plants should be repotted after flowering (usually in March), and it is usually sufficient to repot them every second year. They do not require high temperatures but should be kept at around 50° in winter and 60° in summer, with permanent shading from April to September. Syringe frequently with clear water in summer to maintain a moist atmosphere, but keep a little drier in early autumn when the bulb-like growths (correctly known as pseudo-bulbs) are ripening. Cymbidiums should be ventilated freely in favourable weather. They can be increased by careful division at potting time.

CYNOGLOSSUM *(Hound's Tongue)*

There are annuals, biennials and perennials in this genus and on the whole they are not, perhaps, a particularly distinguished lot apart from *Cynoglossum amabile*, a hardy plant, usually treated as an annual, which is notable for its brilliantly blue flowers. It is a rather sprawling plant, about 2 feet in height, like a coarse and large forget-me-not. Seed can be sown in a greenhouse or frame in March, and the seedlings planted out in May, to flower in July and August. Alternatively seed can be sown outdoors in

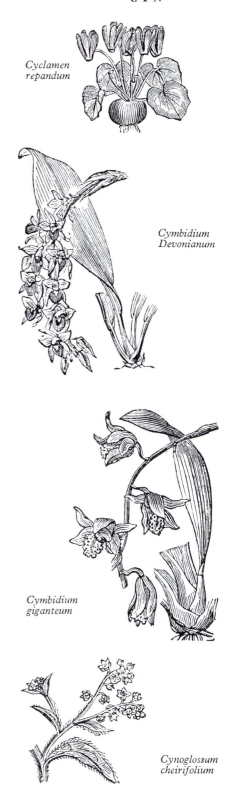

Cyclamen
repandum

Cymbidium
Devonianum

Cymbidium
giganteum

Cynoglossum
cheirifolium

45

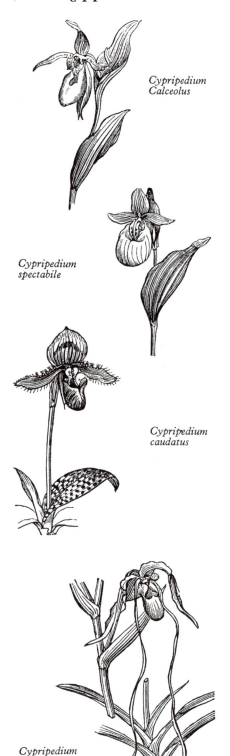

*Cypripedium
Calceolus*

*Cypripedium
spectabile*

*Cypripedium
caudatus*

*Cypripedium
barbatus*

late April where the plants are to flower, when the flowering season will be in August and September. This cynoglossum likes sunny places but is not particular about soil.

CYPRIPEDIUM (*Lady's Slipper*)

The cypripediums, unlike many orchids, do not grow perched up in trees, getting most of their food from the air, but in soil, with a more or less normal root system. Partly for this reason and partly because several kinds of cypripedium can be grown with little or no heat, they are among the best orchids with which an amateur can start.

Several are sufficiently hardy to be grown outdoors. Two of the best of these are *Cypripedium spectabile* which has rose-pink and white flowers, and *C. Calceolus*, with yellow and purple flowers. *C. pubescens*, rather like the last named, has larger flowers. All flower in late spring or early summer and are happiest in cool, rather moist leafy or peaty soils and partly shaded positions.

Of the greenhouse kinds easily the most popular is *C. insigne*, with green and chestnut coloured flowers, a fine and easily grown plant which has given rise to a great number of varieties and hybrids, among the best orchids for the amateur.

Compost for these greenhouse cypripediums consists of 2 parts of good medium loam, 1 part of sphagnum moss chopped fairly finely and 1 part of osmunda fibre well pulled apart. A little coarse silver sand should be added and a sprinkling of hoof and horn meal. Cypripediums mostly flower in the winter and should be repotted in spring when the flowers have faded. They have no marked resting period and must be watered all the year but much less frequently in autumn and winter than in spring and summer. They should be syringed frequently in warm weather and be shaded from hot sunshine.

All can be increased by careful division of the roots in spring. The name Lady's slipper refers to the conspicuous pouch, a feature of the flower of all species.

CYTISUS (*Broom*)

The brooms are among the most showy of spring flowering shrubs. Some of the best are varieties or hybrids of *Cytisus scoparius*, a tall, loose growing shrub with whippy, green branches and showy yellow flowers in May. The varieties and hybrids have flowers of primrose, deeper yellow, crimson, pink and various combinations of these.

There is a fine early flowering pale yellow broom, *C. praecox*, at its best in April; a tall and very graceful white kind named *C. albus*; the more or less prostrate spreading *C. Ardoinii* with yellow flowers; and *C. purpureus*, slightly taller but still spreading, with pale purplish-pink flowers. Very handsome in appearance but slightly less hardy is *C. Battandieri*, with comparatively large, silvery leaves and cylindrical clusters of bright yellow flowers in June. It makes a big, rather sprawling, loose habited shrub and is worthy of a warm and sheltered place.

All these delight in sunny places and rather poor, well-drained soils. They dislike root disturbance and should be raised in pots and transplanted from these to the open ground with as little injury to the roots as possible. They can be planted at any time from November to March inclusive.

They are rather susceptible to wind damage and in exposed places should be securely staked. All can be raised very readily from seed sown in spring in greenhouse or frame or even in the open ground, but seedlings of the hybrids and selected garden forms do not usually come quite true to type and where an exact reproduction of these is required, they must either be grafted (seedling laburnum is often used as a stock) or be raised from cuttings. This is not very easy but it can be done if the cuttings are prepared in August from firm young growths pulled off with a heel of older wood. These should be inserted in very sandy soil in a close frame.

Brooms do not normally require any pruning but if bushes become too big or grow straggly they can be trimmed over lightly immediately after flowering.

DAHLIA

The dahlias grown in gardens are complex, man-made hybrids, painstakingly developed for more than a hundred years. As a result, an extraordinary variety of flower shapes has been produced and for convenience these have been grouped in a classification devised by the National Dahlia Society and accepted by all dahlia growers. Full details are obtainable from the N.D.S. but for ordinary garden purposes it is only necessary to know its broad outlines. These consist of a number of groups such as decorative dahlias with double flowers composed of fairly broad petals; cactus dahlias with double flowers in which each petal is rolled downwards (in the most perfect cactus varieties the petal looks like a curved quill); show dahlias, with almost globular flowers as big as cricket balls and composed of short, almost tubular petals set with almost the precision of a honeycomb; pompon dahlias closely resembling the last but with much smaller flowers; collerette dahlias having single flowers with an extra ring of short petals, usually in a contrasting colour, around the disk-like centre; anemone-centred varieties, with a single row of large outer petals with a cushion-like centre of much shorter petals; true single-flowered varieties, and bedding dahlias which may be either single or double-flowered but are always quite dwarf, usually not above 2 feet in height.

All are grown in the same way except for minor variations necessitated by their height or the purpose for which they are required. All are half-hardy, i.e. they can be grown outdoors in summer but must be protected in winter, and all have tuberous roots. They can be increased either by carefully dividing the roots in spring or by taking cuttings of the young shoots as they appear in spring. The first method is simple and very effective but will not produce a great number of plants as each division must have a piece of the main crown of the plant, i.e. the hard part where stems and roots join. Cuttings enable a

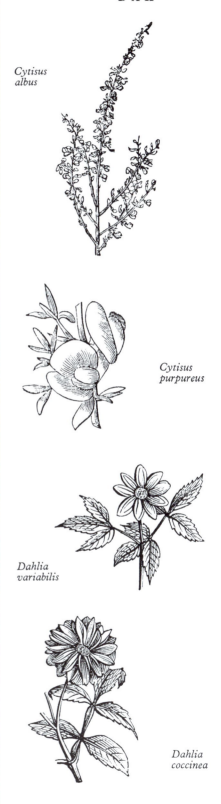

Cytisus
albus

Cytisus
purpureus

Dahlia
variabilis

Dahlia
coccinea

47

*Dahlia
(cactus)*

*Daphne
Genkwa*

*Daphne
collina*

*Daphne
Mezereum*

variety to be multiplied quickly but they must be rooted in a warm greenhouse and then hardened off.

When the cuttings are rooted they are potted singly in good soil (John Innes potting compost No. 1 will do well) and are grown on, first in the greenhouse and later in a frame in which they can be hardened off ready for planting out early in June. Dahlias like a sunny place and a rich soil, well dug and manured. The taller varieties should be staked securely for their stems are heavy and brittle. They like plenty of water. To obtain large flowers the flower buds should be restricted to one per stem.

In the autumn the top growth will be killed by frost. Then the roots should be lifted carefully and stored in a dry, fairly cool but frost-proof place until it is time either to start them into growth for cuttings or to divide and replant them outdoors, which should be done between mid-April and mid-May.

DAPHNE

Many of these beautiful shrubs are extremely sweetly scented. *Daphne Mezereum*, one of the earliest to flower, is deciduous and the purple or white flowers are produced in February or March along the bare stems. It grows about 4 feet high, is a little stiff and ungainly in habit and has a habit of dying unexpectedly without apparent cause, yet despite these defects it is a very desirable shrub because of its earliness and its fragrance.

D. Cneorum, a much smaller and neater evergreen, about a foot in height, bearing neat clusters of pink, fragrant flowers in May, is a good shrub for the rock garden in a sunny place and well-drained rather peaty soil.

Another good kind for the rock garden is *D. Blagayana*, prostrate, with clusters of very fragrant, creamy white flowers in May. It likes stony soils and it is a good plan to place small stones on its sprawling stems from time to time to hold them to the ground. In some ways the best of all is *D. Burkwoodii*, also known as *D. Somerset*, a neat bush about 3 feet high, semi-evergreen, with clusters of fragrant pink flowers in May and June. Both this and the purple flowered *D. collina* like sunny places.

D. odora is evergreen and 2 feet in height. Its purplish-rose flowers appear even earlier than those of *D. Mezereum* and it is desirable to give it a rather sheltered place. As its name implies it is sweetly scented. There are two forms, one with plain green leaves, the other margined with yellow.

Daphne Burkwoodii, *D. Cneorum* and *D. odora* can be increased by July cuttings of firm young growth rooted in a frame. *D. Mezereum* is best raised from seed. *D. Blagayana* usually layers itself and these rooted shoots can be detached in autumn.

DELPHINIUM *(Larkspur)*

Though strictly speaking 'delphinium' is simply the botanical name for the group of plants which should popularly be known as larkspurs, in practice gardeners nearly always mean the annual *Delphinium Ajacis* when they refer to larkspurs and they call the perennial kinds delphiniums. This is a very useful diff-

Erica carnea

Eschscholtzia californica

Epimedium versicolor sulphureum

Erodium Manescavii

Eryngium planum

Eremurus himalaicus

Echinops bannaticus

Erysimum Allionii

Eccremocarpus scaber

Echinacea purpurea

Euonymus europaeus

Felicia tenella

Escallonia langleyensis

Forsythia intermedia
spectabilis

Gazania
[garden forms]

Galanthus
nivalis

Garrya
elliptica

Geranium
grandiflorum

Gaillardia
aristata
[garden form]

Genista
aethnensis

Gentiana
septemfida

Fritillaria
gracilis

Freesia
refracta
[garden
form]

Fuchsia
'Royal Purple'

Galega
officinalis

Gardenia
jasminoides

CNT

erentiation to remember for the annual and perennial kinds need quite different treatment.

The annuals are renewed from seed every year and the finest results are obtained by sowing this in September where the plants are to flower the following summer. Rather smaller plants and later flowers can be obtained by sowing in March or April, also in the open ground. Seedlings should be thinned to 9 or 12 inches. The tall, narrow spikes of bloom are very decorative and pink and white varieties are available as well as several shades of blue, lavender and violet. All are excellent for cutting as well as for garden display.

The perennials flower in June and July, sometimes giving a second display of smaller spikes in August or September, and seedlings usually flower in August in their first year. They may be considered in two groups, the tall 'elatum' varieties, with large spikes of bloom, and the shorter 'belladonna' varieties with small spikes or loose sprays of flowers. All like rather rich, well-drained soils and sunny positions. They may be planted in early autumn on the lighter soils but on heavier soils it is better to plant in March or early April. The large-flowered varieties require staking, preferably one stake to every flower spike, but the belladonna varieties can usually be grown without stakes or at most with a few brushy hazel branches for support.

Delphiniums can be increased either by careful division of the roots in spring, or by cuttings taken at the same season, prepared from young shoots 5 or 6 inches long, cut off close to the crown of the plant and inserted in sandy soil in a frame. The rooted cuttings can be planted out in late May or June.

The elatum delphiniums can also be raised from seed as soon as ripe in August or the following March. Sow in a frame or greenhouse and keep slugs away. The seedlings should be pricked off as soon as they can be handled and should be planted out in late May or early June. Most will flower the same year but there is usually a good deal of variation in the colour and habit of seedlings. However, certain American and English strains come remarkably true from seed.

DEUTZIA

The deutzias suffer from having no popular name and a botanical name that is not easy to remember. If it were not for this they could be as familiar as spiraeas or mock oranges, for they are equally decorative and useful shrubs. All have an erect habit of growth and attractive flowers in dense sprays at the ends of the branches. All are white or are flushed with pink or purple and all flower in June or July. Most of those grown in gardens are either varieties or hybrids of *Deutzia scabra* which is 7 or 8 feet in height and has white flowers. It has several double-flowered varieties one, Pride of Rochester, being suffused with purple and another, *candidissima*, being pure white. A fine rose pink hybrid is Mont Rose, while Avalanche has large white flowers. *D. gracilis* flowers earlier than most, is less tall and is frequently grown as a greenhouse pot plant.

D

Delphinium grandiflorum

Delphinium elatum

Deutzia scabra

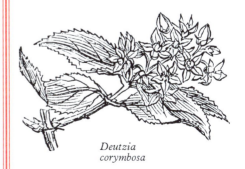

Deutzia corymbosa

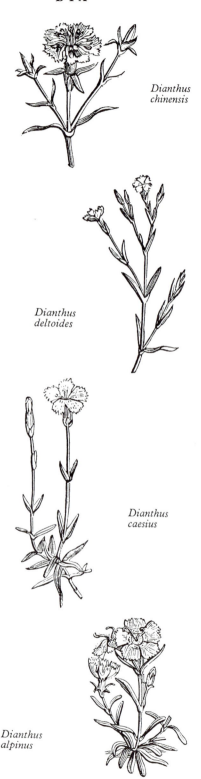

Dianthus chinensis

Dianthus deltoides

Dianthus caesius

Dianthus alpinus

They all like sunny places but are not particular about soil. Old flowering stems can be cut out after flowering, if desired, but deutzias will grow quite happily without any pruning. They can be increased by cuttings of well-ripened young growth in early autumn.

DIANTHUS (Carnation, Pink, Sweet William)

This is one of the great garden families for in addition to numerous wild species suitable for the rock garden, it contains all those lovely summer blooming perennials familiarly referred to as pinks, as well as all the carnations both border and perpetual.

Border carnations are hardy and are grown outdoors, whereas perpetual flowering carnations are a little tender and are grown in greenhouses. Another difference is that border carnations flower once only in June or early July whereas, if carefully managed, perpetual carnations will flower throughout the year.

Most pinks derived from *Dianthus plumarius* flower in June but *Dianthus Allwoodii* hybrids have a longer flowering season, some continuing most of the summer.

All carnations like rather rich, loamy soils preferably containing a little lime. The perpetual flowering varieties may be grown in John Innes potting compost but the loam should be just a little heavier and richer than usual.

Perpetual carnations are raised from cuttings taken between November and March and inserted in pure silver sand or very sandy soil in a close frame at a temperature of about 60°. When rooted they are potted singly and moved on to larger pots as they fill the smaller sizes with roots, until they reach the 6- or 7-inch pots in which they will flower. The growing tips of the young plants are pinched out twice, first when they have seven pairs of leaves and again when the side shoots formed after the first stopping have made about seven pairs of leaves each. Plants can be grown in a deep frame from June to September but after that are better in a greenhouse. They do not need much heat but like an average temperature around 55°. As flower stems lengthen they will need careful staking. For best results the flowers are restricted to one per stem, other buds being removed at an early stage. It is wise to renew stock from cuttings every second or third year.

Border carnations are increased by layers pegged down in July. These should be rooted by September and can be severed from the parent plants, lifted and replanted. They like sunny open places and should be spaced about 18 inches apart. They need not be pinched like perpetual carnations and as they are not so tall, will need less elaborate staking. To get large blooms, restrict the flowers to one per stem but this is not necessary for garden display. Border carnations are classified according to colour, markings and perfume. Those known as cloves have a particularly rich perfume. Fancy carnations have markings of one colour, usually pink, red, crimson or lavender, on a ground of another colour. Self carnations are of one colour throughout. Picotees have a ground of one colour with a narrow margin to each petal of another colour. Bizarres and flakes have heavier and more blotched markings than the fancies.

Pinks are raised from cuttings taken in June or July and rooted in sandy soil outdoors or in a frame. They like open places, are not fussy about soil but appreciate good drainage.

The dianthus species cover a wide range from the cushion forming *Dianthus neglectus*, and trailing *D. deltoides*, to the erect, 2-foot high *D. superbus* with elegantly fringed flowers. They are plants for sunny places and light, well-drained soils. Many do well on walls or in rock gardens and most can be raised from seed sown in a greenhouse or frame in spring. Some can be carefully divided in spring when being transplanted.

Some dianthus are annuals or biennials, or are treated as such. *D. chinensis* and its variety *D. Heddewigii*, examples of the former, are grown as half-hardy annuals, seed being sown in a warm greenhouse in January or February. Seedlings are pricked off into boxes, carefully hardened off and planted out in May in a sunny place.

The Sweet William (*D. barbatus*) is usually grown as a biennial, seed being sown outdoors in May for flowering the following year. Seedlings should be moved to a nursery bed when they can be handled conveniently and finally removed to their flowering beds in September or October. At their best in June, they grow about 2 feet high and have large, flattish heads of brightly coloured flowers, usually pink, scarlet or crimson and white.

DICENTRA *(Bleeding Heart)*

Exceptionally graceful, hardy, June and July flowering perennials which will thrive in partially shaded positions. The three kinds commonly grown are *Dicentra eximia*, about a foot in height, with small carmine flowers; *D. formosa*, taller but otherwise similar; and *D. spectabilis*, at least 2 feet high, with larger pink and white flowers. All have decorative light green, ferny foliage. They can be grown in ordinary soil and are easily increased by division in spring or autumn. *D. spectabilis* is often grown as a pot plant for the unheated or slightly heated house.

DICTAMNUS *(Burning Bush, Gas Plant)*

The only species grown in gardens is *Dictamnus albus* (syn. *D. Fraxinella*). Called burning bush because it is said to give off an inflammable gas, which can be ignited on a warm day, it is a striking and decorative hardy perennial about 3 feet in height with spikes of purple or white flowers in summer. It likes cool shady places and ordinary soils and can be increased from seed or by dividing old roots in spring or autumn.

DIGITALIS *(Foxglove)*

The common foxglove of British hedgerows and woodlands is a biennial or short-lived perennial which, though hardly worth transplanting to the garden in its ordinary purple-flowered form, has given rise to a number of other forms, admirable for rough or shady places. These have larger flowers and the colour range

Dianthus superbus

Dicentra eximia

Dictamnus albus

Digitalis grandiflora

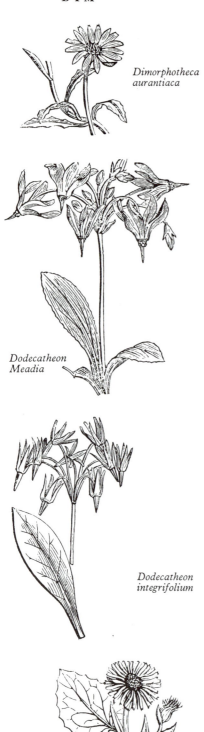

Dimorphotheca
aurantiaca

Dodecatheon
Meadia

Dodecatheon
integrifolium

Doronicum
Pardalianches

is from white and pale pink to crimson, some very beautifully netted with one shade on another. A recent development, known as the Excelsior strain, has flowers held almost horizontally all round the stem instead of drooping on one side only.

All these can be very easily raised from seed sown outdoors in May. The seedlings should be pricked off in a nursery bed, and moved from this in autumn to the place in which they are to flower. They look well among shrubs or in good drifts in thin woodland. There are also perennial species, such as *D. ambigua* with dull yellow flowers.

DIMORPHOTHECA *(Star of the Veldt)*

These are all sun-loving daisies best treated as annuals in this country. They are valuable in the garden because they bring to it a range of colours not commonly found in anything else—shades between orange and apricot, yellow and buff. All grow about 1 foot high and flower in summer according to the time at which they are sown. For the earliest flowers seed should be sown in a greenhouse or frame in March, the seedlings pricked off into boxes and hardened off for planting out in late May or early June. For later flowers seed can be sown outdoors in April or early May where the plants are to flower and the seedlings thinned to 9 inches apart. A position in full sun is essential as in shade the flowers do not open properly. They will grow in almost any soil but prefer that which is fairly light and well drained.

DODECATHEON *(Shooting Star, American Cowslip)*

The dodecatheons are extremely attractive plants for the bog garden. The flowers are not unlike small cyclamens carried on stiffly erect stems which may be anything from 12 to 18 inches in height. That most commonly grown in British gardens is *Dodecatheon Meadia* with rosy-purple or white flowers in May. It thrives best in a very moist place, alongside a pool or a slow moving stream, and it likes peaty soils, though there should be enough grit in them to allow moisture to keep moving freely through them. The best method of increase is by seed sown in spring in a greenhouse or frame in sandy peat.

DORONICUM *(Leopard's Bane)*

These are hardy herbaceous perennials, useful because they flower so early. The bright yellow daisies of the best kind, *Doronicum plantagineum*, are often out in April and are at their best in May. Each bloom is about 3 inches in diameter and as the flowers are carried on good 3-foot stems, they are excellent for cutting as well as for garden display. An improved variety known as *excelsum* or Harpur Crewe has even larger flowers. *D. Pardalianches* is a less showy, very hardy British species.

Doronicums are not at all fussy about soil, will succeed in full sun or partial shade and are readily increased by division in spring or autumn. I have seen them very happily naturalized in grass where they looked like yellow moon daisies.

ECCREMOCARPUS *(Chilean Glory Flower)*

Only one species, *Eccremocarpus scaber*, is grown in gardens. A slender climber with small, ferny leaves, it has tubular orange-red flowers in summer. It comes from Chile and is a little tender in Britain. For this reason, and also because it grows very rapidly from seed, it is often treated as an annual. However, it is a true perennial and it is worth a specially warm and sheltered place, for example, against a wall or fence facing south, for then it will go on from year to year and give a magnificent display. It will reach a height of about 12 feet and cover quite an area. Seed should be sown in a greenhouse either as soon as ripe or in March. Pot the seedlings singly and harden them off for planting out in late May. The plants climb by tendrils so should have some support to which these can cling.

ECHINACEA *(Purple Cone Flower)*

The only species of echinacea grown in gardens is the purple flowered *E. purpurea*. The flowers are like big daisies with a dark central disk in the manner of many rudbeckias (it is sometimes known as *Rudbeckia purpurea*.) The colour is unusual and difficult to describe, rather like the stains of purple plum juice, and is a useful addition to the border. It is a hardy herbaceous perennial easily grown in any fairly moist but reasonably porous soil and open position. It can be increased by division in spring or autumn. The varieties differ a little in the precise shade of their colour and also in height, which varies from 3 to 4 feet. One of the best is The King.

ECHINOPS *(Globe Thistle)*

The globe thistles are distinctly handsome and unusual hardy herbaceous plants. Their flower heads are almost perfect spheres made up of small, closely packed blue flowers which fall off to reveal a striking, spiky, metallic-blue seed head. They are a little coarse in leaf but that is their only fault. All are extremely hardy and easily grown in practically any soil. They like an open position and good drainage and can be increased very readily from seed or, more slowly, by careful division in spring of their long, thongy roots. A third alternative is to take root cuttings in winter and start these in a frame. The names of the various kinds seem to have become rather mixed in gardens and nurseries and that commonly offered as *Echinops Ritro* is not, apparently, that rather dwarf (1 to 2-foot) species but the much larger 5-foot, *E. sphaerocephalus*. Another attractive species often offered is *E. bannaticus*, about 3 feet tall.

EPIMEDIUM *(Barrenwort)*

The epimediums while not showy plants have the merit of attractive foliage which usually colours well in the autumn, small but dainty flowers like those of barberries, to which they are related, and an ability to thrive in quite dense shade. All are hardy herbaceous perennials of comparatively low growth

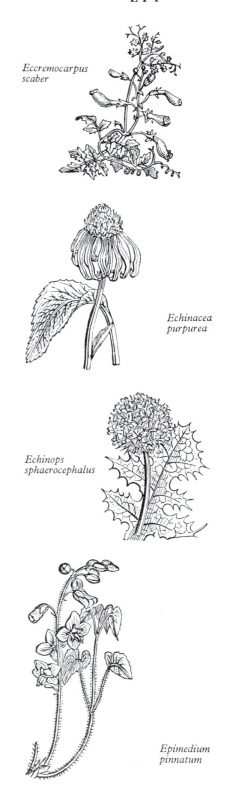

Eccremocarpus scaber

Echinacea purpurea

Echinops sphaerocephalus

Epimedium pinnatum

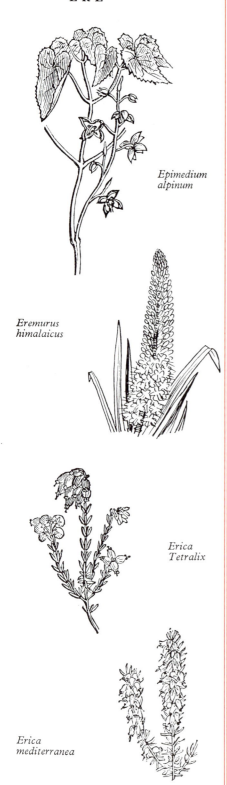

Epimedium
alpinum

Eremurus
himalaicus

Erica
Tetralix

Erica
mediterranea

suitable for planting at the front of the border or as undercover beneath shrubs. The most common kind, *E. versicolor sulphureum*, has pale sulphur yellow flowers in spring. It can be easily increased by division. *E. alpinum* with dull red flowers, *E. pinnatum*, bright yellow and *E. niveum*, white are occasionally seen.

EREMURUS *(Fox-tail Lily)*

The fox-tail lilies are among the most handsome and imposing of all hardy herbaceous perennials but are not very easy to grow. Their fleshy roots spread out from a central crown like the spokes of a wheel and they do not much like being disturbed, let alone broken. Moreover the crowns themselves are a little tender, particularly when starting into growth in early spring and should be protected with small heaps of sharp ashes, coarse sand or dry bracken placed over them in the autumn and left until growth breaks through in the spring.

They like an open, not too dry soil and a sunny position. I have seen them doing well on chalk and also on a light fenland soil, so their range of tolerance in this respect is fairly great. The fleshy roots should be planted in September or October with as little injury as possible, spread out to their full extent in a wide, shallow hole. They do not need more than 4 inches of soil over them. Once established leave them undisturbed for as long as possible. Each year they will send up increasingly large clumps of strap-shaped leaves from which will be thrown up, in June or July, fine stiff stems terminated by huge spikes of white, pink, yellow or apricot flowers. There are many species and hybrids, among the best being *E. Bungei* with 4 or 5-foot spikes of maize yellow flowers; *E. himalaicus*, white, 5 feet; *E. Elwesii*, pink, 5 feet; *E. Olgae*, white, lightly striped with brown; and *E. robustus*, one of the tallest, its pale pink spikes often reaching 9 or 10 feet. The best method of increase is by seed sown as soon as ripe in September in sandy soil in a frame.

ERICA *(Heather, Heath)*

There are a great many different kinds of heather, most of them hardy but a few are either slightly tender and need sheltered places outdoors or are completely tender and must be grown in pots in a greenhouse. They like leafy or peaty soils and most dislike lime though a few, such as *Erica carnea* and *E. darleyensis*, will tolerate it in small quantities.

There are heathers to flower in practically every month of the year and heights vary from the completely prostrate *Calluna Vulgaris minima* to the 8 or 10 feet high *Erica arborea*. Colours range from white and palest pink to deep crimson.

One of the most useful is *E. carnea*, 9 to 12 inches high, compact and early flowering (February-March), with many varieties from white to deep carmine. It will stand some lime. *E. darleyensis* is similar but a little taller and even earlier flowering.

E. cinerea flowers in June and August, *E. vagans* from August to October, *E. tetralix* from June to October, *E. mediterranea*

from February to March and *E. arborea* from March to April.
There are different varieties of all these.

The wild heather of English commons is not an erica at all
but a near relative, *Calluna vulgaris*. It also has numerous
varieties and requires identical treatment.

The most popular greenhouse heathers are *E. gracilis* and *E.
hyemalis*. They require frost protection only and in summer are
best outdoors in a sheltered plunge bed. They need very careful
watering at all times and should be grown in a lime-free, peaty
compost.

All ericas can be increased by layering or by cuttings of young
shoots in summer inserted in a frame.

ERODIUM *(Heron's Bill)*

The erodiums are small rock garden plants, not notably showy
but attractive in a quiet way, and good mat-forming plants some
of which make excellent ground cover for bulbs. Very easily
grown in almost any soil, they like open sunny places and can be
quickly increased by division in spring or autumn. My own
favourite is *Erodium chamaedryoides roseum* (often but, I think,
erroneously, called *E. Reichardii roseum*) because it is so very
neat, with small rounded leaves and the daintiest pale pink
flowers scattered on it like confetti from spring to autumn.
E. guttatum is about 6 inches in height with small clusters of
bright pink flowers in June. *E. chrysanthum* has yellow flowers
and particularly attractive silvery-grey leaves deeply cut into
fine segments. *E. Manescavii* is one of the tallest of all, 1 to $1\frac{1}{2}$
feet high with crude but effective rosy-purple flowers.

ERYNGIUM *(Sea Holly)*

The eryngiums, hardy herbaceous perennials with stiff, rather
spiny leaves, have teazle-like heads of flowers which can, if
desired, be dried and kept for winter decorations. The flowers
are mostly blue, sometimes an odd steely blue that is both unusual and attractive, but at least one, *Eryngium giganteum*, has bone-
white flowers. It is larger than most, often 6 feet in height, and
not a very reliable perennial in our damp, cold winters and is
often treated as a biennial.

They all like light, sandy soils and are less permanent in those
that are heavy and badly drained. The stout, thongy roots pene-
trate deeply into the ground, and they are not very easy to lift
or divide. They can be increased quite readily from root cuttings taken in winter and started into growth in sandy soil in
a frame. Seed also germinates readily in a frame or greenhouse
in spring, and seedlings will flower in their second season.

One of the most reliable is *E. planum*. Individually its blue
flower heads are rather small but they are produced in great
umbers in fine branching sprays and are particularly good for
tting. *E. amethystinum* is amethyst-blue, *E. Oliverianum* is a
fine metallic blue and *E. Violetta* a most unusual violet with a
flush of amethyst. All flower in July and are about 3 feet in
height.

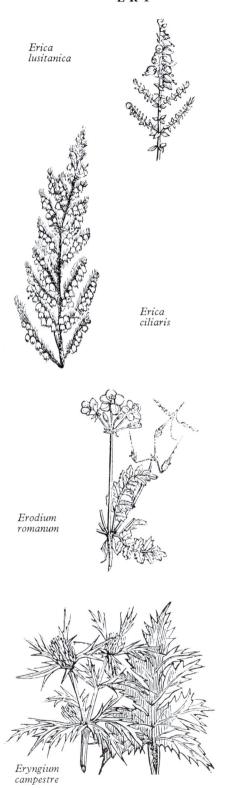

*Erica
lusitanica*

*Erica
ciliaris*

*Erodium
romanum*

*Eryngium
campestre*

55

*Erysimum
Perofskianum*

*Escallonia
macrantha*

*Escallonia
rubra*

*Eschscholtzia
californica*

ERYSIMUM *(Siberian Wallflower)*

This very popular plant is neither a wallflower nor a native of Siberia. Its proper name is *Erysimum Allionii* (not *Cheiranthus Allionii* as it usually appears in seed lists) and it is a native of California. It is one of the showiest plants that can be raised quickly and easily from seed to flower in late spring and early summer. Indeed its one fault is that it continues to produce its vivid orange, wallflower-like flowers for so long that when they do eventually finish, about midsummer, it is getting a little late to replace it with anything else. Seed should be sown outdoors in May the seedlings being transplanted in June to a nursery bed and removed to their flowering quarters in September or October. They should be planted 9 inches to 1 foot apart, preferably in bold masses so that they make a solid sheet of colour when in bloom. They are not at all fussy about soil but they do like sun. *E. Perofskianum* is a yellow or orange flowered annual up to 2 feet in height.

ESCALLONIA

These extremely attractive shrubs, nearly all evergreen, are not quite hardy enough for the coldest parts of the country. They are admirable seaside shrubs and do well in the south and west. Some of the hardiest kinds, such as *E. langleyensis* and *E. edinensis*, will also grow well in many other places if reasonably sheltered.

E. langleyensis, an outstandingly beautiful shrub, makes a big bush of arching branches with neat, glossy foliage and small rosy-carmine flowers all along the stems in June and July. Closely allied and very similar, but with pale pink flowers, is *E. edinensis*.

E. macrantha, stiffer in habit, has larger leaves, is more tender and, therefore, less generally useful.

There are also a number of hybrids such as C. F. Ball, a grand crimson with flowers larger than most; Slieve Donard, with rose-pink flowers and the arching habit of *E. langleyensis*, and Apple Blossom, pink and white, all good but generally less hardy than *E. langleyensis*.

All should be grown in sunny but sheltered positions. They can be grown against walls but this rather spoils their natural grace. I have not found them at all fussy about soil and they can be very easily increased by cuttings prepared from firm young shoots in July or August and rooted in a close frame or under a handlight.

ESCHSCHOLTZIA *(Californian Poppy)*

These are among the most cheerful and the most easily grown of hardy annuals. *E. californica* has finely divided almost fern-like, greyish-green leaves and poppy-like flowers, typically orange, but developed in gardens to include all shades from ivory white to crimson. They love dry sunny places and will often naturalize themselves in such places, coming up year after year from self-sown seed. Seed may be sown in March,

April, May or September where the plants are to flower, the seedlings being thinned to about 9 inches apart. Eschscholtzias grow about 1 foot high, have a sprawling but not untidy habit, and will continue to flower all the summer.

EUONYMUS *(Spindle Tree)*

A family of shrubs and small trees some of which are evergreen and some deciduous. The popular name, spindle tree, only belongs to the latter group, most of which have a rather angular habit and make open shrubs bearing small but brightly coloured fruits in autumn. The evergreen species are much denser in habit for which reason certain kinds are much planted as hedges. For this *Euonymus japonicus* and its numerous varieties are outstanding. The commonest form has dark green, glossy leaves and will grow to a height of 12 or 15 feet. It stands clipping well and thrives in seaside districts. The forms of *E. japonicus* mostly have variegated leaves and differ in the colour and distribution of the variegation, some being yellow, some silver, some margined with the variegation and others with a splash of variegation in the centre of each leaf.

Another good evergreen is *E. radicans*, a shrub which will climb when planted against a wall or, if placed in the open, will spread laterally and not grow above a couple of feet in height. Its leaves are smaller and lighter in colour than those of *E. japonicus* and like that species it has numerous variegated varieties.

Of the deciduous kinds two of the best known are the British spindle tree, *E. europaeus*, and *E. latifolius* which has larger leaves. The first has pink fruits which split open to reveal orange seeds. *E. latifolius* has scarlet fruits with similar seeds and its foliage colours well in the autumn. Even better for autumn colour is *E. alatus*, a shrub with curiously winged branches. Its leaves turn a magnificent crimson or ruby red just before they fall.

All the evergreen kinds can be increased by cuttings of firm young growth taken in early autumn and rooted in a frame. The deciduous kinds are readily raised from seed though, as seedlings may vary a little, specially desirable forms must be increased by cuttings as for the evergreens. None is particular regarding soil and the evergreens will tolerate some shade but the true spindle-trees prefer a sunny position.

FELICIA *(Blue Daisy, Blue Marguerite)*

The best felicia for gardens is *F. amelloides*, a pretty little sun-loving plant often known as *Agathaea coelestis*. Its small, blue daisy flowers are produced most of the summer. It makes a bushy plant 18 inches or more in height eventually, though as it is frequently grown as an annual and then does not have time to reach its full dimensions, it is commonly seen as a small plant 9 to 12 inches high. Not quite hardy enough to winter outdoors except in the mildest places, it can, if desired, be grown as a pot plant for the greenhouse where it is useful both for its long flowering season and its ability to survive with no more than frost

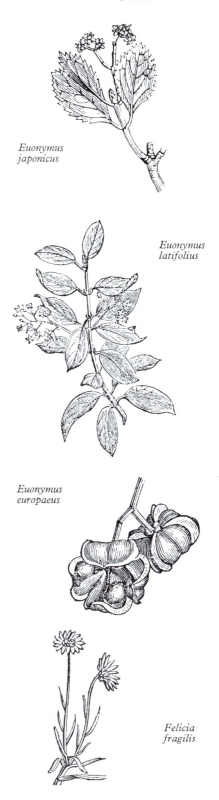

Euonymus japonicus

Euonymus latifolius

Euonymus europaeus

Felicia fragilis

57

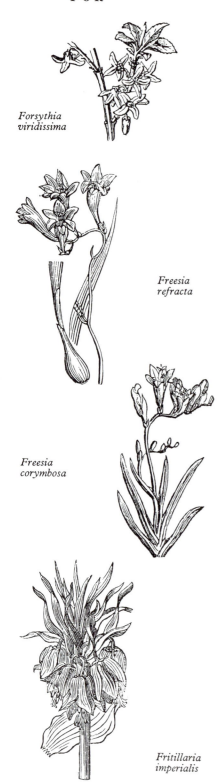

FOR

*Forsythia
viridissima*

*Freesia
refracta*

*Freesia
corymbosa*

*Fritillaria
imperialis*

protection. Seed provides the easiest means of increase and should be sown in a slightly heated greenhouse in February or March. *F. tenella* is an annual, 1 foot high, with similar flowers.

FORSYTHIA *(Golden Bells)*

Forsythias are among the best and most popular of early spring flowering shrubs. Their robustness, ease of culture and free flowering qualities make them general favourites. The best, judged solely on these qualifications, is *F. intermedia spectabilis*, of stiff but not ungainly habit, capable of reaching a height of 10 feet with corresponding spread, though it can be restricted without much difficulty. Its flowers are a particularly bright yellow. It is a pity that its undoubted merits have rather over-shadowed the less spectacular but more graceful *F. suspensa*. This has long, slender arching branches, nearly black in the variety named *atrocaulis*, and paler yellow flowers.

All bloom in March or early April and can be pruned, if desired, by cutting out the old flowering branches as soon as the flowers fade. They can be increased by cuttings of firm young stems taken in autumn and rooted in a frame or sheltered place outdoors.

They are not particular about soil and will tolerate some shade though they prefer an open position. *F. suspensa* can be trained against a fence or wall if desired.

FREESIA

Now that the colour range has been greatly increased and seed has been made available at a comparatively low cost, freesias are becoming very popular as fragrant winter-flowering plants for the cool greenhouse. They make small corms or bulbs and can be grown from these. Alternatively they can be raised from seed and, if this is sown in a warm greenhouse in February or March, the seedlings will flower the same year. They should be grown six or seven together in a 5–inch pot in John Innes compost. During the summer they will be quite happy in a frame as they are nearly hardy (freesias grow outdoors without protection in Cornwall). In autumn they should be returned to the greenhouse and given just sufficient heat to maintain a temperature around 50°. The rather thin flower stems will require some support. After flowering the water supply should be gradually reduced until by about June no water is given at all and the corms are allowed to rest for a few weeks. In late July or early August they can be shaken out of the soil, separated and repotted

Varieties are available in various shades of blue, lavender, mauve, yellow and red and there is also the old white *Freesia refracta alba* and a number of larger flowered white varieties

FRITILLARIA *(Fritillary, Snake's Head, Crown Imperial)*

These are bulbous rooted plants with nodding, bell shaped flowers, but the numerous species differ greatly in stature and appearance. The two most useful in gardens are *Fritillaria*

Meleagris, an uncommon native of Britain which grows freely in some damp meadows near the Thames, and *F. imperialis*. *F. Meleagris* carries its purple flowers, chequered or veined with a lighter shade, in ones or twos on slender, foot high stems. An elegant but rather oddly coloured plant, it is at its best in April and May. It likes damp rich soils and, where conditions suit it, can be naturalized very effectively in grass. Rather similar but with brown and yellow chequering is *F. gracilis*.

F. imperialis is a stout plant with stiff, leafy stems 3 feet high, crowned in May by a complete circle of yellow or reddish flowers of considerable size. A most striking plant for the border, unfortunately it (and particularly its large bulb) has a most unpleasantly pungent smell. It will grow in any ordinary soil and sunny position.

Fritillary bulbs should be planted in September or October, covered with 2 or 3 inches of soil, which will mean taking out quite small holes for *F. Meleagris* and much bigger and deeper ones for *F. imperialis*. Space the former 6 inches and the latter 18 inches apart.

FUCHSIA

The fuchias are fine decorative shrubs just on the borderline of hardiness. Some of the larger-flowered kinds require greenhouse protection in winter, as they can survive little or no frost, while others, mainly those with rather smaller flowers, may be grown outdoors winter and summer in fairly mild or sheltered places. Fine fuchsia hedges are to be seen in some southern and western regions, particularly near the sea where fuchsias nearly always thrive. Even when severely damaged by frost they will usually send up fresh growth from ground level, but under such conditions they do not make the fine specimens found in milder places.

Apart from this difficulty of tenderness, all are very easily grown. They will thrive in most soils and, when grown in pots or tubs, are well suited by John Innes compost. They can be quickly and easily raised from cuttings of firm young shoots, taken at practically any time of year, inserted in sandy soil in a close frame. They do not mind a certain amount of shade though they will also thrive in full sun, and they are excellent town shrubs. No regular pruning is required but dead or injured growth should be removed each spring. In the greenhouse they should be given pots or tubs of ample size to contain their roots and should be watered freely in summer but sparingly in winter. Only enough heat to exclude frost will be required.

GAILLARDIA

Two distinct kinds of gaillardia are commonly grown in gardens, the one annual and the other perennial. The annuals are derived from *Gaillardia pulchella* and its variety *picta*, whereas the perennials are all varieties of *G. aristata*. All have daisy-like flowers mainly in shades of yellow and red, but those of the perennials are larger and more showy and they are altogether

Fritillaria Meleagris

Fuchsia magellanica Riccartonii

Fuchsia magellanica (garden form)

Fuchsia fulgens

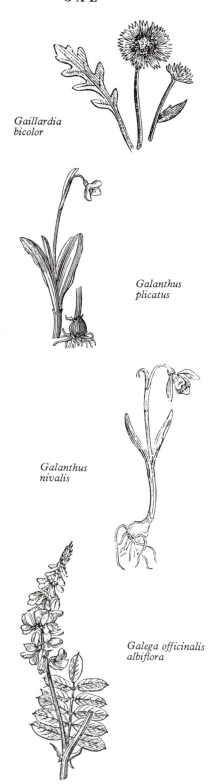

*Gaillardia
bicolor*

*Galanthus
plicatus*

*Galanthus
nivalis*

*Galega officinalis
albiflora*

finer garden plants. Many are yellow with a broad central ring of scarlet. Some are yellow throughout and some are a deep orange or bronze-red. The perennials are about 2 feet in height and the annuals are, in general, a few inches shorter.

Gaillardias are sun loving plants and they like well-drained soils. All tend to have stems a little too weak for the size and weight of their flowers and consequently benefit from some support

Seed of the annuals may either be sown in a greenhouse or frame in March or outdoors in April or May. Under glass the seedlings must be pricked off into boxes and hardened off for planting out 9 to 12 inches apart in May. In the open seedlings may be thinned to 9 inches.

The perennials can also be raised from seed though the seedlings are unlikely to flower until their second year. Alternatively, old plants can be divided in spring or young plants can be raised from root cuttings taken in winter and started into growth in sandy soil in a frame.

GALANTHUS *(Snowdrop)*

The common snowdrop, *Galanthus nivalis*, one of the loveliest spring flowering bulbs, needs no description. There are, however, others equally beautiful but less well known. Outstanding among these are *G. byzantinus*, *G. Elwesii*, *G. Ikariae* and *G. plicatus*, all rather larger than the common snowdrop, with broader leaves, but otherwise having the same gracefully formed, nodding white and green flowers. All flower in late winter or early spring. The double flowered form of *G. nivalis*, though less dainty, is more effective in the mass.

All these are perfectly easy to grow in ordinary soil and cool position. The common kind is admirable for naturalizing in short grass in partially shaded positions, but the others are better in the rock garden or border without the competition of grass and weeds. The bulbs should be planted 4 inches deep in early autumn. Old clumps of bulbs can be lifted and divided in summer after the foliage has died down.

GALEGA *(Goat's Rue)*

The galegas, rather coarse and rampant hardy herbaceous perennials, attractive when carrying their abundant clusters of small, pea-type flowers, will thrive in quite poor soils and rough places. The best species is *Galega officinalis*, 3 or 4 feet high, carrying its bluish mauve flowers from June to early August. It has several good varieties such as *Hartlandii*, pale blue, and Lady Wilson, pinkish lilac.

They will grow in practically any soil and an open or partially shaded position. They can be planted in spring or autumn and are readily increased by division of the roots at either season.

GARDENIA

The gardenia, an evergreen shrub, needs the protection of a warm greenhouse. It is grown mainly for cutting as the waxy white, heavily perfumed flowers are greatly prized as button-holes and for bouquets, shoulder sprays, etc. The kind usually cultivated is *Gardenia jasminoides* which needs an average winter temperature of about 55° (minimum 45°). In summer the temperature can rise a good deal higher provided the plants are freely watered, frequently syringed and lightly shaded. Much less water and overhead moisture is required in autumn and winter and the plants can be kept rather cool and a little on the dry side for a while to rest them. Successive batches can be started into growth from January to March to flower from March to June. This is done simply by raising the temperature a little and increasing the water supply. Gardenias can be increased by cuttings of young shoots in spring, rooted in sand in a propagating case, with a temperature of about 70°.

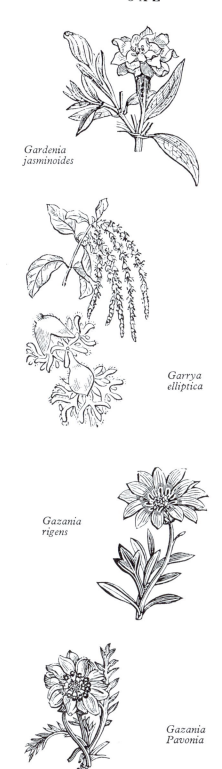

Gardenia jasminoides

Garrya elliptica

Gazania rigens

Gazania Pavonia

GARRYA   *(Silk Tassel Bush)*

In Britain *Garrya elliptica* has no popular name but in America it is known as the silk tassel bush and this is so appropriate that I have used it in the hope that it may be adopted here. It is a fine evergreen shrub, dense and rounded in habit, perhaps as much as 12 feet high when fully grown and unrestricted, but usually seen at about two thirds that height. In mid-winter it produces slender grey-green catkins which gradually lengthen and, in the male form (there are two sexes in this plant) become about 8 inches long and have yellow stamens. The female form has shorter catkins and, of course, no stamens so is not quite as decorative.

A good and unusual shrub, it is worth a little special care. It should be given a sunny sheltered position, indeed I have seen it trained most effectively against a wall though this must have involved a good deal of work as it is naturally a very bushy plant. It appreciates a good but reasonably well-drained soil and does not require regular pruning. Propagation is by cuttings of firm young shoots taken in July or August, rooted in a propagating frame in a greenhouse.

GAZANIA

These are trailing perennials for warm sunny places, have large and very showy daisy flowers, usually in bright shades of orange or orange-red, often with a darker, almost black, zone. The flowers only open in the sun so it is useless to grow them in shady places.

They can be grown outdoors during summer, and in the milder parts of the country some will survive outdoors in winter, but usually it is best to give them frame protection from October to early May. They can be increased easily either from seed sown in a slightly heated greenhouse in spring or by cuttings of firm young shoots taken at almost any time in spring and summer, and rooted in sandy soil in a frame. Gazanias will grow in quite poor soils and like best those that are light and well drained. They are attractive for dry walls, rock gardens, the edges of borders, or summer bedding schemes.

61

*Genista
hispanica*

*Genista
lydia*

*Genista
sagittalis*

*Gentiana
septemfida*

GENISTA *(Broom)*

The popular name 'broom' is shared by both genista and cytisus and there is some botanical confusion between the two genera. The fragrant genista of florists' shops, once known as *Genista fragrans*, is now named *Cytisus fragrans*, and other species have been similarly transferred.

All are sun-loving shrubs with yellow flowers and most are fully hardy. In general they are deciduous but their green stems give them some of the effect of evergreens. They do well in poor, rather dry, well-drained soils. They can all be raised very readily from seed sown in greenhouse or frame in spring, seedlings usually flowering in their second year.

Genista aethnensis is one of the largest, an almost tree-like shrub, 12 to 15 feet in height, with long, nearly pendent, whip-like stems wreathed throughout their length in July with the small yellow flowers.

Equally large but stiffer and more erect in habit are *G. cinerea* and *G. virgata*, both flowering in June and July.

At the other extreme are *G. lydia* and *G. tinctoria*, both almost prostrate, spreading shrubs suitable for the rock garden, the top of a dry wall or the front of a border. *G. lydia* has a particularly delightful habit, its arching shoots producing a wave-like effect. *G. tinctoria* has an attractive double-flowered form and *G. sagittalis* is an interesting but less showy species.

Another popular kind is *G. hispánica*, often known as the Spanish gorse, a fine spring plant about 2 feet high, which might be described as a dwarf and very neat gorse. It will spread over a considerable area and flowers in May and June.

GENTIANA *(Gentian)*

The name gentian conjures up pictures of the most brilliantly blue flowers. This is true of some of the best species but by no means all gentians are of such pure colour, indeed some are not even blue at all. The family is a large one of great variety. *Gentiana verna*, a rare British native, no more than 3 inches high, produces its ultramarine blue flowers in spring. At the other extreme is *G. lutea*, a rather coarse plant, 5 or 6 feet high, bearing yellow flowers in early summer. It is not a particularly desirable garden plant.

Two of the most popular and beautiful are *G. acaulis* and *G. sino-ornata*. The first flowers in spring, the second in autumn. Both have large, trumpet shaped flowers, those of *G. acaulis* deep blue, those of *G. sino-ornata* a much lighter blue striped with white. *G. Farreri* is similar but more difficult to grow. Another of the same character is *G. Macaulayi*, a hybrid between *G. sino-ornata* and *G. Farreri* which has inherited the beauty of both its parents and is easier to grow than either of them.

Good summer flowering kinds are *G. septemfida*, *G. lagodechiana*, and *G. Freyniana*, all with compact clusters of purple flowers. They sprawl about, turning their shoots up to hold their flowers clear of the ground, but are never above 9 inches in height. Some authorities regard *G. lagodechiana* and *G. Frey-niana* as varieties of *G. septemfida*, a little more compact in growth or a few shades darker in colour. All three are easy.

Very different again is *G. asclepiadea*, often known as the willow gentian, presumably because of its gracefully arching habit. It makes slender, more or less erect stems, 18 inches high, carrying loose sprays of deep blue flowers, at their best about mid-summer. Unlike the preceding species, which are sun-lovers, it prefers cool, partially shaded places and may be naturalized in thin woodland.

All gentians like leafy or peaty soils well supplied with moisture in summer but not prone to waterlogging in winter. They are ideal for the rock garden provided the position is not too dry and hot. All those commonly grown in gardens are perennial and quite hardy but some of the more difficult mountain species from high altitudes are better grown in pans in a frame than in the open ground, as they do not like our heavy winter rainfall and variable climate.

All gentians can be increased by seed sown in a frame or greenhouse in spring. Most kinds can also be divided carefully in spring.

GERANIUM *(Cranesbill)*

Here is an outstanding example of a muddle in naming, for the plant that most people commonly call geranium is not the geranium of botanists but a pelargonium. The true geraniums, are hardy herbaceous perennials or rock plants and can all be grown very easily.

One of the best for the herbaceous border is the blue geranium, *G. pratense*. It is a common wild plant in the west of England, about 2 feet in height, bearing its saucer shaped lavender-blue flowers in June and July. Even more showy in the same style is *G. grandiflorum. G. Endressii* has bright pink flowers and both *G. armenum* and *G. phaeum* are magenta.

For the rock garden one of the best kinds is *G. sanguineum*, another native plant often called the bloody cranesbill because of the brilliant purplish red of its flowers. A mat-forming plant, 9 inches or thereabouts in height, it blooms in June and July. An even better variety, *lancastriense*, is lower growing and has clear rose-pink flowers.

Then there are *G. subcaulescens*, a neat growing plant with small brilliantly magenta flowers on 6-inch stems in May and June, and *G. Pylzowianum*, a plant of spreading habit, reminiscent of our native herb robert, with similar bright pink flowers.

All these will grow in any ordinary soil and fairly open position and can be increased by root division in spring or autumn.

GERBERA *(Barberton Daisy, Transvaal Daisy)*

The only species of gerbera grown in British gardens is *G. Jamesonii* a graceful and brightly coloured daisy-like flower for the greenhouse. The long, narrow petals give the flower an

63

Gentiana
acaulis

Geranium
sanguineum

Geranium
sanguineum
lancastriense

Geranium
pratense

Gerbera
Jamesonii

Geum
pyrenaicum

Geum
rivale

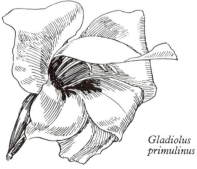

Gladiolus
primulinus

unusually elegant form, and their colours are very varied, some varieties being bright orange, others flame, salmon or pink. All are excellent for cutting as they are carried singly on slender but stiff stems about 18 inches in length.

Gerbera Jamesonii, a South African plant, is not quite hardy in this country. It needs greenhouse protection but not much artificial heat—just sufficient to keep out frost in winter. It likes a very gritty, well-drained but not poor soil and must be watered fairly freely in spring and summer, but very sparingly in autumn and winter. In fact it is not an easy plant to grow, although it can be raised fairly easily from seed. It damps off quickly if grown in soils that are too close or damp, it resents being coddled too much, yet it equally dislikes cold. Some gardeners find that it responds well to the soilless method of cultivation, i.e. grown in coarse gravel fed with a nutrient solution.

Seed should be sown in a cool greenhouse in spring and the seedlings transferred while still small either singly to small pots or about 1 foot apart in beds in which they are to flower.

GEUM (Avens)

There are geums for the herbaceous border and the rock garden but the former are far more popular. All the taller kinds (they average about 2 feet in height) have been derived from *Geum chiloense*, a plant with single scarlet flowers produced in succession during most of the summer. Numerous double flowered varieties have been obtained, of which the best known are Mrs Bradshaw, scarlet like its parent, Lady Stratheden, a good clear yellow, and Fire Opal, coppery red.

Geum Borisii, a smaller plant which may be grown at the front of the border or in the rock garden, is about 1 foot high and bears single bright orange-red flowers. A very good plant indeed, that is seldom without flowers from early summer to autumn.

G. rivale a rather weedy plant, 1½ to 2 feet in height with small old-rose flowers, likes rather damp places. *G. montanum* is a better rock plant, trailing in habit, with large single yellow flowers, and *G. reptans* is similar in habit and bloom.

All are easily grown plants, not fussy about soil, but liking sunny open places. They can be increased by division in spring, or by seed sown in a frame or greenhouse in spring, but there may be some variation in colour and flower form if the double flowered varieties of *G. chiloense* are raised from seed.

GLADIOLUS (Sword Lily)

The gladiolus has been so highly developed by breeding that the wild species have ceased to have much importance for garden display. Three main lines may be discerned to-day, the large-flowered gladioli, for years the most popular of all; the 'primulinus' varieties which are smaller and have the hooded central upper petal derived from *Gladiolus primulinus;* and the comparatively new race of miniatures which are no larger than the primulinus varieties but have wide open instead of hooded flowers and petals which are often crimped or frilled. These miniatures are

Gloxinia
[garden form]

Helianthus
decapetalus
multiflorus

Geum coccineum
[garden form]

Hamamelis
mollis

Gypsophila
elegans

Globularia
cordifolia

Helenium
autumnale
[garden form]

Godetia
amoena
Schaminii

Heliopsis
scabra

Gerbera
Jamesonii

Helianthemum
nummularium

Helichrysum
bracteatum

Gladiolus
[garden form]

CN-T

Hibiscus
syriacus

Hydrangea
macrophylla
Hortensia

Hosta lancifolia

Hyacinthus
orientalis

Impatiens
Sultanii
[garden form]

Hoya
carnosa

Iberis
sempervirens

Helleborus niger

Hippeastrum
[garden form]

Heuchera
sanguinea
[garden form]

Hemerocallis
[garden form]

Hypericum
calycinum

Heliotropium arborescens [garden form]

CN-T

rapidly overhauling the other two classes in popularity because of their grace and their usefulness as cut flowers.

All gladioli make corms which must be protected from frost in winter. The usual practice is to plant the corms outdoors in March, April or early May, covering them with about 3 inches of soil. About six weeks after flowering, the plants are lifted and the tops cut off about an inch above the corms, which are allowed to dry for a week or so. Then the old withered corms can be detached from the bottom of the plump healthy young corms and thrown away. The new corms and also small cormlets or 'spawn' are stored in a dry, cool but frost proof place until planting time in spring.

The cormlets will not as a rule flower the first season but those of expensive varieties are worth growing on in a reserve bed until they reach flowering size in one or two years.

All gladioli like easily worked, well-drained but not dry soils. They do not need much manure but may benefit from dressings of bonemeal and hoof and horn meal before planting. They must be well supplied with moisture in summer.

In addition to these outdoor gladioli there is a race of early flowering gladioli frequently grown as pot plants in the slightly heated greenhouse. They have been derived from *G. Colvillei* and have graceful spikes of small, open, scarlet or white flowers. The corms are potted in autumn, four or five in a 6-inch pot in John Innes compost, and are grown on in a cool greenhouse, with a temperature around 50°. After flowering, watering is decreased gradually and when the foliage has died down the corms are shaken out and stored in a cool dry place until potting time.

All gladioli are readily increased by separating the young corms and cormlets when they are lifted and dried off.

GLOBULARIA *(Globe Daisy)*

This not very well-known family of rock plants is worth cultivation for its neat carpets of shining evergreen leaves and ageratum-like heads of fluffy mauve flowers. The two most commonly seen are *Globularia cordifolia* and *G. nudicaulis*, though *G. bellidifolia* is sometimes grown. All flower in summer, rather later than most alpines, which is an advantage. All are 4 or 5 inches in height and easy to grow in any reasonably well-drained soil and sunny position. They can be increased easily by division of the roots in spring.

GLOXINIA

Tuberous rooted plants for warm greenhouses, gloxinias make fine pot plants for they are neat in habit, have rich green velvety foliage and magnificent, deeply bell shaped flowers in various rich shades of purple, pink and red, often beautifully netted with one or other of these colours on a white base. Tubers can be stored dry from October to February when they are started into growth in shallow trays filled with peat or leafmould and placed in a greenhouse with a temperature of 60–65°.

E

Gladiolus blandus

Globularia cordifolia

Globularia nudicaulis

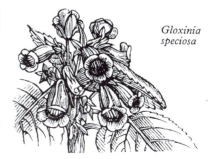

Gloxinia speciosa

*Gloxinia
digitaliflora*

*Godetia
grandiflora*

*Godetia
viminea*

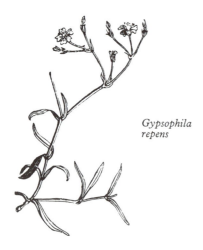

*Gypsophila
repens*

When leaves appear the tubers are potted singly in 3–inch pots in John Innes compost. Later they are moved to 5– or 6–inch pots in which they will flower. Throughout this period they must be kept in a temperature of around 65°, given plenty of moisture at the roots and around the leaves and shaded from strong sunshine. Flowers will be produced throughout the summer, and in autumn the water supply can be progressively reduced to encourage the plants to go to rest by late October.

Gloxinias can be raised from seed sown in February in a greenhouse with temperature around 65°. The seed is very small and requires careful handling and hardly any covering.

GODETIA

These are among the most useful of hardy annuals because they flower freely and are easily grown in practically any soil and sunny or partially shaded positions. The one thing you cannot do successfully with a godetia is to transplant it, so the seed must be sown direct in the open ground where the plants are to flower, in March, April, May or early September. Seedlings should be thinned to 6 to 9 inches apart according to the type being grown. Some are dwarf plants not above 8 inches in height and some are comparatively tall, reaching a height of 2 to 3 feet. Colours vary from white to crimson but some of the loveliest shades are in the pink range where the natural tendency of godetias to run to rather crude shades of carmine, has been curbed.

GYPSOPHILA

Gypsophilas may be regarded most conveniently as either perennials or annuals. The perennials are mostly derived from *Gypsophila paniculata*, which makes one very long tap root and, from that, a fine rounded bush of slender greyish stems and leaves, disappearing about midsummer or just after beneath a cloud of tiny white flowers. These are single in the wild form but there are also good double flowered varieties of which Bristol Fairy is probably the best. A variety with double lilac pink flowers is known, rather optimistically, as Flamingo.

A perennial gypsophila for the rock garden or dry wall, *G. repens* is a pretty trailing plant like a diminished and laxer version of *G. paniculata* and without its tap root. Its flowers, at their best in June, may be white or pale pink.

The annual gypsophilas are derived from *G. elegans*, a plant of loosely sprawling habit, 1 to 1½ feet high, with white flowers much larger than those of the perennials. It can be flowered from June to September by sowing seed in March, April, May and September, thinning the seedlings to 6 inches apart.

All gypsophilas like well-drained soils and *G. paniculata* is particularly happy on chalky soils. They are completely hardy but may succumb to excessive winter wet. The annuals are, of course, raised afresh each year from seed. Seed sown in a frame in spring can also be used to increase the perennials, except the fully double flowered forms of *G. paniculata* which set no seed and must be grafted in spring on to pieces of root of the single flowered variety, a tricky job, for the professional rather than the amateur. Cuttings of short young side shoots will also root in sand in July.

HAMAMELIS (*Witch Hazel*)

Hamamelis mollis is one of the best of winter flowering shrubs for it is quite hardy, easily grown, has showy and very unusual flowers and perfume. In growth it looks very like a nut bush until, in January or February, the bare branches break out into bright yellow flowers looking as if they consisted of twisted tufts of paper or wool. Their fragrance is pleasant.

There are several other species though none quite so good as *H. mollis*. *H. japonica* makes a bigger shrub and has smaller, less brilliant flowers which combine yellow and purple. It has several varieties of which *arborea* is the biggest of all. Another tree-like species is *H. virginiana* which has small yellow flowers in autumn.

They all like good loamy soils and need no regular pruning. Increase is not very easy. Rooted suckers may be detached in autumn when available, or young stems may be layered in early summer. A third possibility is to raise from seed sown in a frame in spring, but seeds may take a year and more to germinate.

Hamamelis virginiana

HELENIUM (*Sneezeweed*)

Hardy herbaceous perennials belonging to the daisy family, extremely useful in the garden because of the solid masses of colour they give in July and August. All are very easily grown in almost any soil and reasonably open place and can be increased by division in spring or autumn.

Colours range from bright yellow to an intense chestnut red and heights vary from 3 to 6 feet. Most of the popular kinds are varieties of *Helenium autumnale*, a 6–foot plant with yellow flowers. Moerheim Beauty is 4 feet high and chestnut red, Chipperfield Orange is 6 feet and deep yellow splashed with red, Riverton Gem is similar, Mme Canivet is pale yellow with a dark centre and about 4 feet, and *pumilum* is yellow and 2 feet.

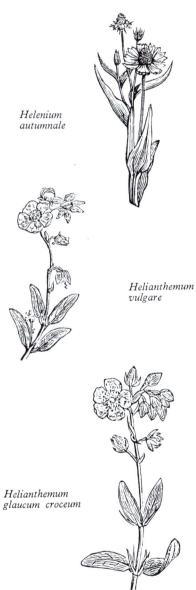

Helenium autumnale

Helianthemum vulgare

Helianthemum glaucum croceum

HELIANTHEMUM (*Sun Rose*)

The helianthemums are very closely allied to cistus, the rock rose, and, in fact are more often called rock roses than they are sun roses. They differ from cistuses chiefly in being on the whole far smaller and, therefore, good plants for the rock garden or dry wall. They are evergreen with thin, wiry stems and flowers which, though they fade quickly, are produced so freely and in such constant succession during May and June that they are among the most useful rock plants at that season.

Colours range from white and pale yellow through deep yellow, orange, copper, and pink to crimson. There are double-flowered as well as single forms.

All are sun lovers and like poor well-drained soils. Pruning is not essential but habit can be improved by trimming the plants

*Helianthus
multiflorus*

*Helianthus
rigidus*

*Helianthus
strumosus*

*Helichrysum
bracteatum*

moderately with scissors or shears after flowering. They can be raised from seed sown in a greenhouse or frame in spring, but seedlings are likely to vary, so selected varieties must be raised from cuttings of half ripe shoots rooted in sandy soil in a frame.

HELIANTHUS *(Sunflower)*

The sunflowers give us both perennials and annuals and with few exceptions are showy plants of the easiest culture.

One fault of some of the perennials is that they are a little too vigorous and invasive. This is certainly true of that otherwise very fine plant *Helianthus rigidus*. It grows 7 or 8 feet high and carries its large yellow flowers in late summer and early August. Unfortunately it spreads by underground shoots which spring up everywhere, choking many less vigorous plants.

Helianthus sparsifolius, also known as *H. Monarch*, superficially rather like *H. rigidus*, has much finer yellow flowers each with a nearly black centre. But so far from becoming a nuisance it is often rather difficult to keep alive as it is one of the few that are not quite hardy. In many places it is necessary to lift some of the roots each autumn and place them in a frame for safety.

A really good garden plant, fully hardy and not unduly invasive, is *H. decapetalus multiflorus* a 5-foot high, August flowering plant with numerous varieties, some with double or semi-double flowers and some with single flowers of extra size.

The giant annual sunflower with huge heads of seed, so often grown for feeding poultry, is *H. annuus*. It is quite hardy and seed should be sown in March or April where the plants are to flower. As they are big seeds they can be dropped in pairs into shallow holes, 2 or 3 feet apart, the seedlings being thinned later to one at each station.

There are also smaller varieties of this species some with flowers variously marked with red, and these are better garden plants for decoration. They should be grown in exactly the same way.

The perennial sunflowers can also be raised from seed if desired, but it is easier to increase them by division.

HELICHRYSUM *(Everlasting)*

There are a number of helichrysums, only a few of which are commonly seen in gardens. The most popular is *Helichrysum bracteatum*, a hardy annual with showy double flowers made up of overlapping hard-textured petals which will retain their colour for many months. This is grown from seed sown in March or April where the plants are to flower, or alternatively, seed may be sown in frame or greenhouse in early March and the seedlings planted out 9 inches apart in May. They should be given a sunny place and a well-drained soil. The flowers are cut just before they are fully open, tied up in small bundles and suspended head downwards in a shed or similar dry but shaded place, for drying. When dry the thin stems will not support the heavy heads and wire will have to be used instead.

Ipomoea Leari

Laburnum
vulgare

Incarvillea
Delavayi

Kalanchoë
Blossfeldiana

antana
Camara

Ixia
hybrida

Lamium
maculatum

Lapageria
rosea

Iris siberica

Kniphofia
Uvaria nobilis

Kerria japonica

Kalmia
latifolia

Jasminum
nudiflorum

CNT

Leycesteria formosa

Lilium speciosum rubrum

Leptosyne maritima

Lavandula Spica

Lathyrus odoratus

Leontopodium alpinum

Limonium sinuatum

Lilium candidum

Leucojum autumnale

Lavatera trimestris

Liatris spicata

Lewisia Tweedyi

CN-T

An attractive plant for a rather warm, sunny place is *H. belli-dioides;* a hardy or near-hardy, low-growing perennial with silvery almost globular flower heads.

H. lanatum is a good grey-leaved shrub not unlike an extremely silvery lavender in appearance and about 3 feet high. Its yellow flowers appear in July but are not particularly attractive. Treatment is as for *H. bellidioides.*

HELIOPSIS

These sunflower-like perennials for the border have the great merit that, unlike so many of the true sunflowers, they do not spread unduly but remain as compact clumps in one place. The best are *Heliopsis scabra* and its varieties *major, patula* and *zinniaeflora,* and *H. laevis.* All are about 5 feet in height and produce deep yellow flowers in August. Most have single flowers but they are double in *H. scabra zinniaeflora.*

All are completely hardy and easily grown in ordinary garden soil and open position. Increase is by division in spring or autumn.

HELIOTROPIUM   *(Heliotrope, Cherry Pie)*

The common heliotrope has long been a favourite summer bedding plant, both on account of its fine heads of small deep purple flowers and because of its rich perfume. Unfortunately many strains to-day seem to have little or no scent though the old fragrance is still available in certain varieties.

Heliotrope will not stand frost and should be kept in a greenhouse in winter in a temperature of around 50°; young plants can be raised from seed sown in a temperature of 60–65° in February or early March, the seedlings being pricked off and later hardened off in a frame for planting outdoors in early June. These seedlings frequently have no perfume and if scented plants are required, it is preferable to raise them from cuttings taken from plants with fragrant flowers. Cuttings may be prepared from young shoots at any time in spring or early summer, and rooted in a propagating frame with bottom heat.

HELLEBORUS   *(Christmas Rose, Lenten Rose, Hellebore)*

None of the hellebores are showy flowers, but several of them have a quiet beauty all their own and nearly all flower in winter or earliest spring when there are few other hardy herbaceous perennials in bloom. The best known are the Christmas rose, *Helleborus niger,* with white, saucer-shaped flowers on stiff 12–inch stems in December and January, and the Lenten rose, *H. orientalis,* with dull pink to purple flowers on rather longer stems, in March and April. *H. corsicus,* a vigorous 3-foot high plant with handsome, divided leaves and great clusters of pale green flowers in January and February is well worth growing.

All these like cool, shady places and soils rich in leaf-mould or peat. They do not like disturbance and often take a year or so to settle in, especially if old clumps are moved. They can be

Heliopsis helianthoides

Heliotropium arborescens

Helleborus olympicus

Helleborus niger

69

*Hemerocallis
fulva*

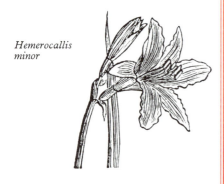

*Hemerocallis
minor*

*Heuchera
cylindrica*

*Hibiscus
Rosa-sinensis*

increased by division after flowering but in many ways it is better to start with seedlings, though seed is sometimes slow in germinating. Sow it in a frame as soon as ripe and transfer the seedlings to their flowering quarters when they have made four or five leaves.

HEMEROCALLIS *(Day Lily)*

These are lily-like flowers mostly in shades of yellow and orange though sometimes with handsome bronze or tawny markings and occasionally verging on apricot or even dull pink. The plants make fine clumps of narrow rather rush-like leaves above which the flowers are carried in clusters on slender but stiff stems 2 to 3 feet high. They open in constant succession during July and August and get their popular name of day-lilies from the fact that individually the flowers only last a day or so though there are plenty of buds to carry on the display.

They will thrive in any ordinary garden soil in either full sun or partial shade. Readily increased by division in spring or autumn, they can also be raised from seed sown in a frame in spring. The two species most commonly seen in gardens are *H. flava* with pale yellow flowers and *H. fulva* with tawny orange flowers. The latter also has a double flowered form known as Kwanso, but this is less graceful than the wild form. There are now a great many hybrids.

HEUCHERA *(Alum Root, Coral Bells)*

Graceful hardy herbaceous perennials for the front row of the border. They make low clumps of rounded leaves, often with bronzy markings, and bear in July and August loose, slender clusters of small pink or red flowers, about 2 feet in height. The most popular species, *Heuchera sanguinea*, is coral scarlet and it has produced a number of garden varieties such as Edge Hall, pink, and *splendens*, deep red. *H. brizoides gracillima* has even smaller but more numerous pink flowers and *H. tiarelloides* is not quite so tall and paler in colour. All will thrive in any ordinary soil and open or even partially shaded position. Propagation is by division in spring or autumn.

HIBISCUS *(Rose Mallow)*

From the garden standpoint the three most important hibiscus are *H. Trionum* a half-hardy annual, 18 inches high, with yellow and maroon flowers in summer, *H. syriacus*, a deciduous shrub which makes a big bush up to 12 feet in height and produces its white, blue or pink flowers in early autumn, and *H. Rosa-sinensis*, a tender shrub for the greenhouse with very showy scarlet, pink, yellow or buff flowers in summer. Seed of *H. Trionum* should be sown in a greenhouse in February or March, seedlings being hardened off for planting out in a sunny place in May or June. *H. syriacus* should be planted in a sunny rather warm place and well-drained soil. Year-old stems can be shortened a little each February. *H. Rosa-sinensis* requires a temperature of around 60° even in winter and must be given plenty of room.

HIPPEASTRUM *(Barbados Lily)*

These are bulbous rooted plants for the warm greenhouse. Their broadly funnel shaped flowers are carried in clusters of two to four at the top of very stout, stiff stems from March to June. They are often very brightly coloured, scarlet, crimson or pink, but there are also white forms. Most of the varieties grown are hybrids. All should be grown in a greenhouse throughout the year, but should be rested from October to February when little water will be needed and the temperature need be no more than 45–50°. After this the temperature should be increased to 60–65° and more water given. After flowering the temperature can be reduced a little and the plants placed on a shelf or staging where they get as much light as possible. A 6– or 7–inch pot will take one good bulb. John Innes compost is suitable.

Hippeastrum psittacinum

HOSTA *(Plantain Lily)*

Hostas are hardy herbaceous perennials chiefly valued for their broad leaves, bright green in some kinds such as *Hosta lancifolia*, *H. ovata* and *H. plantaginea*, grey or blue-green in others such as *H. Fortunei* and *H. Sieboldiana*, and variegated white on green in all the varieties of *H. undulata* and certain varieties of *H. Fortunei* and *H. lancifolia*. All produce loose spikes of long, more or less tubular flowers which are sometimes quite pleasing though their colours are always subdued, lilac, mauve or white. There are few better hardy foliage plants and they will thrive equally well in sun or shade, nor are they particular regarding soil though they succeed best in fairly rich soils that do not dry out too rapidly. All can be increased by division in spring or autumn. These plants are often known as funkias.

Hosta albo-marginata

HOYA *(Wax Plant)*

Hoya carnosa, the kind commonly grown, is a charming climbing plant for the slightly heated greenhouse. It is a twining plant with rather thick leaves and flat circular clusters of pale pink and white flowers that look as if they had been modelled in wax. They are produced in July and August. It is best grown in a border of fairly rich soil with plenty of peat and sand and it must have a good water supply in spring and summer, while it is growing. In winter it can be relatively dry. Thin the stems a little each February to prevent overcrowding. Temperatures should be around 45° in winter, rising to 60° or more in summer. *Hoya bella*, with white and crimson flowers, requires a considerably higher temperature.

Hoya bella

HYACINTHUS *(Hyacinth)*

The common hyacinth is a fine hardy bulb for spring bedding displays and is equally good as a house plant in bowls or as a greenhouse plant in pots or pans. Outdoors, bulbs should be planted in October or November about 8 inches apart and 4 or 5 inches deep in a well-drained, rather light but reasonably rich soil. In pots or pans for the greenhouse John Innes compost

Hyacinthus orientalis

71

Hyacinthus romanus

Hydrangea macrophylla Hortensia

Hydrangea quercifolia

Hypericum officinale

may be used. The bulbs may be set almost shoulder to shoulder and should be potted in August or September. Before being brought into the greenhouse they should be placed for at least 8 weeks in an unheated frame or, better still, in a plunge bed of sharp boiler ashes, in a shady place outdoors where they can be further covered with 2 inches of ashes. Similar general treatment is also required for hyacinths in bowls except that, if the bowls have no drainage holes, soil should be replaced by bulb fibre containing peat, charcoal and crushed oyster shell. Water will be needed from the time the bulbs are potted or placed in their bowls until the foliage begins to die down the following June. They can then be allowed to dry off and the bulbs shaken out and stored in a cool dry place. Outdoor bulbs can be lifted in late June or early July and be treated in a similar manner.

HYDRANGEA

The many varieties of *Hydrangea macrophylla* are among the most showy of summer flowering shrubs. They make rounded bushes from 3 to 8 feet high and at least as much through, carrying fine heads of bloom from July to September. Colours vary according to variety and according to soil, being usually in shades of pink, red and reddish purple in soils containing much lime, and in shades of blue and blue purple in acid soils. There are also white varieties which are unaffected by soil. All will grow in sun or shade. They are reasonably hardy but severe frost sometimes injures the tips of the shoots and may prevent flowering in some varieties.

A hardier species is *H. paniculata* with fine heads of creamy white flowers in July and August. To be seen at its best it should be cut back quite a lot each March whereas the varieties of *H. macrophylla* should not be cut back though the stems can be thinned out a little each March to prevent over-flowering. *H. quercifolia*, also white flowered, has deeply scalloped leaves.

The varieties of *H. macrophylla* also make good pot plants for the slightly heated or unheated greenhouse. They can be grown in John Innes compost in large pots or tubs and must be watered freely from spring to autumn. To obtain blue flowers special blueing powder can be obtained to mix with the soil, or aluminium sulphate may be used at 1 lb. per bushel.

All hydrangeas are very readily increased by summer cuttings of young shoots inserted in a frame and watered freely.

HYPERICUM *(St John's Wort, Rose of Sharon)*

There are herbaceous and shrubby hypericums and some of the former are quite small plants suitable for the rock garden. All are easily grown in almost any kind of soil and almost all are perfectly hardy. The best of the rock garden hypericums are *H. Coris*, *H. olympicum*, *H. fragile*, *H. repens* and *H. reptans*. None of these is above a foot in height and the last three are all trailers. All have showy yellow flowers in June and July and all like sunny places.

The true Rose of Sharon is *H. calycinum*, a low growing,

rapidly spreading evergreen shrub with brilliant yellow flowers in June and July. It will grow in sun or shade and in the poorest of soils and is a fine plant for steep banks and similar difficult places.

H. patulum is a deciduous shrub of compact habit, 3 or 4 feet high and covered in bowl shaped yellow flowers in July and August. Because of its hardiness, ease of culture and freedom of flowering, it is one of the best shrubs of medium size. There are several varieties such as *Henryi, Forrestii* and Hidcote which differ chiefly in having larger flowers.

Finest of all the shrubby hypericums in bloom is Rowallane hybrid which is 4 to 5 feet in height and produces its large golden yellow flowers in late summer. Unfortunately it is not so hardy as most and needs a sheltered position.

All hypericums can be raised from seed. The herbaceous kinds can usually be divided and the shrubby kinds increased by cuttings in summer.

IBERIS *(Candytuft)*

There are both annual and perennial candytufts. The two annuals commonly grown are *Iberis umbellata*, 1 foot high, with flattish heads of white flowers, and *I. coronaria*, a little taller, with stout, short spikes of white flowers. Both can be sown outdoors from March to May or in early September where they are to bloom and seedlings thinned to about 9 inches.

The perennial candytufts commonly seen are *I. correaefolia, I. saxatilis* and *I. sempervirens*, all bushy evergreen plants of spreading habit, not exceeding a foot in height. They have abundant white flowers in May and June and are grand plants for the rock garden or dry wall. They like sun, are not fussy about soil and can be increased by seed sown in spring or by cuttings of young shoots taken in summer and rooted in a frame.

IMPATIENS *(Touch-me-not, Balsam)*

The flowering balsam of gardens is *Impatiens Balsamina* a half-hardy annual with fine spikes of double flowers which may be pink, scarlet, violet, yellow or white. It must be raised anew each year from seed sown in a temperature of 60° from March to May. The seedlings are potted singly in small pots and are moved on to larger pots until they reach the 8– or 9–inch size in which they will flower. John Innes compost suits them well. Plenty of water should be given and frequent syringing in hot weather. The plants will flower from July to October according to time of seed sowing.

In addition there are two other fine but rather similar perennial kinds, *I. Holstii* and *I. Sultanii*. Both are soft stemmed, bushy plants about 2 feet high bearing abundant scarlet or pink flowers during most of the summer. They can be grown outdoors from June to September, but are really more satisfactory as pot plants for the greenhouse. A minimum winter temperature of 50° is sufficient and they can be raised very easily either from seed sown in a temperature of 60–65° in early spring

Hypericum
patulum

Iberis
umbellata

Iberis
coronaria

Impatiens
Roylei

*Incarvillea
grandiflora brevipes*

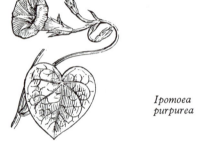

*Ipomoea
purpurea*

*Ipomoea
Leari*

*Iris
susiana*

or by cuttings of young shoots in a propagating box at practically any time while the plants are growing. All these balsams like plenty of water in summer.

INCARVILLEA

These are remarkable hardy herbaceous plants with showy, deeply bell shaped flowers not unlike those of the gloxinia. The flowers are usually rosy red though there is a pink kind named Bee's Pink. All flower in May and June. The species usually seen are *Incarvillea grandiflora* which is about 1 foot high, its variety *brevipes* which is a little more dwarf, and *I. Delavayi*, which is about 2 feet high. All like a sunny place and a good but well-drained soil. They have tuberous roots and can be increased either by very careful division of these roots in spring or by seed sown in a frame in spring.

IPOMOEA *(Morning Glory)*

The ipomoeas are very closely allied to convolvulus and resemble them in their widely funnel shaped flowers. They are all slender but vigorous climbers and mostly have blue flowers— sometimes an intensely pure blue as in the form of *Ipomoea rubro-caerulea* known as Heavenly Blue. *I. Leari* and *I. purpurea* (*Convolvulus major*) have flowers of a deeper hue. All flower in summer and are nearly but not quite hardy. They make good climbers for a slightly heated greenhouse (frost exclusion in winter is all that is required) or *I. caerulea* is sometimes grown as a pot plant with its slender twining stems trained around three of four bamboo canes.

All ipomoeas will grow in any reasonably good soil. They should be watered freely during spring and summer and they require no regular pruning. Propagation is by seeds sown in a warm greenhouse in spring.

IRIS

The iris family is a very large one containing plants of very different character. There are small bulbous rooted irises for the rock garden and larger bulbous rooted irises for the border. There are the very popular bearded irises flowering in May and June which like sunny places and rather dry soils, and there are irises for the bog garden. The only generalization one can make about them is that they are all perennial and nearly all hardy.

First to flower in January are small, bulbous rooted kinds such as *I. histrioides*, light blue, and *I. reticulata*, violet. They need light, well-drained soils and sheltered sunny places and their bulbs should be planted about 2 inches deep in September. The much taller bulbous rooted irises which flower in June and early July and are derived from two species *I. xiphium* and *I. xiphioides*, are divided into three sections—Spanish, English, and Dutch. Their colour range is in blue, yellow and white, and they are first-rate cut flowers. All will thrive in any ordinary soil and open place and all should be planted 3 or 4 inches deep in September.

The May and June flowering bearded irises are hybrids and
they have rhizomes, i.e. fleshy root-like stems lying on the surface of the soil. There are hundreds of varieties differing chiefly in
the colour of their flowers which may be anything from white
and palest yellow or mauve to intense purple, deep yellow or
copper. Heights vary from 2 to 5 feet. These irises may be
planted in spring or autumn, or in late June immediately after
flowering. The rhizomes must be kept almost on the surface
when planting. They like soils well supplied with lime and sunny
places but they will grow in almost any soil and position.

There are also dwarf bearded irises, often known as Crimean
irises, derived from *I. Chamaeiris*. These flower in May and are
suitable for the front of the border or for the rock garden.

Iris sibirica is a fibrous rooted kind with grassy foliage and
it produces its rather small but very graceful blue flowers in
June. It will grow in almost any soil and position but is happiest
near water. It is about 3 feet high. Similar treatment is required
by the tall growing yellow and white *I. ochroleuca*.

A damp soil is essential for *I. Kaempferi* a 3-foot high plant
with very showy purple, violet or blue flowers in June or July.
I. laevigata, which is rather similar in appearance, likes to grow
actually in shallow water though its crowns should not be
covered with more than 3 inches of water.

All the bulbous-rooted irises can be increased by dividing the
clusters of bulbs. The fibrous-rooted kinds and those that
produce rhizomes are increased by division.

IXIA *(African Corn Lily)*

Very beautiful and graceful bulbous-rooted plants which are on
the borderline of hardiness. In mild places they can be grown
outdoors but in many parts of the country they must be grown
as pot plants for the cool greenhouse. All have grassy foliage and
starry flowers carried on slender, 18-inch stems in June. The
colour range is very wide. Bulbs should be planted or potted in
October. Give them a very sunny sheltered place and well-
drained soil. If potted a 4-inch pot will take about 5 bulbs. The
pots should be kept in a frame for two or three months before
being brought into the greenhouse. They should be watered
moderately while they are making their growth and then, after
flowering, the supply should be gradually cut down so that the
bulbs may rest for a couple of months. Propagation is by division
of bulb clusters at planting time.

JASMINUM *(Jasmine)*

The two jasmines commonly grown in gardens are *Jasminum
nudiflorum* which bears its bright yellow flowers in late winter
and earliest spring, and *J. officinale* which is white, fragrant
and summer flowering. Both are grown as climbers but *J. nudiflorum* is a sprawling shrub rather than a true climber and will
need to be tied to suitable supports. Both jasmines are very
easily grown in any ordinary soil and open position. *J. nudiflorum*
will even tolerate a fair amount of shade. Neither requires any

*Iris
pallida*

*Iris
orientalis*

*Ixia
viridiflora*

*Jasminum
officinale*

*Kalanchoë
laciniata*

*Kalmia
angustifolia*

*Kalmia
latifolia*

*Kerria
japonica*

regular pruning and both can be increased either by layering in spring or by striking cuttings of well-ripened young shoots in autumn.

KALANCHOË

These are succulents for the greenhouse and they are useful because of the ease with which most kinds can be grown and because of their brightly coloured flowers. One of the best kinds, *Kalanchoë laciniata* (or *coccinea*) produces its compact scarlet heads on 18-inch stems in summer. Others worthy of note are *K. flammea*, yellow and orange scarlet; and *K. Blossfeldiana* red. All should be grown in John Innes compost in a sunny greenhouse with minimum winter temperature of about 45°. They should be watered very sparingly in winter but moderately at other times. Re-pot when necessary in March and increase by seed sown in a warm greenhouse in spring or by cuttings placed in very sandy soil in spring or early summer.

KALMIA *(Calico Bush)*

The kalmias are evergreen flowering shrubs of great beauty but they are not the easiest of shrubs to grow as they dislike lime and require plenty of moisture, especially in summer when they are making their growth. A deep, cool, rather moist peaty soil suits them best and an open or partly shaded position.

The most popular kind is *K. latifolia* a compact bush 6 or 8 feet high bearing in June, pink flowers, curiously shaped like little Chinese lanterns. *K. angustifolia*, a much dwarfer shrub with rosy-red flowers in June, is occasionally seen and so is *K. polifolia* (*glauca*) which is not over 2 feet high and produces its rose-purple flowers in April. All can be increased by seeds sown in a frame or greenhouse in spring or by layering in early summer.

KERRIA *(Batchelor's Buttons)*

The only species grown, *Kerria japonica*, is usually seen in its double-flowered form, *flore pleno*. The flowers, which appear in April and May, are yellow pompons and it is this that has given the plant its popular name. The ordinary single-flowered form is also worth growing. The kerria makes a loose rather sprawling rapidly spreading shrub with cane-like growths. It is often treated as a climber for which purpose it must be tied up to some suitable support and pruned severely each year after flowering, the flowering stems being cut out to make way for the young shoots. It is perfectly hardy, very easily grown in sun or shade and not in the least fussy about soil.

Propagation is by layering or by summer cuttings which may need a little bottom heat to make them form roots.

KNIPHOFIA *(Red Hot Poker, Torch Lily)*

These are very handsome perennial plants for the border but unfortunately not all are thoroughly hardy. Quite reliable are *Kniphofia Uvaria* and all its many varieties, with stiff, stout

Lonicera
Periclymenum

Lobelia
tenuior

Lysimachia
vulgaris

Lithospermum
prostratum

Lythrum
Salicaria

Linaria
purpurea
[garden form]

Lychnis
chalcedonica

Malcolmia
maritima

Lupinus
polyphyllus
[garden form]

Linum
narbonnense

Lobelia
cardinalis

Magnolia
Soulangeana

Mahonia Aquifolium

Matthiola incana

Meconopsis
betonicifolia

Narcissus
incomparabilis
[garden form]

Narcissus
poeticus

Montbretia
[Crocosmia
crocosmiiflora]

Malus
Lemoinei

Monarda
didyma

Mimulus
luteus

Mesembryanthemum roseum

Malope
trifida
grandiflora

Mirabilis Jalapa

Muscari
botryoides

Myosotis
dissitiflora

flower stems in July, August or September terminated by poker-shaped spikes of scarlet, yellow or scarlet and yellow flowers. Heights vary from 3 to 8 feet. Reliable also is the much smaller and more slender *K. Galpinii* with neat orange 'pokers' carried on 3-foot stems in August. A third species that seems to be quite hardy though it is seldom seen is *K. caulescens*. It has glaucous leaves and branched stems terminated by rather pale red and yellow flower spikes in June.

All these like well-drained but not dry, fairly rich soils, and full sun. They may be planted in spring or autumn but should not be frequently disturbed. They can best be increased by careful division when planting.

LABURNUM *(Golden Rain)*

The common laburnum, *L. vulgare*, is one of the most popular of spring flowering trees. Its long trails of yellow flowers are a familiar sight in May and early June. Its hybrid, *L. Vossii*, is in some respects even better as it has longer flower trails. The other parent of this hybrid, *L. alpinum*, is less familiar but a very graceful tree, a little later flowering and pleasantly fragrant.

All laburnums are easily grown in almost any soil and open position. They are not, as a rule, very long lived and sometimes die suddenly for no apparent cause, but they can be so easily raised from seed sown in spring that losses can be readily made good. No pruning is required.

LAMIUM *(Dead Nettle)*

Most of the dead nettles are weeds but one kind, *Lamium maculatum*, is a useful ground cover for rough places. It is a prostrate, trailing perennial with small, nettle shaped leaves, green with a central blotch of white. The purple flowers appear in March and April and at that season are welcome. This dead nettle will grow anywhere in sun or shade, good soil or poor and can be increased by division at any time.

LANTANA

Once popular greenhouse and summer bedding plants, these for some reason are now seldom seen. In growth they closely resemble verbenas and they have similar flat heads of flowers produced in succession during most of the summer. The colour range is yellow, red and purplish violet with many unusual intermediate shades. Their average height is 3 feet. They can be grown in pots in a frost-proof greenhouse or alternatively may be grown in a greenhouse from October to May and in a sunny place outdoors in summer. They are not fussy about soil but like sun and warmth. Propagation is either by seed sown in a slightly heated greenhouse in spring or by cuttings of young growth in spring or autumn in a frame in the greenhouse.

LAPAGERIA *(Chilean Bellflower)*

The only kind grown is *Lapageria rosea*, a very beautiful tender climbing plant with hanging, bell shaped pink flowers in sum-

Kniphofia
sarmentosa

Laburnum
vulgare

Lantana
montevidensis

Lapageria
rosea

77

Lathyrus grandiflorus

Lavandula Stoechas

Lavandula Spica

Lavatera Olbia

mer. There is also a pure white form. *L. rosea* is nearly hardy and can be grown outdoors in a few very mild places, but must usually be treated as a permanent greenhouse plant. All it needs is frost protection. It is happiest when planted direct in a border of good soil and it should be well watered in summer. The slender stems should be allowed to climb on wires beneath the rafters. A little shade may be required in hot weather and frequent syringing to maintain a fairly damp atmosphere. Increase by layering in spring or early summer.

LATHYRUS (Sweet Pea)

Botanically the familiar sweet pea is named *Lathyrus odoratus*. It is a hardy annual which can be grown from seed sown in spring where the plants are to bloom. For the best results, however, it is preferable to sow in early September in small pots in a frame and to plant out the seedlings in well prepared rich soil the following April. There are also two systems of growing on the seedlings. One is to stick them with brushy hazel branches into which they can clamber quite naturally. By this means the largest possible number of flowers is obtained but some may be rather small. The alternative is to restrict each plant to a single stem, nipping out all side growths and tendrils, and to tie this stem to a long bamboo cane. Usually a double row of such canes is used about a foot apart and a foot from cane to cane with horizontal wires top and bottom to give additional stability. By this 'cordon' system of training the largest possible flowers are obtained, but the plants are more subject to leaf scorch.

There are a great many different varieties of sweet pea and more are added every year. It is usually wise to select up-to-date varieties as these generally give the best results.

LAVANDULA (Lavender)

The common lavender, *Lavandula Spica* (*officinalis*) is one of the most popular dwarf shrubs. It is grown both for its neat grey aromatic leaves which are retained all the winter and for its spikes of lavender blue, fragrant flowers in July. There are numerous varieties varying in height and in depth of colour. Hidcote variety is only a foot high and has deep purplish blue flowers. By contrast Grappenhall Variety is 4 feet high and a fairly pale lavender. There are also other species such as *L. pedunculata* with rather long stemmed flowers and *L. Stoechas* with green leaves and compact heads of purple flowers, but the common lavender is the most useful.

All lavenders like rather light, well-drained soils and sunny places. Winter wet is their enemy and on heavy, wet soils they may prove impermanent. All benefit from being trimmed over after flowering and all can be increased very easily from cuttings either in August in a propagating frame or in October outdoors.

LAVATERA (Mallow)

There are both annual and perennial lavateras and some are not much better than weeds but at least two are first rate garden plants. One is *Lavatera trimestris* (*rosea*) a hardy annual which makes a big, bushy plant 3 or 4 feet high with large, widely opened rose-pink flowers all the summer. It is rather coarse in growth but is immensely showy and as it is also very easy to grow from seed sown in March or April where the plants are to flower, it must be considered one of the ten or twelve best hardy annuals. Seedlings should be thinned to at least 18 inches.

The other outstandingly good kind is *L. Olbia*, the tree mallow, a tall shrub of loose, open habit. It will soon grow to 6 or 7 feet and produce its big, soft pink flowers all the summer. It delights in light, well-drained soils and is a first rate seaside shrub. It is not always very hardy when young and is particularly likely to suffer injury on badly drained soils. It can be quickly raised from seed sown in frame or greenhouse in spring.

LEONTOPODIUM *(Edelweiss)*

This is the alpine around which so much legend has grown up. It is by no means the difficult plant to collect or to grow that it is often supposed to be. It will thrive in any well-drained rock garden provided it is given a sunny, open position well away from the drip of trees. It is notable for its grey, silken-clad, leaves and curiously formed, rayed flowers densely clothed in white wool. It is certainly not a showy plant but it is attractive and unusual. It can be increased by dividing the roots in spring.

LEPTOSYNE

Little known but very attractive hardy annuals with yellow, daisy-like flowers. The kind most commonly seen is *L. Stillmanii* which is about 8 inches high. *L. maritima* is twice as tall. All the leptosynes are sown in April or early May where they are to flower in summer and the seedlings are thinned to 9 inches or thereabouts. They like sunny places and well-drained soils.

LEUCOJUM *(Snowflake)*

Three snowflakes are to be seen in gardens and all resemble the common snowdrop. The spring snowflake, *Leucojum vernum*, has white, green-tipped flowers on 6–inch stems in March or April. The so-called summer snowflake, *L. aestivum*, carries its nodding white, green-tipped flowers on 18-inch stems in April and May. It is followed in October by the autumn snowflake, *L. autumnale*, a smaller and more fragile plant with white, rose-tinged flowers. All like good, rather leafy, cool soils and partially shaded places and both resent disturbance. They are often slow to establish themselves and may disappoint at first. Bulbs of the spring and summer snowflakes should be planted 3 inches deep in September, those of the autumn snowflake the same depth in July or early August. Propagation is by division of the bulb clusters at planting time.

LEWISIA *(Bitterwort)*

The lewisias are extremely beautiful but not very easy rock plants. They require perfect drainage and are sometimes happiest

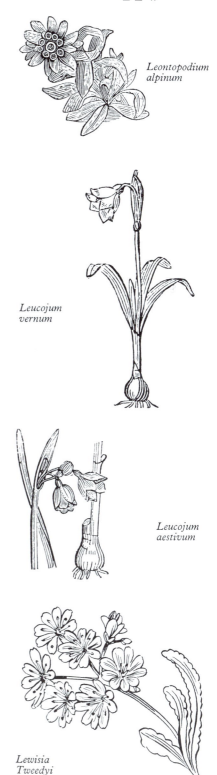

Leontopodium alpinum

Leucojum vernum

Leucojum aestivum

Lewisia Tweedyi

Leycesteria formosa

Liatris spicata

Lilium japonicum

Lilium longiflorum

on a dry wall where their rosettes of leaves can be disposed vertically so that they shed surplus moisture. The leaves are always rather fleshy and the flowers are carried singly or in small clusters on bare stems a few inches to a foot in length. Two of the most popular are *Lewisia Howellii* which has flowers of an unusual pinkish salmon, and *L. Tweedyi* which is not far removed from the colour of a well ripened apricot. Both flower in May and June. There are also numerous hybrids mostly with flowers in some such colours as these. All can be readily raised from seed sown in a frame in spring and as the adult plants are not likely to prove very long lived, however favourable the situation, it is desirable to keep batches of seedlings in reserve.

LEYCESTERIA *(Himalayan Honeysuckle)*

A shrub of very unusual appearance. It makes a large shuttlecock shaped clump of long, bright green, cane-like stems terminated in late summer and early autumn by short trails of chocolate and white flowers. It is hardy but the rather soft growths may be injured by frost in very cold weather. However, the plant always throws up new growths from the base and does not seem to suffer any permanent check—indeed it can, if desired, be cut back almost to ground level each February. It will grow in almost any soil and is equally happy in sun or shade. To increase it suckers can usually be detached with roots attached in either spring or autumn.

LIATRIS *(Blazing Star, Button Snakeroot)*

These curious and beautiful hardy herbaceous perennials belong to the daisy family though one might not guess that last fact from a casual glance at their close, cylindrical flower spikes. These are set with feathery looking reddish purple flowers which start to open from the top downwards. The two commonly seen are *Liatris spicata* and *L. pycnostachya* which are very similar in appearance and which both produce their 3- to 4-foot flower spikes in August. Both have small tuberous roots and both like rather moist, but not waterlogged soils. They should be planted in spring with the crowns of the tubers just below the surface. Give them a sunny place and, if the soil is inclined to dry out quickly, water them freely in summer when it is hot. All can be increased by careful division at planting time.

LILIUM *(Lily)*

This is one of the largest and most complex families of bulbous rooted plants. There are many hundreds of varieties of lily, some quite easy to grow and some distinctly difficult. Most are hardy, but a few, such as the lovely white Easter lily, *Lilium longiflorum*, are sufficiently tender to require cool greenhouse treatment.

It is difficult to generalize about lilies as their needs are so varied. Most can be planted in October or November, but a few, notably the Madonna lily, *Lilium candidum*, and the nearly allied Nankeen lily, *L. testaceum*, are better planted in late July or

Osmanthus Delavay

Omphalodes
cappadocica

Nicotiana
Sanderae

Oxalis
adenophylla

Paeonia
officinalis rubra

Nymphaea
Marliacea

Ornithogalum
umbellatum

Nemesia
strumosa
[garden hybrids]

Nepeta
Faassenii

Olearia Haastii

Nemophila
insignis

Oenothera
fruticosa

Nerine
Bowdenii

Petunia
hybrida

Philadelphus
Lemoinei

Papaver
orientule

Phacelia
campanularia

Passiflora
caerulea

Phlox
subulata

Phlox
paniculata
[garden form]

Penstemon
hybrida

Phygelius
capensis

Perovskia
abrotanoides

Phlomis
fruticosa

Pernettya
mucronata

Pelargonium
zonale

CN-T

early August. Most should be planted so that their bulbs are covered with about twice their own depth of soil but again there are exceptions and the Madonna lily should be just covered with soil and no more. Many lilies dislike lime and thrive best in rather acid soils but there are also many which do not mind lime and a few, such as *L. chalcedonicum*, which positively seem to like it. However, it is probably true to say there is no lily which cannot be grown in a slightly acid, lime-free soil. It is also true that all lilies like an annual top dressing of an inch or so of good leaf mould or peat and that all like to be left undisturbed for a number of years.

All lilies can be raised from seed sown in a frame or greenhouse in spring and a few, such as *L. regale* and *L. philippinense*, will flower in two or three years but most take four or five years to attain flowering size. All can be increased by careful division of the bulb clusters in autumn and many can also be increased by individual scales of bulbs carefully detached and inserted right way up in sand and peat. Some lilies, such as *L. tigrinum* and *L. Henryi*, make tiny bulbs in the axils of the leaves all up the flowering stems and these can be grown on in a few years to bulbs of flowering size.

A few of the most popular lilies are *L. auratum*, the golden-rayed lily of Japan, 6 or 7 feet tall with immense white, fragrant, gold-spotted flowers in July; *L. candidum*, the Madonna lily, 4 feet tall, with fragrant white flowers in July; *L. croceum*, 5 feet high, orange, with maroon spots, June flowering; *L. chalcedonicum*, scarlet, hanging flowers on 3–foot stems in July; *L. Henryi*, orange, purple-spotted flowers on 7-foot stems in late summer; *L. giganteum*, 10 or 12 feet high with narrowly trumpet shaped white flowers in July; *L. longiflorum*, 4 feet with white flowers in September (it is tender and can be flowered in the greenhouse at Easter time); *L. Martagon*, many shades of rose and light purple, 4 feet, June; *L. monadelphum Szovitzianum*, 3 feet, lemon yellow and July flowering; *L. pardalinum*, orange-red with maroon spots, 5 feet high and July flowering; *L. regale*, white fragrant flowers on 4-foot stems in July; *L. speciosum*, white, crimson-spotted flowers in September, 4 feet, rather tender; *L. testaceum*, light apricot, 4 feet, June-July; *L. Thunbergianum*, orange flowers carried erect on 2-foot stems in June-July; *L. tigrinum* the popular tiger lily, orange, maroon spotted flowers, on 5-foot stems in August; *L. umbellatum*, 2 to 3 feet, with yellow to orange-red flowers carried erect in June and *L. Willmottiae*, orange-red pendent flowers on 4-foot stems in July-August.

LIMONIUM (Statice)

These are useful plants with 'everlasting' flowers. There are both annual and perennial kinds. Best known of the annuals are *Limonium sinuatum* and *L. Bonduellii*, the first with white, blue or pink flowers, the second yellow. Both flower in July or August and are grown from seed sown in a slightly heated greenhouse in February or March, the seedlings being hardened off for planting out in a sunny position in late May or early

F

Lilium
canadense

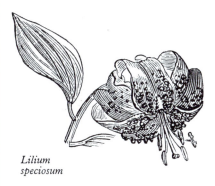

Lilium
speciosum

Lilium
monadelphum

Limonium
sinuatum

*Linaria
purpurea*

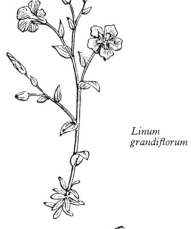

*Linaria
bipartita*

*Linum
grandiflorum*

*Linum
flavum*

June. They should be spaced 9 inches apart in rows 18 inches apart and the flowers should be cut just before they are fully open. They are dried by being suspended head downwards for a few weeks in a cool, dry shed or room.

Best of the perennial limoniums is *L. latifolium*, which makes a large, loose spray of tiny lavender flowers in August. It grows about 2 feet high and, like the white perennial gypsophila which it slightly resembles, is an admirable flower to mix with the larger blooms. It should be planted in a sunny place and well-drained soil and be left undisturbed for as long as possible. It can be increased by root cuttings in winter.

LINARIA *(Toadflax)*

There are many different kinds of toadflax but from the garden standpoint the four most useful are *Linaria marocanna*, a hardy annual about 18 inches high, with small, snapdragon-like flowers in a variety of bright colours in summer; *L. purpurea*, a hardy perennial 3 or 4 feet high, with similarly formed, purple flowers in slender spikes from June to September; *L. pallida* (now usually known as *Cymbalaria pallida*) a small, trailing plant for rock garden or dry wall with pale purple flowers most of the summer, and *L. alpina*, a really good rock plant, tufted, 6 inches high, with purple or shrimp-pink flowers in summer.

L. marocanna is grown from seed sown in March or April where the plants are to flower. It likes a sunny position and any ordinary soil. Seedlings should be thinned to 6 inches. Less familiar, *L. bipartita*, purple and orange, requires similar treatment.

L. purpurea is very easily grown in any soil and fairly open place. It can be planted in spring or autumn and increased by division at either season.

L. pallida likes rather dry, stony places and either sun or partial shade. It is not far removed from being a weed like our own native Kenilworth Ivy, but has flowers of superior size. It can be increased by division at any time of the year.

L. alpina by contrast is worth a good place in the rock garden, in stony, quickly drained soil and a sunny place. It is best increased by seed sown in a frame in spring.

LINUM *(Flax)*

There are annual and perennial flaxes and good garden plants in each. The best annual kind is *Linum grandiflorum* which makes a slender plant about a foot high carrying wide open, scarlet flowers all the summer. It is very easily grown from seed sown in March, April or September where the plants are to flower. It loves sun and does not seem to mind how poor the soil is. Seedlings should be thinned to about 6 inches.

There are several good perennial flaxes. *L. narbonense* and *L. perenne* are very similar in appearance, about 18 inches high, narrow-leaved and carrying fine sprays of light blue flowers from June to August. *L. flavum* has bright yellow flowers and broader leaves and also flowers most of the summer. A neater and still better species with yellow flowers is *L. arboreum* which is not above a foot in height and also flowers all the summer. It is really a tiny, compact shrub.

Then there is *L. salsaloides* which brings us back to the general style of *L. perenne* but it has pearl white flowers in June and July.

All these perennial linums can be raised from seed sown in a frame in spring.

LITHOSPERMUM (Gromwell)

The best of the gromwells is *Lithospermum diffusum*, a low spreading plant of shrubby habit better known to gardeners as *L. prostratum*. It is notable for its intensely blue, forget-me-not flowers which are produced in greatest abundance in May and June but more sparingly for most of the summer. It is a grand plant for a sunny place on a rock garden or dry wall in lime-free soil. It has numerous garden varieties such as Heavenly Blue and Grace Ward which are distinguished by the greater size or superior colour of their flowers. All can be increased by cuttings of young shoots in a frame in July or August.

There are also other useful kinds, such as the grassy-leaved *L. graminifolium*, the loose growing *L. intermedium*, and *L. purpureo-caeruleum*, but none is quite as brilliant as *L. diffusum*.

Lithospermum purpureo-caeruleum

LOBELIA

The common blue lobelia used as an edging plant or ground cover in summer bedding schemes, needs no description, but gardeners are by no means so familiar with the erect growing scarlet and purple flowered lobelias for the herbaceous border. These are derived from three species, *Lobelia cardinalis* and *L. fulgens* both about 3 feet high with scarlet flowers, and *L. syphilitica*, similar in height but with purplish blue flowers. All flower in late summer and early autumn and like rich, cool, leafy soils well supplied with moisture. They may even be grown successfully in a bog garden or near the side of pool or stream. They are not, unfortunately, very hardy and it is wise to lift some roots each autumn and place them in a frame until the spring. They can be increased very readily by division in spring.

The blue bedding lobelias derived from *L. Erinus* are usually treated as half-hardy annuals, seed being sown in a slightly heated greenhouse in February or March and the seedlings hardened off for planting out in May. They should be spaced about 6 inches apart. The trailing lobelia, *L. tenuior*, is treated in the same way and is a popular plant for hanging baskets.

Lobelia Erinus

Lobelia fulgens

LONICERA (Honeysuckle, Woodbine)

This is another family that has surprises for the beginner for in addition to the well-known climbing honeysuckles with their very fragrant yellow or reddish flowers, there are a number of shrubby kinds some of which flower in mid-winter and one of which, *Lonicera nitida*, makes a fine evergreen hedge. This is grown solely for its neat, box-like foliage and it stands clipping well.

Lonicera japonica flexuosa

83

*Lonicera
Brownii*

*Lonicera
Periclymenum*

*Lupinus
polyphyllus*

*Lychnis
chalcedonica*

The two best winter flowering shrubby loniceras are *L. frag-rantissima* and *L. Standishii*. They are rather alike, both making open, 6–foot bushes bearing small cream coloured flowers which are very fragrant. Though hardy themselves their flowers may be destroyed by frost so it is desirable to give them a sheltered position. Otherwise they are not in the least difficult to grow in any ordinary soil.

There are several fine climbing honeysuckles in addition to the common British kind, *L. Periclymenum*. There are, for example, two fine varieties of this known respectively as *belgica* (or early Dutch) and *serotina* (or late Dutch). They have flowers of superior size and colour, one opening in May and June and the other in July and August.

Then there is the nearly evergreen and sweetly scented *L. japonica* and its variety *aureo-reticulata* in which the leaves are veined with gold. *L. tragophylla* has large deep yellow flowers without scent and another scentless kind worth growing for the beauty of its scarlet flowers, is *L. Brownii fuchsioides*. It is a hybrid of the beautiful but rather tender *L. sempervirens*.

All these climbing honeysuckles like rather good, loamy soils and most will grow in partial shade as well as in sun. They can be increased by layering in early summer. *Lonicera nitida* and the other shrubby kinds can be increased by cuttings of well ripened young growth in a frame in autumn.

LUPINUS *(Lupin)*

This is one of the most popular as well as one of the most improved plants for the herbaceous border. The herbaceous lupins have all been derived from *Lupinus polyphyllus*, a vigorous plant with 4-foot high spikes of pale blue or white flowers in June. Under cultivation the form and size of the spikes has been greatly improved and the colour range widened to include yellow, pink, carmine, apricot and many lovely intermediate shades or mixtures of two colours.

All are easily grown in any ordinary soil and sunny position but they do not much like very chalky soils. They can be raised quickly and cheaply from seed sown outdoors in May or in a frame in March, but seedlings usually vary a good deal in colour so selected varieties must be increased by cuttings of young shoots severed close to the crown of the plant in April and rooted in a frame. Lupins can be planted in either spring or autumn.

There is also the tree lupin, *L. arboreus*, a big bushy plant with much smaller spikes of yellow or white flowers in June and July. It is a grand seaside plant and revels in sandy soils but is usually short lived on heavier and richer soils inland. This also is easily raised from seeds or cuttings.

LYCHNIS *(Maltese Cross, Jerusalem Cross, Rose Campion)*

The three best species of lychnis for the garden are *Lychnis chalcedonica*, the Maltese or Jerusalem cross, a 3-foot high hardy perennial with brilliant scarlet heads of cross shaped flowers in July and August; *L. Coronaria*, the rose campion, a grey-leaved plant with magenta flowers in June and July, to be seen in most old cottage gardens, and *L. Viscaria splendens plena* sometimes known as the German catchfly, a smaller plant, not above a foot in height, with short spikes of light carmine, double flowers in June and July. All are sun lovers and all like rather open, well-drained soils. *L. Viscaria splendens plena* may even be grown in a dry wall though it is really a front row plant for the border. All can be increased by careful division in spring.

LYSIMACHIA *(Loosestrife)*

The yellow loosestrife, *Lysimachia vulgaris*, is a very easily grown hardy perennial for shady places and damp soils. It produces 3-foot spikes of yellow flowers in June and July and can be increased by division in spring or autumn. There are other kinds worth growing though none is better than *L. vulgaris*. *L. punctata*, also known as *L. verticillata*, is rather more graceful in habit and *L. clethroides* has white flowers but is not so indestructible.

LYTHRUM *(Purple Loosestrife)*

The two kinds of lythrum commonly grown in gardens have slender spikes of magenta flowers in July and August. They thrive well in damp places but may also be grown quite successfully in the border in ordinary soil and with good drainage. The two species are *L. Salicaria* and *L. virgatum* and they differ chiefly in the fact that the flower spikes of *L. Salicaria* are rather stouter and the individual flowers are larger than those of *L. virgatum*. There are several forms of *L. Salicaria*, two of which, Rose Queen and Lady Sackville, have flowers of a pure rose-pink colour. All can be increased by division in spring or autumn.

MAGNOLIA *(Cucumber Tree, Yulan, Lily Tree)*

Most of the popular magnolias are either large shrubs or small trees and they are grown for the beauty of their flowers. These are carried erect in most of the spring flowering kinds such as *M. denudata*, *M. Soulangeana*, *M. Kobus*, *M. salicifolia* and *M. stellata* and are not unlike a tulip in shape for which reason they are often referred to as tulip trees though this name properly belongs to *Liriodendron tulipifera*. In contrast there is a summer flowering group of magnolias, including *M. sinensis*, *M. Watsonii*, *M. highdownensis* and *M. Sieboldii* in which the flowers are saucer shaped and hang downwards. They are white with a central boss of crimson and are both beautiful and fragrant. The spring flowering kinds are not, as a rule, so powerfully scented (some are not scented at all) and their flowers are white, pink or purple. All these are deciduous. In addition there are two notable evergreen kinds, *M. grandiflora* which has large shining green leaves not unlike those of a laurel, and fine white flowers shaped like water lilies, and *M. Delavayi* with darker, less shining leaves and

Lychnis
Viscaria

Lythrum
virgatum

Magnolia
grandiflora

Magnolia
denudata

85

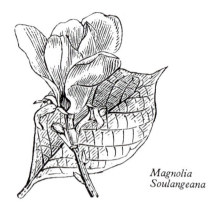

*Magnolia
Soulangeana*

*Mahonia
Aquifolium*

*Malcolmia
maritima*

*Malope
malacoides*

white flowers which are not so freely produced.

Magnolias prefer slightly acid soils though many of them will grow on neutral or even slightly alkaline soils. They do not like being disturbed and are not always easy to transplant but the best time to move them is in spring or early autumn. They are hardy enough but as some flower so early it is advisable to give them a sheltered position as protection for their bloom.

The usual methods of propagation are by layering the young stems in late spring or early summer or by grafting on to nearly allied species which may themselves be raised from seed.

MAHONIA

These evergreen shrubs are closely allied to the barberries. They are easily grown but not all are completely hardy. One of the best, *Mahonia Aquifolium*, has holly-like leaves, makes a compact shrub 3 or 4 feet high and produces its clusters of small, clear yellow flowers from February to May. It is fully hardy. *M. japonica* and the very similar *M. Bealei* flower in winter and their yellow flowers are borne in a circle of radiating spikes like the spokes of a wheel. They are extremely handsome shrubs and are fairly hardy but need a sheltered place because of their winter flowering. *M. lomariifolia* makes great rosettes of long, pinnate leaves and is a very handsome foliage plant quite apart from the beauty of its yellow flowers, but it is rather apt to get bare at the base and acquire a gaunt, ungainly habit and it is not very hardy.

Mahonias will grow in most ordinary soils, none needs any regular pruning and all can be increased by autumn cuttings. *M. Aquifolium* can also be increased by division in spring or autumn.

MALCOLMIA *(Virginian Stock)*

The Virginian stock, *Malcolmia maritima*, is a pretty little annual, quite hardy and so easily raised from seed sown where it is to flower, that it can be grown practically anywhere. It is 6 inches or so in height, has confetti-like flowers in various shades of pink, lilac and white, and, if sown successively from March to May with a final sowing in September, will give a supply of flowers most of the summer. It is particularly useful as an edging plant, for filling bare places in the rock garden or for crevices between paving slabs.

MALOPE

The usual species of malope grown in gardens, *M. trifida*, is a hardy annual which makes a big, bushy plant not unlike a lavatera in habit and flower, but rather more crude in colour. The widely open, funnel shaped flowers are a rather fierce magenta, effective in the right place but not always easy to associate. This is a very easily grown plant not in the least fussy about soil but preferring sunny places. Seed should be sown in March, April and September where the plants are to flower and the seedlings should be thinned to about 18 inches apart.

MALUS *(Apple)*

There are numerous kinds of crab apple as well as other nearly allied species of malus which are useful ornamental trees or large shrubs. One of the best of these, *M. floribunda*, a small tree, bears small but abundant flowers in April and early May. They are red in bud but pale pink when fully open. *M. Lemoinei* makes a rather larger tree, perhaps 25 feet high when full grown, and it has bigger, deep carmine flowers and purple foliage. Very similar in appearance are *M. aldenhamensis* and *M. Eleyi* and all three usually carry good crops of purple, cherry-like fruits. Then there are the true crab apples such as Dartmouth, with round purplish red fruits and John Downie with oval yellow and red fruits. The Siberian crab has smaller, round fruits very freely produced, yellow in one variety and red in another.

They will grow in any ordinary garden soils and open positions. They need not be regularly pruned but can be thinned out and cut back a little in autumn if they become overgrown. All can be raised from seed sown outdoors in March but there is usually some variation in the seedlings, for which reason selected varieties are usually grafted in spring or budded in summer.

MATTHIOLA *(Stock)*

There are several very distinct types of stock grown in gardens but they have all been derived from one native seaside plant, *Matthiola incana*. The principal garden kinds are the ten-week stocks which are grown as half-hardy annuals, East Lothian stocks which may be treated as half-hardy annuals or as hardy biennials and Brompton stocks which are always grown as hardy biennials. All make bushy plants with fine spikes of fragrant flowers which may be single or double though the doubles are always more highly prized. The colour range is from white and palest mauve or pink to pale yellow, deep purple and crimson.

Seed of the ten-week stocks is sown in a greenhouse or frame, in a temperature of 55° in March, seedlings being pricked off and then hardened off for planting out in late May or early June. Alternatively seed can be sown in late June to give seedlings to flower in a warm greenhouse in winter.

The East Lothian stocks can either be sown in February and treated like ten-week stocks when they will flower in late summer, or they can be sown in August, the seedlings overwintering in a frame and planted out in April to flower in July.

Brompton stocks are sown outdoors towards the end of June, the seedlings being transferred to a nursery bed of good soil in an open place as soon as they can be handled conveniently, and finally removed to their flowering quarters in October or March. In cold districts they are best overwintered in a frame.

MECONOPSIS *(Himalayan Poppy, Blue Poppy, Welsh Poppy)*

The most famous species of meconopsis is undoubtedly *M. betonicifolia*, the Himalayan blue poppy, a beautiful hardy peren-

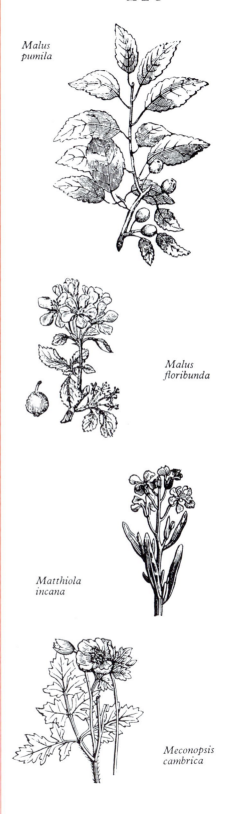

Malus
pumila

Malus
floribunda

Matthiola
incana

Meconopsis
cambrica

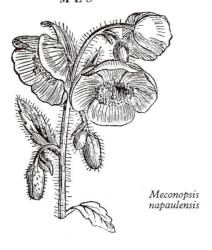

Meconopsis
napaulensis

Mesembryanthemum
crystallinum

Mesembryanthemum
acinaciforme

Mimulus
luteus

nial 3 to 5 feet high bearing large, saucer shaped sky blue flowers in July and August. It is not the easiest of plants to grow as it is fussy about soil and position, liking best a deep cool, leafy or peaty soil and a partially shaded place. It can be raised from seed sown in sandy peat in a frame in spring but seedlings often vary considerably and many may give flowers of an inferior amethyst.

There are many other species mostly with similar requirements and many of them not long lived. Typical of the family is *M. integrifolia*, the Chinese yellow poppy, 3 feet high with large pale yellow flowers. It always dies after flowering and so must be frequently renewed from seed. *M. napaulensis* (*Wallichii*) has pale blue flowers and very handsome foliage covered with tawny hairs. *M. cambrica*, the Welsh Poppy, is rather like a miniature Iceland poppy with pale yellow flowers and in half shady places it often takes complete control, reproducing itself so rapidly from self-sown seed that it ousts everything else.

MESEMBRYANTHEMUM (Ice Plant)

These half-hardy succulent plants, mostly of trailing habit, have highly coloured flowers which have a superficial resemblance to those of the daisy family though they are, in fact, quite unrelated. There are a great many kinds and naming is rather confused. Among the best for garden purposes are *Mesembryanthemum aurantiacum*, more erect than most and with fine orange flowers; *M. Brownii*, not unlike the last but smaller in all its parts and, if anything, even brighter in colour; *M. criniflorum*, prostrate, red, pink or white and one of the few annuals in the family; *M. roseum*, trailing and with rose pink flowers, and *M. crystallinum*, the true ice plant, so-called for the glistening, translucent pustules which cover it. It is a trailing annual with whitish or very pale pink flowers. In seaside districts the vigorous *M. acinaciforme* often grows wild.

All love sun; it seems to be impossible to find a place too hot and dry for them and they delight to scramble over stones or to cascade down sunny walls. The perennials can be increased by cuttings of young shoots in summer or early autumn and the annuals by seed sown in a warm greenhouse in spring. As they are all likely to be killed by a few degrees of frost, it is wise to keep some stock in a frost-proof greenhouse or frame in winter.

MIMULUS (Monkey Flower, Musk)

There are both annual and perennial species of mimulus, several of which are gay plants for garden or greenhouse. The perennials are mostly moisture lovers which can be grown in damp parts of the rock garden, at the side of pools or streams or even in the bog garden. Examples of this kind are *Mimulus luteus* and *M. guttatus*, two very similar plants, 12 to 18 inches high with yellow, red-spotted flowers in summer, and *M. cupreus*, half as high and copper coloured. There are many garden varieties of these, one of the finest of which is the dwarf and very brilliant Whitecroft Scarlet.

The annual kinds are usually hybrids and they are often de-

scribed as *M. tigrinus*, a name of doubtful validity. They produce
large, pouched flowers in various shades of yellow and crimson
usually heavily spotted or blotched with one colour on the other.
Seed should be sown in a slightly heated greenhouse or frame in
February or March and the seedlings pricked out and hardened
off for planting out in late May. They like fairly rich and well-
watered soil.

The old-fashioned musk, famous for the fact that it has mysteriously lost its scent, is little grown nowadays. It is *M. moschatus*, a plant for the cool greenhouse in which it can be grown
either from seed sown in March or from cuttings of young
growth in spring or summer.

MIRABILIS   (Marvel of Peru, Four O'clock Plant)

The only kind of mirabilis likely to be seen in English gardens
is *Mirabilis Jalapa*. It has been called the four o'clock plant
because its fragrant yellow, red, white or variously blotched
flowers tend to open in the afternoon and keep closed when the
sun is shining brightly. It is a perennial, very readily raised from
seeds sown in a warm greenhouse in spring and quickly making
large, tuberous roots which plunge deeply into the soil. It can
be grown outdoors in summer in warm, sunny positions but is
killed by frost so must either be renewed annually or be overwintered in a greenhouse. It grows about 3 feet high, makes a
fairly big, leafy plant and flowers profusely from midsummer
until the autumn.

MONARDA   (Bergamot, Bee Balm)

Hardy herbaceous perennials related to the sages and with a
pleasant aromatic perfume. The only species commonly grown
is *Monarda didyma* but this has numerous garden varieties differing in colour. All are bushy plants 2 to 3 feet high. The common
form has scarlet flowers but there are varieties with white,
mauve, violet, purple and pink flowers. All are very easily grown
in any ordinary soil and fairly open position, and all can be
increased by division in either spring or autumn.

MONTBRETIA

The familiar garden plant which everyone knows as a montbretia will be found in modern botanical works of reference as
Crocosmia crocosmiiflora. It is a hardy plant producing innumer-
able small corms by separating which it can be easily and rapidly
increased. It loves warm, sunny places and does not seem to
mind how poor the soil is so long as it is fairly well drained. The
orange coloured flowers are borne on slender spikes in August
and September. There are many improved varieties with flowers of greater size and extending the colour range from clear
yellow to crimson, but few of these are either as hardy or as
easy to grow as the common type. Some must even be lifted
each autumn and overwintered in a frame to be planted out the
following April and most of these improved forms prefer fairly
rich, well-worked soils such as would be prepared for gladioli.

89

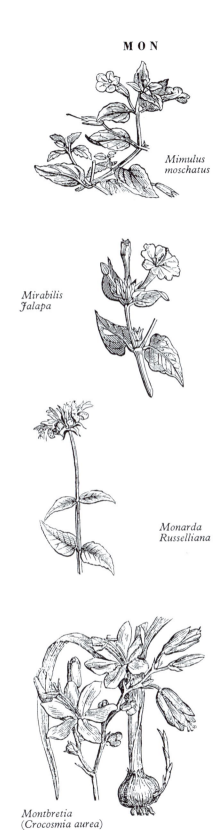

Mimulus
moschatus

Mirabilis
Jalapa

Monarda
Russelliana

Montbretia
(Crocosmia aurea)

Muscari
racemosum

Myosotis
sylvatica

Narcissus
triandrus

Narcissus
Bulbocodium

MUSCARI *(Grape Hyacinth)*

Small early flowering, bulbous-rooted perennials that are ideal for the front of a border or for massing in the rock garden or beneath shrubs. The most popular kind is *M. botryoides* which has 6-inch high spikes of clear blue flowers. It has numerous varieties including a white and one named Heavenly Blue which is a deeper and purer blue. There is also an interesting kind known as the feather hyacinth, *M. comosum monstrosum*. This has much larger flower spikes, which may be 12 inches long but arch or flop more or less horizontally. The blue flowers have a feathery appearance and are most attractive.

Bulbs of these and other grape hyacinths should be planted in autumn, 2 to 3 inches deep in ordinary soil and a sunny position. They can be increased by dividing the bulb clusters at planting time. It is not desirable to lift the bulbs annually.

MYOSOTIS *(Forget-me-not)*

All the familiar kinds of forget-me-not are hardy perennials but the common kinds used for spring bedding and derived from several species, including *Myosotis caespitosa*, *M. dissitiflora* and *M. sylvatica*, are not easy to keep after flowering and are so readily raised from seed that they are nearly always treated as biennials. Seed is sown outdoors in June or early July, the seedlings are pricked out in a nursery bed and are transferred to their flowering quarters in October. They will grow in practically any soil or place and do not object to some shade. In wild parts of the garden they will often naturalize themselves, coming up year after year from self-sown seed without any attention.

There are also choicer and more compact kinds of forget-me-not for the rock garden, such as *M. alpestris*, and for the edge of the water garden or the bog there is the true forget-me-not, *M. palustris (scorpioides)*. This is a rather looser plant with pale blue flowers each with a yellow eye.

NARCISSUS *(Daffodil)*

One of the most popular families of hardy bulbous rooted plants and one which has been so highly developed in gardens that varieties run into thousands. To avoid confusion these have been arbitrarily divided into a number of sections distinguished by the form and general colour of the flowers. Those with long central crowns are known as trumpet daffodils and those with short crowns as small-cupped narcissi. Then there are double-flowered varieties and varieties which bear numerous small flowers on one stem. The poet or pheasant-eye narcissi all have very small flat cups, the colour of which is ringed in the manner of *Narcissus poeticus*. The jonquils have small very fragrant flowers in clusters.

In addition there are the numerous wild species some of which are extremely beautiful and distinctive. There is, for example, the cyclamen-flowered daffodil, *N. cyclamineus*, only a few inches in height and with tubular crowns and narrow, reflexed perianth segments. It is an exquisitely dainty flower. So is the hoop-petticoat daffodil, *N. Bulbocodium*, another miniature with the crown shaped like a tiny crinoline and the surrounding segments very narrow. The angel's-tears daffodil, *N. triandrus*, is 6 to 9 inches in height and has clusters of small, nodding white flowers and *N. Tazetta* is also multiflowered.

All these thrive in good loamy soils and should be planted in August, September or October. Cover their bulbs to about twice their own depth. They can be naturalized in grass but the grass must not be cut until the daffodil foliage has died down in late June or early July.

Propagation is by division of the bulb clusters in July but it is not desirable to lift daffodils annually. They are best left undisturbed until they become overcrowded.

Narcissus Tazetta

NEMESIA

There are few more beautiful annuals than *Nemesia strumosa* and its many garden varieties, but it is a plant that needs a little more care than many annuals. The thing to avoid above all others is to get the seedlings starved and prematurely in flower before they are planted out. For this reason it is wise not to start too early. Seed can be sown in a greenhouse or frame in late March or early April and the seedlings pricked off into good soil as soon as they can be handled. They should then be hardened off carefully for planting out in late May or early June. Give them a sunny position and rather rich soil and space them 6 to 9 inches apart. The average height of the plants is about 12 inches but there are dwarf forms not exceeding 6 inches. The colour range includes yellow, orange, red, blue and white.

Nemesia floribunda

NEMOPHILA (Baby Blue-eyes)

Nemophila insignis is a pretty blue-flowered hardy annual which deserves to be better known than it is. It only grows about 6 inches high and may be had in flower most of the summer if three or four sowings are made between mid-March and mid-May. Sow the seed where the plants are to flower, preferably in a sunny place but in any ordinary soil, and thin the seedlings to 4 inches apart. *N. maculata* has white purple-spotted flowers.

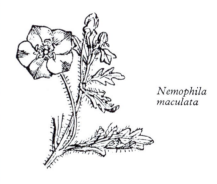

Nemophila maculata

NEPETA (Catmint)

The catmints are hardy perennials mostly with rather aromatic leaves. The best known is the plant always listed, though incorrectly, as *Nepeta Mussinii* (its real name is *N. Faassenii*). It is a bushy plant usually about 15 inches high, though there are taller forms, with greyish leaves and slender spikes of small lavender blue flowers. The effect is very attractive and the plant goes on flowering almost all the summer. It likes well-drained places and does not seem to mind how poor the soil is. It makes an excellent edging to a border and is also very happy in a dry wall. It is quite hardy but tends to die in winter on cold, wet soils. It is very easily propagated by division in the spring.

A very different kind is *N. hederacea* (*Glechoma*) a slender

Nepeta hederacea

91

*Nerine
sarniensis*

*Nicotiana
Tabacum*

*Nymphaea
caerulea*

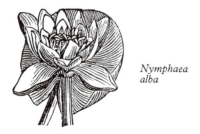

*Nymphaea
alba*

trailing plant with light blue flowers. It has a variety with silver variegated leaves which is sometimes grown in hanging baskets and window boxes. It is quite hardy, not in the least fussy and easily increased by division.

NERINE *(Guernsey Lily)*

The name Guernsey lily is really applied to one nerine only, *Nerine sarniensis*, which has roundish heads of scarlet flowers carried in early autumn on leafless stems 18 inches tall. The leaves appear as the flowers fade. This kind is too tender to be grown outdoors and needs the shelter of a frost-proof greenhouse which is also true of the kind commonly known as *N. Fothergillii*, which is very similar in general appearance, and of the many hybrids which are sold under fancy names and which have flowers in various shades of red and pink. By contrast the rose pink flowered *N. Bowdenii* can be grown outdoors in very sunny, sheltered places, as at the foot of a wall facing south. It is not quite so tall and flowers in late summer.

All these nerines have bulbous roots. The greenhouse varieties should be potted in July or August, in John Innes compost, one bulb in a 4-inch pot or three bulbs in a 6-inch pot. Water moderately during the flowering and growing period, roughly from late August to May, but keep almost dry in June and July. They like full sun at all times.

Bulbs of *N. Bowdenii* should be planted in July, being covered with about 3 inches of soil.

NICOTIANA *(Tobacco)*

The true tobacco is *Nicotiana Tabacum*, a large, rather weedy annual which is grown solely for its leaves. There are, however, numerous ornamental kinds of nicotiana of which the best are *N. alata grandiflora* (*affinis*) often known as the sweet scented tobacco or the jasmine tobacco, and *N. Sanderae* the red flowered tobacco. These are both grown as half hardy annuals, seed being sown in a warm greenhouse in February or March and the seedlings pricked out and hardened off for planting outdoors in late May or early June. Both make plants 3 or 4 feet high with showy flowers which are white in *N. alata*, carmine in *N. Sanderae*. They are not particular about soil and will thrive in full sun or partial shade. The fragrance is most marked at night.

NYMPHAEA *(Water Lily)*

The hardy water lilies are all species of nymphaea and there are also some kinds, such as *N. caerulea*, the blue lotus of Egypt and *N. stellata*, the blue lotus of India, that are tender aquatics which must be grown in a warm greenhouse. All must have their roots in water all the year but there are individual preferences as to the depth of the water. For example *N. alba*, the common white water lily, and *N. Gladstoniana*, another kind with large white flowers, both like fairly deep water, say 2 feet or even 3 feet. By contrast *N. tetragona*, the pygmy water lily, with small white flowers, and its pale yellow variety *helvola*, both thrive best in water no more than 4 or 5 inches deep. The majority of the popular hybrids, known under the general name *N. Marliacea*, will grow well in water 1 to 2 feet deep.

Most make fleshy or tuberous roots and should be planted just as growth is starting in April or May. They can be planted in ordinary soil in the bottom of a pool or may be planted in boxes, baskets or wire cages filled with good rich soil and then sunk in position. Propagation is by division at planting time.

OENOTHERA *(Evening Primrose)*

The common evening primrose, *Oenothera biennis*, is a tall, rather weedy biennial with very beautiful pale yellow flowers of fragile build which open in the evening. It is a good plant for rough places and one that will thrive in very poor soils and sunny or partially shaded positions. It flowers in July and August. It is easily grown from seed sown in May or June where the plants are to bloom the following year.

A better garden plant is *O. fruticosa*, a bushy perennial 18 to 24 inches high, delighting in rather light, well-drained soils and producing a profusion of bright yellow flowers in July and August. It has several varieties such as *Youngii* and *major*, differing mainly in being rather more compact in habit or even more showy in flower. All are good perennials in well-drained soils and all can be increased by division in spring.

There are also dwarf oenotheras for the rock garden, notably *O. missouriensis*, a low-growing, grey-leaved plant with fine light yellow flowers in late summer; *O. mexicana* with soft pink flowers, and *O. acaulis* *(taraxacifolia)* with white or pink tinted flowers. All want the best possible drainage and full sun.

OLEARIA *(Daisy Bush)*

There are many kinds of olearia but unfortunately most of them are a little too tender to be fully reliable outdoors except in the mildest parts of the country. All are evergreen shrubs with daisy-like flowers. One of the best for general planting is *Olearia Haastii*, a big bush of dense, rounded habit with neat oval leaves and masses of small white daisy flowers in July and August. Hardy enough for most places, it is not in the least fussy about soil and usually does well in towns.

Another good kind, *O. stellulata* *(Gunniana)*, is about 5 feet high, has small grey leaves and white flowers. It is not as hardy as *O. Haastii* but does well in many parts of the country.

Very different in appearance is *O. macrodonta*, which may grow to a height of 20 feet but can be kept much smaller by a little judicious pruning each spring, and has large holly-like leaves and white flowers. In some mild places it is grown as a hedge.

All can be increased by cuttings of firm young shoots in July or August in a propagating frame.

OMPHALODES *(Navel-wort)*

These are small and very pretty perennial plants with blue flowers rather like forget-me-nots. One of the best is *Omphalodes*

Nymphaea micrantha

Oenothera Drummondii

Oenothera biennis

Olearia stellulata

93

*Omphalodes
verna*

*Ornithogalum
narbonense*

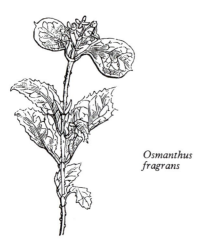

*Osmanthus
fragrans*

*Oxalis
rosea*

Luciliae, a neat tufted plant about 6 inches high which flowers in May. *O. verna* is coarser in growth and sprawling in habit, 8 or 9 inches high with abundant blue flowers in April and May. It is sometimes called the creeping forget-me-not. *O. cappadocica* has blue-grey leaves and the usual blue flowers.

Both *O. verna* and *O. cappadocica* will grow in shade or sun and almost any kind of soil. *O. Luciliae* needs sun and reasonably well-drained soil. It is really a plant for the rock garden. All can be increased by division in the spring.

ORNITHOGALUM (*Star of Bethlehem*)

The true star of Bethlehem is *Ornithogalum umbellatum*, a hardy bulbous-rooted plant with loose, foot high sprays of starry white flowers in June. Not unlike it but with narrower spikes and nodding flowers is *O. nutans* which flowers at the same time. Both are useful plants for odd corners and difficult places for they will thrive in almost any soil and do not mind full sun or partial shade. Both can be increased by division in the autumn.

OSMANTHUS (*Fragrant Olive*)

Without doubt the best osmanthus for general garden planting is *Osmanthus Delavayi*, a first-class evergreen shrub, freely branched and dense in habit, with small, very dark green leaves and tiny white tubular flowers produced with great freedom in April. They are notable for their extremely sweet fragrance which is often air-borne for many yards around a plant. Another occasionally grown, principally for its dark green holly-like leaves, is *O. Aquifolium*. Both like good, loamy soils and though both may be considered hardy in most parts of the country, *O. Delavayi* should be given a little protection until it is firmly established and growing well. Neither requires any regular pruning and both can be increased by cuttings of firm young shoots in a propagating frame in July or August. *O. fragrans*, up to 30 feet high, requires greenhouse protection.

OXALIS (*Wood Sorrel*)

The British wood-sorrel, *Oxalis Acetosella*, is a pretty carpeting plant with clover-like leaves and fragile pearl white flowers in spring, but it spreads so rapidly that it must be considered a bad weed in gardens. Not so *O. adenophylla* and *O. enneaphylla*, two lovely rock plants which never spread far or make themselves a nuisance. Both have tuberous roots and grey leaves but the fine flowers are white veined with lilac pink in *O. adenophylla* and white in *O. enneaphylla*. Neither exceeds 3 inches in height and both revel in sun and rather light, well-drained soils. Another very popular kind is *O. rosea* (or *rubra*) a prostrate plant with clover-like leaves and loose sprays of light rose flowers most of the summer. It loves sun and warm dry places and may often be seen in old cottage gardens tucked in under a sunny wall or growing in the crevices of a path. It also makes a useful pot plant for a sunny window.

O. rosea can be easily increased by division at practically any time of the year. *O. enneaphylla* can also be divided in spring but *O. adenophylla* must be raised from seed sown in a greenhouse or frame in spring.

PAEONIA *(Peony)*

Three types of peony are commonly grown in British gardens, the common peony derived from *Paeonia officinalis*, the Chinese peonies derived from *P. albiflora*, and the tree peonies derived from *P. suffruticosa (Moutan)*. The first and second are hardy herbaceous perennials, usually about 3 feet high with single or, more commonly, large double flowers in June. They differ in that though the colour range in both is from white, through pink to crimson, there is a greater variety of shades in the Chinese than in the common peony and they are fragrant. Many of the loveliest flowers are to be found in the Chinese type.

Varieties of *P. suffruticosa* are all rather soft-stemmed shrubs and they are not quite so easy to grow as the other two groups. Plants average 6 feet in height and they produce their very large, usually fully double flowers in June. The colours are varied and often very beautiful, covering white, pink, crimson, apricot and many intermediate shades or combinations of two or more colours.

They like good, rich, loamy soils not inclined to dry out too severely, and thrive in sun but will succeed in light shade. They dislike being moved and usually take a year or so to recover and start flowering freely again.

All can be planted in spring or autumn. The herbaceous kinds are usually increased by division, the tree peonies by grafting, often on to herbaceous peony roots though this is not really a practice to be commended.

PAPAVER *(Poppy)*

The poppies are a gay lot and all are easy to grow. There are both annual and perennial kinds, the two most important in the first class being the Shirley poppies and the opium poppies, and the two best in the second group, the oriental poppies and the Iceland poppies.

The Shirley poppies are derived from our own native field poppy, *Papaver Rhoeas*, but instead of being all scarlet like that brilliant but troublesome plant, they have flowers of every shade from white and palest pink to scarlet, some combining two shades, some single flowered and some double and all beautiful.

The opium poppies are derived from *P. somniferum*, a rather more robust plant with smooth greyish green leaves. Most modern strains have large double flowers and the colour range is from white to purple.

Both these annual poppies are grown from seed sown in March, April, May or September where the plants are to flower. The seedlings should be thinned to 9 inches, or thereabouts. They like a sunny place and do not mind how poor or dry the soil is.

*Paeonia
suffruticosa*

*Paeonia
albiflora*

*Papaver
Rhoeas*

*Papaver
somniferum*

95

Papaver nudicaule

Papaver orientale

Passiflora edulis

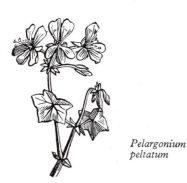

Pelargonium peltatum

The oriental poppies are derived from *P. orientale*, a sturdy, leafy plant with large scarlet flowers blotched with black within. They appear in June. White and pink varieties have also been produced and some with fringed petals, They like sunny places and well-drained soils and can be raised from seed sown outdoors in May or by root cuttings in winter. Seedlings may vary a little from their parents.

The Iceland poppy *P. nudicaule*, though a perennial, is usually grown either as an annual or as a biennial, seed being sown in a greenhouse in February or March and the seedlings planted out in May for July and August flowering, or sown in a greenhouse or frame in June to be planted out in August or September for flowering early next summer. They need a sunny place and well-drained soil. The flowers are very dainty, carried on slender but firm stems, 12 to 18 inches high, and the colour range includes yellow, pink, orange and tangerine.

PASSIFLORA *(Passion Flower)*

These are vigorous climbing plants many of which are too tender to be grown outdoors in this country. *Passiflora caerulea*, however, will succeed on warm and sheltered walls where it will soon make a mass of growth extending to 15 or 20 feet and freely covered in late summer with remarkable pale blue, white and purple flowers. There is a pure white variety named Constance Elliott.

P. edulis, sometimes known as the purple grenadilla, has white and purple flowers followed by large, egg-shaped fruits which are edible. *P. antioquiensis (Van Volxemii)* also has edible fruits and very showy, scarlet flowers. Both these must be grown in a warm greenhouse.

All passion flowers are readily and quickly raised from seed sown in a warm greenhouse in spring. They like good, loamy soils and plenty of sun.

PELARGONIUM *(Geranium)*

This is one of those flowers the nomenclature of which has become very confused in gardens. What everyone calls geranium is, in fact, a pelargonium, and the true geraniums are hardy herbaceous plants which are not often seen though several of them are well worth growing.

The pelargoniums may conveniently be considered in three groups—the popular zonal-leaved varieties so largely used for summer bedding, the ivy-leaved pelargoniums popular for window boxes, hanging baskets, etc., and the show or regal pelargoniums grown as pot plants for the greenhouse.

Best known of the zonal-leaved varieties is the scarlet flowered Paul Crampel, but there are newer and better varieties such as the semi-double Gustav Emich. There are also varieties with white, pink and carmine flowers and a number with variegated leaves. All are bushy plants which will flower all the summer outdoors, or most of the winter under glass if the summer buds are picked off. All like sun and warmth and will grow in almost any soil. They can be increased by cuttings of firm young growth

Primula
polyantha

Polygonatum
multiflorum

Prunus serrulata
'Kanzan'

Phyteuma
Scheuchzeri

Platycodon
grandiflorum

Primula
malacoides

Polygonum
affine

Potentilla
fruticosa

Polemonium
caeruleum

Pulmonaria
officinalis

Plumbago
capensis

Pyracantha
coccinea

Rosa [Floribunda type]

Rhus typhina

Rudbeckia speciosa

Ramonda Myconi

Romneya Coulteri

Rosa Moyesii

Rodgersia pinnata

Reseda odorata

Rhododendron ponticum

Ribes sanguineum

Ranunculus asiaticus

Saintpaulia ionantha

Rosmarinus officinalis

CNF

in a frame in late summer or a warm greenhouse in spring.

The ivy-leaved pelargoniums are grown in exactly the same way except that they are trailing plants which can be allowed to fall over the edge of something, be tied up to a stake or other support, or simply be allowed to sprawl over the ground. The popular varieties nearly all have pink, double flowers, but there are also red varieties.

The show and regal pelargoniums are bushy plants not unlike the zonals in habit but they have much larger flowers usually pink more or less heavily blotched with crimson or maroon. They flower in late spring and early summer and are grown as pot plants in moderately heated greenhouses, usually being stood outside or in a frame during July and August to rest. In other respects their treatment is as for zonal pelargoniums.

Pelargonium denticulatum

PENSTEMON *(Beard Tongue)*

There are dwarf, more or less shrubby penstemons such as *Penstemon rupicola*, *P. heterophyllus* and *P. Scouleri* which can be grown in the rock garden, but the most popular are the many large-flowered kinds collectively known as *P. gloxinoides* and distinguished by fancy names such as Newbury Gem and Garnet. Some are not quite hardy and may need the protection of a frame in winter, but others are quite hardy in many parts of the country. They grow about 2 feet high and have spikes of fine tubular flowers, the general effect at a short distance being not unlike that of antirrhinums. Colours range from white through pink to scarlet and purple and the flowering season from June to October. All like sun though they will put up with some shade. They are not fussy about soil and can be readily increased by cuttings of non-flowering shoots in a frame in August or September.

Pelargonium zonale

Penstemon heterophyllus

PERNETTYA *(Prickly Heath)*

The only kind much grown in gardens, *Pernettya mucronata*, is a freely branching evergreen shrub 2 or 3 feet high with neat glossy green leaves, small white flowers in May, followed by large berries in the most remarkable colours, bright rose pink, lilac, purple, red, crimson, near black and white. This is a first-class dwarf shrub for rather moist and cool peaty or leafy soils. It likes sun and requires no pruning. As it suckers very freely it can be increased by detaching these with roots in autumn or early spring. It can also be raised from seeds sown in a frame in spring.

PEROVSKIA

Only one kind is commonly cultivated, *Perovskia atriplicifolia*, a shrub that is apt to be killed to near ground level each winter and then throws up a number of straight 4–foot stems bearing small grey leaves, and, on the upper half, small lavender blue flowers. The whole effect in August is extremely charming, a grey-lavender mist of colour. This is a shrub for the sunniest places and the best drained soils, but not poor soils. It resents

Pernettya mucronata

G

*Petunia
axillaris*

*Philadelphus
grandiflorus*

*Philadelphus
coronarius*

*Phlomis
fruticosa*

root disturbance and should be raised in pots so that it can be planted with the minimum of damage. It is best propagated by root cuttings in winter.

PETUNIA

These popular half-hardy annuals have been greatly developed as summer bedding plants. For this purpose very free-flowering varieties, with flowers of medium size and usually of one colour throughout, are preferred to the larger flowered and usually striped or blotched varieties of former years. Double-flowered varieties are also available.

All can be raised from seed sown in a warm greenhouse in February or March. Seedlings must be pricked out and hardened off for planting outdoors in late May or early June. Petunias like sun, warmth and good drainage and are not so happy on cold, wet soils. Most modern bedding varieties grow about 1 foot high. The colour range is in blue, violet, purple, pink, rose, crimson and white.

PHACELIA

The most popular phacelia in Britain is *Phacelia campanularia*, a very attractive hardy annual 6 to 8 inches high, spreading in habit, with flowers of the clearest possible blue. There are other annual species such as *P. minor*, *P. Whitlavii* and *P. viscida*, but *P. campanularia* is the best. All can be grown from seed sown outdoors in April where the plants are to flower in July. A sunny position and well-drained soil should be chosen for preference and the seedlings should be thinned to 6 or 8 inches.

PHILADELPHUS   (Mock Orange)

The mock oranges are free flowering shrubs with white flowers in June or July and many are extremely fragrant. They grow vigorously in almost all soils and are not in the least difficult. They prefer sunny positions and need no regular pruning but, if desired, to reduce the size of the bushes, flowering stems can be removed as soon as the flowers fade.

There are many kinds some being hybrids known as *Philadelphus Lemoinei* and having names such as Virginal, Belle Étoile, and Beauclerk. Some have single, some double flowers and heights vary from about 4 to 8 feet. There are also some good species, notably *P. coronarius*, 8 to 10 feet high with single, very fragrant flowers; *P. grandiflorus*, large flowered but scentless, and *P. microphyllus*, no more than 5 feet high with exceptionally fragrant, rather starry flowers. *P. purpureo-maculatus* is a hybrid with single white flowers carrying a purple blotch at the base of each petal. All can be increased by cuttings of firm young stems in autumn.

PHLOMIS   (Jerusalem Sage)

The common Jerusalem Sage, *Phlomis fruticosa*, is a grey-leaved shrub with rather soft, sappy shoots which are all the better for a little pruning to keep them as stiff as possible. The whorls of fine, yellow, sage-like flowers are produced in June or July and as soon as they fade the flowering stems can be shortened a little. The bush grows about 3 feet high but tends to flop and spread. It is an attractive plant for a warm sunny place and even if it is cut back by frost in winter it usually breaks away strongly from the base next spring. It can be increased by cuttings of firm young shoots in summer in a propagating frame.

PHLOX

There are phloxes for the herbaceous border and phloxes for the rock garden or dry wall and all are useful, easily grown plants. The border phloxes are mostly derived from *Phlox paniculata* (*decussata*) and there are a great many varieties designated by fancy names such as Brigadier, Border Gem, Frau Antonia Buchner, Sweetheart and Mrs Ethel Prichard. All flower in July or August and have fine trusses of fragrant flowers, the colour range being from white and palest pink or mauve to scarlet, crimson and violet. They are grand plants for sunny or partially shaded places in good, rich soil which does not dry out too rapidly. Heights vary from about 2 to 5 feet and all can be increased by division in spring or autumn or by root cuttings in winter.

Among the best of the rock garden phloxes are the many varieties derived from *P. subulata*, sometimes known as the moss pink. These are mat-forming plants with narrow leaves and almost stemless rose-pink, lilac, mauve or white flowers in May and June. All can be increased by summer cuttings in a frame.

PHYGELIUS (*Cape Fuchsia*)

The Cape fuchsia, *Phygelius capensis*, is an interesting and attractive perennial with 4-foot high stems bearing in summer curved, tubular flowers that are a brilliant orange-scarlet. It is hardy enough for a great many parts of the country but it likes a warm, sunny spot and a fairly well-drained soil. It can be very readily increased by division in the spring.

PHYTEUMA (*Horned Rampion*)

These are very attractive rock plants with curiously formed flowers which at a short distance look rather like little bladders terminating in a tiny horn or spike. These are usually blue or white, and are produced in late spring or early summer. Very typical of the family and one of the best to grow is *Phyteuma comosum* which makes a low, spreading clump 4 to 6 inches high with purple and lilac flowers. Other good kinds are *P. Scheuchzeri*, and *P. orbiculare*, blue, 1 foot; and *P. hemisphaericum*, blue, 3 to 4 inches. All like sunny places and well-drained soils and all can be increased either by division in spring or by seed sown in a frame at the same season.

PLATYCODON (*Balloon Flower*)

Only one kind of platycodon is grown in gardens but it has several varieties. It is a hardy herbaceous plant named *Platycodon*

Phlox
Drummondii

Phlox
procumbens

Phlox
paniculata

Phyteuma
orbiculare

99

*Platycodon
grandiflorum*

*Plumbago
capensis*

*Polemonium
caeruleum*

*Polygonatum
officinale*

grandiflorum and it flowers in July and August. It grows 12 to 18 inches high and has bell shaped light blue flowers which are very similar to those of some campanulas. It is in bud that the plant is most striking for the buds are large and inflated like so many small, blue balloons. This is a good and slightly unusual plant for a sunny place and a good, loamy soil. There are varieties with white flowers and one, named *Mariesii*, which is rather dwarfer than most and has blue flowers of deeper colour and greater size. All are readily increased by division in spring.

PLUMBAGO (*Leadwort*)

Plumbago capensis is a beautiful and easily grown greenhouse climber with trusses of pale blue, phlox-like flowers in summer. It is a perennial and is best planted directly in the greenhouse border though it can be grown in a tub or large pot. It likes good loamy soil and plenty of water in summer. It should be trained around a pillar or to wires strained beneath the rafters and may be kept to moderate dimensions by cutting back all the previous year's shoots to 8 or 9 inches each March. Only enough heat is required in winter to keep out frost. Increase by cuttings taken with a heel in April and rooted in a propagating frame.

POLEMONIUM (*Jacob's Ladder*)

These are hardy herbaceous perennials, the only one of which at all commonly seen in gardens is *Polemonium caeruleum*. It is called Jacob's ladder because of the ladder-like appearance of its pinnate leaves. The blue flowers are carried in short spikes on foot-high stems in early summer and are as freely produced in partial shade as they are in full sun. This is, in fact, a very easy plant to grow in almost any soil and position and used to be a great favourite in cottage gardens. It is easily increased by division in either spring or autumn.

POLYGONATUM (*Solomon's Seal*)

The best known and most generally useful of this family is *Polygonatum multiflorum*. It is a graceful plant making arching stems reaching a height of about 3 feet and bearing smooth greyish green leaves which are themselves decorative. In May and June tubular creamy white flowers hang downwards along the upper half of these stems. It is the curious seal-like marks on the tubers that have suggested the popular name Solomon's seal. This plant likes cool, leafy, rather moist soils and partially shaded positions and may be naturalized in thin woodland. It is also first rate in shady borders. It can be increased very readily by division in spring or autumn.

POLYGONUM (*Knotweed*)

Some of the knotweeds really are weeds of the most obnoxious kind, penetrating far and wide and, once admitted to the garden, not easily dismissed from it again. But among them are some useful and entirely safe garden plants. Two of the best of these are

Saponaria
Vaccaria

Salvia
splendens

Saxifraga Burseriana

Sedum
spurium

Saxifraga
umbrosa

Salpiglossis
sinuata

Scabiosa
caucasica

Schizanthus
hybridus

Sanguisorba
obtusa

Scilla
hispanica

Santolina
Chamaecyparissus

Salvia patens

Saxifraga
[mossy hybrid]

Spiraea Vanhouttei

Solidago
canadensis

Spartium
junceum

Sisyrinchium
angustifolium

Sidalcea
malvaeflora

Silene
Schafta

Sempervivum
calcareum

Solanum
jasminoides
album

Stachys
lanata

Senecio
laxifolius

Strelitzia
Reginae

Skimmia
japonica

Shortia
uniflora
grandiflora

CN·T

trailers for the rock garden or dry wall, *Polygonum affine* and *P. vaccinifolium*. Both make carpets of growth from which arise in late summer and early autumn dainty spikes of pink flowers. *P. vaccinifolium* is the smaller and neater of the two, but *P. affine* scores in having fine autumn foliage effects as an additional attraction. Two kinds for the herbaceous border are *P. Bistorta sanguineum* and *P. campanulatum*, the first with slender spikes of deep red flowers on 2–foot stems and the second with small sprays of pale pink flowers on 3–foot stems. Both flower without break from July to October and both are easy to grow in almost any position but *P. campanulatum* needs plenty of moisture in summer. All these knotweeds can be increased by division in spring or autumn. *Polygonum baldschuanicum* is a rampant climber with white, pink tinged flowers from July to October. It is useful for covering sheds, fences, pergolas and walls.

Polygonum Bistorta

POTENTILLA *(Cinquefoil)*

The potentillas are fine plants for rather dry, sunny places. They do not seem to mind how poor the soil is, indeed they usually flower more freely when it is rather poor. Most are hardy herbaceous perennials, some, such as *Potentilla nitida*, with silvery leaves and pink flowers, and *P. nepalensis* with cherry red flowers, being small enough for the rock garden, and others, such as the numerous varieties of *P. atro sanguinea* being better suited to the herbaceous border. *P. atro sanguinea* itself has single scarlet flowers but there are other forms which are double or semi-double and range in colour from yellow through orange and scarlet to crimson. All are about 18 inches in height with the exception of Gibson's Scarlet which is almost prostrate, and all flower from June to August. Division in spring or autumn is the simplest method of increasing all these potentillas. *P. fruticosa* is a shrubby species which grows up to 4 feet high. It has yellow flowers borne in summer and there are many beautiful varieties with flowers larger and deeper in colour or paler than the type.

Potentilla nitida

PRIMULA *(Primrose, Polyanthus, Auricula)*

A number of most popular hardy and greenhouse plants are to be found in this family. Our native primrose is *Primula vulgaris* and this has given rise not only to many coloured garden forms but also, with the cowslip, to the multi-flowered polyanthus (*P. polyantha*). There are all shades of pink, yellow, orange, scarlet, crimson and blue and there are double-flowered forms of the primrose as well as the more familiar singles. They are plants for rather good, loamy or leafy soils and cool perhaps partially shaded positions, and all can be increased either by careful division after flowering or by seed sown in spring in a frame.

The popular auricula is botanically *P. Auricula*, a plant with rather leathery leaves, more or less heavily dusted with grey meal, and clusters of brightly coloured flowers in spring on 8–inch stems. It has been greatly developed in gardens and there are many different colours.

Primula Auricula

Primula cortusoides

101

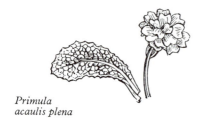

*Primula
acaulis plena*

*Primula
sinensis*

*Prunus
communis*

*Prunus
Laurocerasus*

Then there are a great many primulas for the rock garden, some with flowers in round clusters such as the pale blue *P. denticulata* or violet *P. capitata*, some with flowers in loose heads, such as the pink *P. frondosa*, bright rose *P. rosea* and lilac *P. Edgeworthii*, some almost stemless such as the wine coloured *P. Juliae* and at least one, *P. Vialii*, with its purple flowers in spikes. Most of these like cool, rather leafy or peaty soils.

There is another group of hardy primulas that is happiest in the bog garden or at the side of a pool or stream. The yellow flowered *P. Florindae* and *P. helodoxa* and magenta *P. japonica* and *P. pulverulenta* are of this type and they are vigorous plants growing 2 to 4 feet in height and often renewing themselves by seed where conditions suit them.

Finally there are the greenhouse primulas of which *P. obconica*, *P. sinensis* and *P. malacoides* are the best known examples. All these have numerous garden varieties differing in colour and size and form of flower and all flower in winter. They should be renewed annually from seed sown in April for *P. sinensis* and *P. obconica* and in June for *P. malacoides*. The seedlings are grown on singly in small pots, being moved on as they require it and usually flowered in the 5-inch size. Very little heat is needed, just enough to prevent the temperature from falling below 45°.

PRUNUS *(Cherry, Plum, Peach, Almond)*

Some of the best ornamental trees of moderate size are to be found in this family. The Japanese cherries derived from *Prunus Lannesiana* and *P. serrulata* are particularly good. They have a considerable range of habit from the erect Amanogawa, with branches ascending like those of a Lombardy poplar to the spreading Fugenzo which when fully grown may cover 30 feet or more of ground. Colours range from white and bluish pink to quite a warm pink and there are single and double-flowered forms. All flower in April or early May. Then there is the lovely autumn-flowering *Prunus subhirtella autumnalis* with small but abundant white or shell-pink flowers and the weeping form of *P. subhirtella* which flowers in spring. *P. yedoensis* is white-flowered and exceptionally free in March and April and *P. Sargentii* has pink flowers at the same season and foliage which is bronze in spring and orange-scarlet in autumn. These are all cherries.

Among the plums the two best are the popular purple-leaved *P. cerasifera Pissardii* which produces its small pale pink flowers in February and March and *P. cerasifera Blireana* which has larger, deeper pink semi-double flowers.

The ornamental peaches are all varieties of *P. persica*. One of the best, Clara Meyer, has very double rose-pink flowers in April. Iceberg is a pure white and Russell's Red a good carmine.

The almonds flower a week or so earlier than the peaches and the commonest kind, *P. communis (Amygdalus)*, is also the best.

The common cherry laurel used for hedging is *P. Laurocerasus*.

One other prunus which merits special mention is *P. triloba flore pleno*. The young branches of this are wreathed in very double pink flowers each April but it is a little more tender than most and really needs a warm sheltered wall. It is often grown as a pot plant in a cool greenhouse.

All these prunus like good, loamy soils and sunny positions. They need no regular pruning. Increase by budding in summer.

PULMONARIA *(Lungwort)*

The lungworts, useful hardy perennials because they flower very early, will grow well in partial shade and several have distinctly decorative foliage. This is particularly true of *P. officinalis* and *P. saccharata*, both of which have green leaves spotted with white. Their flowers are red fading to purple. Better from the point of view of flowers is *P. angustifolia* with clear blue flowers. All are quite dwarf plants for the front of the border and all will grow in any reasonable soil. They can be increased by division in spring or autumn.

PYRACANTHA *(Firethorn)*

These are evergreen shrubs naturally bushy and branching in habit but often trained against walls. For this *Pyracantha coccinea*, with clusters of small white flowers in early June followed by scarlet berries in autumn is often used. It has a very fine form named *Lalandii* in which the berries are larger and of a more orange-scarlet. Then there is *P. Gibbsii* with smaller, deep red berries produced with even greater profusion, and *P. Rogersiana fructu luteo* which has yellow berries.

All these like good loamy soils but may be grown almost anywhere. They will thrive in sun or shade and are excellent for clothing north walls. Pyracanthas are increased by seeds sown in spring or by cuttings made from side shoots pulled off with a heel in July or August and rooted in a propagating frame. When grown as bushes they need not be pruned but when trained against a wall it will be necessary to cut back badly placed side shoots each summer.

RAMONDA

The ramondas are those rather rare things, rock plants that prefer shade to sun. They make flat rosettes of rather leathery leaves that like to press themselves flat against the face of a vertical crevice in a wall or between large stones. But for them to be perfectly happy the crevice should face north. The flowers, which are not unlike those of a potato in form, are produced in twos or threes on 6–inch stems in May and June. They are soft bluish lilac in the popular *Ramonda pyrenaica (Myconi)*, but there is also a white-flowered form of this and one that is not far removed from clear pink. *R. Nathaliae* has bluer flowers and is very attractive. All like cool, peaty or leafy soils and can be raised from seeds sown in a frame in March or by leaf cuttings in early summer.

RANUNCULUS *(Buttercup, Fair Maids of France)*

No one wants to cultivate common buttercups, pretty though they are, but the ranunculus family is a large one and contains

103

Pulmonaria (Mertensia) virginica

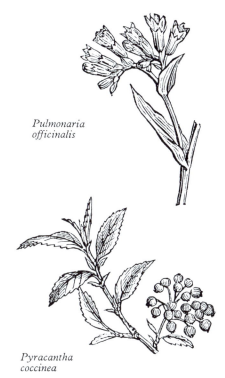

Pulmonaria officinalis

Pyracantha coccinea

Ramonda pyrenaica

*Ranunculus
aconitifolius*

*Reseda
odorata*

*Rhododendron
ponticum*

*Rhododendron
Thomsonii*

many species very different from the yellow weeds of our meadows and lawns. One of the most striking of these is *Ranunculus asiaticus*, familiarly known as the turban ranunculus. The garden forms of this always have fully double flowers like brightly coloured balls, some yellow, some scarlet, some crimson, all beautiful. They are carried on 9-inch stems in May and June and are excellent for cutting. The plants have small tuberous roots which should be planted 2 inches deep in good loamy soil and a warm sunny position. If the soil is really well drained they can be planted in November but in damp, cold places it is better to wait until late February or early March. In July the tubers should be lifted carefully and stored in a cool dry place until planting time. *R. aconitifolius* is a white flowered hardy perennial, loveliest in its double form.

RESEDA *(Mignonette)*

The mignonette, *Reseda odorata*, is one of the most pleasantly fragrant of annuals and though its broad spikes of small, pale green and red flowers are not showy, they make a pleasant change in the annual border from the more brightly coloured plants. It is a hardy annual, seed of which should be sown in March, April or early May where it is to flower. The seedlings should be thinned to 6 or 8 inches. Mignonette likes sunny places and is not fussy about soil though many gardeners believe that it does best where there is chalk. It can also be grown in pots as a greenhouse plant.

RHODODENDRON

This is one of those huge families about which it is difficult to generalize without being completely misleading. All rhododendrons are shrubs but some are so small that they can be grown quite easily in the rock garden and some are so big that they appear like trees. The shrubs commonly known as azaleas are, in fact, rhododendrons but for the sake of clarity they have been kept separate in this book.

All the rhododendrons with which we are concerned here are evergreen and almost all dislike limy or chalky soils. They like peat or leaf mould though this is not essential to them and they will grow well in any loamy soil that is not alkaline. There are hundreds of species some, such as *Rhododendron impeditum* and *R. racemosum*, with quite small flowers, while others such as *R. Griffithianum* and *R. Falconeri* have very large flowers. In addition there are great numbers of garden hybrids many of which are hardier and easier to grow than the species though they may lack some of their grace. The peak flowering period for these hybrids is May and early June and most make big, rounded bushes with handsome leaves and fine trusses of bloom. Colours range from white and pale pink to scarlet, crimson and purple.

Rhododendrons are easy to transplant and are best obtained in autumn or early spring. Most prefer a little shade and are happiest in thin woodland, but many of the hardy hybrids will also grow well in full sun. All benefit from an annual top dressing of peat or leaf mould which may be applied in spring or autumn.

Most of the good hybrids are increased by grafting in a warm greenhouse in spring, *R. ponticum* usually being used as a stock, but even better plants can be raised from layers pegged down in early summer. They may take 18 months or more to form roots.

RHUS (Sumach)

Several of the shrubs formerly known as rhus have now been transferred to another genus named Cotinus where they will be found in this book. Here we are principally concerned with the stag's-horn sumach, *Rhus typhina*, a handsome small tree with long, pinnate leaves which turn scarlet or crimson before falling in autumn. The fruits are also curious and beautiful— erect conglomerations of tiny crimson fruitlets which look a little like red horns and presumably have suggested the popular name. A variety of this has leaves so much divided that they look almost like the fronds of a fern. This sumach will grow in any ordinary soil and open position. It reaches a height of about 12 feet and suckers freely. These suckers, detached in autumn with some root, provide a ready means of increase.

*Rhododendron
arboreum*

RIBES (Currant)

Most of the currants are utilitarian rather than ornamental but the American currant, *Ribes sanguineum*, is a showy early flowering shrub with short trails of rose pink flowers in March ınd April. It makes a big, dense bush as much as 8 feet high and it has numerous varieties, some with pale flowers and some deep carmine. Two of the best of these are King Edward VII and Pulborough Scarlet. All are very easily grown in practically any soil and sunny or partially shaded position. They can be readily increased by cuttings of firm young shoots in the autumn.

*Rhododendron
caucasicum*

RODGERSIA

These very attractive hardy perennials have handsome leaves and branched sprays of small flowers a little like those of some spiraeas. They like damp places but will also grow quite well in ordinary soil provided it does not dry out too severely.

One of the best kinds is *Rodgersia pinnata* the leaves of which are made up of several separate leaflets. The flowers are rose pink and carried on 3 to 4–foot stems in July. *R. tabularis* has larger, undivided leaves not unlike those of some ornamental rhubarbs and the flowers are white. All can be increased by division in spring or autumn.

*Rhododendron
maximum*

ROMNEYA (Californian Tree Poppy)

This is one of those plants that is not quite a shrub and yet not quite a herbaceous plant either. It makes a woody crown from which are thrown up each year 6–foot cane-like stems carrying blue-grey leaves and terminated in summer by a succession of large white poppies each with a central boss of golden stamens. In winter these stems usually die down to the base again to be replaced by a new crop the following year. The Californian tree

*Ribes
sanguineum*

105

*Rosa chinensis
flore pleno*

*Rosa
Banksiae*

*Rosa
bracteata*

*Rosa
centifolia*

poppy, a beautiful plant for rather poor, stony soils and sunny positions, is hardy in most parts of the country but does not survive bad drainage and dislikes cold, wet soils. It is difficult to transplant and a start should be made with small plants from pots so that they can be transferred to the ground with a minimum of root disturbance. Propagation is by root cuttings in winter.

The kind usually grown is *Romneya Coulteri*, but *R. trichocalyx* is sometimes seen. They are very similar.

ROSA *(Rose)*

The rose is the most highly developed of all flowers. It has been bred and hybridized for centuries and, as a result, it has developed an immense variety of forms, colours and habits.

To-day the most popular classes of rose for garden display are the hybrid teas, the floribundas, the dwarf polyanthas, the hybrid musks, the climbing roses mainly of H.T. origin and the ramblers mainly derived from *Rosa Wichuraiana* and *R. multiflora*.

The hybrid teas are bush roses usually 2 to 4 feet in height and mostly with large double flowers, though a few singles are still grown. They flower throughout the summer with a main flush of bloom in June and early July and a secondary peak in September. The colour range includes practically everything except blue and many new varieties are added to the list every year.

The floribundas are mainly derived from the roses once known as hybrid polyanthas. They are also bush roses similar to the H.T.s in habit though usually a little more vigorous and freely branched. Their flowers are of medium size, usually produced in fine clusters, and their flowering season is similar to that of the H.T.s. They are the bedding roses *par excellence* to-day.

The dwarf polyanthas are bush roses usually of more dwarf and compact habit. Their flowers are quite small, like those of rambler roses, and are similarly produced in large clusters. They flower continuously throughout the summer.

The hybrid musks look very much like the floribundas but on the whole make even larger bushes, some of them reaching a height of 7 or 8 feet. Their flowers are small to medium, produced in big clusters and though they are all-summer flowering they are particularly good in the autumn.

The climbing roses grow to a height of 10 or 12 feet and mostly have rather large flowers similar to those of the H.T.s from which many of them are derived. They do well trained against walls or on pillars and they have a fairly long season in bloom.

The rambler roses are much more vigorous, often reaching a height of 15 feet or more, and their flowers, though small, are produced in very large clusters. Most of them flower in June or July and do not give any earlier or later display. These are the best roses for covering pergolas or large screens.

In addition there are miniature roses growing no more than 6 or 8 inches high and a great many other classes some so old that they have almost been forgotten. The rose species, too, provide valuable material for the shrub border and some, such as *Rosa Moyesii*, are worth growing for their scarlet heps as well as for their flowers.

All roses like good loamy soils. They thrive best in sunny places though a few kinds, such as the rambler Alberic Barbier and climber Mermaid, will succeed in shade. All are best planted in autumn though they can be moved at any time between October and April. Pruning must be varied to suit particular varieties and this is a subject which must be left for specialist books. Propagation is usually either by cuttings of firm young stems in autumn or by budding in July.

ROSMARINUS *(Rosemary)*

The common rosemary, *Rosmarinus officinalis*, is a delightful evergreen shrub, usually 4 to 5 feet high, with narrow aromatic leaves and small, pale blue flowers in May. It is a little tender and apt to be damaged by severe frost or cold winds, but can be grown outdoors in most parts of the country. It likes good but well-drained soils and warm, sunny places and needs no regular pruning. Propagation is by cuttings of firm young shoots in a frame in July or August. There are numerous varieties, one with white flowers and several with flowers of a deeper blue. The completely prostrate rosemary often known as *R. prostratus* is really *R. lavendulaceus* and is much less hardy than the common rosemary.

RUDBECKIA *(Coneflower)*

These are hardy herbaceous and hardy annual plants very closely related to the sunflowers and looking much like them. In several kinds the central disk is raised and cone-shaped instead of being flat, hence the popular name coneflower. Three of the best perennial kinds are *Rudbeckia speciosa* (*Newmannii*) 2 to 3 feet high with orange yellow, black-centred flowers; *R. nitida* Herbstonne, 6 or 7 feet high with bright yellow, green-centred flowers, and *R. laciniata* Golden Glow, 7 to 8 feet tall, with double yellow flowers. All flower in August and September.

Best of the annual rudbeckias is *R. hirta* which grows about 2 feet high and has yellow flowers. There are a number of hybrids of this with a colour range from yellow to deep chestnut red. All are readily grown from seed sown in April where the plants are to flower. Seedlings should be thinned to a least a foot apart.

SAINTPAULIA *(South African Violet)*

The only species grown in gardens is *Saintpaulia ionantha* but this is a variable plant and it has produced a number of varieties. Typically it is a low growing greenhouse perennial with soft, velvety green leaves and violet blue flowers carried in small clusters on 6–inch stems. In a warm greenhouse it will go on flowering almost the entire year. The varieties differ mainly in colour, from near white to pink and deepest violet, but there

107

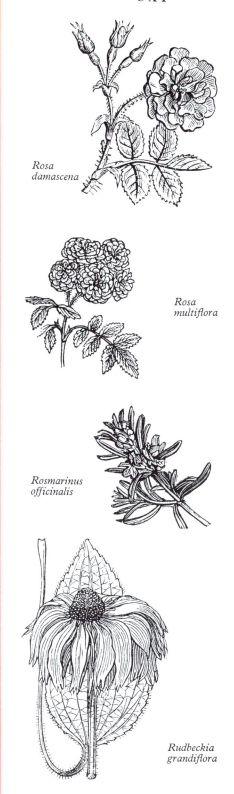

Rosa
damascena

Rosa
multiflora

Rosmarinus
officinalis

Rudbeckia
grandiflora

*Salpiglossis
sinuata*

*Salvia
splendens*

*Salvia
Grahamii*

*Salvia
patens*

are also some double flowered forms. All like a compost with plenty of peat or good leaf mould and thrive best in a fairly warm moist greenhouse. A minimum winter temperature of around 55° rising to 65° in summer suits them admirably. They will grow equally well in sun or shade, should be watered freely in summer and moderately in winter and may be raised from seed in February, by careful division in March or April, or by leaf cuttings in summer.

SALPIGLOSSIS

These lovely plants are not the easiest of half-hardy annuals to grow well. Their trumpet shaped blooms are carried all summer on stems 3 feet in height and are usually purple, rose, scarlet, cream or rose, in many cases veined with gold. The effect is delightful and the salpiglossis is worth a little trouble. Seed should be sown in a moderately heated greenhouse in February or March and the seedlings either pricked out and hardened off, if they are to be flowered out of doors, or potted singly if they are to be grown in pots for the greenhouse. Outdoors they should be given a warm sunny position and good but well-drained soil. Plant at the end of May or early in June and space at least 1 foot apart. In the greenhouse they can be flowered in 5- or 6-inch pots and should be grown in John Innes compost.

SALVIA *(Sage)*

The common sage, *Salvia officinalis*, though primarily a herb, is in its variegated forms not a plant to be despised in the ornamental garden. There are, however, many other purely ornamental kinds of salvia, some hardy plants for the herbaceous border, some half-hardy plants for summer bedding and several poised rather uneasily both between hardiness and tenderness and between a shrubby and a herbaceous habit. An example of this last class is *Salvia Grahamii*, a rather softly shrubby plant 3 feet in height, which produces scarlet flowers in constant succession from July to October if only one can find a place warm enough to suit it.

Far more generally useful and much more popular is the genuinely half-hardy *S. splendens*, the familiar scarlet salvia of summer bedding schemes. This can be treated as a half-hardy annual if seed is sown in a warm greenhouse in January or early February, the seedlings being potted singly and hardened off for planting out in early June. Alternatively cuttings can be rooted in a warm greenhouse between January and March and treated in a similar manner. A plant that loves sunny places and does best in warm summers, it grows 18 to 24 inches high and produces its abundant spikes of vivid scarlet flowers from July until the first autumn frost.

Best of the hardy herbaceous salvias is that usually known in gardens as *S. virgata nemorosa* though its correct name is *S. superba*. It grows about 3 feet high and produces its slender purple spikes in July and August. It is quite hardy, very easily grown in any ordinary soil and open position and is certainly one of the

Syringa
vulgaris
[garden form]

Streptocarpus
hybridus

Thalictrum
dipterocarpum

Tigridia
Pavonia

Symphoricarpos
racemosus

Trollius
europaeus

Tamarix
pentandra

Tagetes patula
[garden form]

Trillium
grandiflorum

Thymus Serpyllum

Tropaeolum
majus

Tradescantia
virginiana

Wisteria
sinensis

Viola
tricolor
[pansy]

Weigela
florida

Vinca
minor

Verbascum
Brousa

Veronica
spicata

Venidium
fastuosum

Tulipa
Gesneriana
[garden
form]

Zinnia elegans
[garden form]

Viburnum
Carlesii

Yucca
filamentosa

Verbena
venosa

Viburnum
Opulus

Sanguisorba officinalis

best dozen or so border plants. *S. Sclarea* and its variety *turkestanica* are worth growing for their large, hairy leaves as well as for their 3–foot spikes of pale blue or pinkish flowers, and *S. uliginosa* is one of the truest blue flowers of late summer. Finally there is the tuberous rooted *S. patens* which has gentian blue flowers in summer but is not entirely hardy and may need to be lifted and placed in a frame for the winter.

SANGUISORBA *(Burnet)*

The plants which the botanist calls sanguisorba the gardener very often calls poterium and in nursery catalogues they are as likely to be found under the one name as the other. The two best are *Sanguisorba canadensis* and *S. obtusa*, the first with bottle-brush spikes of fluffy white flowers and the second similar in style but pink in colour. Both flower in August and September and are hardy herbaceous perennials. They like sunny places and can be increased by division in the spring.

SANTOLINA *(Lavender Cotton)*

The lavender cottons are technically shrubs but they are comparatively soft-stemmed and low-growing and are usually grown in the herbaceous border, frequently as edgings in the manner of lavender or catmint. The most popular, *Santolina Chamaecyparissus*, has tiny silvery leaves and grows 18 to 24 inches high. It has yellow, tansy-like flowers in summer, but it is grown for its silver foliage rather than for these. It can be increased by careful division in the autumn or by cuttings of firm young shoots taken in July and rooted in a propagating frame.

Santolina neapolitana

SAPONARIA *(Soapwort)*

The common soapwort, *Saponaria officinalis*, is a hardy herbaceous plant 18 to 24 inches high with heads of pink flowers in August and September. It is usually seen in its double flowered form and is a showy though somewhat coarse plant. Perhaps more generally useful is the sprawling and trailing *S. ocymoides*, a fine plant for a steep bank or a dry wall. It will quickly cover several square feet of space with its loose mounds of growth which disappear in June and July beneath a cloud of small pink flowers.

Both these plants are perennials. There is also a useful annual kind, *S. Vaccaria*, which makes slender 18-inch stems carrying very dainty pink or white flowers that are excellent for cutting. It can be raised from seed sown in March, April or May where the plants are to flower.

All these like sunny places and all thrive in any ordinary soil. *S. officinalis* can be increased by division in spring, *S. ocymoides* by seed in a frame or greenhouse in spring.

Saponaria officinalis

SAXIFRAGA *(Saxifrage)*

This is one of the great families of rock garden plants and there are so many different kinds that it is necessary to consider them in their respective groups rather than as individuals.

First to flower are the cushion or Kabschia saxifrages, all of

Saxifraga Cotyledon

109

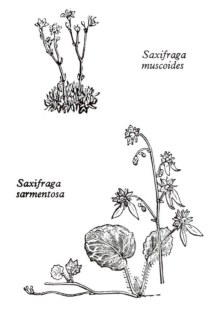

*Saxifraga
muscoides*

*Saxifraga
sarmentosa*

*Saxifraga
hypnoides*

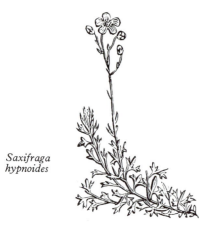

*Saxifraga
Geum*

which make compact hummocks of growth from which the flow-ers are produced in March and April, usually on short stems though some kinds appear almost stemless. There are white, yellow and pink kinds and all are beautiful. These are plants for sunny places in the rock garden in really well-drained soil which may contain as much as 50% of stone chippings. Because of their habit of flowering very early, many gardeners grow them in pans and allow them to bloom under glass so that they are not spoiled by the weather. Fine examples of this group are *Saxifraga Burseriana*, white, and *S.* Cranbourne, pink.

Next come the silver saxifrages which make fine rosettes of firm-textured leaves often heavily silvered along the margins. Their flowers are borne in loose clusters which are often of con-siderable size. The commonest colour is white, sometimes speckled with red as in the popular *S. Cotyledon caterhamensis*, but there are yellow and pink varieties. All like to grow in crev-ices between rocks or between stones in a dry wall. The position should be open and sunny.

By contrast the mossy saxifrages like cool, rather moist soils and partially shaded positions. They make soft mounds of bright green leaves and flower in May, the flowers varying con-siderably both in size and in the length of the stems on which they are borne. White, pink and red are the commonest colours in this group. Two fine examples are *S. Wallacei* and *S. hyp-noides*.

The familiar London pride is a saxifrage belonging to yet another group. Its name is *S. umbrosa* and it makes rosettes of green leaves bearing in May and June, loose sprays of small pink flowers. It will grow practically anywhere in sun or shade.

In addition to these there are saxifrages, such as *S. Griesbachii*, which make silver rosettes of leaves from which ascend flowering stems clothed in crimson bracts, and saxifrages such as *S. opposi-tifolia* which lie flat on the ground and carry their flowers stem-less on this carpet.

Almost all saxifrages can be increased by careful division after flowering and many can also be raised from seed sown in a frame or greenhouse in spring.

SCABIOSA *(Scabious)*

There are a number of species of scabious but two are of out-standing importance for the garden. One is *Scabiosa caucasica*, a hardy herbaceous perennial, and the other is *S. atropurpurea*, a plant invariably grown as an annual.

S. caucasica carries its large flat blue, mauve or white flowers on stiff 2 to 3–foot stems and it blooms continuously from July to October. It is not a plant that ever makes a great show at one time, but it is excellent for cutting. It likes fairly well-drained, but not dry, soils and open, sunny positions. It resents autumn disturbance and should always be planted in spring and it can be increased by careful division at that season.

S. atropurpurea is very different in appearance as the flowers are bee-hive shaped and the colour range is much more varied, from white and palest pink or mauve to an almost black purple. Seed can be sown in March in a frame or greenhouse, the seedlings being pricked out and hardened off for planting out in late May, or alternatively seed can be sown outdoors in April directly where the plants are to flower. This scabious grows about 3 feet high and should be spaced a foot apart.

SCHIZANTHUS *(Butterfly Flower)*

Among the most graceful of half-hardy annuals, the garden hybrids of *Schizanthus hybridus grandiflorus* have attractively marked flowers in shades of pink, mauve, purple, carmine, crimson and white with deeper markings of the ground colour or of yellow or bronze.

Best grown in the warm greenhouse, seed sown in John Innes compost in March or April in a temperature of 55° to 60° will produce plants to flower in August and September while seed sown in late August or early September will provide flowers in April or May. Seedlings should be potted on regularly until they reach 7, 8 or 9–inch pots in which they will flower. Growing tips should be pinched out when the plants are three or four inches high. Do not repot between November and February inclusive. Careful staking will be required, and cool, airy conditions are needed after germination. Water fairly freely in spring and summer, sparingly in autumn and winter.

SCILLA *(Bluebell, Squill)*

The common bluebell, *Scilla nonscripta*, needs no introduction, but it has a number of useful relatives that are not so well known. The one that most closely resembles it is the Spanish bluebell, *Scilla hispanica* (*campanulata*). This is a more robust plant with broader leaves and taller, stiffer flower spikes. In addition to the blue form there are good pink and white varieties. It thrives under exactly the same conditions as our native bluebell and is a useful bulb to naturalize beneath shrubs.

Then there is the Siberian squill, *Scilla sibirica*, a much smaller plant with dainty spikes of bright blue flowers on 3 to 4–inch stems in March and April. It is a good bulb for the rock garden or for the front of the border and it likes sunny places.

By comparison *S. peruviana*, with its very broad spike of purple or white flowers, is a rather clumsy plant. It looks a little like a very squat and ungainly hyacinth.

All these scillas should be planted in autumn, 2 to 3 inches deep with the exception of the bluebell which can be as much as 6 inches deep. They can be increased by division of the bulb clusters.

SEDUM *(Stonecrop)*

The stonecrops are a large family of succulent plants most of which are hardy. They are useful for the rock garden and for walls and nearly all of them like warm sunny places. They vary a great deal in character from the completely prostrate *Sedum lydium* with tiny bronzy leaves to the 2–foot high *S. maximum*

Scabiosa Columbaria

Schizanthus pinnatus

Scilla peruviana

Scilla sibirica

111

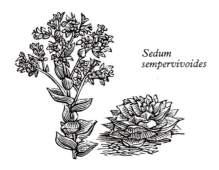

Sedum
sempervivoides

Sedum
acre

Sempervivum
arachnoideum

Sempervivum
soboliferum

with quite large beetroot coloured leaves.

Two of the most popular stonecrops are *S. spathulifolium atropurpureum*, a prostrate spreading plant with thick, spoon-shaped leaves, plum-red in colour, and *S. spectabile* an 18–inch tall plant with large, flattish heads of pink flowers in early autumn. At that season it is one of the best plants for the front of the border.

There are a great many more kinds, mostly prostrate or low-growing plants which spread rapidly. All can be grown with the greatest of ease in almost any soil and open place. There is even one, *S. pulchellum*, with rosy-purple flowers, that likes rather moist soils and partially shaded positions. All can be increased by division in spring or autumn with the exception of *S. caeruleum* which is an annual and *S. pilosum* which is biennial. Both these must be renewed every year from seed.

SEMPERVIVUM *(Houseleek)*

The common houseleek, *Sempervivum tectorum*, got its name because of its ability to grow on the roofs of buildings with no more soil than might have been caught in the angle between one tile and another. In this respect it is a very typical member of its family for most of the sempervivums are happiest when spreading their stiff rosettes of leaves over the surface of a rock or the face of a wall. They all love, sun, warmth and good drainage and they can survive with a minimum of soil. They are grown primarily for their leaves which vary from the small, reddish, cobweb-covered rosettes of *Sempervivum arachnoideum* to the magnificent 8-inch bronze and red rosettes of *S. Boutignyanum*. Some, such as *S. calcareum* and *S. Greenii*, have grey-green leaves tipped with red and some, such as *S. tectorum* itself, are green throughout. All produce in summer, very stiff and solid flower spikes like little lighthouses, each bearing a cluster of starry pink or reddish flowers. They are curious rather than beautiful. All are hardy and perennial and all can be increased by division at almost any time of the year.

SENECIO *(Groundsel, Cineraria)*

The common groundsel is one of the most troublesome of garden weeds but it has some distinguished relatives that are first-rate garden or greenhouse plants. Probably the most popular of these is the plant that every gardener knows as cineraria but which the botanist calls *Senecio cruentus* (see Cineraria).

A very different plant is *Senecio laxifolius*. This is a hardy shrub 3 to 4 feet high with rounded grey leaves and masses of yellow daisy flowers in July. It likes warm, sunny places and fairly well-drained soils and is easily raised from cuttings of firm young shoots in July or August.

Yet another useful senecio is the dusty miller, *S. Cineraria*, a half-hardy, grey-leaved plant often used for summer bedding. It grows about 2 feet high and makes an admirable foil for the scarlet flowers of pelargoniums. It can be raised from cuttings of firm growth in spring or late summer.

SHORTIA

These are very beautiful, low growing perennials for the wood-land or shady places in the rock garden. The two kinds usually seen are *Shortia galacifolia* and *S. uniflora*. Both are very similar, only a few inches high, and making wide clumps of shining green leaves from which appear in spring, fragile, bell shaped, pale pink flowers. They need cool leafy or peaty soil which is open enough to be well drained in winter and yet spongy enough to hold plenty of moisture in summer. They can be increased by careful division in spring. Also included in this family now as *S. soldanelloides* is the plant most gardeners know as *Schizoco-don soldanelloides*. It needs similar treatment and has clusters of pale pink, fringed flowers in spring.

*Shortia
soldanelloides*

SIDALCEA

From the garden standpoint the most important sidalceas are the numerous varieties of *Sidalcea malvaeflora*, a hardy herba-ceous perennial which carries slender spikes of pink flowers in summer. They are at their best in August. The varieties differ in height, varying from about 2 to 5 feet, and in colour from palest pink to near crimson. All are excellent border plants easily grown in any ordinary soil and reasonably open situation. They can be increased by division in spring or autumn.

*Silene
acaulis*

SILENE   *(Catchfly)*

There are both annual and perennial catchflies, the former usu-ally being represented in British gardens by *Silene pendula*, a fragile plant with clusters of pale pink flowers in summer. It is a very easily grown plant, being quite hardy and not in the least fussy about soil. Sow it in March or April where it is to flower and thin the seedlings to a few inches apart.

The two most popular perennial kinds are *S. Schafta*, which makes a loose, tumbling mass of rather weedy growth which disappears in late summer beneath a cloud of rose-pink flowers, and *S. alpestris* which makes much neater tussocks of shining green leaves on which stand the small white flowers on slender 6–inch stems in June and July. *S. acaulis* is even closer and more compact in habit and has stemless, pink flowers, but is shy about producing them. These are all plants for sunny places in the rock garden or dry wall and all can be increased by division in spring.

*Silene
Schafta*

SISYRINCHIUM   *(Blue-eyed Grass)*

The common name, blue-eyed grass, really only applies to two sisyrinchiums, *S. Bermudiana* and *S. angustifolium* (*anceps*) and is very appropriate to them as both make grass-like leaves from which small violet-blue flowers appear intermittently all the summer. They are not plants to make a fuss about but are useful for their foliage and long-flowering season. As they are no more than 1 foot in height, they are most suitable for the rock garden or the extreme front of the border.

*Sisyrinchium
grandiflorum*

H

113

Skimmia
japonica

Solanum
jasminoides

Solanum
macranthum

Solidago
Virgaurea

Very different is *S. grandiflorum*, a beautiful but extremely fragile plant with rush-like leaves and nodding, silken-textured flowers, the colour of amethysts. There is also a white variety. This is a plant for a specially selected and sheltered place in the rock garden with well-drained soil and perhaps a pane of glass in April to protect its flowers from rain. Alternatively it can be grown in pots or pans in the alpine house.

All these sisyrinchiums can be increased by division in the spring.

SKIMMIA

The skimmias are compact evergreen shrubs which have the triple merits of good foliage, abundant white flowers and fine red berries. Moreover they are very easily grown in practically any soil and situation and they will even flower and berry quite well in shady places. The kind commonly grown, *Skimmia japonica*, suffers from the slight drawback that it has male and female flowers on separate plants and only the females will produce berries and then only if there is a male nearby to fertilize them. But there are other kinds which produce both sexes on the same bush, notably *S. Fortunei*, which is lower growing than *S. japonica*, usually not exceeding 2 feet, and *S. Foremanii* which reaches 3 to 5 feet as does *S. japonica*. All can be increased by layering in spring.

SOLANUM

The potato is a solanum but there are other species of the same genus which are grown solely for ornament. One of the best known of these is a greenhouse pot plant grown for its scarlet, cherry-like fruits at Christmas time. Its name is *Solanum Capsicastrum* and it is generally grown from seed sown in February or early March in a temperature of about 65°. The seedlings are potted singly, and repotted as necessary in John Innes compost. Pots 5 to 6 inches in diameter are usually large enough for the final potting in late May or early June. From June to September they are best plunged outdoors in a sunny sheltered place where they should be well watered, but by October they must be back in a greenhouse with an average temperature of 50°.

Another and very different kind is *S. crispum*, a vigorous climber for a sunny sheltered place. It will reach a height of 15 to 20 feet and it produces in summer, loose clusters of pale bluish-purple flowers not unlike those of the potato. Even more beautiful but a little more tender is *S. jasminoides* with similar habit and white flowers. These climbing solanums need no regular pruning and are increased by cuttings of young growth in spring in a propagating box with bottom heat.

SOLIDAGO (*Golden Rod*)

These are very easily grown hardy herbaceous perennials mostly flowering in late summer or early autumn and with fine sprays of small yellow daisy flowers. The commonest kind which is to be seen in almost every garden, is *Solidago canadensis*, which has a great many garden varieties and hybrids with names such as Golden Wings, Golden Mosa and Leraft. These vary in height from 2 to 6 feet and in colour from pale to deep yellow. There is also a fine hybrid known as *S. missouriensis* (correctly *Solidaster luteus*) which is more rounded in habit, 2 to 3 feet high and lemon yellow in colour. All these golden rods will grow in almost any soil but prefer a sunny position. They can be increased very readily by division.

SPARTIUM *(Spanish Broom)*

Only one kind of Spanish broom is grown in gardens, *Spartium junceum*, a shrub with green, almost leafless stems, and slender spikes of bright yellow, sweetly scented pea-flowers from June to August. It likes sun and good drainage and does not seem to mind how poor the soil is, for which reasons it is often seen at its best near the sea. It will grow 8 or 10 feet high but can be kept a good deal shorter if it is pruned moderately each spring. The simplest method of increasing it is by seed sown in a frame in spring. This is in every way an outstanding member of the broom family for it is showy, easily grown and long flowering.

SPIRAEA

Most of the herbaceous plants that are familiarly known to gardeners as spiraea are, in fact, astilbes, and the true spiraeas are nearly all shrubs. There are some excellent kinds among them and they vary quite a lot in style. Two of the earliest and most popular are *Spiraea arguta* and *S. Thunbergii*, both making very twiggy bushes 4 to 6 feet high, smothered in April with tiny white flowers. A little later, in May, comes *S. Vanhouttei* which is a little stiffer but still very graceful in habit and carries its clusters of white flowers along the arching branches. One of the most useful kinds is *S. japonica*, especially in its variety Anthony Waterer. This makes a dense shrub with erect 4 to 5– foot stems terminated in July and August by flattish heads of pink flowers. These are carmine in Anthony Waterer and the leaves are usually flecked with cream. It is an ideal shrub for small gardens as it can be limited in size by a little careful cutting back each spring.

At the other extreme of size are *S. arborea* and the very similar *S. Lindleyana*. Both will grow 12 to 15 feet in height and produce great plumes of creamy white flowers in July and August. They are extremely handsome shrubs.

Another distinct group is represented by *S. Douglasii, S. Menziesii* and *S. salicifolia*, all of which have short bottle-brush-like spikes of fluffy pink flowers in late summer. They spread rather rapidly by suckers, which can be a nuisance, but they are fine, trouble-free shrubs for rough places.

Spiraea Aruncus, often known as goat's beard, is a very vigorous herbaceous plant which will grow 5 or 6 feet high and produce very fine plumes of creamy white flowers in June and July. Botanists no longer call it a spiraea but have named it *Aruncus sylvester*.

Spartium
junceum

Spiraea
japonica

Spiraea
Douglasii

Spiraea
Lindleyana

115

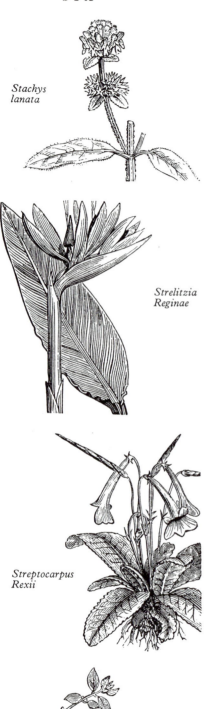

Stachys lanata

Strelitzia Reginae

Streptocarpus Rexii

Symphoricarpos albus

All shrubby spiraeas can be increased by cuttings of firm young stems in a frame in July or August and quite a number can also be increased by detaching suckers or offsets in autumn.

STACHYS *(Betony, Woundwort, Lamb's Ears)*

In general the betonys are not very choice garden plants but *Stachys lanata* has long been popular because of its extraordinarily soft and silky grey leaves. The spikes of reddish-purple flowers are also enveloped in grey down and it is this densely hairy nature that has earned it the popular name, lamb's ears. It is an indestructible hardy perennial which keeps close to the ground except when it throws up its 18–inch flower stems in summer. It will grow in any soil and reasonably open place and can be increased by division at practically any time of the year.

STRELITZIA *(Bird of Paradise Flower)*

The only species grown in gardens, *Strelitzia Reginae*, is one of the most extraordinary of all flowers. The flowers are shaped rather like the head of a bird with long purplish beak and a crest of orange and blue. These very handsome blooms are carried in May and June on long, stiff stems above leaves like those of a banana or very large canna. As might be expected this is a semi-tropical plant requiring warm greenhouse treatment in this country. It should be grown in large pots in John Innes compost and should be given a temperature of around 55° in winter rising to at least 65° from April onwards. It should be watered very freely from April to September and kept in a moist atmosphere but may be relatively dry in winter. Propagation is usually by division in spring.

STREPTOCARPUS *(Cape Primrose)*

The popular name of the streptocarpus is rather misleading for anything less like a primrose than this predominantly blue, trumpet-shaped flower it would be difficult to imagine. There are also pink and white varieties but yellow is conspicuous by its absence. Most of those grown in gardens are hybrids and all are greenhouse plants though they do not require high temperatures. They are usually raised from seed sown in a temperature of 65°, in January or February if the plants are to flower in early autumn, or in July if they are wanted in the summer. The seedlings are grown on in John Innes compost and are gradually worked on into 4 or 5–inch pots in which they will flower. They require a good deal of water while they are making rapid growth in spring and summer and at this period the atmosphere should also be kept as moist as possible, but in winter they need to be kept rather dry. An alternative method of propagation is by mature leaves pegged to a bed of sandy peat in a close frame with bottom heat. This can be done at almost any time in spring or summer.

SYMPHORICARPOS *(Snowberry)*

The common snowberry of British hedgerows is *Symphoricarpos albus* (*racemosus*). It makes a dense bush of rather thin, twiggy growth and is notable for its globular white berries in autumn. At that season it is very decorative and though not, perhaps, a shrub for the more select parts of the garden it is well worth a place on the outskirts. It will thrive anywhere, even in competition with trees, and is a good cover shrub. There are other kinds less frequently seen, one of the best of which is *S. orbiculatus* often known as the coral berry on account of its rose-purple berries. Unfortunately it does not usually fruit sufficiently freely in this country to be effective. It should be given a warm and sunny situation. These shrubs can be increased by detaching offsets or suckers in autumn.

SYRINGA (Lilac)

The common lilacs are all derived from *Syringa vulgaris*, a tall shrub or small tree with pale purple flowers. The garden varieties have, in general, larger individual flowers and finer clusters, and they have a colour range from white and palest lavender to a deep reddish purple. There are single and double-flowered forms. In addition to these numerous varieties of common lilac, there are also several other species well worth growing, as well as hybrids between some of these species. There is, for example, the Hungarian lilac, *S. Josikae*, with elegantly formed clusters of lilac flowers. *S. reflexa* is a Chinese lilac which has small pink flowers in drooping clusters and *S. villosa*, which also comes from China, has very long flower clusters. A series of hybrids has been made between *S. reflexa* and *S. villosa* and these are often known as the Preston lilacs. They contain some very elegant and attractive shrubs with smaller flowers than those of the common lilac but more gracefully formed. *S. emodii* is very like *S. villosa*.

All these lilacs like fairly rich soils and open, sunny positions. They are quite hardy and easy to grow and they require no regular pruning. The species are easily raised from seed sown in spring in a frame, but the garden varieties do not come true to colour and form from seed and so are increased by grafting on to seedlings of the common lilac, by layering in spring or early summer, or by detaching suckers in autumn, if the plants are on their own roots and have not been grafted.

TAGETES (Marigold)

Not all the plants commonly called marigold belong to the tagetes family for the common pot marigold is a calendula, but the African marigold is *Tagetes erecta* and the French marigold is *T. patula*. There is also a very pretty little dwarf marigold with small single orange flowers which is named *T. signata pumila*. All these are annuals readily raised from seed sown in a greenhouse or frame in March. The seedlings should be pricked out as soon as possible into boxes of good soil, and should then be hardened off for planting outdoors in late May. All these marigolds like a sunny place. Though they will grow in almost any soil, for really good results the French and African varieties should have a rather rich soil—certainly a good deal richer than would be advisable for most annuals.

117

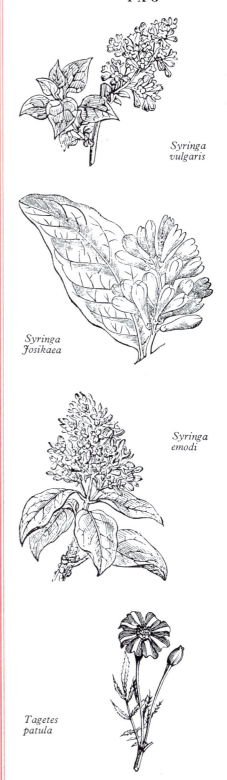

Syringa vulgaris

Syringa Josikaea

Syringa emodi

Tagetes patula

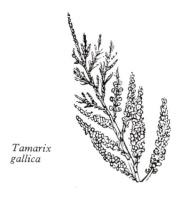

*Tamarix
gallica*

*Thalictrum
aquilegifolium*

*Thalictrum
minus*

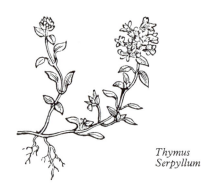

*Thymus
Serpyllum*

The African marigolds are mostly between 2 and 3 feet tall and have very big, almost globular flowers in shades of yellow and orange. The French marigolds are shorter, usually about 18 inches, and they have rather smaller but more perfectly formed double flowers usually yellow with crimson or chestnut red markings.

TAMARIX *(Tamarisk)*

These very graceful shrubs thrive especially well near the seaside and are happiest in light, well-drained soils. All have very slender branches set with tiny green leaves not unlike those of heathers and their small flowers are produced in fine feathery plumes which are most graceful. One of the best is *Tamarix pentandra* which has pink flowers in August. There is also a variety of this named *rubra* in which the flowers are almost red. To extend the season there is *T. tetrandra* which bears its pink flowers in May. For finest results *T. pentandra* should be cut back hard each spring and *T. tetrandra* should be similarly pruned as soon as it has finished flowering. All species of tamarisk can be increased by cuttings of well ripened growth in autumn. *T. anglica* and *T. gallica* are frequently used for hedging in exposed sea side places.

THALICTRUM *(Meadow Rue)*

The loveliest of all the meadow rues is *Thalictrum dipterocarpum*, but it is not one of the easiest to grow. A rather tall herbaceous plant very sparsely branched and open in habit, it has small, round leaves and produces, in July and August, loose sprays of nodding lilac and yellow flowers. The effect of a well grown plant 5 or 6 feet high is very beautiful. There is also a double flowered form named Hewitt's Double. Both these plants need good but well-drained soils and rather warm positions. They are apt to be killed in winter on cold, wet soils.

Far easier to grow but not so graceful is *T. aquilegifolium* which has leaves very like those of a columbine (aquilegia) and clusters of small purplish flowers on 3-foot stems, in early summer. *T. glaucum* is rather taller and has pale yellow flowers and attractive grey foliage. *T. minus* (*adiantifolium*) is not above 18 inches high, has leaves like those of maidenhair fern and greenish yellow flowers in summer. All can be increased by careful division in spring.

THYMUS *(Thyme)*

The thymes are useful plants for the rock garden and also for the crevices between paving slabs. Several of them are quite prostrate in habit and of these one of the finest is *T. Serpyllum* and its numerous varieties. This makes a carpet of rooting stems set with tiny leaves and smothered in June and July by the heather-pink, carmine or white flowers. There is an attractive variety named *lanuginosus*, the leaves of which are clothed with whitish down. The lemon-scented thyme, usually sold as *T. citriodorus*, is in fact a variety of *T. Serpyllum*. It has an attractive golden leaved form. *T. nitidus* is one of the best of the erect, shrubby kinds, a neat, 18–inch high bush with grey-green, fragrant leaves and masses of soft pink flowers in May.

All thymes like well-drained soils and open sunny positions. The creeping kinds can be easily increased by division in spring but the shrubby kinds must be increased by cuttings of firm young shoots in July or August in a frame.

TIGRIDIA *(Tiger Flower)*

The tigridias are bulbous-rooted plants which are not quite hardy enough to be reliable outdoors except in the south and west. They like warm, sunny places and light, well-drained soils and are excellent plants for a sheltered border at the foot of a south wall. They are well worth a little trouble as they are extremely unusual and beautiful in flower. The species usually grown is *Tigridia Pavonia* which grows 2 to 2½ feet high and has widely opened flowers that look a little like three petalled tulips (there are actually six petals but three are very small). The colours are bright yellow, rose, red etc., usually spotted with a deeper colour. Though each flower only lasts a day, a succession of blooms is produced for several weeks in August. The corms should be planted in April and lifted in October and stored like those of gladioli.

TRADESCANTIA *(Spiderwort)*

Several of the tradescantias are greenhouse plants, one *Tradescantia fluminensis*, being a popular trailing plant for the edges of greenhouse stages or even for growing beneath the staging. It has several useful variegated varieties.

There is also one kind, *T. virginiana*, which is a perfectly hardy herbaceous perennial valuable for its long-flowering season and ability to thrive almost anywhere, in good soil or poor, sun or shade. It grows about 2 feet high, has broadly grass-like leaves and clusters of three-petalled flowers which open in succession from June to September. The wild species is purple-flowered but there are many garden varieties some of which are a clear lavender-blue or violet and some rose. All can be increased by division in spring or autumn.

TRILLIUM *(Wood Lily)*

These are very beautiful plants for shady places and cool leafy, or peaty soils. They grow 12 to 18 inches tall and carry their broad green leaves in threes. The flowers are also three-petalled (or appear so). One of the best is *Trillium grandiflorum* with white to rose flowers. *T. erectum* is rather a dull purple and perhaps more interesting than beautiful and another with purple or green flowers is *T. sessile*. All can be increased by careful division in March. They flower in April or May.

TROLLIUS *(Globe Flower)*

The globe flowers resemble very large, almost globular buttercups and all flower in spring or early summer, though they often

119

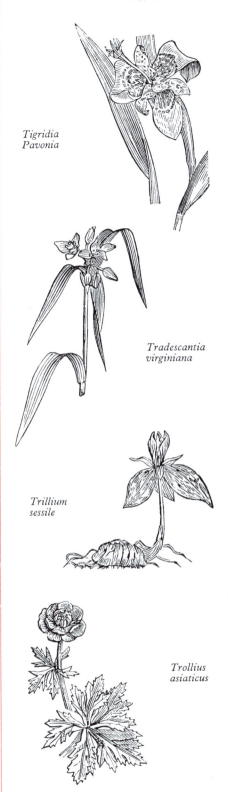

Tigridia Pavonia

Tradescantia virginiana

Trillium sessile

Trollius asiaticus

*Tropaeolum
speciosum*

*Tropaeolum
polyphyllum*

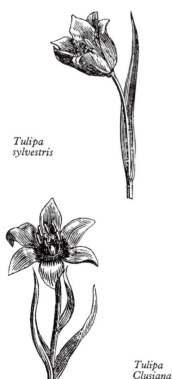

*Tulipa
sylvestris*

*Tulipa
Clusiana*

give a second flush of bloom in August. They like cool places and rather moist soils and though they can be grown in the herbaceous border they are really happier at the side of a stream or in damp soil near the edge of a bog garden. *Trollius europaeus* is the kind most commonly grown and this has numerous varieties or hybrids differing mainly in the precise shade of their flowers which may be anything from pale yellow to orange. All are about 2 feet high. *T. Ledebourii* is rather taller and flowers later, a further difference being that its orange flowers are more widely opened and less ball shaped. *T. asiaticus* is very much like *T. europaeus* and has colour forms varying from light to deep yellow. All can be increased by careful division in spring.

TROPAEOLUM *(Nasturtium)*

The popular annual which everyone knows as nasturtium is, in fact, *Tropaeolum majus*. This is a climbing plant in its natural form but it has a great many varieties some of which, like the Tom Thumb nasturtiums, are compact and bushy. All are plants of the easiest culture, growing in any soil however poor, and even tolerating shade, though they flower most freely in sunny places. The flowers are either yellow or some shade of red or crimson and are produced throughout the season. Though really quite tender *T. majus* grows so rapidly that it can be treated as a hardy annual by sowing the seed outdoors in April where it is to flower.

There are also fine perennial kinds of tropaeolum of which two of the best are *T. speciosum* (the flame flower) and *T. polyphyllum*. The first is a slender climber with small scarlet flowers in summer. It is a plant that likes to scramble up through an evergreen shrub such as a holly or rhododendron, which it will then drape with its gracefully divided leaves and vivid flowers. Though not a very hardy plant it does not like dry heat and does best in the damper parts of the country, especially in some parts of Scotland. *T. polyphyllum*, by contrast, loves sun and warmth and is a good plant for a sunny bank. It has a tuberous root and trailing stems set with grey-green leaves and bearing bright yellow flowers. It must be increased by seed but *T. speciosum* can be propagated by division of its roots.

TULIPA *(Tulip)*

The tulip is a plant which has been highly developed in cultivation over a period of several centuries and it is, therefore, not surprising that to-day there are thousands of varieties grouped in a dozen or more main classes. These range from the quite dwarf and very early Duc van Thol tulips which are really only suitable for forcing in the greenhouse, to the tall and late-flowering Darwins which are such favourites for bedding displays in May. The early-flowering tulips bloom in April and are further subdivided into single and double-flowered varieties. A little later come the Mendel and Triumph tulips which occupy an intermediate position between early-flowering and Darwin groups. Then in May, in addition to the Darwins, there are the so-called cottage tulips and their offshoot, the lily-flowered race. Cutting across these various groups are the parrot tulips which may be early or late but all of which have curiously twisted or slashed petals and colours usually splashed with green and contrasting shades in a very distinctive manner. An entirely new race of rather dwarf early-flowering tulips has been produced from *Tulipa Kauffmanniana* and another new race of tall late-flowering tulips with notably brilliant colours is being raised by hybridizing *Tulipa Fosteriana* with other groups. The Rembrandt tulips are Darwins with broken colours, i.e. one colour splashed or streaked on a base of another colour. There are also double May-flowering tulips which have flowers not unlike those of peonies.

All these beautiful types, with the exception of the Duc van Thols, can be grown outdoors in any reasonably good and well-drained soil. Their bulbs should be planted 4 or 5 inches deep in October or November and are best lifted again in July when the foliage has died down. They should then be stored in a cool dry place until planting time. Propagation is by division of the bulb clusters when they are lifted.

VENIDIUM

The best known species is *Venidium fastuosum*, a rather coarse annual about 3 feet high and bearing, in summer, large and immensely showy daisy flowers which are orange with a central zone of black. There are other kinds, such as *V. calendulacea* which is shorter and less strikingly marked and there are also many hybrids in a wide range of colours. Seed of all may be sown in a greenhouse or frame in March, the seedlings being pricked out and hardened off for planting out in May. *V. calendulacea* may also be treated as a hardy annual, seed being sown outdoors in April where the plants are to flower.

VERBASCUM *(Mullein)*

The mulleins are mostly rather tall plants with long, tapering spikes of flowers which may be yellow or buff coloured or, in *Verbascum phoeniceum*, purple. Some are good perennials but many are biennials or usually behave as such and these must be renewed from seed every year. This can be sown outdoors in May in a sunny place and well-drained soil. Among the best of the perennial kinds are *V. Chaixii*, *V. thapsiforme (densiflorum)* and *V. nigrum*, all of which are yellow and about 5 feet high, and various hybrids such as Cotswold Queen, buff; Gainsborough, lemon yellow; and Pink Domino, mauve. The common mullein, *V. Thapsus*, covered with grey hair, grows to 7 feet tall, but a better plant, equally woolly but shorter, is *V. Brousa*. All perennial kinds can be increased by root cuttings in a frame in winter.

VERBENA *(Vervain)*

The best known verbenas are the half-hardy trailing kinds used for summer bedding. These all have brilliantly coloured flowers in shades of red, pink, purple and violet. They are fine carpeting

121

Tulipa acuminata

Tulipa Gesneriana

Verbascum ovalifolium

Verbascum phoeniceum

*Verbena
bonariensis*

*Verbena
canadensis*

*Veronica
spicata*

*Veronica
speciosa*

plants for sunny places and may also be grown on the top of terrace walls or in tubs, earthenware vases and hanging baskets. They are almost hardy and only require frame or cool greenhouse protection in winter. All can be readily raised from seed sown in a warm greenhouse in January or February, and selected forms can also be increased from cuttings taken in late summer and rooted in a frame.

In addition to these there are several hardy or near hardy kinds which may be grown in the herbaceous border or rock garden. *V. chamaedryfolia* has scarlet flowers, is a trailer and only thoroughly hardy in the milder parts of the country. *V. venosa (rigida)* is a good hardy perennial, a foot high, with close spikes of purple flowers from July to September, and *V. bonariensis* is a rather tall and sparse perennial with clusters of deep purplish blue flowers in August and September. All these can be increased by division in spring.

VERONICA *(Speedwell)*

There are both herbaceous and shrubby veronicas and botanists have separated most of the latter into a new genus under the name Hebe. However, as few gardeners have adopted this change, sensible though it seems, all the species are here treated as veronicas. All the shrubby kinds are evergreen and many of them are near the borderline of hardiness. Nevertheless there are such beautiful kinds among them that they are worth a little risk. *Veronica speciosa* is a late-flowering kind about 5 feet high which makes a shapely rounded bush and produces its short spikes of violet, purple, red or pink flowers from August to October. It does well by the seaside but is often severely damaged by frost inland. *V. salicifolia* has narrow leaves and slender, partially drooping spikes of white flowers from July to September. It is a very graceful evergreen but again is liable to be badly damaged by frost.

One of the hardiest is *V. Traversii*, a rounded, densely bushy shrub, 4 to 5 feet high with neat rounded leaves and short spikes of white flowers in July. Another very distinctive kind is *V. cupressoides*, a small shrub 18 to 24 inches high with such tiny leaves that it looks more like a conifer than a broad-leaved evergreen.

The herbaceous veronicas range from the completely prostrate, blue-flowered *V. rupestris*, an admirable carpeting plant for the rock garden, to the 6 foot tall, bluish-white *V. virginica*. *V. incana* has grey leaves and violet-blue flowers and is a good edging plant 9 to 12 inches high. *V. spicata* is taller, 1 to 2 feet, and it has slender spikes of blue, pink or white flowers. *V. longifolia subsessilis* is one of the best with fine spikes of blue-purple flowers in August and there are also several varieties of *V. latifolia*, 2 to 3 feet high, with narrow flower spikes which may be purple, pink or white.

All these herbaceous kinds are quite hardy and will grow in any ordinary soil and open position. They can be increased by division in spring or autumn. The shrubby kinds can be increased by cuttings of firm young growth in a frame at practically any time in summer or early autumn.

VIBURNUM *(Guelder Rose, Snowball Tree, Laurustinus)*

There are two viburnums that are called snowball trees because they have almost globular heads of white flowers. One of these is *Viburnum Opulus sterile*, a variety of the British guelder rose, and the other is *V. tomentosum plicatum*, often referred to as the Japanese snowball to distinguish it from the native kind. It has a very attractive habit, with horizontal branches, and the flower heads are not quite as large as those of *V. Opulus sterile*. There are also other varieties of *V. tomentosum* which have more or less flat heads of flowers borne all along the branches and these are quite as decorative as the globular headed varieties. All these flower in May and early June and are deciduous.

The popular laurustinus is *Viburnum Tinus* and is one of the best of evergreen winter flowering shrubs. It will grow 8 or 10 feet high and makes a very dense, rounded bush. The flower heads are pale pink in bud, white when open and they continue from January to April.

Another fine winter-flowering kind, this time deciduous, is *V. fragrans*, a rather stiffly branched shrub, 8 to 10 feet high which produces its small clusters of very fragrant white, pink-tinged flowers from November to February. It is perfectly hardy and even its flowers will survive a considerable amount of frost. In April and May comes *V. Carlesii*, another very fragrant shrub with clusters of white, pink-tinted flowers. It grows 5 or 6 feet high.

V. rhytidophyllum is an evergreen worth growing for its large, deep green leaves which have a remarkably wrinkled surface. It makes a big shrub, 10 or 12 feet high and carries large trusses of rather dull whitish flowers in June which are followed by red berries. There is an attractive variety in which the flower buds are pink.

All these viburnums will grow in any reasonable soil. They can be increased by cuttings of firm young shoots in July or August.

VINCA *(Periwinkle)*

The periwinkles are creeping evergreen shrubs which are useful for ground cover in shady places. They do well on banks or beneath trees that are not too closely planted, and they all flower in spring. The two principal kinds are *Vinca major* and *V. minor* but the latter is more useful as a garden plant as it has produced a number of varieties some with single and some with double flowers, a colour range from white and palest blue to purple and rose, and at least two forms with variegated leaves. All are of the easiest cultivation in almost any soil that does not dry out too much. They are naturally woodland or hedgerow plants and these are the conditions that suit them. They can be increased by division of the roots in autumn.

123

Viburnum
Tinus

Viburnum
Opulus

Viburnum
macrocephalum

Vinca
major

*Viola
odorata*

*Viola
lutea*

*Weigela
rosea*

*Wisteria
Sinensis*

VIOLA *(Pansy, Violet)*

The common bedding viola, the pansy and the violet are all members of the same genus, known to botanists as Viola. This can be a trifle muddling to the gardener until he gets used to it. The bedding viola is a good perennial which can be propagated either by careful division of the roots in spring or by cuttings of young shoots in early autumn. It will grow almost anywhere but likes best rather good, porous soils that contain enough humus to keep them cool and moist even in warm weather. It has tufted growth and is an ideal plant for edging or for making a carpet beneath taller plants. The flowering season is from May to September and the colour range includes almost everything except red.

Pansies differ from violas in being more straggly and less tufted in growth, in having flowers usually with strong markings, often black on yellow, purple, blue or bronze, and being less reliable perennials. They can be increased by cuttings as for violas but it is common practice to renew them annually from seed sown in a frame or greenhouse in February or March. The seedlings are pricked out and hardened off for planting out in good soil in May.

Violets are divided into single and double-flowered varieties, the latter being less vigorous and more difficult to grow. All thrive in fairly rich soils well supplied with moisture though not badly drained. They can be increased by careful division in spring but a better method is to make cuttings from the runners in early autumn and root them in a frame. They are planted out in good soil the following April and will make sturdy clumps for flowering the following winter.

WEIGELA

These very decorative deciduous shrubs are sometimes known in gardens by an alternative but discarded botanical name, Diervilla. All make rather large well-branched shrubs which tend to become arching in habit with age. The trumpet shaped flowers are borne in small clusters all along the stems and make a very fine display in late May and June. Often there is a second lot of flowers in late summer. Most of the varieties cultivated are hybrids. Among the best are Abel Carriere, pink, Eva Rathke and Newport Red, both deep carmine, and *styriaca*, rose. All will grow in practically any soil and situation but prefer one that is fairly sunny. They do not need regular pruning but flowering branches can be cut back when the flowers fade. All can be increased by cuttings of half-ripe shoots in a frame in July or by firmer cuttings outdoors in autumn.

WISTERIA

These are among the loveliest and most popular of hardy climbing plants. There are several kinds, all very vigorous and producing long, trailing spikes of soft lavender or mauve flowers in May and early June. The most popular is *Wisteria sinensis*, the Chinese wisteria, but *W. floribunda*, the Japanese wisteria, has longer flower trails, particularly in its variety *macrobotrys* in which they may be as much as 3 feet. There are several other varieties of this wisteria, one with pale pink flowers, and there are white flowered forms of both the Chinese and Japanese wisterias.

All like good soils and warm sunny places. They are happiest trained against a sunny wall but may also be grown over pergolas or can even be trained in the open to form standards or large bushes. Though regular pruning is not essential it is often convenient to shorten sidegrowths to four or five leaves each July. The best method of increase is by layering the long stems in early summer.

YUCCA *(Adam's Needle)*

The yuccas are all very exotic looking plants with stiff rosettes of long, sword-shaped leaves, sometimes carried almost on the ground, as in *Yucca filamentosa* or *Y. flaccida*, and sometimes carried on a short trunk as in *Y. gloriosa*. The flowers are creamy white and produced in July or August, in long erect spikes which have a very striking appearance. It is often stated that they take a great many years to flower but this is quite incorrect as plants that are growing well in a warm, sunny place and reasonably good but well-drained soil, usually flower quite regularly every year.

Most of the species are not too hardy and are most suitable for the mild southern and western counties or for seaside gardens, but *Y. filamentosa* and *Y. flaccida* usually succeed quite well in most parts of the country. In very cold places the leaves may be tied together in early winter to form a tent-like protection to the heart of the rosette. Yuccas are increased by seeds sown in a greenhouse in spring and also by rooted offsets detached in March.

ZINNIA *(Youth and Old Age)*

These very popular and brightly coloured, half-hardy annuals need to be sown a little later than most other plants of this class. Sow in a cool greenhouse in late March or an unheated frame in early April and grow straight on without either check or forcing. In too much heat the seedlings are apt to damp off. Zinnias like good soils and warm, sunny places. They grow about 3 feet high and should be spaced at least a foot, preferably 18 inches, apart. For late summer flowers it is wise to sow some seeds in early May directly in the open ground where they are to bloom and to thin the seedlings to the necessary distance.

There are several different types of zinnia. The best known is the large-flowered type with rather broad, flat petals, making an almost ball-like flower. A more recent development is the chrysanthemum-flowered type in which the petals are rolled and the bloom has a spiky appearance. There is also a race of pompon or miniature-flowered zinnias. All have the full zinnia range of colours including particularly strong reds and crimsons, fine yellows, pink and rose shades.

125

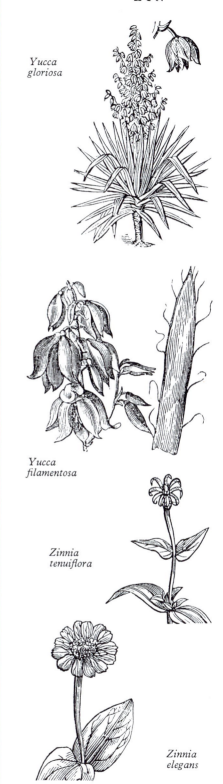

Yucca
gloriosa

Yucca
filamentosa

Zinnia
tenuiflora

Zinnia
elegans

INDEX

to popular and catalogue names

GARDEN PLANTS
IN COLOUR

GARDEN PLANTS
IN COLOUR
an Amateur Gardening encyclopaedia

BY A. G. L. HELLYER, F.L.S.

illustrated from watercolour drawings

BY CYNTHIA NEWSOME-TAYLOR

and from line drawings

BY G. R. KINGBOURN

FOREWORD

'Plants in Colour' is not so much a sequel to 'Flowers in Colour' as a companion to it. In the earlier volume I concentrated upon those plants most commonly grown in gardens, whereas in this second book I have endeavoured to introduce the reader to some of the most beautiful and interesting plants, whether they are familiar or not. Some of the genera have already appeared in 'Flowers in Colour' but I have taken the opportunity to bring in other species or varieties, particularly those that I regard as of special merit. An example of this is the michaelmas daisy Marie Ballard, one of the most perfect varieties of Aster novi-belgii ever raised and a worthy representative of the achievement of that great breeder of michaelmas daisies, the late Ernest Ballard.

But in the main the genera dealt with in 'Plants in Colour' are those which were omitted from its predecessor simply because they did not rank among the most popular with gardeners. That in no way reflects on their merit and is an added reason why they should be introduced with the aid of the best possible pictorial representation.

In this I have again had the assistance of Cynthia Newsome-Taylor who has prepared all the colour illustrations from living material. This has involved an enormous amount of work spread over a period of rather more than two years and I am greatly indebted to her for having stuck to it so patiently and produced plant portraits which are at once so lifelike and so decorative. Her paintings for 'Flowers in Colour' were awarded a Silver Grenfell Medal when exhibited at the Royal Horticultural Society and the present series is certainly in no way inferior—personally I think that her skill has increased still more.

For the line illustrations, which keep pace with the text, I enlisted the help of another gifted artist, George R. Kingbourn, who has also been busily engaged in making drawings for the book for more than two years. These have involved him in numerous journeys to the Royal Horticultural Society's gardens at Wisley where he has been able to find a great many of the plants he has needed. He is himself a very keen and successful gardener, and it is, no doubt, his deep interest in plants that has enabled him to portray so successfully their character as well as their likeness.

The assembly of so much living material for these two artists would have been quite impossible without the assistance of a great many people. I am particularly indebted to the Royal Horticultural Society for allowing me to use the Wisley gardens so freely and to Mr Frank Knight, the Director, and Mr Francis Hanger, the Curator for bearing so cheerfully all my importunate demands for plants and flowers. Mr W. M. Campbell, the Curator of the Royal Botanic Gardens, Kew, is another who has helped again and again with characteristic generosity.

But even these two rich sources have not proved sufficient for the varied material I sought and I have had to go far afield for some plants. Among those who have helped are Mr R. J. Wallis, head gardener at Wakehurst Place; the late Mr Thomas Carlile and his daughter, Miss Wendy Carlile, who now manages the Loddon Nurseries, Twyford; T. W. Sanders Ltd., who at the time I was preparing this book still had their nurseries at St. Albans; Mr A. Westall, the Supervisor of Bedgebury National Pinetum; Mr J. R. B. Evison, Superintendent of the Brighton Parks; Mr Reginald Perry of Perry's Hardy Plant Farm, Enfield; Mr Alan Bloom, Bressingham, Diss; Messrs Wallace and Barr, Tunbridge Wells; Mr Charles Puddle, head gardener at Bodnant; Mr N. Edland, secretary to the National Rose Society; Mr C. J. Marchant, Keeper's Hill Nursery, Wimborne, Dorset; Mr Will Ingwersen, East Grinstead, Sussex; Mr Christopher Lloyd; Mrs Margery Fish; Captain G. K. Mooney; Mr L. Maurice Mason; and Commander T. Dorrien-Smith, whose garden at Tresco Abbey in the Isles of Scilly contains so many treasures. There are many more, too numerous to mention individually, and I tender my grateful thanks to them all.

Rowfant, 1958   A. G. L. HELLYER

THE PLATES

Abelia floribunda

Abies nobilis

GARDEN PLANTS IN COLOUR

ABELIA

Graceful but unspectacular shrubs, several of which have the merit of producing their small tubular flowers from midsummer until early autumn. This is true of *Abelia grandiflora*, with pale pink flowers, *A. schumanii* (Plate 1) which is a little deeper in colour, and *A. chinensis* which is pure white and scented. All these are deciduous but *A. floribunda*, with rose coloured flowers, is evergreen. It is a little more tender and usually needs the protection of a sunny wall. Similar in many respects and also evergreen, is *A. grandiflora*, a hybrid with *A. floribunda* as one of its parents. Being hardy it may be preferred for outdoor planting but it is not really quite as beautiful as *A. floribunda*. All make slenderly branched bushes 3 to 6 feet high and need no regular pruning. They like warm, sunny positions and well-drained soils and are readily increased by half-ripe cuttings in July.

ABIES *(Fir)*

A great many of the firs are far too large for anything but forest or woodland planting, but a few make good specimens for large gardens. One of the best is the Spanish Fir, *Abies pinsapo*, which has unusually short, blue-grey leaves set all round the branchlets instead of in two opposite rows. The Caucasian Fir, *A. nordmanniana*, is a bigger and faster growing tree which makes a very handsome, conical specimen. *A. concolor*, the Colorado Fir, has glaucous green foliage which is blue-grey in certain forms and always strikingly handsome. *A. nobilis* is notable for the size of its cones, which stand erect on the branches, and also for its handsome grey-green foliage. There is one interesting and attractive dwarf fir, *A. balsamea hudsonica*, a form of the Balsam Fir. It makes a flat-topped rather spreading little tree rarely above 2 feet high and grey-green in colour. All these are hardy trees which can be grown in any reasonable soil, though they thrive best in deep, loamy, well-watered soils. The ordinary types can be raised from seed, but specially selected forms are usually increased by grafting on to seedlings of the parent species.

ACANTHOLIMON *(Prickly Thrift)*

Rock plants with tufts of narrow, sharp pointed leaves and clusters of small flowers on short stems produced for many weeks in summer. Only one species, *A. glumaceum* (Plate 1), has become really familiar in gardens. It is a first rate plant for a sunny ledge or crevice, in gritty, well drained soils. Its flowers are produced on 6-inch stems in July and August and are pink, which slightly increases its very superficial resemblance to a thrift. It can be increased by seed or can be layered by working sandy soil down into the matted tufts so that they form roots, after which

10

they can be detached or the whole plant may be lifted and carefully divided.

ACER *(Maple)*

Many of the maples are forest trees, too large to be considered for ordinary garden planting, but there are some notable exceptions and the Japanese Maple (*Acer palmatum*) is one of the best foliage trees suitable even for quite small gardens. It grows slowly, taking a long time to reach 12 or 15 feet, and it has numerous forms, some with leaves deeply dissected into narrow, ferny lobes, as in *A. palmatum divisilobum*, some richly coloured purple or yellow, and all taking on fine autumn hues before they fall. Numerous varieties have been named, one of the finest for autumn colour being Osakazuki (Plate 1). All succeed best in good loamy soils and sheltered, partially shaded positions.

The Snake-bark Maples are grown for their handsome bark which is at first bright green, striped with white. There are several rather similar species, including *A. davidii*, *A. hersii*, and *A. pensylvanicum*. They will grow 20 or 30 feet high fairly quickly.

A. griseum is also grown for its bark which is cinnamon coloured and is constantly peeling off in large, ragged flakes which gives it a very distinctive appearance. It makes a most attractive small tree.

A. negundo is usually planted in its variegated form in which the light green leaves are heavily bordered with white. The young wood is also bright green. This is a favourite town-garden tree, growing eventually about 30 feet high. *A. nikoense* is also a fairly small tree and slow growing into the bargain. It colours well in autumn.

The common sycamore, *A. pseudoplatanus*, is too big for any but large gardens but there are some good varieties of it, notably *brilliantissimum* the young leaves of which are pink and gold. Similarly the Norway Maple, *A. platanoides*, also a large tree, has a fine variety named Goldsworth Purple with deep purple foliage.

Acers need no regular pruning but can be thinned or shaped in winter. They are best increased by seeds except for selected colour forms which are grafted on to seedlings of the species of which they are varieties.

ACIDANTHERA

Slightly tender plants closely allied to gladiolus and making similar corms. The only kind familiar in British gardens is *A. bicolor murielae* (Plate 1), which produces its fragrant, white, maroon-blotched flowers on slender 2 foot spikes in late summer. It is a very beautiful plant but a little too tender to be left outdoors in winter except in mild districts and well drained soils. In most parts of the country it is better to treat it much like a gladiolus, to which it is related and which it in some ways resembles. The corms are lifted and stored dry in a frost proof place until March or April when they can be replanted 3 inches deep and 6 inches

Acer palmatum divisilobum rubrum

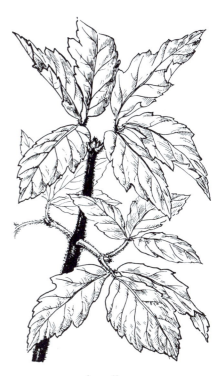

Acer nikoense

11

Adonis vernalis

Aesculus parviflora

apart in a sunny place. Acidantheras are best increased by separating the small corms when the plants are lifted in autumn. In places too cold to grow this beautiful plant outdoors it can be grown in pots in an unheated greenhouse.

ADONIS *(Pheasant's Eye)*

The species most commonly seen in gardens is the Summer Pheasant's Eye, *Adonis aestivalis* a hardy annual with finely divided ferny leaves and crimson flowers on 18-inch stems in summer. Seed of this should be sown in a sunny place in April and early May, seedlings being thinned to a few inches apart. There are also perennial species of which the best known is the Spring Pheasant's Eye, *A. vernalis* (Plate 1), with similar ferny leaves and bright yellow flowers on 10-inch stems in April and May. It will grow in sun or light shade and likes a good, well-drained soil. Similar but even earlier flowering is *A. amurensis*. Increase of all the perennial kinds is by division immediately after flowering.

AESCULUS *(Horse Chestnut, Buckeye)*

The common Horse Chestnut, *Aesculus hippocastanum*, is really too large and fast growing a tree for any but big gardens, but it is extremely handsome, very hardy and will grow in any reasonable soil. The candelabra-like flower spikes are always white and the so-called Red Horse Chestnut is a hybrid between the common Horse Chestnut and another species of aesculus. It is a smaller tree but even so may soon reach a height of 30 to 40 feet. There are, however, still smaller kinds, notably the Red Buckeye, *A. pavia*, a shrub 10 or 12 feet high, with rose-pink flowers in June, and the Dwarf Buckeye, *A. parviflora*, which is similar in height and has white flowers in July and August, later than most other kinds. *A. octandra*, the Sweet Buckeye, is a fairly large tree with yellow flowers and it has produced some useful garden hybrids with *A. pavia* as the other parent, these being more useful than *A. octandra* because they are usually much smaller. One of the loveliest of all the species is the Indian Horse Chestnut, *A. indica*, a big tree with smooth, shining green leaves with flowers which give the impression of being soft pink though, in fact, they combine white, rose pink, and yellow. It has a reputation for being less hardy than the Common Horse Chestnut, probably because it is called 'Indian', but in fact it appears to be perfectly hardy.

All these chestnuts thrive best in fairly good, loamy soils but are not fussy. They need no regular pruning. The species are best increased by seed sown outdoors in late winter or early spring, but the hybrids are budded, usually on seedlings of the Common Horse Chestnut.

AKEBIA

Vigorous hardy climbers which ascend by twining. Two species are grown and both have clusters of small maroon or deep purple flowers followed, in favourable seasons, by sausage-shaped vio-

12

let or purple fruits. *A. trifoliata* has three leaflets to each leaf, *A. quinata* (Plate 1) usually five leaflets. A further difference is that the flowers of *A. quinata* are fragrant. Both kinds thrive in any fairly rich soil and sunny position. The rather curious and quite small flowers appear in spring and are most likely to be followed by fruits in a warm season. Plants should be given plenty of room to climb up a trellis, over a dead tree or some other substantial support. Propagation is by layering in late spring or by seed sown in a greenhouse.

ALSTROEMERIA (Peruvian Lily)

The commonest of the Peruvian Lilies, *Alstroemeria aurantiaca*, is so free-growing a plant that it not infrequently becomes almost a nuisance in gardens, spreading far by means of its thick white roots and producing its orange, black-speckled flowers with the utmost freedom in July and August. Considerably choicer and correspondingly more difficult to manage is *A. ligtu* and the many hybrids raised from it (Plate 1). These have loose heads of flowers in a great range of delicate shades of pink, rose, salmon, apricot and flame. Slugs are fond of the young growth and seedlings, in particular, must be protected from these pests. The roots should be planted about 5 inches deep in good, preferably fairly light, and certainly well-drained soil, in a sunny, open position and should thereafter be left undisturbed as long as possible to multiply. The flowers are produced in July.

Two other charming species are *A. chilensis* and *A. haemantha*, the former with deep red or soft pink flowers, the latter bright red and orange with purple spotting and veining. Though both are classed as hardy they certainly need a warmer, more sheltered position and a better drained soil than *A. aurantiaca*.

Whereas the Orange Peruvian Lily can be easily increased by division of the roots in spring or autumn, *A. ligtu* and its hybrids, and also *A. chilensis* and *A. haemantha*, are best raised from seed sown in a greenhouse or frame in spring or, better still, as soon as ripe in late summer. The seedlings should be allowed to grow undisturbed the first year and transplanted in March.

AMARANTHUS (Love-Lies-Bleeding)

Half-hardy annuals of which the only species commonly cultivated in the Britsh Isles is *A. caudatus* (Plate 1). This grows 3 or 4 feet tall and produces long, hanging trails of vivid, red-purple flowers. It is a very handsome plant either as a pot specimen in the greenhouse or for summer bedding for which it is often used as a 'dot' plant. Seed should be sown in a warm greenhouse in February or March, seedlings being potted individually and gradually hardened off for planting outdoors in late May or early June. This amaranthus likes a fairly rich soil and a sunny position.

ANAGALLIS (Pimpernel)

The pimpernel most commonly grown in gardens, *A. linifolia*, although a perennial, is invariably grown as an annual. In warm,

Alstromeria ligtu hybrid

Alstroemeria aurantiaca

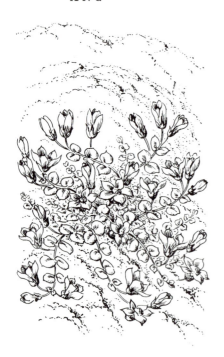

Anagallis tenella

Anchusa italica

sheltered places seed can be sown outdoors in April or early May, but in most gardens it will be better to treat it as a half-hardy annual and to sow in March or April in a cool greenhouse or frame. The seedlings should then be pricked off and hardened off for planting outdoors 6 inches apart in May. They should have as sunny a place as possible to open their deep gentian blue or bright red flowers. In habit *A. linifolia* is trailing. There are several garden forms of this plant, usually with flowers of superior size, such as *monellii*, a fine deep blue, *parksii*, (Plate 1), with big red flowers, and Napoleon III, the deepest red of all.

One other species occasionally grown is *A. tenella*, the Bog Pimpernel. It is also a creeping annual with pearly pink flowers in summer. It thrives in wet soil by the side of a stream or pool.

ANCHUSA *(Alkanet)*

In gardens the most familiar species is the Italian Alkanet, *A. italica*, a plant for the middle or back of the herbaceous border, remarkable for its brilliant blue flowers, like huge forget-me-nots, in June. Very different and by no means so well known as it deserves is the plant known in gardens as *Anchusa caespitosa* (Plate 1). The true owner of this name is a dwarf Cretan plant suitable for the rock garden and with typical blue anchusa flowers, but the plant which wrongly bears its name in gardens is 12 to 15 inches high and a first-class plant for the front of the border. It has gentian blue flowers in June and July. Like the Italian Alkanet it is perennial but not very long lived and should be renewed every few years from seed or by cuttings made from the young shoots in spring. It also resembles *A. italica* in liking sunny places and well-drained soil. The Italian Alkanet can also be raised from seed but specially selected garden forms are often increased by root cuttings in winter. These, if made from pieces of root about 2 inches long, inserted right way up in sandy soil so that they are just covered, will make shoots very readily and may be planted out in a nursery bed in June for final transference to flowering positions the following autumn or spring.

ANEMONE *(Windflower)*

This large and varied genus has already been described in *Flowers in Colour* but I was not there able to give a picture of the loveliest of the small, early blooming windflowers, *A. blanda* (Plate 1). This tufted perennial, in habit much like *A. apennina* but less rampant and with finer blue flowers, is one of the best plants to bloom in the rock garden in March. Unlike the wood anemones it prefers a sunny place though it will put up with some shade. It likes warmth and the soil should be cool, deep and well drained but not dry, treatment which also suits *A. apennina* admirably so that the two plants may be grown together, if so desired. Propagation is by division after flowering.

ANTENNARIA *(Cat's Ears)*

A. dioica, the only Cat's Ears at all commonly grown in gardens, is a pretty native plant forming a close mat of small grey leaves studded in spring with small pink or white, rather chaffy flowers. The pink form is usually distinguished with the varietal name *rosea* (Plate 2). These are excellent carpeting plants for the rock garden, easily grown in any reasonably drained soil and sunny position. They may also be planted in crevices between paving slabs. They are easily increased by division at almost any time.

ANTHURIUM

Very striking tropical perennials which are quite easy to grow, provided they can be given a really warm greenhouse (an average temperature of 60 to 65° F. in winter, rising to 75° or more in summer). The leaves are dark velvety green, and are held like shields. The flowers are densely packed in a long, cylindrical spadix like that of the arum lily and in the popular kinds stick out from a flat, oval, highly coloured spathe which is the most conspicuous part of the flower. The two species most commonly grown are *A. andreanum* (Plate 2), with vermilion, rose or white spathes, and *A. scherzerianum*, which has a number of varieties ranging in colour from white to blood red, some splashed with white on a red ground. All make fairly big plants and need to be grown in pots 8 to 12 inches in diameter as they reach maturity. They like a rich, peaty potting compost, plenty of water in spring and summer and a really humid atmosphere. In winter they can be kept drier but are never allowed to rest completely. They flower in late spring and early summer and are increased by detaching offshoots in March, which is a good potting time.

ARENARIA *(Sandwort)*

This large genus has not produced many really good garden plants but one is certainly outstanding and several others are useful. The outstanding plant is *A. montana* (Plate 2) which might be likened to a handsome and highly refined stitchwort. It makes slender, sprawling stems set with narrow leaves and, in early summer, bearing numerous quite large white flowers, the whole plant not exceeding 6 inches in height. Its proper place is the rock garden in a sunny place and any reasonable soil. One of the useful plants is *A. verna caespitosa* which makes a low, rounded hummock of growth, rather like moss. The white flowers are small to the point of insignificance but the plant is worth growing for its own sake as ground cover, particularly for small, early flowering bulbs. It also has a variety named *aurea* with yellow-green leaves. Either will grow anywhere, in sun or shade. Another excellent ground-cover plant is *A. balearica* which makes a close carpet of bright green smothered in small white, almost stemless flowers in spring. It is happiest in a rather cool soil not liable to dry out rapidly in summer, and will grow in sun or partial shade. All these sandworts can be increased by division at almost any time.

ARGEMONE *(Prickly Poppy)*

Poppy-like plants which, though perennial in their natural surroundings, are best treated as annuals in the garden. The

Anthurium scherzerianum

Arenaria balearica

15

Arisaema candidissimum

Aristolochia heterophylla

best known is *A. mexicana* (Plate 2), a plant with rather handsome blue-grey, prickly leaves and abundant pale yellow or cream coloured flowers in summer. *A. grandiflora* has bigger flowers and leaves that are scarcely prickly. Both grow about 2 feet high, like warm sunny places and well-drained soils and should be sown thinly in April where they are to flower, the seedlings being thinned out to at least 9 inches apart.

ARISAEMA (Dragon Root, Jack-in-the-Pulpit)

Herbaceous perennials allied to the arum lilies and with somewhat similar inflorescences consisting of a spathe folded around a narrowly cylindrical spadix which carries the true flowers. None is showy but several have an elegance of form and delicacy of colouring which make them well worth growing. One of the best is *A. candidissimum*, a small plant not above 12 inches in height which produces white, purple-striped, hooded flowers in early summer. It likes a cool, moist soil and a shady position and can be increased by careful division of its tuberous roots in spring. Less graceful but better known is the true Dragon Root, *A. dracontium*, a plant often known in gardens as *Arum dracontium*. It grows about 2 feet high, has deeply divided leaves rather like the fingers of a hand, stems handsomely mottled with purple, and green spathes. *A. triphyllum* is the plant known as Jack-in-the-Pulpit, a pretty little North American species with narrowly divided leaves and spathes handsomely netted and striped with purple, the whole plant being under a foot in height. All are easily grown in any ordinary soil not liable to dry out rapidly, and cool, partly shaded positions.

ARISTOLOCHIA (Dutchman's Pipe)

Nearly all aristolochias are climbing plants, the handsomest all requiring greenhouse protection, though there are also several interesting species hardy enough to be planted outdoors. Of these the best is the Dutchman's Pipe, *A. durior*, a vigorous, deciduous climber with large, handsome leaves and curiously shaped flowers from which it derives its popular name. They are tubular, curved, inflated at the mouth, and combine yellow-green with brown. *A. heterophylla* is another, less well-known, species hardy enough to be grown outdoors in the south and west. The flowers have the same curious formation and are yellow with a nearly black mouth. One of the most handsome species is the Calico Flower, *A. elegans* (Plate 2), in which the widely inflated mouth of the flower is white, netted with purple. It needs a moderately heated greenhouse and plenty of room to climb. All species like a fairly rich, loamy soil and a sunny position. They can be raised from seed in a warm greenhouse in spring or by cuttings in summer or early autumn rooted in a warm frame.

ARTEMISIA (Southernwood, Mugwort)

A large and rather confused genus of shrubby, sub-shrubby and herbaceous plants mainly valued for their grey or silvery foliage

Akebia
quinata

Amaranthus
caudatus

Acer
palmatum
'Osakazuki'

Anemone
blanda

Anchusa
caespitosa

Abelia
schumanii

Acidanthera
bicolor
murielae

Adonis vernalis

Anagallis
linifolia
parksii

Alstroemeria
ligtu hybrid

Acantholimon glumaceum

Begonia
semperflorens

Aristolochia
elegans

Azalea
'Hinomayo'

Asperula
arcadiensis

Arenaria
montana

Astrantia major

Aucuba
japonica
[female]

Antennaria
dioica rosea

Argemone
mexicana

Anthurium
andreanum

Aster novi-belgii
'Marie Ballard'

though one kind, *Artemisia lactiflora*, is grown for its fine, plumy sprays of creamy-white flowers in late summer. This is the best of the truly herbaceous species, a perfectly hardy plant, 5 feet high, with green foliage and thriving in semi-shade just as well as it grows in sunnier places.

Most of the grey-leaved kinds are sun lovers and do best in fairly well-drained soils. Typical of these is *A. ludoviciana*, a sub-shrubby plant 2 feet high with silver-grey leaves. It is first rate for the front of the herbaceous border. There are many other kinds, some small enough for the rock garden, and some, such as *A. frigida*, with very much divided, ferny foliage. This finely divided foliage is also seen in the Southernwood, *A. abrotanum*, a rather soft-wooded shrub 3 feet high with aromatic leaves. It likes a sunny place and well-drained soil.

Many artemisias can be increased by division in spring, but those that will not divide must be increased by cuttings of firm young shoots in summer in a propagating frame.

ARUNDINARIA *(Bamboo)*

This is one of the principal genera of hardy bamboos, the other being phyllostachys. There are numerous hardy species differing in height and leaf character. One of the most vigorous is *Arundinaria fastuosa*, a magnificent plant that may reach 20 feet in height in good soil. The canes are stout and strong, the foliage dark, shining green. By contrast *A. vagans* is only a couple of feet high, a dense carpeting plant with narrow leaves. *A. japonica* is of intermediate height, about 10 or 12 feet, with very long leaves and a particularly dense habit. *A. nitida* gets its name from its dark canes which are slender and very freely produced. It is exceptionally hardy as is also *A. murielae*, another very graceful kind. Both are 10 to 12 feet high. *A. auricoma*, a much shorter plant seldom above 4 feet high, has green leaves striped with yellow. *A. palmata* is notable for the great size of its leaves. All these bamboos like fairly good, loamy soils and a position sheltered from cold winds. All will grow in shade and *A. nitida* prefers a shady place and a rather moist soil as it quickly suffers from drought. All can be increased by division in spring and in some it is fairly easy to dig out rooted offsets or suckers but others make such compact clumps that they must be literally chopped into pieces.

ASPERULA *(Woodruff)*

The woodruffs range from rock plants delighting in stony soil and perfect drainage, to low-growing woodland plants that will thrive in any reasonable soil. Typical of the woodlanders and a very charming plant in the right place, is the British *A. odorata* which makes a loose, tumbling mass of growth 8 or 9 inches high, freely decked with fragrant white flower clusters in spring. There is no difficulty about growing it in any cool and shady place. By contrast the mountain species *A. arcadiensis* (Plate 2) and the very similar *A. suberosa* detest dampness and shade and are happiest on a sunny ledge or slope in the rock garden in soil

Arundinaria fastuosa

Asperula odorata

Aster acris

Aster ericoides

liberally mixed with stone chippings. They make spreading tufts of fragile stems set with small leaves densely covered with soft, grey down and bearing in early summer, abundant clusters of baby-pink flowers. They are the kind of plants that need a pane of glass over them in the winter or are, perhaps, best grown throughout in a pan. *A. odorata* can be divided easily, *A. arcadiensis* and *A. suberosa* with more difficulty. Both can be increased from seed sown in spring.

ASTER (*Michaelmas Daisy*)

This great genus of hardy herbaceous perennials has provided plant breeders with some wonderfully malleable material so that, in *A. novi-belgii* in particular, they have been able to develop both the size and the colour of the flowers to such an extent that they appear to have little in common with the wild species from which they are derived. Garden varieties are very numerous and constantly being added to so that names quickly become dated, but Marie Ballard (Plate 2) is typical of the type of large double flower which gardeners appear to have set as their ideal in form. Colours range from white and palest lavender, mauve or pink to violet-blue and crimson, and heights from less than a foot to 6 feet. Almost the only features they may be said to share are glossy foliage and a flowering season in September and October.

By contrast the less numerous varieties of *Aster novae-angliae* have slightly hairy foliage and a tendency to close their flowers at night. All are about 5 feet high and the colour range is confined to pink, rose and purple.

The numerous varieties of *A. amellus* flower a little earlier, in August and the first week or so in September, and all are bushy plants about 2 feet or a little more in height. Moreover, so far this species has not produced any varieties with double flowers. Colours are mainly blue, violet and mauve, for though 'pink' varieties are listed, they are not bright or clear pinks such as are found among the *A. novi-belgii* varieties. *A. amellus* is peculiar, also, in disliking disturbance in the autumn, whereas most other Michaelmas daisies can be moved just as safely in autumn as in spring.

The light lavender-blue *A. frikartii* is similar to *A. amellus* but even more branching and bushy in habit. It also dislikes being transplanted in autumn.

Another useful kind is *A. acris*, an intensely bushy plant with narrow leaves and dense masses of starry lavender-blue flowers. It grows about 2 feet high and will grow in any sunny place. This is true also of the pretty little yellow-flowered *A. linosyris*, a plant often known as Goldilocks. It grows about 18 inches high and flowers in August.

Some of the later asters with small flowers are very useful for mixing with the large-flowered garden varieties to lighten the effect. This is true of *A. ericoides*, a plant with a peculiarly angular method of branching, with small narrow leaves and abundant, though very small, white flowers. It grows 2 to 3 feet tall. *A. cordifolius*, which is nearer 5 feet, has a graceful arching habit and loose sprays of small white, mauve or pale lavender flowers.

The alpine asters are smaller in stature but mostly larger in flower, typical of the group being *A. subcaeruleus* which makes spreading clumps of leaves from which in June arise straight stems of 9 inches or so each terminated by one large violet blue flower. It is a showy and useful plant.

All these perennial asters can be grown in any ordinary soil and many will put up with a certain amount of shade though they prefer an open, sunny situation. They can be increased by division and the vigorous kinds are all the better for being divided annually, or at least every second year, to prevent the individual plants becoming so large that they starve themselves.

ASTRANTIA *(Masterwort)*

Unspectacular hardy herbaceous perennials which nevertheless have a quiet and distinctive beauty entirely their own. The small, pale pink or whitish flowers are crowded into little clusters surrounded by a ruff of papery looking bracts which give them the appearance of tiny Victorian posies. The most familiar kind is *A. major* (Plate 2), a plant 2 feet high with pink flowers more or less suffused with green. *A. carniolica* is not unlike it but rather smaller and more white than pink, and *A. minor* is smaller still, certainly not above 1 foot high, with near-white flowers. All like cool, partially shaded places and are admirable for the front of the border or for edging woodland paths. They can all be increased by division in spring or autumn.

AUCUBA *(Spotted or Variegated Laurel)*

Only one species, *A. japonica* (Plate 2), is commonly grown in this country. At one time it was grossly overplanted in shrubberies and to form hedges, but recently it has been almost completely neglected. It is a laurel-like, evergreen shrub, 6 feet or more high with several varieties one of which has leaves rather unpleasantly spotted with yellow, a characteristic which earned it the name Spotted Laurel. It was the over-planting of this spotted form which gave the aucuba a bad name, but there are other more desirable forms, notably the female plants of the plain green-leaved aucuba which, if planted with an occasional male bush for pollination, will usually produce good crops of bright scarlet fruits in autumn, well set off by the bright green foliage. The aucuba will grow in any soil and place, even under quite large trees and in deep shade. It is an excellent town shrub and will stand any amount of pruning to keep it in shape or within limited bounds. It is very easily increased by cuttings in autumn.

AZALEA

All the azaleas are, botanically, rhododendrons and require similar lime-free soil and cool, partly shaded situations. From a gardening standpoint it is convenient to consider them apart because of their generally much lighter effect. Many are deciduous and those that are evergreen have small leaves.

Most of the popular azaleas are hybrids, often of rather com-

Astrantia carniolica

Aucuba japonica variegata

19

Azalea vaseyi

Azalea schlippenbachii

plex parentage, but they may be roughly grouped into about half-a-dozen main classes.

Largest flowered are the mollis and sinensis azaleas which have been interbred to the point at which it is difficult if not impossible to draw a line between them. They make quite large, freely branched bushes, are deciduous and have clusters of very large flowers, often in brilliant shades of orange, flame or crimson though there are also softer salmons, apricots and yellows. The flowers are very widely funnel shaped and they open in April or early May before the leaves.

The Ghent varieties are also deciduous shrubs but a little later in flowering time so that their flowers open with the leaf buds. The flowers are not quite so large, are less widely opened and more trumpet-shaped and, like the wild yellow *A. lutea*, have the added attractions of fragrance and good autumn foliage colour. The colour range of the flowers is the same as that of the mollis and sinensis azaleas. The varieties known as *rustica flore pleno* are really double flowered forms of the Ghent type.

The kaempferi hybrids are again deciduous and notably free flowering with widely opened flowers, principally in shades of pink, rose, and red and also with good autumn foliage colour.

A. obtusum is an evergreen species usually represented in gardens by the intensely magenta *A. obtusum amoenum*. This is a comparatively dwarf, spreading bush 2 to 3 feet high and usually considerably more through, with small evergreen leaves and very numerous, though individually small, flowers.

All the varieties known as Kurume or Japanese azaleas (Plate 2) are closely related to this and have similar evergreen foliage and small flowers. They are at their peak in May and are grand plants for the rock garden, for the front of a shrub border or the edge of a woodland path. Colours range from white through palest mauve and pink to scarlet and carmine and many have garden names such as Hinomayo and Hinodegiri. They are not quite so hardy as most of the deciduous azaleas.

Yet another group is known as Malvatica hybrids. These are evergreen and small-leaved, but in general they are taller and less spreading in habit than the Kurume azaleas and they have larger flowers. The colour range is similar.

The so-called Indian azaleas are too tender to be grown out-doors and are treated as greenhouse plants. Large numbers are forced each year for the shop trade at Christmas and after and some of these get grown on from year to year, but they are not the easiest of plants to manage as they are grown in almost pure peat or very peaty soil which needs to be watered carefully and, moreover, if they are not kept growing steadily all the spring and early summer, they are apt to miss a season in flowering. They are best outdoors from June to September. The flowers are quite large, usually double and in various shades of pink and red with or without white.

There are, in addition, numerous delightful species such as *A. schlippenbachii*, *A. ledifolium* and *A. vaseyi*. Some of these, and particularly the pale pink *A. schlippenbachii*, have a delightful butterfly grace of flower.

All azaleas like cool, peaty or leafy soils not liable to dry out too quickly in summer. They can be readily raised from seed, but seedlings of the hybrids are likely to vary greatly in colour so that named or selected varieties are more usually increased by cuttings in July in a frame, preferably with bottom heat.

BEGONIA

Of all the numerous kinds of begonia none is more generally useful than the dwarf, fibrous-rooted varieties that are grown from seed for summer bedding. They are all derived either directly or as hybrids from *B. semperflorens* (Plate 2) and many have been given distinguishing garden or 'fancy' names. The colour range has been considerably extended to cover almost everything from white and palest pink to crimson. Height averages 1 foot in the best varieties and some have beetroot-red or coppery-purple foliage as an additional attraction. All are readily raised from seed sown in a temperature of 60° to 65° F. in February or March, the seedlings being pricked off and later hardened off for planting out in early June. They will thrive in sun or partial shade, the one essential being ample moisture. Though the plants are perennial it is more convenient and satisfactory to treat them as annuals and renew from seed each year.

The summer flowering tuberous rooted begonias may also be used for summer bedding but the very large, double-flowered varieties are nearly always grown as greenhouse plants, the individual stems carefully staked and tied to support the weight of the flowers. They can be raised from seed sown, like that of *B. semperflorens*, in a warm greenhouse, but usually a little earlier. There is always some variation in seedlings, however, and for this reason specially selected or 'named' varieties are grown from tubers started into growth in January, February or March in seed boxes filled with peat or leaf mould and later potted individually. They do not need a great deal of heat; about 60° to 65° to start the tubers and then little or no artificial heat as the outside temperature increases. Indeed in summer the problem is rather to keep the atmosphere sufficiently cool and moist than the reverse. In autumn they are allowed to dry off.

The many varieties of *B. rex* are grown for their handsomely marbled and often very large leaves. They like the same cool, rather moist conditions that suit the tuberous rooted begonias, but as their roots are fibrous they have no resting season and must be kept moderately watered even in winter.

That is also true of many other fibrous-rooted greenhouse begonias, some of which are quite as handsome in their way as the *B. rex* varieties. Two of the most popular are *B. socotrana* and *B. manicata*, both with large leaves and small sprays of single pink flowers in winter. These flourish with less warmth than the more showy winter flowering begonias of the Gloire de Lorraine type which are hybrids between *B. socotrana* and a white flowered species named *B. dregei*, and produce an abundance of very

21

Begonia manicata

Begonia haageana

Berberis gagnepainii

Berberis verruculosa

elegant sprays of pink flowers. Other winter flowering races have been raised by crossing *B. socotrana* with summer-flowering tuberous-rooted begonias. Yet another deservedly popular and easily grown fibrous-rooted species is *B. haageana*. It has handsome velvety-green leaves and sprays of pale pink flowers in spring and summer.

The pendulous begonias, so useful for hanging baskets in summer, are simply forms of the tuberous rooted summer flowering begonias and are grown in exactly the same way, except that instead of being potted they are placed in April or May in baskets lined with moss and filled with good potting soil.

BELOPERONE *(Shrimp Plant)*

Beloperone guttata (Plate 3) is a delightful and unusual greenhouse plant that will grow well in a quite moderate temperature and make a good specimen in a 5- or 6-inch pot. The whole plant grows about 18 inches high and the white, purple-spotted flowers are borne in a dense, arching spike. These flowers, however, can scarcely be seen as they are surrounded and almost covered by light, pinkish-brown bracts, produced over a long season in summer. It is easily grown in ordinary John Innes compost in a greenhouse with a minimum winter temperature of 45°F. and in summer no artificial heat is needed. Propagation is by cuttings of firm young shoots and the plant must be watered throughout the year, though much more sparingly in winter than in summer.

BERBERIS *(Barberry)*

This big genus of shrubs includes a number of excellent garden plants some, such as *Berberis aggregata* and *B. wilsonae*, mainly valued for their abundant crops of coral red berries, some, such as *B. darwinii* and *B. stenophylla*, with beauty of foliage and flower as their principal qualifications, and a few, such as *B. thunbergii* and its variety *atropurpurea*, grown mainly for their rich foliage colour. All are hardy and easily grown in any reasonable soil.

The genus can be divided into evergreen and deciduous kinds and it is naturally the evergreens, such as *B. darwinii*, *B. stenophylla*, *B. verruculosa*, *B. gagnepainii*, *B. linearifolia* (Plate 3) and the very similar hybrid *B. lologensis*, that are highly regarded as foliage plants. All these are also very showy in flower, with clusters of small orange or orange-yellow flowers in March and April, at which season they are among the most showy shrubs that are suitable for planting almost anywhere as they are quite hardy and will grow in any reasonable soil.

By and large the deciduous species are far less spectacular in flower but *B. jamesiana* (Plate 3) is capable of making a very good display with its long trails of lemon yellow flowers which are followed by equally long clusters of uncommonly fine green and coral-red fruits. Many of these deciduous species cross readily one with another so that a great many hybrids have also been raised and some of the best have been given names. Like their parents they are all very spiny plants, dense in growth and usually with thin, arching stems.

All these shrubs can be raised from seed and often the deciduous kinds will seed themselves about so that all that is necessary is to lift the seedlings in autumn and transfer them to a nursery bed. Cuttings of firm young growth will also root in a propagating frame in July and this is the way in which all the hybrids should be increased as they may vary considerably from seed.

BETONICA *(Betony)*

The common betony is a British wild plant, showy enough with its red-purple flowers in summer but too widespread to be worth transplanting to the garden. But *Betonica grandiflora* (Plate 3) from Asia Minor is certainly worth consideration for the front of the herbaceous border for it is like a giant betony with bolder foliage and larger flowers. It is perfectly hardy, very easily grown in any ordinary soil and open position and it will flower for several weeks immediately after midsummer.

There are several colour forms ranging from reddish purple to violet and there is said to be a white variety but I have not seen it. This fine betony is not seen anything like so much as it deserves. Propagation is by division in spring or autumn.

BILLBERGIA

Although in nature these handsome tropical plants are epiphytes, that is they grow perched up on the limbs or trunks of trees with their roots suspended in the air, in cultivation they are mostly grown as normal pot plants, though in a rather peaty or leafy compost. The most popular is *B. nutans* (Plate 3), a plant with long narrow saw-edged leaves and gracefully arching flower spikes bearing nodding green and blue flowers and red bracts. It is an unusual and arresting colour scheme. This billbergia is so easily grown that it is often used as a house plant. It will grow quite happily in a cool greenhouse, only needing sufficient artificial heat to exclude frost, but equally it is quite ready to enjoy much higher temperatures. It should be watered fairly freely in spring and summer, rather sparingly in winter. Potting is best done in March and offsets or suckers can then be removed carefully and potted separately if more stock is required. An attractive hybrid from this easy growing plant, with *B. decora* as its other parent, is named *B. windii* and is notable for its near-crimson bracts. It is, if anything, an even more handsome plant than *B. nutans* and requires much the same treatment but appreciates a little more warmth.

BOUVARDIA

Tender evergreen shrubs with fragrant flowers (Plate 3), produced during the autumn and winter. They are not difficult to grow and used to be very popular, but the fact that they need a winter temperature around 60°F. is against them under present economic conditions.

Billbergia windii

Bouvardia 'Alfred Nenner'

Brassavola digbyana

Brassocattleya hybrid

Bouvardias can be grown from both stem and root cuttings, the former being more often employed. They are prepared from young shoots in March or April, rooted in small pots in a propagating frame with bottom heat and a temperature around 70°. When rooted and a little hardened, the cuttings are potted singly and moved on as they require it. From mid-summer until mid-September the plants are as happy in a frame as in a greenhouse, but must be returned to the house before there is any risk of frost. It is best to pinch out the points of shoots occasionally to produce a more bushy habit. The plants must be kept watered and growing well all winter and, after flowering, can be pruned back fairly severely, partly to keep them compact, partly to encourage the production of strong young shoots for cuttings.

Despite their names, some of which might suggest that they are species, all the garden bouvardias appear to be hybrids. Good kinds are *jasminiflora*, white, Alfred Nenner, double white, President Garfield, double pink and Dazzler, scarlet.

BRASSAVOLA

These hot-house orchids have many points in common with the better known and more popular cattleyas and are grown in exactly the same way. There are not many species, the most important from the garden standpoint being *Brassavola digbyana*, a plant with very large white, or greenish-white flowers remarkable both for their fragrance and for the heavily fringed lip which gives the flower an extremely handsome and distinctive appearance. This fine orchid flowers in summer.

BRASSOCATTLEYA

These very opulent looking orchids are bi-generic hybrids between brassavola and cattleya. From the first parent they have acquired a fringe to the large lower petal, or labellum, and the second parent has given them rich colourings. Cultivation is exactly as for cattleya. The huge and richly coloured flowers of the brassocattleyas are much sought after by florists and are certainly among the most handsome of the whole orchid family.

BRUNFELSIA

Tropical evergreen shrubs of which only one is at all commonly grown in British greenhouses. This is *Brunfelsia calycina* (Plate 3), a neat bushy plant bearing fine violet blue flowers almost throughout the year. The flowers are, in fact, tubular but the tube is so narrow and is so widely folded back at the mouth that the casual impression is of a nearly flat flower a good 2 inches in diameter. This brunfelsia can be grown as a pot plant or planted out in good, rich soil in the greenhouse border. It likes a fairly warm temperature with a minimum of 50°F. even in winter and something nearer 60° in spring and summer. It should be watered freely in spring and summer, much more sparingly in autumn and winter though at no season should it be permitted to become dry. It can be increased by cuttings of young shoots in spring in a propagating frame with bottom heat.

BRUNNERA

The plant often known in gardens as *Anchusa myosotidiflora* is, according to botanists, *Brunnera macrophylla*. It is a hardy herbaceous plant, low growing and sprawling, with rather big coarse leaves and loose sprays of blue flowers very like forget-me-nots. Its twin merits are that it flowers early in spring and will grow practically anywhere in sun or shade. It is useful for the front row of the herbaceous border or may be naturalized in thin woodland. It is easily increased by division immediately after flowering.

BUDDLEIA

The purple buddleia, *B. davidii*, is everyone's favourite and one of the easiest shrubs to grow, but the very distinctive *B. alternifolia* is nothing like so well known despite the elegance of its habit. Instead of the rather stout, erect or spreading stems of the purple buddleia it has thin, wiry stems which arch over and hang down. Moreover, the small purple flowers, produced in June, instead of being crowded into large, pointed spikes, are strung out along almost the whole length of these thin stems, giving them the appearance of lengths of purple braid. It can be grown as a natural bush 12 feet or more high, but looks even better if run up on a short main stem like a half-standard tree, with a big head of branches, as this permits the weeping habit to be fully developed. It should be thinned a little after flowering.

Equally distinctive and different from the popular idea of a buddleia is *B. globosa* with small, quite globular orange-yellow flower heads in early summer. They look for all the world like little orange-yellow balls suspended on the branches. This species is even more apt to become gaunt and open in habit than some varieties of *B. davidii* and it is very desirable to prune it back quite a lot each year immediately after flowering to keep it in shape. There is also a hybrid (*B. weyeriana*) between this species and *B. davidii* in which the flowers are intermediate both in form and colour. It is a variable plant and some forms are better than others, but none is, in my view, really attractive.

A most interesting and beautiful species for the more favoured parts of the country is *B. colvillei*, a very tall shrub with pendent clusters of quite large maroon-purple flowers. It is quite unlike any of the other species but unfortunately it is also much more tender so that it can only be grown in the mildest places.

All buddleias are easily satisfied as regards soil, prefering those that are well drained to the point of dryness. All can be readily raised from half-ripe or ripe cuttings and also from seed.

BULBOCODIUM

There is only one species, *Bulbocodium vernum* (Plate 3), and this is an attractive little spring flowering plant, much like a crocus in appearance, with purple flowers before the narrow leaves appear. It also resembles a crocus in making corms which should be planted in autumn 2 or 3 inches deep in any light soil, and a

Brunnera macrophylla

Buddleia colvillei

Caladium hybrid

Calanthe bella

warm sunny position. It can be increased by division of the clusters of corms.

BUTOMUS *(Flowering Rush)*

Butomus umbellatus (Plate 3) has been described as the most beautiful British wild plant and it is certainly impressive when well established near the bank of a stream, canal or pool. The leaves are rush-like and the stiff, 3 to 4 foot flower stems terminate in a loose head of fine pink flowers in July and August. Being a native it is a plant of unquestionable hardiness and can be easily grown in any open, sunny place. It likes best to have its crown covered by 2 to 3 inches of water and should be planted in April or May. It can be increased by division at planting time.

CAESALPINIA

Three species are suitable for planting outdoors in the milder parts of the country and all are extremely handsome. Two of them, *C. japonica* (Plate 3) and *C. sepiaria*, are so much alike that there is doubt as to whether they really are distinct species. Both are very vigorous, sprawling or climbing shrubs fiercely armed with large thorns and carrying in June and July large, erect sprays of bright yellow, or yellow and red, flowers. The third hardy, or nearly hardy, caesalpinia is *C. gilliesii*, a shrub or small tree 20 feet or more high where it can be grown without suffering frost damage and with deep yellow flowers enlivened by scarlet stamens in July and August.

All these plants require sun, warmth and good drainage. It may be necessary to protect them with sacks or bracken in winter, and weather-damaged growth should be removed each spring. A position near the foot of a sunny, sheltered wall may prove most desirable, especially for a border-line species such as *C. gilliesii*. Propagation is by seed sown in a greenhouse in spring or by layering in late spring.

CALADIUM

Tropical American plants grown for the beauty of their large shield-shaped leaves (Plate 3). These are coloured in many ways, usually with white, silver, green and pink in various combinations. They have tuberous roots or rhizomes which need to be rested in autumn, when watering can be discontinued and the plants stored in a warm, dry place until March. From then onwards they should be grown in a warm greenhouse (temperature 65°F. or more) with plenty of water both at the roots and in the air. This will involve daily syringing in summer besides frequent damping down and shading from direct sunshine. March is the best month for potting and the compost should be fairly rich and contain plenty of peat. Propagation is by seeds sown in a temperature of 75° in spring.

CALANTHE

Lovely and unusual orchids with long, slender spikes of flowers. Two of the most popular are *C. vestita* (Plate 3) and *C. veitchii*, the first with white and red flowers in November and December, the second with rose coloured flowers in January and February. There is also a very beautiful rose-pink hybrid named *C. bella*. *C. veratrifolia* has pure white flowers with a yellow crest on the lip and is not in flower before spring. The conical pseudo-bulbs of all these are striking in appearance and silvery in colour and the leaves die down before the flower spikes appear. These are terrestial orchids which should be grown in a compost of loam, peat or leaf-mould and sphagnum moss in about equal parts. Potting is best done in March and from then on plants should be kept watered and syringed, and shaded as the sun gains power. When the leaves die down, far less water will be needed and none at all from the time the flowers fade until new growth is seen to be starting in spring. Calanthes do not require high temperatures—around 50°F. in winter rising to 60°, or more with sun heat, in spring and summer.

CALCEOLARIA *(Slipper Flower)*

It is the greenhouse calceolarias, varieties of the hybrid *Calceolaria herbeohybrida* (Plate 4), that have been most developed in gardens. Not only has the size of the pouch-like flowers been greatly increased and the colour range extended, but also height and habit have been varied. There are now dwarf and compact races as well as large and spreading ones, so that the needs of the small greenhouse can be as readily met as those of larger ones. The cultivation of all is the same. Seed sown in early summer will give plants to flower the following spring. Throughout treatment should be cool and airy with a minimum winter temperature of 45°F. and shade in summer from all strong, direct sunshine. Although the plants are perennial, they are invariably treated as annuals and are discarded after flowering. Watering is the most tricky part of their cultivation as, though they like plenty of moisture at the roots, they do not like to be wet at the base of the leaves and care should be taken not to let water run down the leaves so that it collects in the crowns.

The bedding calceolarias, varieties of *C. integrifolia*, are very different in habit and treatment. If left to themselves in a sufficiently mild climate they would make shrubby plants several feet in height and even when annually renewed from cuttings, as they are for bedding, they show something of their shrubby habit. The pouched yellow or reddish-brown flowers are individually small but freely produced throughout the summer and plants will thrive in partially shaded as well as fully sunny places. Cuttings will root readily in a frame in late summer and young plants produced in this way are unlikely to exceed 18 inches.

There are also some interesting hardy species for the rock garden, notably *C. darwinii*, a lovely little plant, no more than 6 inches high with quite large yellow and chestnut-red flowers in summer. It likes cool, leafy soil and a sheltered place as does tufted *C. polyrrhiza* with yellow flowers spotted with purple. Both these can be increased by division in spring. *C. mexicana*, with clusters of pale yellow flowers on 9-inch stems is a hardy annual for a warm corner.

Calceolaria mexicana

Calceolaria darwinii

27

Callirhoe pedata

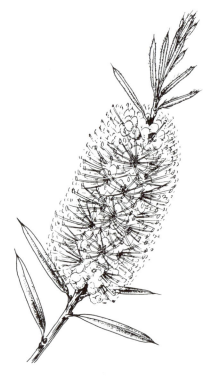

Callistemon salignus

CALLA *(Water Arum)*

The only species grown, *Calla palustris* (Plate 4), resembles a small arum lily with greenish white spathes on 9-inch stems. It is hardy enough to be planted outdoors in bog gardens or the very damp soil at the margins of pools or streams. It will not object if its crowns are actually submerged in an inch or so of water and it is of perfectly easy culture, soon spreading into a good clump of glossy leaves and being readily increased by division in the spring.

CALLIRHOE *(Poppy Mallow)*

Very showy plants which need a sunny place and porous, well-drained soil if they are to thrive. There are both annual and perennial kinds, the most important being *C. involucrata* (Plate 4), a foot high perennial with brilliant magenta flowers 2 inches or more across, produced for many weeks in summer. It is a native of Texas and Mexico and is imperfectly hardy, for which reason it is often grown as a half-hardy annual, no attempt being made to save it after flowering. Seed, in any case, provides the most satisfactory means of increasing it and is best sown in a warm greenhouse in March. Seedlings should be pricked off into boxes and hardened off for planting out in late May. The same treatment suits the truly annual *C. pedata* with crimson flowers.

CALLISTEMON *(Bottle Brush)*

These evergreen Australian shrubs or small trees are remarkable for the unusual formation of their flowers which have very long stamens, rather like bristles, and are crowded into dense spikes which have the appearance of highly coloured bottle brushes. Most are on the borderline of hardiness, which means that they can be grown outdoors only in a few very sheltered and mild gardens, particularly in Cornwall and the extreme west. Elsewhere they must be grown in frost-proof greenhouses, no artificial heat being required except in cold weather to keep out frost.

The species most frequently seen are *C. coccineus*, red and yellow, *C. salignus*, yellow, *C. citrinus*, also known as *C. lanceolatus*, red, its improved crimson form *splendens* (Plate 4), and *C. speciosus* which is deep red with yellow stamens. Callistemons will grow in any reasonable soil and need no regular pruning except when grown in pots, when it is desirable to cut them back a little after flowering to prevent them growing too big. They make good pot plants provided they can be given room, but are even better if they can be planted directly in a bed of soil in the greenhouse, so that they can develop freely and make bushes.

Propagation is by seeds sown in a temperature of 60°F. in spring or by cuttings of ripe one year shoots in autumn, rooted in a propagating frame.

CALLISTEPHUS *(China Aster)*

The annual plants which most gardeners know as China asters, in fact belong to the genus callistephus. There are many different types, the most popular being the Ostrich Plume (Plate 4), with large double flowers composed of a shaggy mass of narrow petals, the Comet (Plate 4), which is also double but has a smoother, more regular, better groomed flower, the Pompon which resembles the Comet but is far smaller both in size of plant and of flower, and the Singles which have but one row of petals to their yellow centred daisy flowers. In all these classes the colour range is from white, pale pink and pale mauve to crimson and royal purple. All are grown from seed, which is best sown in late March or early April in a cool greenhouse or frame (temperature 50° to 55° F). Seedlings need plenty of light and ventilation to prevent damping-off disease. They should be pricked off early into fairly deep seed boxes and hardened off for planting out in late May. They will thrive in sun or partial shade and should be planted at least 1 foot apart. Alternatively the single asters may be sown early in May where they are to flower, the seedlings being thinned to from 9 to 12 inches apart. All flower in late summer and early autumn.

CALLUNA *(Heather)*

The common heather, often known as the Scotch heather, is not a species of erica, but a calluna, its name being *C. vulgaris*. It is variable in colour, flower, form and habit, quite hardy and easily grown in almost any lime-free soil. The common wild type is light purple and 2 to 3 feet high, but there are garden varieties ranging from white and pale pink to crimson. Two forms have unusually coloured leaves; *aurea*, yellow and *cuprea*, yellow turning to bronze. One variety, *foxii*, is almost completely prostrate. From the garden standpoint one of the most valuable forms is H. E. Beale (Plate 4) which is heather-pink and has double flowers crowded up rather tall, erect stems. Because of their substance and lack of sexual organs, the flowers last exceptionally well.

Callunas like sunny, open places and well-drained, lime-free soils. They benefit from annual trimming with shears after flowering in late summer and early autumn. They can be propagated by layering in May or by cuttings of firm young shoots in July rooted in sand or very sandy soil in a frame.

CALOCHORTUS *(Mariposa Lily)*

Elegant and unusual perennials which thrive best in sunny, sheltered places and well-drained soils. Alternatively they may be treated as pot plants for the unheated or slightly heated greenhouse. They form corms which should be planted a couple of inches deep in March or April. The showy flowers are a little like small, wide-open tulips. Later the foliage dies down and then the corms should be lifted and stored in a dry, frost proof place like those of the gladiolas. Colours are varied and flowers are often streaked or spotted with one colour on another; purple or rose on a base of cream or white being common combinations. Flower stems are usually about 2 feet high though some dwarf kinds do not exceed 6 inches. The best known

Callistephus sinensis (Ostrich Plume)

Calluna foxii nana

Calochortus venustus

Camassia esculenta

species is *Calochortus venustus*. Propagation is easily effected by the natural multiplication of the corms which can be separated when they are lifted in the autumn.

CALYCANTHUS *(Allspice)*

Deciduous shrubs of which the best for garden planting is *Calycanthus floridus* (Plate 4), the Carolina Allspice. This makes a rather loose, spreading shrub 5 to 6 feet high and more in diameter, with fragrant, dull reddish-purple flowers in June and July. It is by no means a showy shrub, but it is an interesting and rather unusual one and it has the added attraction of aromatic branches and leaves. Although it comes from the warm south-eastern states of the U.S.A. it is reasonably hardy provided it can be given a sunny, fairly sheltered situation. It likes a good, rich, loamy soil, needs no regular pruning and can be increased by layering in May or June or by natural suckers in autumn.

CAMASSIA

Attractive but little known herbaceous perennials with bulbous roots, rosettes of narrow, sword-shaped leaves and stiff spikes of flowers. *C. cusickii* (Plate 4), *C. esculenta* and *C. quamash* all follow the same general pattern and have soft blue or greyish-blue flowers. They are easily grown in almost any soil and reasonably open position and are readily increased by division of the bulb clusters in autumn. All flower in early summer and are between 2 and 3 feet in height. Though not by any means spectacular plants they are worthy of a place in the herbaceous border because they are so very different from anything else in flower at their season.

CAMELLIA

In addition to the many varieties of *C. japonica*, some of which have been in cultivation for a hundred years and more, there are more recent hybrids, some of great beauty. Among the most useful of these are those raised by crossing *C. japonica* and *C. saluenensis* which have been given the general name of *C. williamsii*. Typically these have single, broadly funnel-shaped flowers in shades of pink, but there are also several magnificent double-flowered varieties of which Donation (Plate 4) is one of the best. It has very large, bright pink flowers in late winter and early spring. Salutation is not unlike it but has different parentage, being the result of a cross between *C. reticulata* and *C. saluenensis*.

C. sasanqua is another very beautiful shrub with large, single white or blush-pink flowers which have the grace of a wild rose and are produced in late autumn and winter. Because of its flowering season it should be given a specially sheltered situation. There are now a number of named varieties of *C. sasanqua* differing in colour as well as in size and form of flowers.

All these camellias thrive under the same conditions as *C. japonica*, namely in slightly acid soils well provided with humus. None will tolerate lime. They make excellent companions for rhododendrons and, like them, appreciate light shade such as may be found in open woodland, though they can also be grown in full sun provided the soil does not dry out too much in summer. All are evergreen and can be increased by cuttings of firm young shoots in July or by well-developed leaves cut off with an axillary growth bud and a slip of stem. Such cuttings or leaves should be inserted in peat and sand in a close but not heated frame.

CAMPANULA *(Bellflower)*

In addition to the many excellent species of campanula, which range from prostrate plants for the rock garden to tall plants for the herbaceous border, there are a number of garden forms that have special qualifications for consideration. One such is the variety of *C. lactiflora* known as Loddon Anna (Plate 4), a 5-foot tall herbaceous perennial with fine, pyramidal sprays of flowers differing from those of the wild species in being soft mauve instead of pale blue. It is a plant that will thrive in shade, as well as in sun, and it flowers in July and August. Then there are numerous garden varieties of *C. persicifolia*, all 2 or 3 feet high and June to July flowering, but differing in colour and some with double instead of single flowers. Excellent examples are Telham Beauty, lavender blue, Blue Bell, deep blue, Delft Blue, double-flowered lavender blue, and Fleur de Neige, double-flowered white.

An excellent plant for the front of the herbaceous border is *C. glomerata* which bears its light violet flowers in clusters on the top of 18-inch stems. This, too, has improved garden varieties such as *dahurica* (Plate 4) in which the flowers are both larger and a deeper, more intense violet-purple. *C. glomerata* flowers in June and July.

The rather stiff *C. latiloba* (*grandis*) has a deeper blue garden form known as Highcliffe Variety. It grows 3 feet high, flowers in June-July and, like its parent, will thrive almost anywhere.

There are also numerous good varieties of the rock garden campanulas and several fine hybrids. The 9-inch high *C. carpatica* with big, erect, cup-shaped flowers, has a deep violet-blue form named Mrs de Frere, a very light china blue variety named Chewton Joy and a white variety, Alanah.

The dwarf, fairylike *C. cochlearifolia* (*pusilla* and also *bellardii*) has several varieties such as Miranda, china blue, and alba, white.

An old and much admired form of the prostrate, starry-flowered *C. garganica* is W. H. Paine. It differs from the soft blue type in being a deeper colour and having a white eye to each flower.

Two fine hybrids for the rock garden are Birch Hybrid, the result of a cross between the truly bell-flowered *C. portenschlagiana* and the more starry, looser growing *C. poscharskyana*, and *C. stansfieldii*, a neat, 6-inch plant with hanging pale violet bells, which is said to have *C. carpatica* and *C. waldsteiniana* for its parents.

All these rock garden campanulas thrive in sun or partial shade and any reasonable soil. Almost all perennial campanulas,

Camellia sasanqua 'Tojo'

Camellia japonica 'Adolphe Audusson'

Campanula garganica

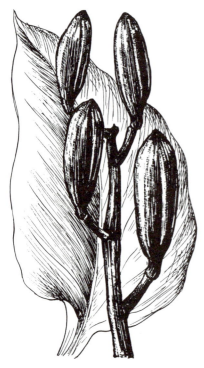

Cardiocrinum giganteum (seed pods)

rock or herbaceous, can be increased by division in spring and the species can also be raised very readily from seed sown in a greenhouse or frame in spring. The hybrids and selected garden forms are unlikely to breed entirely true from seed though the variations obtained may be pleasing.

CAMPSIS *(Trumpet Creeper, Trumpet Flower)*

These not-too-hardy, deciduous climbers have suffered from a multiplicity of botanical names, having been at different times known as *Bigonia*, *Tecoma* and, most recently, *Campsis*. They are all vigorous and immensely showy plants, common in the Mediterranean region where their scarlet, orange or yellow trumpet-shaped flowers are to be seen on many a sunny wall. In Britain they need all the sun and shelter they can be given if they are to flower freely each August and September. The hardiest kind is *Campsis radicans* with scarlet and orange flowers but, good though it is, it is surpassed in beauty by *C. chinensis*, better known as *grandiflora* (Plate 5), which has even larger flowers. Hybrids between these two species have been raised and distributed under the collective name *C. tagliabuana*. They are variable and not all equally good but the form known as Madame Galen is almost as handsome as *C. chinensis* itself. *T. radicans* will support itself by aerial roots like an ivy but *T. grandiflora* must be tied to wires or a trellis. Both should be pruned each winter, when all long, young shoots made the previous year should be cut back to within two or three buds of the older wood. They can be increased by layering in May or June.

CARDIOCRINUM

The giant Himalayan woodland lilies used to be classified as *Lilium* along with the true lilies, but have now been given a separate genus of their own with the name *Cardiocrinum*. In consequence the plant that most gardeners know as *Lilium giganteum* now becomes *Cardiocrinum giganteum* (Plate 5). There is something to be said for this change on horticultural as well as botanical grounds because these giant lilies differ in their cultural requirements from the ordinary lilies in several important points. For one thing the bulb dies after flowering, leaving as a rule, offset bulbs to carry on. In order to get the best results these offset bulbs must be lifted when the parent bulb has flowered and be replanted with plenty of space so that each has a good chance to grow on and, in three or four years time, produce a towering spike of white trumpet flowers. This transplanting is best done in the autumn before the ground gets too cold and wet.

C. giganteum grows 6 or 12 feet high and flowers in July or August. It likes to grow in thin woodland, in deep, rich, leafy soil which can, with advantage, be enriched with manure. The bulbs must not be planted deeply like most lilies, but should be just covered with soil. They should be widely spaced—at least 2 feet apart.

There are two other species, *C. cordatum* and *C. cathayanum*, neither quite so tall nor so imposing as *C. giganteum* for which

Calanthe
vestita

Bulbocodium
vernum

Billbergia
nutans

Berberis
jamesiana

Butomus
umbellatus

Beloperone
guttata

Caesalpinia
japonica

Betonica
grandiflora

Caladium bicolor
[garden form]

Bouvardia
hybrida

Berberis
linearifolia

Brunfelsia
calycina

Camellia
williamsii
'Donation'

Calceolaria
herbeohybrida

Callistemon
citrinus
splendens

Campanula
lactiflora
'Loddon Anna'

Calluna
vulgaris
'H.E. Beale'

Callistephus chinensis
Ostrich Plume

Comet

Campanula
glomerata
dahurica

Camassia
cusickii

Calycanthus floridus

Callirhoe
involucrata

Calla
palustri

reason, no doubt, they have never been so freely planted.

Cardiocrinums can be increased by the offsets naturally produced or by seed sown in a frame or greenhouse in spring.

CARPENTARIA

The only species, *Carpentaria californica* (Plate 5), is an exceptionally lovely but none too hardy, evergreen shrub, 6 feet or a little more in height, bushy in habit and with fine white flowers, each with a golden boss of anthers in the centre. It is one of the best evergreen shrubs in flower around midsummer, comparable in this respect with the eucryphias and, like them, requiring a sheltered and sunny position. It is not fussy about soil provided drainage is reasonably good. No regular pruning is either necessary or desirable. It can be raised from seed sown in a greenhouse or frame in spring.

CASSIA *(Senna)*

Though there are a great many sennas, some shrubby, some herbaceous and all tender, only one has been much grown in Britain. This is *Cassia corymbosa* (Plate 5), one of the showiest of shrubs for a cool greenhouse. It is evergreen, rather loose in habit and about 10 feet in height. Often in the greenhouse it is treated almost as a climber, being trained against a back wall or encouraged to grow up under the rafters where it can display its magnificent sprays of bright yellow flowers for many weeks in summer and early autumn. It is not difficult to grow, requiring only sufficient heat to keep out frost in winter and, if grown in large pots, it can actually be stood outdoors in a sunny, sheltered place from June to September, but really it is seen to best advantage if planted permanently in a bed of good, well-drained soil in the greenhouse. It should be watered freely in summer, sparingly in winter and should be pruned in January sufficiently to keep it in good shape or prevent it from occupying more space than can be spared. It is increased by cuttings of half-ripened shoots in June or July in a propagating frame.

CATALPA *(Indian Bean Tree)*

Deciduous trees notable for their large leaves, showy erect flower clusters, which bear a superficial resemblance to those of a horse chestnut, and their broadly spreading habit which makes them useful shade trees. The best for general planting is *C. bignonioides*, known as the Indian Bean Tree. It is usually about 20-30 feet high, but may be 30 to 40 feet in width. The leaves are light green (yellowish-green in the variety *aurea*) and are specially large if the branches are pruned back fairly severely each winter, treatment which also greatly restricts the tree in size. The flowers appear in July and August and are white speckled with purple and yellow.

This fine tree thrives well in town as well as country gardens. It likes a good, loamy soil and a warm, fairly sheltered but sunny place. It can be raised fairly rapidly from seed sown in a greenhouse or frame in spring but the golden-leaved form does not

C

Catalpa bignonioides

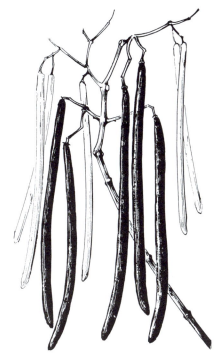

Catalpa bignonioides (seed pods)

Cattleya hybrid

Centaurea babylonica

come true from seed and must be raised from cuttings in July in a warm frame.

CATTLEYA

In some ways these are the most opulent looking of all orchids; large and often richly coloured flowers which last well when cut and are, therefore, much in demand for floristry. The cattleyas are epiphytes, which means that they grow with their roots mainly in the air rather than in soil. In cultivation they are usually grown in pots liberally supplied with drainage and filled with a mixture of three parts of chopped sphagnum moss and two parts of osmunda fibre with a little charcoal to assist in keeping it sweet. Potting is done as growth starts in spring or early summer. A minimum temperature of 55° F. is needed even in winter and it can rise considerably in summer, provided the atmosphere is kept moist and the plants are shaded from direct sunlight. Water must be given moderately in spring, rather freely in summer and sparingly after flowering, at which period the plants rest for a time. There are cattleyas to bloom at almost every month of the year. The flowers are usually white and purple or mauve with yellow markings, but there are also pure white forms. A great many of the most popular kinds are hybrids but there are also a number of good species such as *Cattleya gigas* with lilac-rose and purple flowers in July; *C. citrina*, yellow in colour and summer flowering; *C. gaskelliana*. which may be purple-violet or white and flowers in late summer; *C. labiata* with rose-lilac and purple or white and purple flowers in autumn; *C. trianae*, in many variations of pink, purple and yellow, all winter flowering, and *C. mossiae* (Plate 5) another extremely variable plant in flower during May and June.

CELASTRUS

Vigorous twining deciduous climbing plants grown for their showy fruits in autumn. The best species is *Celastrus orbiculatus* (Plate 5), often known as *C. articulatus*, and the small, green fruits give no hint of their beauty until they ripen and split open in autumn to reveal the scarlet seeds against the bright yellow interior coat of the fruit. It is a plant of the easiest culture in any reasonably good soil. It will soon scramble up a tree or drape itself over quite a large shed and the only difficulty is that plants frequently produce flowers of one sex only, some being all male, some all female. Only the females will produce fruit and then only if there is a male somewhere in the vicinity to provide pollen. As celastrus is usually raised from seed and seedlings will vary in sex, there is often no means of knowing what sex one is planting until flowers are produced. There is also a hermaphrodite variety, which should be obtained if possible. Celastrus needs no regular pruning.

CENTAUREA *(Cornflower, Sweet Sultan)*

The Common Cornflower, *Centaurea cyanus*, is a hardy annual easily raised from seed sown in spring or early autumn where the plants are to flower. It is perfectly hardy, loves sun and does not mind rather poor, sandy soils. There are pink and white as well as the familiar blue varieties and also dwarf varieties as well as those of the normal 3 to 4 foot height.

Rather more difficult to grow well is the Sweet Sultan, *C. moschata* (Plate 5). Although classed as a hardy annual it is not so tough as the cornflower and needs a sunny, rather warm place and a well drained though not poor soil, if it is to do well. There are numerous colours and the flowers are excellent for cutting. Plants may be had in flower throughout the summer by successional sowing, as for cornflower, and they grow about 18 inches high.

There are, in addition, a number of useful herbaceous perennial cornflowers all quite hardy and ranging from the 18-inch, blue or white flowered, *C. montana*, to the 6-or 7-foot, yellow flowered *C. babylonica*, a very handsome plant for the back of the herbaceous border. Other attractive perennials are *C. dealbata*, pink flowered and 2 feet high, *C. ruthenica*, rather taller and yellow flowered, and *C. macrocephala* with larger yellow flowers.

All these perennials are summer flowering and easily increased by division in spring or autumn. In addition there are several slightly tender perennial kinds grown not for their flowers but for their white or silvery-grey foliage. These are *C. cineraria*, *C. gymnocarpa* and *C. ragusina* and all three are much used in summer bedding schemes for which purpose they are usually raised from spring or autumn cuttings in greenhouse or frame and are given protection against frost in winter.

CERCIS *(Judas Tree)*

By far the best cercis, and the only one at all freely planted in this country, is *Cercis siliquastrum* (Plate 5). This is a delightful small tree, very graceful in leaf and with clusters of small purplish-red, pea-type flowers in May and early June. It is in every way an admirable tree for the smaller garden and should be planted more freely in the warmer parts of the country. It grows about 20 feet high and makes a good, branching head of rather thin branches. It likes a sunny place and well-drained soil, needs no regular pruning and should be raised from seed sown in spring in a greenhouse or frame. Seedlings usually show some variation in the colour and size of their flowers so when buying trees it is just as well to see them in flower first.

CESTRUM

Tender or half-hardy shrubs and climbing plants with clusters of hanging, tubular flowers. *C. aurantiacum* (Plate 5) is typical. It climbs to a height of 8 or 10 feet, produces its orange-yellow flowers in late winter, and will succeed in a moderately heated greenhouse, minimum winter temperature of 45°F. *C. newellii* is rather more hardy and will grow outdoors in some very sheltered places in Britain though it is more frequently treated as a cool greenhouse climber. It will reach 10 feet or thereabouts and has very showy crimson flowers in spring. Both plants will grow

Centaurea montana

Cestrum newellii

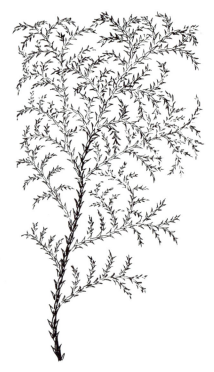

Chamaecyparis pisifera plumosa

in any reasonable soil, like sun and need no regular pruning. They can be raised from cuttings of the young growths struck in a propagating frame with bottom heat.

CHAMAECYPARIS *(False Cypress)*

Evergreen conifers all of which are better known to gardeners as Cupressus, a name now restricted to a few species only such as *Cupressus macrocarpa* and *C. arizonica*. There are three very popular species of chamaecyparis, *C. lawsoniana*, *C. obtusa* and *C. pisifera*, and each has produced a great number of garden forms differing in habit, leaf form and leaf colour.

Typically *C. lawsoniana* is a tall, conical tree with small green leaves on frond-like branchlets. Some forms, such as *allumii* and *erecta viridis*, are narrower and more columnar in habit; some, such as Triomphe de Boskoop are blue grey; others such as *stewartii* are golden yellow; others, such as *fletcheri* are very slow growing and take years to reach a height of 10 feet; yet others, such as *filifera* and *pendula*, are weeping in habit. A few, such as *ellwoodii* and *minima*, can be grown in the rock garden.

C. obtusa does not grow as fast or make as large a tree but it has a more feathery appearance. There are several very handsome golden-leaved forms, such as *crippsii* and *aurea*, and a few really dwarf varieties, such as *minima*, *lycopodioides* and *pygmaea*, which are suitable for the rock garden.

C. pisifera is not as good a tree in its wild form but it has produced some delightful garden varieties one of which, *plumosa aurea*, is outstanding as a feathery, golden-leaved tree of moderate size. Another variety, *filifera*, is remarkable for the cord-like appearance of its branchlets. It seldom exceeds 6 feet, is spreading in habit and has golden forms.

All these False Cypresses are hardy and easily grown. All can be clipped and some make excellent hedges, best for this purpose being *C. lawsoniana* and some of its forms. The wild species can be raised from seeds but garden forms are usually grafted though they can also be raised from cuttings.

CHIASTOPHYLLUM

The showy, yellow-flowered rock plant which most gardeners know as *Cotyledon simplicifolia* (Plate 7) is, in fact, *Chiastophyllum oppositifolium*. It is a succulent for warm, well-drained places as in a sunny dry wall or crevice. The drooping spikes of yellow flowers are borne in May and June. Increase is by division in spring.

CHLOROPHYTUM

The plants now known by this name will be more familiar to many gardeners by their former name, antericum. They are foliage plants for the greenhouse or dwelling house, with long narrow leaves usually striped with white or cream in the varieties favoured by gardeners. The most popular is *Chlorophytum capense variegatum* (Plate 5) but *C. comosum variegatum* is also a handsome plant, well worth growing. Both will thrive in ordin-

Chamaecyparis pisifera filifera

Cestrum
aurantiacum

Cardiocrinum giganteum

Celastrus
orbiculatus

Chlorophytum
capense
variegatum

Centaurea
moschata

Campsis
grandiflora

Cercis
siliquastrum

Carpenteria
californica

Cattleya
mossiae

Cassia
corymbosa

Clematis
macropetala

Chrysanthemum
[Korean]

Clematis
florida
bicolor

Cissus
discolor

Coelogyne cristata

Chrysanthemum
[anemone centred]

Clematis
tangutica

Codonopsis ovata

Clethra
delavayi

Codiaeum
variegatum
pictum

Cistus
purpureus

Chrysanthemum carinatum
[garden forms]

Cimicifuga
racemosa

C. Newsome-Taylor.

ary John Innes compost. They need frost protection in winter but otherwise have a wide tolerance of temperature. They should be shaded from direct sunlight in summer, watered freely during spring and summer, and frequently syringed to maintain a damp atmosphere (this will not be possible, of course, in a dwelling house). In winter they should be watered moderately. Propagation is by division in March, the best month for potting.

CHRYSANTHEMUM

In addition to the many different groups of large or medium-flowered chrysanthemums, which are the most popular with exhibitors and cut-flower growers, there are several groups of small-flowered chrysanthemums which make excellent garden plants. Among these are the Korean chrysanthemums (Plate 6), which are sufficiently hardy to be left outdoors in winter. They produce large, freely branched sprays of flowers in late summer and autumn, typically single though there are also double-flowered varieties. They can be grown readily from seed sown in a greenhouse or frame in spring and will flower in their first year. Selected varieties are usually raised from cuttings in late winter or early spring like the larger flowered chrysanthemums, but they can also be increased by division in spring.

C. rubellum flowers in July and August, is 2 to 3 feet tall and typically has soft pink flowers, but it has also given rise to a large number of colour forms, some single, some double flowered. It is an excellent border plant to be grown in a similar manner to the Korean chrysanthemums.

Pompon chrysanthemums are so called because their flowers are small, double and button-like. Because the petals are short and firm they are not easily damaged by wind and rain and so the August and September flowering pompons make first-rate garden plants. Later kinds may need to be flowered under glass but require a minimum of heat. Pompons are usually raised from cuttings like large-flowered varieties.

A neglected but very beautiful class of greenhouse chrysanthemum is the Rayonnante, with very narrow, spider-like petals usually in delicate shades of pink and apricot. They are grown from cuttings and given greenhouse protection from late September onwards.

Further interesting developments are the Charm chrysanthemums, very freely branching, bushy plants with masses of small single flowers, and the Cascade chrysanthemums which closely resemble the Charm varieties in flower, but are gradually trained downwards to make a hanging cascade of growth. Both types can be raised from either seed or cuttings.

The Anemone-centred chrysanthemums (Plate 6), like the Rayonnantes, are unusual in the form of their flowers rather than in method of cultivation. They may be likened to singles which have developed a 'pad' of short petals in place of the usual central yellow disk. In some varieties this 'pad' is of a different colour from that of the ray petals. There are both early and late flowering anemone-centred varieties.

Chrysanthemum (Pompon)

Chrysanthemum (Rayonnante)

37

Chrysanthemum maximum
'Fringed Beauty'

Cimicifuga racemosa

The hardy herbaceous chrysanthemums, derived from *C. maximum*, have also been greatly developed in gardens to include numerous varieties with fully double flowers as well as very large-flowered varieties and some with fringed petals. The singles are all extremely easy to grow in almost any soil and place but the doubles are often more difficult, demanding much better winter drainage and occasionally even needing frame protection in winter where the soil is very wet and cold. These double varieties should only be moved in spring.

All the hardy annual chrysanthemums, derived from *C. carinatum* (Plate 6) and *C. coronarium*, are easy plants to grow in any sunny place and ordinary soil. The contrasted rings of colour in the *C. carinatum* varieties makes them particularly attractive.

The common bedding marguerite is also a chrysanthemum, the species being *C. frutescens*. There is a yellow variety as well as the popular white and a particularly good form is known as Jamaica Primrose. In common with other forms of the marguerite it should be increased by cuttings of firm young growths which can be rooted in a frame or greenhouse at practically any time.

CIMICIFUGA *(Bugbane)*

Hardy herbaceous perennials with slender spikes of small white flowers in late summer. There are several kinds but the two most frequently seen are *C. racemosa* (Plate 6), a rather tall plant for the back of the border, and *C. simplex*, which is about 4 feet high. Both like rather moist soils and cool, partially shaded places, but can be grown almost anywhere. They have a light and elegant appearance in flower which makes them useful as a foil for more solid flowers. Both can be increased by division in spring or autumn.

CISSUS

Tender climbing plants closely allied to the vine and grown for their ornamental foliage. The two best known are *Cissus discolor* (Plate 6), a hothouse plant with leaves reddish-purple beneath and deep green variegated with white above, and *C. antarctica*, which is popular as a house plant and only needs enough heat to exclude frost. It is often known as the Kangaroo Vine and it has green leaves. Other kinds sometimes grown as house plants are *C. gongylodes* and *C. sicyoides*. *C. discolor* likes a temperature in the seventies and plenty of moisture in the soil while it is in growth. It is increased by spring cuttings rooted in a propagating box with generous bottom heat. The other species will thrive in ordinary cool greenhouse or living room conditions, should be watered freely in spring and summer, moderately in autumn and winter, and can be increased by cuttings.

CISTUS *(Rock Rose)*

I have already dealt with this genus of evergreen shrubs in *Flowers in Colour* and would only add to what I said there, that further observation suggests that *C. purpureus* (Plate 6) is hardier

than I supposed. No doubt in this respect it cannot compete with
C. laurifolius, *C. ladaniferus* or *C. cyprius*, but it is so beautiful
a shrub that it is certainly worth a trial in all but the coldest
gardens. The flowers are very large, rose with a deep purple
blotch at the base of each petal. It should be given really well-
drained soil and a sunny position sheltered from cutting winds.
Like all other rock roses it grows readily from seed, but is a
little variable in colour, so specially desirable forms may be
increased by cuttings in July.

CLEMATIS *(Virgin's Bower)*

It is the showy hybrid varieties of clematis, the plants with
large, highly coloured flowers and fancy names, like Nelly Moser
and Comtesse de Bouchard, that are, and will probably always
continue to be, the most popular with gardeners. But their
undoubted excellence and the ease with which most of them can
be grown in any soil that is reasonably cool and moist in summer
without becoming waterlogged and sour in winter, should not
blind gardeners to the existence of numerous excellent species.
These may fall short of the hybrids in display, but they make
ample amends in quality and character. Some, indeed, are so
unlike the ordinary garden varieties that at first it is difficult
to realize that they belong to the same genus. This is true of
C. tangutica (Plate 6) with its stout, bright yellow sepals folded in
to form a helmet-shaped flower, and also of the lovely blue-
mauve *C. macropetala* (Plate 6) with row upon row of narrow
sepals which give the nodding flowers the appearance of being
double. The seed heads of *C. tangutica* are particularly silvery
and attractive and, as the plant flowers late and continues for a
considerable time, flowers and seed heads are to be found at the
same time. By contrast *C. macropetala* flowers early, in May, but
often gives a second crop in summer.

These are both plants of the greatest beauty and as easily
grown as any of the hybrids. So too is the evergreen *C. armandii*
except that it is not quite as hardy as some and may need the
protection of a south or west facing wall in the colder parts of
the country. It is one of the first to bloom, its clusters of white
flowers appearing in late March and continuing throughout
most of April. *C. florida bicolor* (Plate 6) is another very distinctive plant with white flowers each with a kind of 'anemone
centre' of short purple petal-like segments. It needs a warmer,
more sheltered spot than most species and flowers in summer.

A free growing and easy species is *C. flammula* with masses of
small, white, fragrant flowers in late summer. Even more vigorous and rapid growing is the mountain clematis, *C. montana*, a
plant that will quickly climb to 20 feet or more and each
May produces an abundance of its white or soft pink flowers
each a couple of inches in diameter and fragrant in some
forms.

C. jouiniana has its soft lilac-blue petals folded in so closely
that they appear to form a tube, a peculiarity also to be noted
in pale yellow *C. rehderiana* and the similar *C. veitchiana*.

Clematis armandii

Clematis veitchiana

Clematis integrifolia

Codonopsis convolvulacea

In addition to all these there are several herbaceous species which may be planted in the border along with other herbaceous perennials. Perhaps the best of these is *C. heracleifolia davidiana*, a rather cumbersome name for a very pretty 4-foot plant with nodding, bell-shaped blue flowers in late summer. *C. integrifolia* is not unlike it and deeper in colour.

All the climbing clematis can be increased by layering in May or June and most species also by seed sown in a frame or greenhouse in spring, though seed is often slow and irregular in germination. The herbaceous kinds are increased by division.

CLETHRA *(Sweet Pepper Bush)*

Clethra alnifolia is an attractive hardy deciduous shrub 6 or 7 feet high with close spikes of fragrant white flowers in August. It is not a showy plant, but it is pretty and unusual and it has the additional merit of thriving in damp places, like the alder which its leaves resemble. It is a plant that suckers freely, so the easiest means of increase is to detach rooted suckers in autumn. Even more attractive but, unfortunately, also rather tender are *C. arborea*, sometimes known as the Lily of the Valley Tree, an evergreen 20 feet or more in height with loose spikes of white flowers in late summer, and *C. delavayi* (Plate 6), a deciduous species said to make a tree up to 40 feet though usually much smaller. The white flower spikes are narrower and denser than those of *C. arborea* and appear in July.

CODIAEUM *(Croton)*

These exotic plants (Plate 6) are grown for their foliage colours and shapes which are astonishingly varied. Green, yellow and red are mixed in various combinations and shades and leaf shapes vary from very narrow to broadly lance-shaped. All are varieties of *C. variegatum*, a tropical evergreen shrub 5 or 6 feet high, but in gardens more often seen as a pot plant a couple of feet or thereabouts in height. Codiaeums need a good deal of warmth and moisture, certainly a temperature which does not fall below 55°F. in winter. They need plenty of water in summer and a moderate supply even in winter, and are best grown in a fairly rich compost containing plenty of leaf mould or peat. Propagation is by air layering of the young stems or by cuttings of half-ripened shoots with ample bottom heat.

CODONOPSIS

Small herbaceous plants, most of them climbing or sprawling and allied to the campanulas though, in general, more difficult.

Typical of the genus are *Codonopsis clematidea* and *C. ovata* (Plate 6), two plants very similar in appearance and evidently much confused in gardens. They grow about a foot high, need some kind of support or a rock to sprawl over and produce a succession of blue, bell-shaped flowers during the summer. *C. convolvulacea* is a slender twiner with similar blue flowers. All are sun lovers and may need a specially sheltered position or some protection in winter. The soil must be well drained and it is desirable to raise a few young plants annually from seed and overwinter in a frame in case of casualties outdoors.

COELOGYNE

Orchids, most of which are not well known or likely to become popular, though one is a favourite plant with gardeners because of its neat habit and ease of culture. This is *C. cristata* (Plate 6), a charming plant with sprays of fragrant white flowers which cluster at the base of the leaves. It can be grown in a pot or suspended basket and thrives in a compost of three parts chopped sphagnum moss and one part osmunda fibre. It flowers from January to May, should be watered freely in spring and summer, sparingly in winter and needs an average temperature of 65°F. in summer falling to 55°F. in winter. It is increased by division at potting time immediately after flowering.

COLUMNEA

Very handsome trailing plants for the well-warmed greenhouse. The most popular is *Columnea gloriosa* (Plate 7) with orange-scarlet flowers in summer. It should be grown in a basket suspended from the rafters or other convenient place, and, being epiphytic needs a compost of leaf-mould or peat with enough sand to keep it open. It should be watered freely in spring and summer, moderately in autumn and winter, and at all times have plenty of atmospheric moisture. It can be increased by summer cuttings in a propagating box with plenty of bottom heat.

CONVOLVULUS *(Bindweed)*

The common bindweed of gardens is a horrible weed which everyone wants to destroy but some of its exotic relatives are delightful garden plants which, so far from being a nuisance require a little nursing if they are to be kept alive. This is certainly true of *Convolvulus mauritanicus* (Plate 7), a beautiful trailing plant for a sunny, sheltered ledge in the rock garden. It sprawls over the ground rather like an elegant periwinkle and produces a profusion of soft blue, widely funnel-shaped flowers throughout the later summer. But it is none too hardy.

C. *cneorum* (Plate 7), a silvery-leaved bushling about 2 feet in height with white or blush-white flowers in summer, is another excellent species for a sunny rock garden.

C. *althaeoides* is another sprawler with finely divided leaves and magenta pink flowers. Like the others it is more a plant for southern than for northern gardens.

All the foregoing are perennials to be raised from cuttings of firm young growth in a propagating frame. Quite different in its requirements is C. *minor* (*tricolour*) a sprawling hardy annual with light or dark blue flowers in summer. This must be raised anew each year from seed sown in April where the plants are to flower. Like all the rest it is a sunlover.

CORNUS *(Dogwood, Cornel, Cornelian Cherry)*

These deciduous shrubs and small trees are described in *Flowers in Colour* and I return to them here principally to give

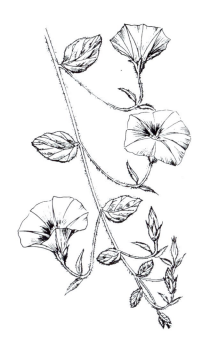

Convolvulus mauritanicus

Cornus mas

41

Cornus kousa

Coronilla glauca

a special recommendation to *C. florida rubra* (Plate 7), in my opinion the loveliest of them all, where it can be grown well. It likes warmth, good ripening of the wood in autumn and reasonable freedom from late spring frosts. It makes a small tree 15 feet or so in height and as much through, producing its lovely soft pink 'flowers' (they are really bracts surrounding the true flowers) in May. It likes loamy soil and needs no pruning.

An excellent shrub or small tree, generally overlooked, I believe, because it is badly grown, is *C. mas*, the Cornelian Cherry, so called because of its edible red fruits which, however, are seldom produced in any quantity. Its yellow flowers are individually tiny but they are produced with such freedom in February and March that it can make quite a striking picture. It should be planted in a sunny place in reasonably good soil.

Some dogwoods fruit well in suitable surroundings and this is true of *C. capitata*, which is rather tender and has sulphur coloured bracts, and *C. kousa*, which has very showy white bracts. The fruits are a little like strawberries.

Most species of cornus can be increased by layering in May. *C. mas* often suckers and these can be detached in autumn.

COROKIA

The only species likely to be found in British gardens is *Corokia cotoneaster* (Plate 7), a curious evergreen shrub with thin, curiously contorted branches. The leaves are small and very sparsely produced which simply serves to emphasize the odd tracery of the branches. The flowers are small and yellow, produced in May. This is not a very hardy shrub, and in many places may need the protection of a sunny wall, but it can be grown in the open in the milder counties and will then make a densely twiggy bush 5 or 6 feet high and at least as much through. It is not fussy about soil and needs no pruning. Propagation is by cuttings of well-ripened young wood in autumn in an unheated frame.

CORONILLA

The most attractive species is *Coronilla glauca* (Plate 7), an evergreen shrub with small, blue-grey leaves and clusters of small, bright yellow, sweetly scented pea-flowers produced more or less continuously throughout the summer. It would rank high among evergreen shrubs if it were a little hardier but, in fact, it requires wall protection in many places and is really only suitable for planting completely in the open in the mildest parts of the country. There it will make a well-branched bush 4 or 5 feet in height.

A much hardier plant is *C. emerus*, the Scorpion Senna, a deciduous shrub of loose, open habit 7 or 8 feet high with small clusters of yellow flowers also produced successively throughout the summer. *C. emeroides* is very like it.

All these coronillas like good, loamy, well-drained soil and sunny, sheltered places. They can be increased by seed or by cuttings of firm, young shoots in a propagating frame in July.

CORTADERIA *(Pampas Grass)*

The Pampas Grass of the Argentine is the most handsome of all grasses, a plant capable of making very large clumps of its long narrow leaves from which in autumn spring the great plumy silver heads of flowers. This is *Cortaderia argentea*, a plant hardy in all but the coldest parts of the country and easily grown in any reasonable soil. It should be planted in spring and it is wise to cut back the previous year's foliage each April. There are several varieties of pampas grass, some, such as Sunningdale Silver (Plate 7), superior in the size and silkiness of their plumes, others, such as *pumila*, not so tall. All can be increased by division at planting time.

CORYLOPSIS

Delightful early flowering shrubs or small trees with small, soft yellow, fragrant flowers in short trails. There are numerous species, some closely alike. One of the best known is *C. spicata* with flower trails a little over an inch in length, but *C. willmottiae* and *C. platypetala* have flower trails twice as long and should be more widely planted than they are at present. *C. pauciflora* (Plate 7), has the shortest trails of all, indeed they are little more than clusters of two or three, freely produced along the length of the hazel-like stems. All flower in April, like good loamy soils and fairly sheltered positions. They will do well in thin woodland provided they get some sun and they should not be planted in frost pockets as their young growth is tender. All can be increased by seed sown in spring or by cuttings in autumn rooted in a frame.

COTONEASTER

I have dealt with these handsome, berry-bearing shrubs in *Flowers in Colour* and return to them here merely to point out that some of the most effective are hybrids. Such are *Cotoneaster watereri* (Plate 7) and *C. cornubia*, evergreen bushes with heavy crops of large scarlet berries in autumn. *C. hybrida pendula* is prostrate, or, when grafted on a stem, makes a pretty weeping plant very suitable for small gardens. All are easily grown in any ordinary soil and reasonably open place and must be increased by cuttings or grafting.

COTYLEDON *(See Chiastophyllum)*

CRASSULA

This large genus of succulents contains many interesting or odd plants and one species of outstanding decorative merit, *C. falcata*. This makes a well-branched plant, 2 feet high, with fleshy, grey, sickle-shaped leaves and flat clusters of vivid scarlet flowers in summer. There are varieties of it, some much paler in colour, some combining white and red. All make excellent pot plants for the frost-proof greenhouse. They do not need much heat in winter, 45° to 50°F. being ample, but in spring and summer the temperature may be allowed to rise considerably

43

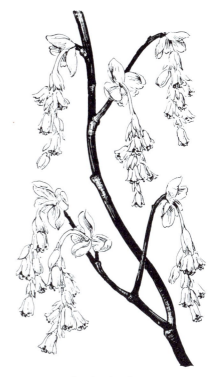

Corylopsis spicata

Crassula sarcocaulis

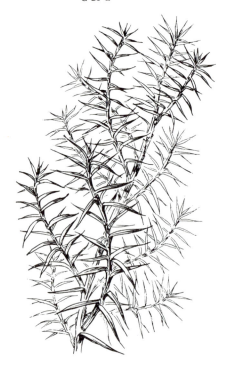

Cryptomeria japonica elegans

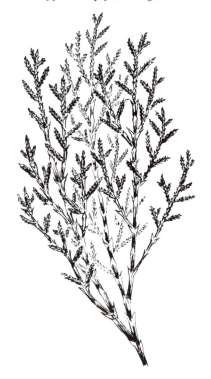

Cupressus sempervirens

with sun heat. They will thrive in an ordinary, rather porous potting compost, make good specimens in 5- to 7-inch pots and should be watered moderately in spring and summer, very sparingly in autumn and winter. March is the best time for repotting and cuttings can be rooted at the same time in very sandy soil in a frame or propagating box.

C. sarcocaulis is a quaint succulent like a tiny shrub with a profusion of pink flowers in summer. It grows 8 or 9 inches high and can be planted outdoors in very sunny, sheltered places but is safer as a pot plant in the alpine house.

CRYPTOMERIA *(Japanese Cedar)*

The wild form of the Japanese Cedar, *Cryptomeria japonica* (Plate 7), is not much planted as an ornamental tree in this country as it is apt to be a little sparse in habit and disappointing in performance. But it has produced a very distinctive and beautiful variety named *C. japonica elegans* which is a very popular evergreen shrub or small tree, especially in the milder parts of the country. It is exceedingly dense and bushy in habit with elegant feathery foliage which has the peculiarity of turning reddish brown in parts in the autumn so that at this season there is a striking contrast between it and the normal softly grey-green foliage. It is usually seen as a big bush or small tree up to about 20 feet in height. It likes a good, loamy soil not liable to dry out too badly in summer and should be given a fairly sheltered situation. It can be pruned in spring if it grows too large. The species can be raised from seed but selected forms must be propagated by cuttings in a frame in autumn.

CUPRESSUS *(Cypress)*

Many of the coniferous trees that are known by gardeners as Cupressus, in fact belong to the nearly allied genus Chamaecyparis, the false cypresses. However, the popular *Cupressus macrocarpa* really does belong to the true cypresses. It is a very quick growing tree which will submit to considerable restriction and so has been much used as a hedge plant. In maritime regions and mild districts it is very suitable for this purpose, and also for use as a wind-break, but is apt to be severely damaged by frost and wind in cold regions. It has rather feathery, bright green foliage and is a very handsome tree, eventually reaching a height of 50 to 70 feet. It is columnar when young but usually spreading when old. By contrast *C. arizonica* (Plate 8), which is very similar in leaf, is narrowly conical in habit and blue-grey rather than bright green. It is hardier and makes a delightful specimen tree of about the same ultimate height as *C. macrocarpa*.

C. sempervirens is the cypress commonly found in the Mediterranean region, its narrowly erect variety, *stricta*, being one of the most characteristic features of Italian gardens. This is genuinely spire-like in habit but unfortunately all forms of *C. sempervirens* are a little tender, especially when young. This tenderness is even more marked in *C. funebris*, the lovely weeping species known as the Mourning Cypress. It can only be grown outdoors

Columnea
gloriosa

Convolvulus
mauritanicus

Corylopsis
pauciflora

Cornus
florida
rubra

Convolvulus
cneorum

Coronilla
glauca

Corokia
cotoneaster

Cotyledon
oppositifolia

Cryptomeria
japonica

Cotoneaster
watereri

Cortaderia argentea
[Sunningdale Silver]

C Newsome-Taylor.

Cyclamen
neapolitanum

Daphne
odora

Datura
suaveolens

Davidia
involucrata

Dendrobium
hybrid
'Sunburst'

Daboëcia
cantabrica

Cytisus
supinus

Cupressus
arizonica

Curtonus
paniculatus

Delphinium
'Pink Sensation'

Cytisus battandieri

Desfontainea
spinosa

in the mildest and most sheltered places and elsewhere must be treated as a pot plant for the cool greenhouse.

All kinds of cupressus are best raised from seed sown in a frame or greenhouse in spring. They are not fussy about soil.

CURTONUS

The only species at all familiar in British gardens, and that by no means a common plant, is *Curtonus paniculatus* (Plate 8), better known as *Antholyza paniculata*. This looks rather like a tall and uncommonly luxuriant montbretia, with more narrowly tubular scarlet flowers produced in late summer in branching sprays. The leaves are broadly sword-shaped. The large corms should be planted in autumn, 3 inches deep in good well-drained soil and a warm, sunny position. This is a plant suitable for the milder counties and one which deserves to be more widely planted in south and west. It is propagated by division of the corm clusters at planting time but should not be frequently disturbed as it improves by being allowed to remain and form large clumps.

CYCLAMEN

The greenhouse cyclamen derived from *C. persicum* are so popular and showy that they tend to detract attention from the far smaller but exquisite hardy species. Typical of these is *C. neapolitanum* (Plate 8), with ivy-shaped leaves usually attractively marbled, and rose-pink or white flowers carried in early autumn on 4- or 5-inch stems. *C. coum* is even shorter, the small deep magenta flowers almost nestling in the dark green leaves in February and March. Very like this but with slightly marked foliage is *C. hiemale*. *C. europaeum* is carmine and late summer flowering, continuing into autumn and sometimes even going on to produce some flowers in spring. *C. vernum* is winter and spring flowering and *C. atkinsii*, which is a hybrid between *C. coum* and *C. vernum*, has light green leaves marked with silver and very pretty light rose or white flowers from January to March.

All these hardy cyclamen make large corms like those of the greenhouse kind and these corms do not like being disturbed. It is best, therefore, to start with small plants, preferably from pots to avoid overmuch root injury. They like leafy soils and cool places, partially shaded or even in full sun so long as the soil does not dry out badly. They are best increased by seed sown in spring, either in a frame or unheated greenhouse, or in a carefully prepared seed bed in the open.

The greenhouse cyclamen, derived from *C. persicum*, has been so 'improved' in gardens that its large, full flowers in a variety of shades from white to crimson bear little resemblance to the dainty pink blooms from which they have been developed. In the process of breeding the pleasant fragrance of the wild flowers has also been lost though efforts are being made to get it back again.

These more tender cyclamen are raised from seed sown in May or August, the seedlings being potted individually at an early stage in John Innes compost and grown on in a cool house

Cyclamen Hiemale

Cyclamen persicum

Cytisus 'Porlock'

Cytisus praecox

to flower the second winter after sowing. Thereafter they can be grown on for years provided the plants are rested for a couple of months each summer in a cool, shady frame. They can then be repotted in August and returned to the greenhouse not later than October. They require little heat, just sufficient to maintain a winter minimum of about 45°F.

CYTISUS (Broom)

Of all spring-flowering shrubs the brooms are the quickest to give a return in flower for they can be raised easily from seed and seedlings will usually flower freely in their second year. Indeed many brooms will seed themselves about so that seedlings will appear in all kinds of unexpected places, even in the crevices of wall or between the slabs in a paved path. But this readiness of reproduction is an indication of the naturally rather short life of most brooms so that they must be frequently renewed if they are to be preserved in good condition.

Most handsome are the many varieties of *Cytisus scoparius*, the Common Broom, a shrub varying greatly in habit from sprawling bushes not above 3 feet in height to erect shrubs 6 or 7 feet high. The colour range, too, is wide, from pale yellow to crimson and there are no more showy shrubs in the garden in May.

The White Portugal Broom, *C. albus*, flowers at the same time and is a little taller and more graceful in habit. The small flowers are white.

The first broom to flower is usually *C. praecox*, a soft yellow flowered hybrid at its best in late April. The flowers have an unpleasant smell but this is not very noticeable in the garden.

Another fine hybrid broom is *C. kewensis* which is low growing and spreading in habit and has pale yellow flowers. It is an admirable shrub for the rock garden.

C. purpureus is seldom seen but it is an interesting and distinctive plant of sprawling habit producing its pale purple flowers in May. It suckers freely and can be easily increased by digging up these rooted suckers in autumn.

Quite distinct from all these and a very attractive shrub of loose, open habit with silvery leaves and upright spikes of yellow flowers is *C. battandieri* (Plate 8). It soon makes quite a big shrub 12 feet or more in height and it may need some support as, like most brooms, it is none too well anchored in the soil.

Very different from this but equally distinctive is *C. supinus* (Plate 8), a dwarf, compact plant about 3 feet high with erect stems terminated in July and August by a cluster of yellow flowers.

C. Porlock is a surprisingly hardy hybrid between two rather tender species, *C. monspessulanus* and *C. racemosus*, the latter better known to most gardeners as the fragrant 'genista' of florist's shops. Porlock resembles it and flowers in May and June. It makes a dense, evergreen bush 5 or 6 feet high.

DABOECIA (St Daboec's Heath)

There is only one species of daboecia, *D. cantabrica* (Plate 8), often known as *D. polifolia*, and in general appearance it resembles the heathers to which it is related. It is a low-growing evergreen, 18 inches to 2 feet high, with narrow, heather-like leaves. The flowers are little pendant magenta urns drawn in at the mouth and they are produced in constant succession from mid-summer to autumn. There is also a white flowered variety and some others with deeper purple flowers. Like most of its family it dislikes lime and thrives in acid soils such as those that suit heathers and rhododendrons. It likes peat but can get on without it. What is essential is good drainage. Propagation is by seed sown in sandy peat in spring or by cuttings of half-ripe shoots in similar soil in a propagating frame in July. Early each spring plants may be trimmed over with shears or secateurs to prevent them from becoming straggly.

DAPHNE

Shrubby plants some of which are sufficiently dwarf to be planted in the rock garden, others of medium height and excellent for small borders. The most popular is *Daphne mezereum*, a rather stiff deciduous shrub which produces its very fragrant, mulberry purple or white flowers before its leaves in February or March. Early though it is, it is preceded by a choicer and less well-known evergreen species, *D. odora* (Plate 8), which in a favourable season may open its paler purple but equally fragrant flowers in January. It is reputed to be rather tender and, probably for that reason, has not been planted as much as it deserves, but it has a variety with yellow-margined leaves which is hardier than the green-leaved form and is certainly worth trying in all but the coldest gardens. It makes a well branched bush a couple of feet high and rather more in diameter and is ideal for a south-facing border protected by a fence or wall.

D. *burkwoodii*, also known as *D. somerset*, is deciduous and in some ways the most useful of all because it is hardy, easily grown and makes a compact, rounded bush about 3 feet high smothered in May with fragrant soft pink flowers. It is a hybrid and one of its parents, *D. cneorum*, might claim to be the most beautiful of all daphnes so freely does it flower and so bright is its particular shade of rose pink. It is intensely fragrant and makes a very neat, evergreen, widely spreading shrub no more than a foot high, and for that reason very suitable for the rock garden, but it is not always an easy shrub to grow. It likes sun and good drainage but not a dry soil. An even dwarfer form is known as *eximia*.

D. *blagayana* is also a species for the rock garden, a completely prostrate evergreen plant with clusters of ivory-white fragrant flowers in March and April. D. *collina* grows about 18 inches tall and makes a dense evergreen bush with fragrant purple flowers in April and May. It likes sun and can be grown in the rock garden or at the front of the shrub border.

D. *retusa* is a very slow growing evergreen making a tight, compact little plant smothered beneath fragrant rose flowers in March. It is often grown as a pot plant for the alpine house.

Most daphnes can be increased by cuttings of the current year's growth taken in July and rooted in a propagating frame.

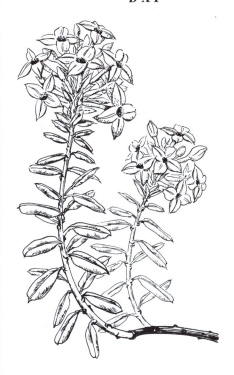

Daphne cneorum eximia

Daphne collina

47

Datura sanguinea

Delphinium (Belladonna)

DATURA *(Angel's Trumpet)*

The popular species of datura are all vigorous loosely branched shrubs, but they are mostly too tender to be grown in the open, except during the summer. Sometimes they are used as greenhouse plants but they need a fairly big house. More frequently they are grown for summer bedding and may often be seen in the elaborate, sub-tropical schemes favoured in public parks. The hardiest species and also one of the smallest is *Datura cornigera*, often known as *D. knightii*. The large, white or pale cream, trumpet-shaped flowers hang down and are very showy, particularly in the double-flowered form which is most popular. In sheltered gardens in Devon and Cornwall it sometimes lives outdoors winter and summer making a bush about 4 feet.

D. *suaveolens*, the commonest species, is similar in appearance but much more vigorous and is often known as Angel's Trumpet, a name also applied to the rather similar *D. arborea*. *D. suaveolens* is also most popular in its double-flowered form (Plate 8) and is very fragrant.

D. *sanguinea* is the showiest of all because its long, pendent flowers are bright orange-red. It is usually grown as a greenhouse plant permanently planted in a border of good, loamy soil.

All the daturas appreciate a rather rich soil and plenty of water in spring and summer while they are making their growth. They may be pruned quite severely in autumn to prevent them becoming too big and straggly and this also eases the problem of winter storage when they are used for summer bedding. In winter they need a greenhouse with a minimum temperature of about 45°F. They can be increased by cuttings of firm young shoots in spring or early summer but root most readily in a soil-warmed frame or propagating box.

DAVIDIA *(Handkerchief Tree, Dove Tree, Ghost Tree)*

One very handsome but rather uncommon tree notable for its fine, broadly conical habit and the large white bracts which surround the small ball-shaped heads of red or white flowers. These bracts may be over 6 inches long and 4 inches broad in a good specimen and a tree in full bloom does look rather as if hundreds of white handkerchiefs had been attached to it. The only species is *Davidia involucrata* (Plate 8) and it has two varieties, *laeta* and *vilmoriniana*, which do not differ greatly from it. All make shapely, fairly quick growing trees, eventually 40 feet or more in height. *D. involucrata* thrives in any reasonable soil that does not dry out quickly in hot weather. A rather heavy, moist loam suits it best of all. It can be increased from seed sown in a cool greenhouse or frame in spring. No pruning is required.

DELPHINIUM *(Larkspur)*

There are both perennial and annual races of delphinium that have been highly developed as garden plants, the annuals from a pretty Mediterranean plant named *Delphinium ajacis*, the

Epacris
longiflora

Elaeagnus pungens
aureo-variegata

Edraianthus
serpyllifolius

Draba
aizoides

Dierama
pulcherrimum

Dracaena
deremensis
bausei

Diascia
barberae

Dryas
octopetala

Dianthus plumarius
'Casser's Pink'

Dipelta
floribunda

Erinus
lpinus

Euphorbia
fulgens

Eucryphia
nymansensis

Erinacea
pungens

Exacum
affine

Eucharis
grandiflora

Eriophyllum
lanatum

Eucomis
comosa

Erythronium
dens-canis

Erigeron
'Charity'

Erica
mediterranea

Erythrina
crista-galli

Euphorbia
wulfenii

perennials mainly from *D. elatum* and *D. cheilanthum*, but with other species creeping in to complicate the picture.

The annual larkspurs are quite hardy and may be sown out-doors at any time in March, April or September where they are to flower. They carry their flowers in narrow spikes usually 3 or 4 feet high and the colour range includes white as well as many shades of pink, rose lavender, blue and violet. They flower in summer, the precise time depending upon when they were sown, and they like a sunny place and reasonably good soil.

The big perennial delphiniums will repay better cultivation; deeply dug and well manured ground and a certain amount of thinning out of the young growths each spring to concentrate their strength on a few of the best stems. The flower spikes are often 6 or 7 feet in height and the normal colour range is from white and palest mauve to intense purple and violet.

There have, however, been some interesting developments in the perennial kinds, particularly in the widening of the colour range to include pink, lilac and delicate pastel shades of parma-violet. The first break to pink in these hybrid perennial delphin-iums occurred in Holland in a variety named Pink Sensation (Plate 8). It was the result of a cross between an ordinary garden delphinium and a slender, red-flowered species named *D. cardin-alis*. It is in many respects intermediate in type, 4 feet in height with slender spikes of soft-pink flowers. It is hardy and perennial but needs a well-drained soil, and should be renewed every few years from cuttings of firm young shoots taken when 4 or 5 inches long in April and rooted in sandy soil in a frame.

Other crosses between garden delphiniums and species, made in America, produced further breaks in colour and the development of varieties that can be raised remarkably true to colour from seed, provided the plants are hand fertilized with their own pollen. In general they are tall plants with rather loose spikes of remarkably large flowers. *D. nudicaule*, another red-flowered species not as a rule much over a foot in height and tuberous rooted, has also been used by American breeders to produce some remarkably coloured but not very easily grown hybrids.

The so-called 'Belladonna' delphiniums are the varieties derived from *D. cheilanthum* and are sometimes known as Gar-land Larkspurs, presumably because of their graceful sprays (not spikes) of flowers. They average 3 or 4 feet in height, branch freely and are excellent plants for cutting, with a colour range from white and pale blue to violet.

The typically British race of tall, spire-flowered delphiniums can be raised from seed but the colours do not come true in this way, seedlings often differing widely from their parents. For this reason selected, or 'named' varieties are usually increased by cuttings of firm young shoots in March or April inserted in sandy soil in a frame. The same method is used for the Bella-donna delphiniums, most of which are sterile and produce no seed, but the American giant delphiniums have been specially

D

Delphinium nudicaule

Delphinium elatum (pips)

Dendrobium 'Gatton Monarch'

Dianthus barbatus

bred to be reproduced from seed and as a rule do not do well from cuttings. Seed may be sown either as soon as ripe or in March and seedlings must be protected from slugs.

DENDROBIUM

This very large genus of orchids contains such widely different species that it is difficult to generalize about them. Some have solitary flowers, some clusters of flowers, some arching sprays of bloom (Plate 8). Most require a fair amount of warmth, especially from January to September when most are flowering and making their growth. During this period a temperature around 65°F. is ideal, but during the resting period in autumn the temperature may fall to 55°F. Water should be given freely while plants are in growth and the astmosphere should also be very moist. In autumn considerably less water and atmospheric moisture are needed. The compost should be entirely of sphagnum moss and osmunda fibre, usually about twice as much fibre as moss. Repotting should be done in April or May as new growth starts but care should be taken not to overpot the plants as they flower best when rather restricted for pot room. Many dendrobiums make excellent cut flowers, lasting well in water and often handsomely blotched or edged with another colour.

DESFONTAINEA

The only species, *Desfontainea spinosa* (Plate 8), is a beautiful evergreen shrub, often mistaken for a holly until it produces its tubular scarlet flowers a little after midsummer. It is then a very striking sight and the display continues until early autumn. Unfortunately it is none too hardy. It thrives in Cornwall and in many sheltered places on the west coast, but in colder inland gardens it must either be grown in a greenhouse or be given the protection of a south-facing wall. It grows 8 or 10 feet high, makes a densely branched bush with shining, dark green, spined and holly-like leaves, requires no pruning and can be raised from seed sown in a greenhouse in spring. It is not fussy about soil but it likes moisture in soil and atmosphere which, perhaps, accounts for the way in which it thrives in some western Scottish gardens.

DIANTHUS *(Pink, Carnation, Sweet William)*

So varied is this astonishing genus that whole books have been written about it, some even about one or other of its most important sections such as the hardy Border Carnation or the more tender Perpetual Flowering Carnation. Though these two popular and highly developed plants differ greatly in their requirements in the garden, they have been produced from the same species, *Dianthus caryophyllus*. The border carnations can be grown outdoors and are raised from layers pegged down around the parent plants in July. The perpetual flowering carnations need greenhouse protection, at any rate in winter, and are usually grown under glass throughout the year. They are raised from cuttings in winter and they can be had in flower at any time of the year, whereas the border carnations have a comparatively short flowering season in June and July. Attempts have been made to combine the best qualities of both races by interbreeding them and the Perpetual Border Carnation is one result.

Similarly the great race of garden pinks, derived from *D. plumarius* and blooming for a short season outdoors in June, has been crossed with perpetual flowering carnations to lengthen its flowering season and with border carnations to improve the size and formation of its flowers. The results are to be seen in *Dianthus allwoodii*, a race of pinks flowering for most of the summer, and in the show pinks which are much grown by exhibitors. Again there has been a tendency to carry over some of the less desirable features of the parents so that these hybrid pinks are not always as hardy and easily grown as the old-fashioned garden varieties such as Mrs Sinkins and Pink Mrs Sinkins. But they have a much greater colour range and some of the best are very good garden plants easily raised, like other pinks, from cuttings or pipings in summer.

The early summer flowering Sweet William, *D. barbatus*, has for long been a favourite on account of its fine heads of fragrant flowers, often very strikingly coloured with a ring of deep colour on a paler base. It is a perennial but so easily raised from seed that it is often treated as a biennial, seed being sown each May to give young plants to be put in their flowering beds in September or October. But there are plants obviously related to the sweet william which have such double flowers that they are unable to produce any seed. These must be increased by careful division in spring or by cuttings whenever they can be obtained. One such plant is Casser's Pink (Plate 9), a remarkable, rather sprawling plant with clusters of vivid scarlet, double flowers. It thrives in light, well-drained soils and sunny places and is probably not long lived unless frequently renewed from cuttings or divisions.

There are, in addition to all these, a great many small dianthus species whose proper place is the rock garden or the dry wall. Here belong the lovely, tufted *D. neglectus* with rose and buff flowers, the trailing *D. deltoides* which may be pink, rose or crimson, and the Cheddar Pink, *D. gratianopolitanus* (it used to have the much nicer name *D. caesius*) which looks like a very neat rose-coloured garden pink. *D. alpinus*, a neat little plant with variously coloured flowers, has been hybridized and developed to produce a number of garden varieties and *D. plumarius* itself, in its old and unimproved single-flowered forms, is a first rate plant for rock garden or dry wall.

Most of these rock garden pinks can be easily raised from seed but, as there is likely to be variation in colour and habit, specially desirable forms should be increased by cuttings or by careful division in spring.

Seed is the only method of increasing the annual pinks such as *D. chinensis* and its variety *heddewigii*, immensely showy plants for the summer garden, best raised in a warm greenhouse and hardened off for planting outdoors in late May. Here again

51

Dianthus allwoodii 'Doris'

Dianthus (show-pink) 'Show Beauty'

Dierama pulcherrimum

Draba aizoides

the hybridist has been at work crossing these plants with sweet williams and other species of dianthus to widen still further the variety at the gardener's disposal.

DIASCIA

Nearly all the reference books describe *Diascia barberae* (Plate 9), as a half-hardy annual. It is perfectly true that this rather fragile plant can be raised from seed sown in a warm greenhouse in March and be planted out in May or early June to give a display of its pretty, salmon-pink flowers the same summer, but it is equally true that, if the position is open and the soil well drained, it may be left to grow on without protection for years. It is, in fact, a hardy herbaceous perennial suitable for a front position in the border or a sunny ledge in the rock garden. The flowers are produced all through the summer in short spikes and are unusual both in shape and colour so that, though this is not a spectacular plant, it is one that almost always attracts attention. It is increased by seed sown under glass in spring.

DIERAMA *(Wand-Flower)*

Here is an example of a popular name perfectly fitting the plant to which it is applied. *Dierama pulcherrimum* (Plate 9) is a hardy herbaceous perennial which makes clumps of long, grass-like leaves from which grow, in June and July, very long slender, arching stems weighed down and swaying beneath the weight of a dozen or more tubular flowers, pale magenta in the common form but varying from white to intense crimson in garden varieties. The wand-flower likes a fairly rich soil not liable to dry out rapidly in summer but reasonably well drained in winter. It is fully hardy in all except the coldest districts where it may need a little winter protection. It can be raised readily from seed sown in a greenhouse or frame in spring, but seedlings are apt to vary a little in the colour of their flowers, so selected forms should be increased by division of the clusters of corms in spring.

DIPELTA

Hardy deciduous shrubs closely resembling weigela and having a similar rather loose, arching habit and tubular flowers expanded at the mouth. There are several species but only one is likely to be met in gardens and that rather occasionally. This is *Dipelta floribunda* (Plate 9) with very pale pink flowers, a little flushed with gold in the throat. It is a pretty and free flowering shrub, at its best in early June. It is perfectly hardy, will grow in any ordinary soil and, if it is desired to restrict its size, it may be pruned, like a weigela, after flowering by cutting back the flowering stems as far as the first non-flowering shoots. Left to its own devices it will reach a height of 10 to 12 feet but pruning will keep it well below this. It can be increased by cuttings of half-ripe shoots in a propagating frame or box in July or by cuttings of fully ripe growth inserted in a sandy soil outdoors in October.

DRABA

The drabas are not exciting rock plants but they are very attractive ones because of their neat, cushion habit and the freedom with which they produce their very small flowers, usually on thread-like stems only an inch or so in length. Some species are a little difficult and need moraine treatment in the garden, or may be grown in a very stony compost in well-drained pans in the alpine house or frame. But many drabas are easily grown plants in any fairly sunny place and reasonably well-drained soil. Examples of this type are *Draba aizoides* (Plate 9), yellow; *D. brunifolia*, yellow; *D. bryoides*, yellow and *D. dedeana*, white. All flower in spring and can be increased by division immediately after flowering.

DRACAENA *(Dragon-tree)*

These plants are often mistaken for palms though, in fact, they are quite unrelated. They are also much confused with Cordyline, which they do resemble and to which they are closely allied. They are tropical trees or shrubs with long, narrow leaves in a rosette or head which gives the palm-like impression. In gardens they are grown as greenhouse pot plants and are prevented from assuming their natural proportions. They are useful foliage plants with a considerable variation of colour and the ability to withstand quite rough treatment for short periods, which makes them suitable for temporary use as house plants. They should be grown in John Innes compost in fairly large pots in a warm greenhouse. They enjoy warmth and moisture which encourages rapid and vigorous growth and the most handsome leaf development. Repotting should be done in spring. Propagation may be by cuttings made from short lengths of stem inserted in sandy peat in a close frame within the greenhouse, with soil-warming or bottom heat to encourage rapid rooting. This can be done at any time in spring and summer. Dracaenas can also be grown from seed, provided a temperature of 65°F. or more can be maintained for germination. Sometimes dracaenas are increased by rooting the whole top of a plant or air-layering it, a useful method of restoring balance to a plant that has become too long-stemmed and has acquired a leggy look. *D. deremensis bausei* (Plate 9) has green leaves broadly banded with cream and is a popular variety. *D. draco* is the true Dragon-tree, 40 feet or more in height in its native habitat in the Canary Islands but grown in this country as a greenhouse pot plant. *D. fragrans* has several varieties with variegated leaves, and so has *D. hookeriana*. The coloured leaved plants known as *D. indivisa* are in fact varieties of *Cordyline indivisa*.

DRYAS

Creeping, evergreen plants which are admirable for the rock garden in a sunny place and any ordinary, reasonably well-drained soil. Dryas is a useful plant for chalky gardens as it has no objection to a high degree of akalinity but it is not dependant

Dracaena fragrans

Dryas suendermannii

Edraianthus pumilio

Epacris hybrid

upon chalk. The leaves are neat and dark green and the flowers, like single roses, sit close down on this highly effective carpet. The species commonly grown is *Dryas octopetala*, (Plate 9), which has white flowers, but there is also a species named *D. drummondii* with yellowish flowers and a hybrid between the two, named *D. suendermannii*, which starts with a suggestion of yellow but soon pales to white. *D. octopetala* is the best. All can be increased by pegging the trailing stems into sandy soil and, when they are rooted, detaching and lifting them, or by seed sown in a greenhouse or frame in spring, but seedlings are rather slow in attaining flowering size.

EDRAIANTHUS

Most of the plants grown in gardens under the name *Wahlenbergia* in fact belong to this genus. It is closely allied to *Campanula* and the bell-shaped blue or violet flowers of such species as *Edraianthus pumilio* and *E. serpyllifolius* (Plate 9) do closely resemble those of some of the alpine campanulas. They are tufted, rather sprawling plants with narrow leaves and very slender stems and they have an air of good breeding, warning, quite correctly, that they are not the easiest of plants to grow. They need perfect drainage of the type one gets in the moraine and they do not take kindly to our uncertain winters, so many enthusiasts prefer to grow them in pots or pans and give them the protection of the alpine house or frame in winter and spring. They can be raised from seed or by careful division in spring.

ELAEAGNUS *(Oleaster)*

One of the finest variegated evergreen shrubs is *Elaeagnus pungens aureo-variegata* (Plate 9). This makes a big bush, 10 feet or more high, with fairly large, glossy leaves which are broadly variegated with yellow down the centre. In the very best forms this yellow band is so wide that at a short distance the bush appears entirely golden. It is a perfectly hardy shrub thriving in any ordinary soil and reasonably open position.

There are other good species of elaeagnus but none so valuable in the garden as this. *E. macrophylla* is an evergreen shrub with big leaves which are green above and silver beneath. Its silvery flowers are not very conspicuous but they are fragrant and produced in autumn when few shrubs are in bloom.

E. argentea has wholly silver leaves and yellow flowers produced in May. Unlike the other two it is deciduous and it also produces suckers freely, which, if desired, may be dug up with roots attached, in autumn or winter, and planted elsewhere.

The two evergreen species are best increased by cuttings of half-ripe shoots in July in a propagating frame. No pruning is essential but, if plants become too big, they may be pruned to shape in April.

EPACRIS

Greenhouse evergreen shrubs which bear a superficial resemblance to the greenhouse heaths and require similar treatment, though they are botanically unrelated. There are numerous species, among the best being *Epacris longiflora* (Plate 9) with crimson and white flowers, *E. purpurascens* which is white and purple, *E. impressa*, a valuable plant with flowers which may be anything from white to deep red, and *E. rigida* which is pure white, but many of the plants grown in gardens are hybrids. All make plants 1½ to 2 feet high if grown in 5- or 6-inch pots. For potting a compost should be used consisting mainly of peat, with sufficient sand to keep it open, and the plants should be potted firmly. Little artificial heat is needed in spring and from July to September pots may be stood in a frame. They should be returned to the greenhouse before there is danger of frost and throughout the winter only enough heat should be used to maintain a minimum temperature of 45°F. At all times they should be given all the light possible and as much ventilation as the weather will allow. They should be watered moderately. Most kinds flower in winter or early spring. After flowering the young stems should be cut back considerably and as soon as new growth appears repotting should be done. Propagation is by cuttings of young shoots in May or June in sandy peat in a propagating frame or box.

ERICA *(Heather, Heath)*

Some of the finest heathers for garden display are forms of species that have been discovered growing wild or have been raised from seed. In either case they have to be kept true to type by vegetative propagation—either by cuttings of firm young shoots inserted in sand in a frame in July, or by layering in early summer.

Erica carnea Springwood White is typical of these selected garden varieties; a very superior form of white, winter-flowering heather with long spikes of flowers. Springwood Pink has the same habit and clear pink flowers. King George has the typical tufted habit of the wild *E. carnea* but starts to flower a month or so earlier, often as early as mid-November.

Some of the most richly coloured heathers are varieties of *E. vagans*, the Cornish Heath, notably Mrs D. F. Maxwell which is a brilliant carmine and *rubra* which is rosy red. For contrast there is St Keverne, bright pink and Lyonesse, pure white. All flower in late summer and early autumn.

The summer flowering *E. cinerea*, the Fine-leaved Heath, has also produced excellent garden forms such as P. S. Patrick, which has deep purple flowers; coccinea, which is purplish red; *atro-rubens*, ruby red; C. D. Eason, rose, and Apple Blossom, pale pink.

In addition to these dwarf heathers there are some much taller kinds, often known as tree heathers, principal of these for outdoor cultivation being *Erica arborea*, *E. mediterranea* (Plate 10) and *E. terminalis*. All will stand drier conditions than the dwarf heathers and *E. arborea* is definitely a little tender. It thrives best in the mild south-western and western counties. *E. arborea* is the true Tree Heather and makes a big, erect shrub

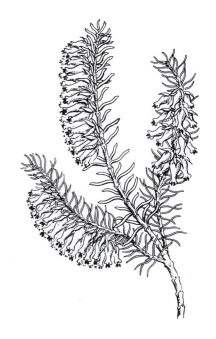

Erica carnea

Erica vagans

Erica darleyensis

Erigeron mucronatus

as much as 20 feet high in very favourable places, though usually only half that height. Its off-white flowers appear in March and April. There is a hardier and dwarfer variety named *alpina*.

E. australis comes from Spain and Portugal not, as one might imagine, from Australia. It grows 8 feet high and has purplish red flowers from April to June.

E. mediterranea is very variable, 10 feet high in some forms, half that in others. There is a wide colour range too, from white to red, but all flower at the same time from February to March. *E. darleyensis* is a hybrid of this with *E. carnea* as its other parent and it is intermediate in habit, being bushy and about 2 feet tall—taller, that is, than *E. carnea* but a good deal shorter even than short forms of *E. mediterranea*. It produces its soft, heather-purple flowers from November to April and is a most desirable plant.

E. terminalis is sometimes called the Corsican Heath but it comes from the western Mediterranean regions. It is 5 to 8 feet high and has rosy-pink flowers from June to November.

ERIGERON *(Fleabane)*

Hardy herbaceous perennials with daisy-flowers resembling those of the Michaelmas daisy but produced in June and July. Most kinds grow about 2 feet tall and are, therefore, excellent for small borders or for middle or front positions in larger borders. Many of the varieties commonly grown in gardens are hybrids with 'fancy' names such as Felicity, Charity (Plate 10) and Quakeress, and these have flowers varying in colour from pale mauve, lavender and soft pink to violet or purple. In addition several species are grown, notably *Erigeron aurantiacus*, which is unique in having orange flowers and is rather more difficult to grow than most as it is liable to die in winter unless the soil is sandy and well drained; *E. glaucus*, which is little over 6 inches high and has big lavender flowers; *E. macranthus*, often wrongly called *E. mesa-grande*, 2 feet high with large violet-purple flowers, and *E. philadelphicus*, with much smaller flowers than the rest, soft pink, borne freely in small sprays. *E. mucronatus* is smaller still, in flower and stature, a pretty little pink and white flowered plant which sometimes seeds itself about so freely in dry walls or between the crevices of paving stones that it becomes a weed. It is not completely hardy and may be killed in cold winters.

All can be increased by division in spring. All like rather well-drained soils but few, except *E. aurantiacus* and hybrids from it, are really fussy about soil.

ERINACEA *(Hedgehog Broom)*

Erinacea anthyllis (Plate 10), which will be more familiar to most gardeners as *E. pungens*, is a remarkable evergreen shrub no more than a foot high, but usually considerably more in diameter, making a firm mound of extremely spiny growth, grey-green with lavender-blue pea-flowers freely produced in May and June. The name Hedgehog Broom is fairly appropriate but Hedgehog

Gorse would be more so in view of the spininess of the whole plant and its dense habit, far more like a tiny gorse bush than a broom. It is at home in the rock garden or on a dry wall and thrives in full sun and a well-drained soil. It can be grown from seed sown singly or in pairs in small pots in spring so that it may be grown on in these pots until ready for planting out, as it resents root disturbance.

ERINUS

Small rock plants making neat rosettes of leaves and bearing short spikes of pink, carmine or white flowers in May and June. The species commonly grown is *Erinus alpinus* (Plate 10), a first-rate plant for a dry wall or for growing in narrow crevices between rocks in the rock garden. It likes sun and good drainage, is readily increased from seed and often seeds itself. Seedlings usually vary a little in colour so selected forms, such as the very bright rosy-carmine Dr Hanele, should be increased by division in spring.

ERIOPHYLLUM

Hardy herbaceous perennials mostly white or grey because of the dense hairs which clothe their stems and leaves. They belong to the daisy family and have typical daisy-flowers. *Eriophyllum lanatum* (Plate 10) is a sprawling plant 8 or 9 inches high but a good deal more in diameter. The flowers are bright yellow, showy and very freely produced. It is hardy but likes a warm, sunny place and a rather light, well-drained soil and is most suitable for a sunny ledge in the rock garden. *E. caespitosum* is similar in character but less densely white woolly. A third species, covered in silken hairs, is. *E. leucophytum*. Propagation is by division in spring or by seed sown in a greenhouse or frame in spring.

ERYTHRINA *(Coral-tree)*

There are several species of erythrina but the name Coral-tree is commonly applied to *Erythrina crista-galli* (Plate 10), a remarkable herbaceous plant, 6 feet or more high, with leathery, pinnate leaves of considerable size and very showy spikes of big, deep scarlet, pea-type flowers in summer. It is not a hardy plant though it may sometimes be grown outdoors in very mild places, especially if given some protection in winter. More commonly it is grown as a pot plant under glass or is started into growth in spring in a greenhouse and then planted outdoors in early June when danger of frost is past. Roots should be potted in March in John Innes compost and should be grown in a temperature of 55° to 60°F. for a while. Later they may be gradually hardened off, expecially if they are to be planted out. Plants should be brought back into the greenhouse before there is danger of frost and the water supply gradually reduced. From November to February no water need be given. Propagation is by seed or by cuttings of young shoots taken in spring with a heel of older growth and rooted in a propagating frame with soil warming or other means of providing bottom heat.

Erigeron glaucus

Erythrina crista-galli

57

Erythronium americanum

Eucharis amazonica

ERYTHRONIUM *(Dog's Tooth Violet)*

Small, bulbous rooted plants, often with handsomely mottled or marbled leaves and nodding, cyclamen-like flowers on stems usually 6 to 8 inches long, but as much as 18 inches in the very vigorous, cream-flowered *E. californicum*. The best known species is the true Dog's-tooth Violet, *E. dens-canis* (Plate 10). This has exceptionally handsome leaves mottled with purple and white, and rose-coloured flowers on 6-inch stems and is often known as the Trout Lily. *E. americanum* is similar in height and has yellow flowers. *E. revolutum* is nearly twice as tall and has cream, purple-tinted flowers. There are numerous other species such as *E. grandiflorum*, yellow, *E. montanum*, white and orange, *E. citrinum*, pale yellow and *E. tuolumnense*, yellow and white. All are spring flowering, the season extending from about March to May. All like cool, rather leafy or peaty soils and partially shaded positions. They should be planted in autumn, 2 or 3 inches deep, and can be increased either by seed sown in a cool greenhouse or frame in spring or by division of the bulb-clusters at planting time.

EUCHARIS *(Amazon Lily)*

Tender, bulbous-rooted plants which make beautiful pot specimens for well-heated greenhouses. The best known kind is *Eucharis grandiflora* (Plate 10), often called *E. amazonica*. The white, tubular flowers are borne in clusters on a stout 2-foot stem from March to October. It needs a rather rich soil, such as a John Innes compost with a little well-rotted farmyard or stable manure added. Bulbs should be potted in May. Once they are established and growing, the plants should be watered and syringed freely and kept in a temperature around 75°F. Watering should be greatly reduced in autumn and almost discontinued in winter, when the bulbs are at rest, though even then a temperature of 60° to 65°F. is desirable. Annual repotting is not required provided the bulbs are not overcrowded, are top dressed each spring with rich compost and fed, while in growth, with liquid manure. Propagation is by removal of small bulbs when potting, which should be potted singly in 6-inch pots.

EUCOMIS *(Pineapple Flower)*

Bulbous-rooted perennials to be grown as pot plants in the greenhouse. The best known and most generally useful is *Eucomis comosa* (Plate 10), often called *E. punctata* in gardens, a nearly hardy plant with long, strap-shaped leaves and stiff, purple-spotted flower stems, 2 feet long, bearing close, cylindrical spikes of green flowers in mid-summer. Though not a showy plant it is an arresting one because of its unusual appearance. It is easily grown in a frost-proof greenhouse in John Innes compost and will only need artificial heat in really cold weather. Bulbs should be potted singly in September or October, watered rather springly in winter, fairly freely in spring and summer. Repotting is only necessary when the pots become overcrowded with roots.

EUCRYPHIA

These beautiful trees or large shrubs suffer from the handicap of being on the border-line of hardiness, but several kinds succeed in the milder counties and one, *Eucryphia glutinosa*, is hardy enough to be planted in sheltered places in most parts of the country. It is an erect growing, deciduous shrub, 12 feet or more high, with large white flowers, each with a cluster of golden anthers in the centre, the whole effect being a little like a single rose. It dislikes alkaline soils and succeeds under the same conditions as rhododendrons and heathers.

E. cordifolia is similar in flower but evergreen and tree-like in habit, often attaining a height of 40 feet or more. It flowers in August and is one of the most beautiful trees in the garden then, but it is decidedly tender and most suitable for the climatically favoured parts of the south and west.

A hybrid between those two species, *E. nymansensis* (Plate 10), is in many respects intermediate between them as it grows 30 feet or a little more in height and is hardier than *E. cordifolia* though not quite as hardy as *E. glutinosa*. It is evergreen and the white flowers appear in August.

All eucryphias should be planted in autumn in sunny but sheltered places. They need no pruning and are increased by cuttings of half-ripe shoots in a close frame in July.

EUPHORBIA *(Spurge)*

This vast genus of annuals, perennials, shrubs and trees contains a great many weeds and worthless plants, but also a few that are useful in the garden or greenhouse and two or three that are outstandingly beautiful.

In the last category must be included *Euphorbia fulgens* (Plate 10), a shrub to be grown in a warm greenhouse. Its orange scarlet flowers are borne in mid-winter along the length of gracefully arching branches which are excellent for cutting. It likes a temperature in the upper 60's, enjoys plenty of moisture, except for a few weeks after flowering, and thrives in a rather rich soil.

Much the same can be said of *E. pulcherrima*, better known as the Poinsettia, a tender shrub grown for its large, scarlet bracts produced in mid-winter. Both plants can be increased by cuttings of firm young shoots inserted in sand and peat in a propagating frame or box with bottom heat of around 75° to 80°F.

E. splendens, known as the Crown of Thorns, is an intensely spiny, succulent shrub with very showy scarlet flowers in summer. It also needs a warm greenhouse, but a drier atmosphere and less water.

Quite different in appearance and cultivation are the hardy euphorbias of which *E. wulfenii* (Plate 10) is one of the most handsome, and *E. cyparissias*, the Cypress Spurge, perhaps the prettiest. *E. wulfenii* is a perennial of almost shrub-like habit, with stout stems 4 feet high, bearing large heads of greenish flowers surrounded by yellow bracts. By contrast *E. cyparissias*

Eucryphia glutinosa

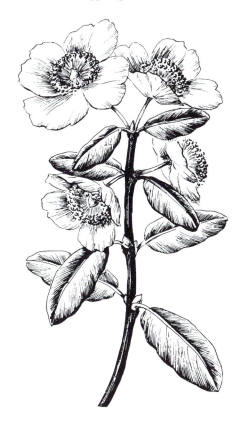

Eucryphia cordifolia

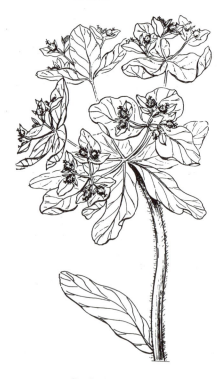

Euphorbia epithymoides

Exochorda racemosa

is quite a slender plant, no more than 1 foot high, with greenish-yellow inflorescences and a habit of taking on enchanting autumn tints before its leaves fall in the autumn. It spreads by underground shoots and can be increased by division in autumn or spring, as can most of the herbaceous euphorbias, but *E. wulfenii* is a little more difficult to divide and may be more readily raised from seed. Yet another attractive hardy species is *E. epithymoides*, better known in gardens as *E. polychroma*, which makes a low, dome-shaped mound of grey-green leaves covered over in early summer with flowers surrounded by showy, bright yellow bracts. *E. pilosa major* is not unlike this and often colours well in the autumn, and *E. myrsinites* is a trailing plant with grey-green leaves and the usual yellow bracts in summer.

EXACUM

Only one species is at all commonly grown and that nothing like as much as its merits deserve. This is *Exacum affine* (Plate 10), a bushy little annual or biennial about a foot high, with small, flat, lilac-blue, fragrant flowers each with a central cluster of golden yellow stamens. It is readily raised from seed sown in January or February (or, for earlier flowering, in September) in a temperature of 60° to 65°F. The seedlings should be potted singly in John Innes compost and later moved on into 5- or 6-inch pots in which they will flower the following summer or early autumn. Throughout the plants must have plenty of water and a temperature of 60°F or more. The John Innes compost will suit them well.

EXOCHORDA *(Pearl Bush)*

Beautiful deciduous shrubs which are strangely neglected as they are hardy and not difficult to grow. *Exochorda racemosa* (Plate 11), better known as *E. grandiflora*, is one of the best, a very bushy shrub, 8 or 10 feet high, producing a great many short spikes of white flowers in May. *E. geraldii* is more vigorous and has slightly smaller flowers. *E. macrantha*, a hybrid with *E. racemosa* as one of its parents, closely resembles that species and is said to be even freer-flowering.

All exochordas like good loamy soils and sunny positions. They are improved by pruning immediately after flowering, when the weaker stems should be removed to give the stronger ones more room to develop. They can be readily increased by detaching rooted suckers in autumn.

FATSIA

Fatsia japonica (Plate 11) is often seen as a house plant—an evergreen, shrubby plant with very big, dark green, shining leaves a little like those of a fig. It is a very good pot plant but it is equally at home outdoors where it will make a spreading shrub or small tree 10 or 12 feet high and, in a favourable season, produce club-like clusters of creamy flowers in great profusion in October and November when there is little of interest in the garden. It is hardy enough to be grown in all except the coldest districts, provided it is given a sheltered position. It does not mind semi-shade, will thrive in any reasonable soil and requires no pruning. It can be planted at any time from October to March. Propagation is by cuttings of nearly ripe shoots taken in late summer, but they need some bottom heat and should be inserted in a propagating frame in a greenhouse.

FOTHERGILLA

Hardy deciduous shrubs chiefly valuable for the splendid autumn colour of their foliage. Their fluffy clusters of creamy-white flowers, looking rather like small bottle-brushes, appear in April and are pleasantly fragrant. The two best kinds are *Fothergilla major* and *F. monticola* (Plate 11), both shrubs ultimately about 6 feet tall but slow growing, with hazel-like leaves which turn yellow, orange and copper before they fall. Both are quite hardy and easily grown in any reasonably good soil and sunny or slightly shaded position. No pruning is required. Fothergillas can be planted at any time from November to March and are best increased by layering in May or June.

FRANCOA *(Bridal Wreath)*

Herbaceous perennial plants which are on the borderline of hardiness and, for that reason, are usually grown as greenhouse or window pot plants, though in some sheltered gardens they will grow outdoors. The two commonest kinds are *Francoa ramosa* (Plate 11) and *F. sonchifolia*, both about 2 feet high, with slender, curving spikes of small flowers in July, white in *F. ramosa*, soft pink in *F. sonchifolia*. Both are very easily grown in almost any soil. Outdoors they seem to prefer a sunny position, but as pot plants they will thrive in a window for years despite the very much lower light intensity. They make excellent plants for the unheated or only very slightly heated greenhouse and should be planted or potted in March, at which time roots may be divided if desired.

FREMONTIA

Very beautiful deciduous shrubs which, in gardens, are almost invariably treated as climbers trained against a sunny wall. They are not fully hardy and are only suitable for planting outdoors in the milder counties. Elsewhere they may be grown in cool greenhouses, either as pot plants or planted in borders.

There are two species, both very alike. *Fremontia californica* (Plate 11) has bright yellow flowers, *F. mexicana*, deeper coloured more orange-yellow flowers produced from May to July. The leaves of both kinds are a curious dull green and the whole plant has a pleasantly aromatic smell.

Fremontias should be planted in April from pots, as they dislike root disturbance. They like a light, well-drained soil. They need no pruning, except to keep them in shape when they are grown on walls, which should be done in spring. Seed provides the best means of increase, sown in spring in a greenhouse or frame.

61

Fothergilla major

Fremontia californica

Fritillaria meleagris

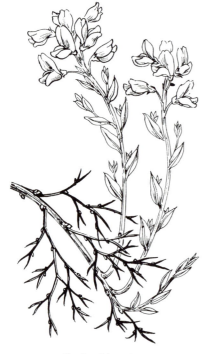

Genista hispanica

FRITILLARIA *(Fritillary, Snake's Head, Chequered Lily, Crown Imperial)*

This is a big genus of plants with some 80 or more known species, many of great beauty but by no means all easy to grow. They are plants that have attracted the attention of specialists and collectors and at least one whole book has been devoted to them. But there is nothing at all rare or mysterious about the Crown Imperial, *Fritillaria imperialis* (Plate 11), a stately, bulbous-rooted herbaceous plant producing in May its pendent clusters of yellow or orange flowers on stiff 3-foot stems with a curious top-knot of leaves above them. It is a favourite with cottage gardeners and no doubt would be even more widely grown were it not for the unpleasant, foxy smell it emits. There is a variety of it, named *inodora*, which is said to lack this smell, but I have never had the good fortune to meet it. *F. imperialis* is easily grown in any ordinary soil and sunny position. The bulbs should be covered with 4 or 5 inches of soil and thereafter be left to grow undisturbed until the clusters become so overcrowded that flowering suffers. Then they should be lifted and divided in July or August, the best planting months, though it is rarely possible to purchase bulbs before September.

Another easy species to grow is *F. meleagris*, the Snake's Head or Chequered Lily. This delightful plant has nodding lantern-shaped flowers in spring, chequered all over in shades of dull red, or red and white or yellow, each carried singly on a slender, foot-high stem. There is also a pure white variety. It is a rare native of Britain found in damp meadows near the Thames and elsewhere and this gives a clue to its successful cultivation in gardens. It can be naturalized in grass or planted in rock gardens and borders in good, rich, rather moist soil. The bulbs should be planted in autumn and be covered with 2 or 3 inches of soil. They should not be lifted and replanted annually but left to multiply naturally and form ever-spreading clumps.

GALTONIA *(Giant Summer Hyacinth)*

Though there are two or three species of galtonia, only one is at all commonly found in gardens. This is *G. candicans* (Plate 11), a hardy, bulbous-rooted plant with tall spikes of pendent white flowers in summer. The whole effect is rather like a giant white hyacinth with unusually loose and open flower spikes. The stem may be as much as 4 feet high and the plant looks well in the middle row of a herbaceous border. It will grow in any reasonable soil provided drainage is good. There is no need to disturb the bulbs annually. Plant them 6 or 7 inches deep in September or October and leave them undisturbed until they become overcrowded, when they may be lifted, divided and replanted at the usual planting time.

GENISTA *(Broom)*

The distinction between genista and cytisus is a purely botanical one and this is one of those instances where botany tends to confuse rather than to clarify the issue so far as gardens are concerned. All the genistas are shrubs, most are deciduous, and all the important garden kinds are yellow flowered. But they differ enormously in habit and height, from the sprawling, spreading carpets of *Genista tinctoria pleno* (Plate 11), to the 15-foot grace of *G. aethnensis*. These two I rate very high in the genus, the first because it is such a useful ground coverer in warm, sunny places, flowering with the utmost profusion in June, the second because of its extremely elegant, semi-weeping habit and the fact that it flowers in July when there is often rather a lack of colour in the shrub border.

The Spanish Broom, *G. hispanica*, also makes good ground cover but it is a taller plant than the double-flowered *G. tinctoria*, making mounds of very dense, spiny growth about 2 feet high, rather like a dwarf and compact gorse. It flowers in May.

Another low and spreading plant, but of more open habit, is *G. lydia*. The stems arch over so that it looks best when planted in a dry wall or rock garden, but may also be used at the front of the shrub border. Its very bright yellow flowers are produced in late May and June.

G. virgata is often known as the Madeira Broom but despite its name it is quite hardy and a showy shrub of considerable size, often 12 feet or more high and as much through, with abundant yellow flowers in June and July. *G. cinerea* is very like it but not quite so tall.

All these genistas like warm, sunny places and reasonably well-drained soils, but none is fussy and they have wide adaptability. Most can be raised from seed but, if this is not available, cuttings may be taken in July or August and rooted in nearly pure sand in a propagating frame.

GENTIANA *(Gentian)*

This large and important genus of rock plants was included in *Flowers in Colour* and I return to it here principally to show illustrations of two of the most useful and easily grown kinds, and two, incidentally, which are markedly different in character. One is *Gentiana freyniana*, a summer-flowering species with rather pale blue flowers clustered at the ends of spreading stems. It is much like *G. septemfida* and *G. lagodechiana* and all three are plants which will grow readily in any reasonable rock garden soil and sunny, open position. The graceful willow gentian, *G. asclepiadea*, 18 inches or so in height, has flowers spread out along the arching stems in a spike-like spray in mid-summer. It can be grown at the front of the herbaceous border or on the edge of a woodland glade, just as easily as in the rock garden and is a plant of great charm. There is a white variety.

All these gentians can be raised from seed and also by division in spring.

GESNERIA

Tropical South American perennials which make excellent pot plants for a well-warmed greenhouse. They have tuberous

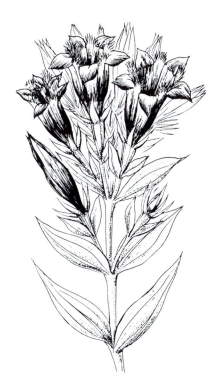

Gentiana freyniana

Gentiana asclepiadea

Gesneria 'Orange King'

Gillenia trifoliata

roots, handsome, usually velvety leaves and showy spikes of tubular flowers, commonly yellow, orange or red. There are numerous species such as *Gesneria cardinalis* (Plate 11) but in gardens it is hybrids that are most grown.

Cultivation is not unlike that of tuberous rooted begonias but, for preference, with more heat. Tubers are rested in winter, with no water and a temperature of about 55°F, and are started into growth any time from March to May simply by bringing them into a temperature around 65° to 70°F and giving them water. From then on they should have plenty of moisture at the roots and in the air. In summer they must be shaded from direct sunlight. The flowering season extends from about July to December according to variety and time of starting. After flowering, water is reduced and, a little later, withheld altogether so that plants may rest.

Gesnerias are usually grown, one tuber in each 5-inch pot, in a compost containing rather a lot of peat, some loam and a little sand. The tubers should be just covered with soil.

Gesnerias can be raised from seed sown on the surface of a mixture of peat and sand, or by the natural multiplication of the tubers. Mature leaves can also be slit across the veins and pegged to the surface of a sand and peat compost in a close frame with bottom heat. If kept moist they will soon form plantlets at the slits. Again the likeness to some begonias will be observed.

GILLENIA *(Indian Physic)*

The only species at all commonly grown, and that still a rather rare plant in gardens, is *Gillenia trifoliata*, a pretty and graceful hardy herbaceous perennial with loose sprays of small, white, starry flowers surrounded by red calyces. The stems are very slender and the whole plant no more than 3 feet in height. It flowers in early summer and will thrive in an open or partially shaded situation. It is not fussy about soil and can be increased by division in the spring.

GLADIOLUS *(Sword Lily)*

The familiar garden gladioli are all hybrids of rather complex parentage and, for the sake of convenience, they have been split up into several groups such as the Large Flowered, Primulinus, Miniature and Butterfly. These are, however, entirely arbitrary divisions, and continual interbreeding tends to blur still further whatever clear lines of demarcation may have existed between them. In consequence some of the large flowered varieties show traces of the hooded upper petals which should distinguish the primulinus varieties and many of the latter have become so large and open flowered that they seem to differ little from the smaller varieties of the large flowered group. The miniature gladioli originated in Canada and mostly have gracefully crimped petals, in contrast to the butterfly gladioli which originated in Holland and are, in the main, smooth petalled. Both these and the primulinus gladioli are exceptionally good for flower arrangements.

Fothergilla monticola

Galtonia
candicans

Fatsia
japonica

Exochorda
racemosa

Fremontia
californica

Gesneria cardinalis

Francoa
ramosa

Fritillaria
imperialis

Genista tinctoria
plena

adiolus
zantinus

Hebe
'Midsummer Beauty'

Hedera colchica
dentata variegata

Halesia
carolina

Haemanthus
coccineus

Hieracium
aurantiacum

Hesperis
matronalis

Gloriosa
rothschildiana

Hencherella
'Bridget Bloom'

Haberlea
rhodopensis

Hepatica
triloba

Helleborus
corsicus

Halimium
alyssoides

The colour range in these hybrid gladioli is astonishingly wide and constantly being still further extended. All flower in late summer, the precise time depending to some extent upon the time at which the corms are planted. This may be between early March and late May and the corms should be given a sunny place, in rich well-drained soil, and be covered with about 3 inches of soil. About six weeks after flowering the plants are lifted, the leaves cut off an inch or so above the corms and the latter placed in boxes in a shed or greenhouse to dry off. After a week or so the old withered corms can be broken from beneath the new corms and discarded and these new corms stored for the winter in any cool but frost-proof place such as a cupboard indoors.

No such precautions are required for *G. byzantinus* (Plate 11), a hardy species with spikes of rather narrow, vividly magenta flowers in early summer. This neglected plant will look after itself in any warm, sunny spot and well-drained soil, and need never be lifted until its clumps become too big and overcrowded, when it can be divided like any herbaceous plant.

More exacting are the early flowering gladioli known as *G. colvillei* which have slender spikes of scarlet or white flowers and are usually grown in cool greenhouses to give cut flowers in May and June. For this purpose the corms are potted or boxed in autumn and rested in summer after flowering. During the winter, when other gladioli are resting, the colvillei varieties should be growing in a temperature of 50° to 60°F.

GLORIOSA

Often known as the Climbing Lily, *Gloriosa rothschildiana* (Plate 12) is a remarkable greenhouse plant with slender stems, climbing by means of tendrils, and showy yellow and red flowers, in form not unlike those of *Lilium speciosum*. It flowers in summer.

This and other gloriosas should be grown in pots in a half-and-half mixture of peat and loam with a little sharp sand. February is the month for potting, one bulb in each 7- or 8-inch pot. They need a really warm temperature, 70° to 75°F, and plenty of moisture throughout the spring and summer, but in autumn and winter they rest and need no water. At this period the pots may be laid on their sides, but still a fairly warm temperature (60° to 65°F) should be maintained. Do not shake out the bulbs when repotting, but tease away a little of the soil and replace with fresh soil. Small bulbs may be removed very carefully and potted on their own, and plants can also be raised from seeds sown singly or in pairs in small pots in February in a close frame with a bottom temperature of 75°F or thereabouts. Gloriosas have brittle roots and do not like these being broken, so great care should be taken when repotting not to cause any injury.

HABERLEA

Shade-loving rock plants closely allied to and resembling the ramondas. They have similar flat rosettes of leathery leaves and

Gladiolus primulinus hybrid

Gladiolus colvillei

Haemanthus albiflos

Halesia monticola

clusters of flowers like tiny gloxinias on 6-inch stems in April or May. The best known is *Haberlea rhodopensis* (Plate 12), a charming little plant, normally with lilac flowers though there is a pure white variety named *virginalis*. *N. ferdinandi-coburgi* is very similar, more vigorous and considerably more uncommon.

All haberleas like cool, leafy or peaty soils and are happiest when growing on their sides in vertical, or near vertical, crevices in the rock garden or dry wall. A north aspect suits them best though they will grow well in full sun also, provided they do not get too baked and dry. They can be increased by seed sown in a frame or greenhouse in spring, or by leaf cuttings in June in sandy peat in a close frame. Well-grown leaves are detached and their stalks inserted in the sandy-peat.

HAEMANTHUS *(Blood Lily)*

Bulbous-rooted plants for the moderately heated greenhouse. All have broadly strap-shaped leaves, stout flower stems and rather curious, compact flower clusters looking a little like broad pincushions because of the long stamens. These rounded flower heads are surrounded by wide petal-like bracts which are often the same colour as the flowers—white in *Haemanthus albiflos*, deep red in *H. coccineus* (Plate 12), crimson in *H. katherinae* and light scarlet in *H. puniceus*. With the exception of *H. coccineus*, which flowers in early autumn, all these flower in summer.

Bulbs should be potted in March but annual repotting is undesirable as plants flower most successfully when rather pot-bound. Ordinary John Innes compost may be used and the bulbs should be completely covered. They should be watered moderately at first and kept in a minimum temperature of 55°F., rising with sun heat. More water will be needed towards flowering time, but a few weeks after flowering the water supply should be gradually reduced and the bulbs allowed to rest for a time in a cooler atmosphere before they are started into growth anew in the spring; but at no time should the soil be completely dry, nor should the temperature ever fall below 45°F. Small bulbs, or offsets, can be removed at potting time as a means of increasing stock.

HALESIA *(Snowdrop Tree)*

Beautiful hardy deciduous trees suitable for sheltered positions in good, loamy soil. There are several species but only two, *Halesia carolina* (Plate 12) and *H. monticola*, are at all familiar in British gardens and even they are surprisingly rare considering their beauty and comparative ease of culture. Both produce similar hanging clusters of white bell-shaped flowers in May, though they are rather larger in *H. monticola* which is also a larger tree. It is said to grow up to 100 feet in its native habitat in the United States, but no trees of anything approaching this size are known in this country. *H. caroliniana* makes a spreading tree 20 feet or so high. Neither species requires any pruning and both can be raised from seed sown in a frame or greenhouse in spring or by layering in May or June.

HALIMIUM

Small evergreen shrubs closely allied to the sun roses (*helianthemum*) and often included in that genus. They relish the same conditions of well-drained soil and warm, sunny position and are admirable for rock gardens, dry walls and banks. Among the best species are *Halimium alyssoides* (Plate 12), a 2-foot shrub with bright yellow flowers; *H. libanotis*, about 3 feet high and also yellow-flowered, but with a small dark spot at the base of each petal; *H. umbellatum*, a little more dwarf, with smaller white flowers marked with yellow at the centre; *H. ocymoides*, 2 feet or a little more with yellow flowers heavily blotched with deep purple, and *H. lasianthum formosanum*, 2 feet high but very spreading and also with yellow, purple-blotched flowers in July.

All can be increased by seed, or by cuttings of half-ripe shoots in July in a propagating frame. They can be lightly pruned after flowering to keep them neat in the same manner as helianthemums.

HEBE *(Veronica)*

Many name changes made by botanists, though doubtless excellent on botanical grounds, are merely annoying to gardeners as they involve learning new names without any advantage in clarity or understanding. Not so the separation by botanists of the great genus of *Veronica* into two separate genera under the names *Veronica* and *Hebe*, with the herbaceous and rock garden species remaining under the first name and the evergreen shrubby species transferred to *Hebe*. This is a change that makes for simplification for there is little similarity between the culture and garden use of the two groups. Moreover the new name is as pretty and easily remembered as the old one, which makes it all the more surprising that it has been almost completely ignored by gardeners.

Nearly all species of hebe come from New Zealand and many of them are tender or on the borderline of hardiness. Nevertheless there are some splendid shrubs among them, none better than *Hebe speciosa* and the many garden forms and hybrids of it. These make well-branched, shapely, evergreen bushes usually about 4 feet high, with dense spikes of flower from July to October (later still, sometimes, if the autumn is mild). They do well by the sea but also succeed in inland gardens if they do not get too severely frozen. The colour range is from pale blue and pink to violet, purple and crimson. Simon Delaux, crimson flowered, is an outstanding example. Autumn Glory with violet flowers, is also related to *H. speciosa* but is not above 2 feet high, has smaller leaves and is much hardier. *H. salicifolia* is looser and more graceful in habit, 5 or 6 feet high, occasionally considerably more, with narrow leaves and long, slender spikes of white or mauve-tinted flowers in late summer and autumn. It is probably just a little hardier than *H. speciosa* but not as hardy as *H. brachysiphon*, which is apparently the correct name of the shrub every gardener knows as *H. traversii*, a dense small-leaved evergreen, 4 or 5 feet high, with short spikes of white

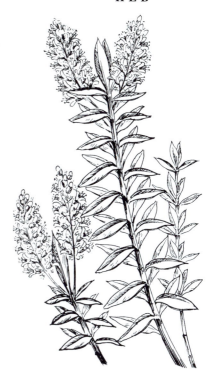

Hebe traversii

Hebe salicifolia

67

Hedera helix conglomerata

Hedera helix sagittaefolia

flowers produced very freely in July. This is hardy in all except the very coldest places and one of the best flowering evergreens. It makes an excellent hedge.

A lovely hybrid hebe, which probably owes something to *H. speciosa* and more to *H. salicifolia*, is *H.* Midsummer Beauty (Plate 12). This makes a bush 3 or 4 feet high with long spikes of lavender flowers. It is at least as hardy as *H. salicifolia*.

Very different from these are *H. cupressoides*, *H. buchananii* and *H. hectori*, small shrubs, 1 to 2 feet high with tiny leaves so tightly packed along the branches, one over another, that the whole effect is remarkably like a cypress. Their proper place is the rock garden in a sunny, sheltered situation.

H. hulkeana is another highly distinctive plant, a loosely branched evergreen, 3 feet or more high, with lavender flowers in large sprays instead of the usual spikes. It is rather tender and in all except the mildest parts of the country will probably need the protection of a sunny wall. Alternatively it can be grown as a pot plant in the cool greenhouse.

All the hebes thrive in well-drained soils and sunny places. If desired they can be lightly pruned after flowering to prevent them from becoming too large. All are very easily raised from cuttings at almost any time.

HEDERA *(Ivy)*

Though the ivy has been given a bad name, it is an admirable self-clinging evergreen climber with a great many very beautiful varieties differing in the shape and colour of their leaves. Most of the good garden ivies are varieties of the British ivy, *Hedera helix*, but perhaps the most beautiful of all ivies, *H. colchica dentata variegata* (Plate 12), belongs to an Asiatic species that has been called the Persian Ivy. It has very large leaves almost without indentations and the colour is pale green, broadly banded with yellow. It will grow as readily as the common ivy in almost any soil and place. The plain green-leaved form of this ivy is also worth growing.

Among the best varieties of the common ivy are *caenwoodiana*, which has small very deeply lobed leaves; *digitata*, with very large deeply lobed leaves; the various forms of *marginata* in which the leaves are bordered with white, cream, yellow or red, *sagittae folia*, with very narrow, almost arrow-like lobes, and *conglomerata*, an extraordinary slow growing, bushy plant with small leaves densely huddled on the rather contorted stems.

When the common ivy is full grown it produces bushy growth with ball-like clusters of yellowish-green flowers in October, followed by black berries. If cuttings are taken of this adult growth, the resultant plants remain bushy and never climb. This form of the ivy is sometimes known in gardens as tree ivy or *arborescens*.

The Canary Island Ivy, *H. canariensis*, has very large leaves and is much grown as a house plant, particularly in its variegated form. A number of other varieties of ivy has been specially developed as house plants.

Jacobinia
carnea

Iris
histroides

Juniperus
sabina
tamariscifolia

Ixora
[garden form]

Ipheion
uniflorum

Hypericum
repens

Kniphofia
galpinii

Hoheria
lyallii

Hippophaë
rhamnoides
[female form]

Inula
oculus-Christi

Humea elegans

Ilex aquifolium
aurea marginata

Lilium auratum platyphyllum

Layia elegans

Lagerstroemia indica

Leonotis leonurus

Leptospermum scoparium nicholsii

Lathyrus grandiflorus

Lachenalia 'Burnham Gold'

Kolkwitzia amabilis

Ivy will grow in almost any soil and sunny or shady position. When grown on walls it can, with advantage, be trimmed over with shears each spring. Cuttings taken at practically any time in summer or autumn root readily in a frame.

HELLEBORUS (Christmas Rose, Lenten Rose, Hellebore)

Hardy herbaceous perennials which have the twin merits of flowering in winter or early spring and of thriving in shady places. The Christmas Rose, *Helleborus niger*, has white flowers, a little like single roses, borne on naked stems, about a foot long in the common variety but as much as 2 feet and heavily red spotted in the fine variety *altifolius* which also starts to flower a little earlier—November, in an average season, against December for the common form.

The Lenten Rose, *H. orientalis*, carries its flowers in clusters, starts to flower in March and has a wider colour range than the Christmas Rose, from white to maroon.

H. foetidus and *H. viridis* are both green-flowered and have handsome, dark green leaves, but better still in this style is *H. lividus*, better known as *H. corsicus* (Plate 12), a bigger plant 3 feet high when well grown, with large deeply-toothed leaves and fine clusters of apple-green flowers in winter, lasting until about March. At its season it is one of the handsomest plants in the garden.

All these hellebores like good, rich rather leafy soils not liable to dry out too quickly in summer. They will grow in sun or shade, but prefer the latter, resent root disturbance and are best planted in autumn. They can be increased by seed, which is usually rather slow in germinating, or by careful division at planting time.

HEPATICA

Low-growing hardy perennials, very closely related to anemone. Two species are commonly grown in gardens, *Hepatica triloba* (Plate 12) and *H. transsilvanica*, better known as *H. angulosa*. *H. transsilvanica* is the stronger growing, 9 or 10 inches high, with sky-blue flowers. *H. triloba* is not above 6 inches high and has slightly smaller flowers which are also sky-blue in the common form, but there are several varieties differing in colour, *alba* being white and *rubra* pink, and there are also delightful double-flowered forms. All flower in February and March. All are delightful little plants to border a woodland path or a shady border or to grow in a cool and shaded part of the rock garden. They like a leafy, woodland type of soil, thrive in chalk or limestone localities and should be planted in autumn or in spring immediately after flowering. They are most readily increased by division at planting time.

HESPERIS (Dame's Violet, Sweet Rocket)

The common Sweet Rocket, *Hesperis matronalis* (Plate 12), is a hardy herbaceous perennial, but it is often a rather short-lived

Helleborus niger

Helleborus foetidus

Hesperis matronalis flore pleno

Hieracium villosum

one and, as it is apt to increase itself readily from seed, it is often regarded as a biennial. It grows about 3 feet tall and produces, in May and June, long sprays of small white or purple flowers which are fragrant in the evening. It is a rather untidy plant for the herbaceous border, but first rate in the wild garden where it will often naturalize itself and spread considerably. Far choicer is the Double Sweet Rocket (*H. matronalis flore pleno*), with fully double white or purple flowers, but it is more difficult to grow and, as it produces no seed, must be increased by cuttings of short, non-flowering shoots in sandy soil in a frame in spring or early summer. Both double and single forms like a rich, rather moist soil with plenty of humus to keep it open.

HEUCHERELLA

In *Flowers in Colour* I described as *Heuchera tiarelloides* a dainty plant with sprays of soft pink flowers. Botanists have now given a new name to this plant, which is, in fact, a bi-generic hybrid between *Heuchera brizoides* and *Tiarella cordifolia*. The new name is *Heucherella tiarelloides* and it has also acquired a lovely companion named Bridget Bloom (Plate 12) which is taller and more closely resembles a soft-pink heuchera. This is a hybrid between an undisclosed heuchera and *Tiarella wherryi*. These are all easily grown hardy herbaceous perennials for the front row of the border, valuable because they are even lighter and more airy in effect than the heucheras and thrive just as readily under a wide range of conditions. They will grow in sun or partial shade in any reasonable soil and can be increased by division in spring or early autumn, the best planting seasons.

HIERACIUM (Hawkweed)

Mostly these are horrible weeds but at least two species of hieracium are worth a place in the garden, especially in poor, stony soils and sunny dry positions. These are *Hieracium aurantiacum* (Plate 12) with brilliant orange-red, dandelion-like flowers, and *H. villosum* with similar bright-yellow flowers and leaves densely covered with long, silvery hairs. Both plants are mat forming and flower most of the summer. They are readily increased by division at practically any time and the only precaution necessary is not to plant them near any small rock plant or other treasure which they will certainly swamp with their rather invasive growth.

HIPPOPHAË (Sea Buckthorn)

Hippophae rhamnoides (Plate 13) is a small deciduous tree or large shrub with narrow, silvery leaves, inconspicuous flowers and orange berries with a very staining juice. The berries are freely produced, but only on female plants as the sea buckthorn produces male and female flowers on separate plants. In order to ensure crops of berries a male plant must be grown fairly near the female plants so that pollen may be blown by wind from male to female flowers. Once this essential fact has been grasped, the cultivation of sea buckthorn is quite simple as it will grow in any reasonable soil and open, sunny position. It is a first rate sea-side plant and may sometimes be seen naturalized on waste land or sand-dunes near the sea, but it grows equally well inland. It is said to make a tree 30 feet or more in height, but is more usually seen as a bush about 10 or 12 feet high. It needs no pruning and is increased by seed sown in spring.

HOHERIA

These large shrubs or small trees are grown for their clusters of white flowers about midsummer when the shrub border can easily lose interest. All are very quick growing and not, as a rule, very long lived but they are readily increased by seed and in favourable places sometimes seed themselves about so that there is no difficulty about keeping up a succession of young plants. The naming of the genus is a little involved as it has at different times been known as *Plagianthus* and *Gaya* and the species have also been confused. Probably the best known kind is *Hoheria lyallii* (Plate 13), a plant with softly downy leaves that have a slightly greyish appearance. The variety known as *glabrata* very closely resembles it but has smooth green leaves. *H. populnea* and *H. sexstylosa* are both evergreen in a mild winter but unfortunately are a good deal less hardy and only really suitable for the mildest parts of the country.

All like well-drained, fairly rich soils and warm, sunny places. Even the deciduous kinds may be cut back fairly severely in cold winters but they usually break into growth again from below the damaged area and, because of their rapid growth, soon make good specimens again. No regular pruning is needed except when damage of this kind occurs, when all dead wood should be removed as soon as it is detected.

HUMEA *(Incense Plant)*

The only species grown in gardens, *Humea elegans* (Plate 13), is a biennial with long, arching sprays of tiny reddish-brown flowers and large, rather coarse leaves with the perfume of incense. It is a tender plant mainly grown for the greenhouse, but it is sometimes planted outdoors in summer in sub-tropical bedding schemes. It is raised from seed sown in May, June or July in an unheated frame. Seedlings are potted singly, as they appear, in John Innes compost and are moved on into larger pots as necessary, until by the following March or April they reach the 8-, 9- or 10-inch pots in which they will flower in summer. Greenhouse protection will be needed from late September onwards but only enough artificial heat to maintain a minimum temperature of 45 F. The two most important points are not to break the roots when repotting and not to overwater. A little shading may be needed in summer while the flower sprays are being produced. On good plants these sprays may be 6 feet tall.

HYPERICUM *(St. John's Wort, Rose of Sharon)*

This very large genus contains many pretty weeds, some excellent plants for the rock garden or dry wall and a few good

Hoheria populnea

Hypericum 'Hidcote'

Hypericum calycinum

Hypericum fragile

shrubs. A few of the alpine hypericums are quite prostrate plants, such as *Hypericum reptans* which makes a carpet of leaves closely following the outline of rock or soil and studded with fine yellow flowers sitting close down on the slender stems, but most are more shrubby and branching in habit. These range from free-growing but sprawling plants only a few inches in height, of which *H. fragile* and *H. repens* (Plate 13) are excellent examples, to erect little bushes, such as the foot-high *H. coris* and 18-inch *H. olympicum*. In general the colour is bright and shining, not far removed from buttercup yellow, but *H. olympicum* has two forms, one of the typical hypericum shade the other, named *citrinum*, a pale moon-yellow. All are sun-lovers and, with the possible exception of *H. reptans*, which is occasionally a little temperamental, all are indestructible plants in any reasonably drained soil. They are all readily raised from seed and will sometimes seed themselves about.

Most important of the shrubby hypericums are *H. calycinum*, the Rose of Sharon, and the numerous varieties of *H. patulum*. The former is an extremely vigorous sprawling evergreen shrub not above 18 inches in height but capable of spreading indefinitely, rooting as it does, so that it is an indefatigable coverer of ground but also, in the wrong place, a nuisance and even a weed. It will thrive in sun or shade in any kind of soil but with a special partiality for chalk and its flowers are large, bright yellow, very showy and produced in July and August. It is an admirable plant for covering a difficult bank or smothering the weeds beneath taller shrubs but it needs to be kept in its place. It can be increased at any time simply by digging up rooted pieces and replanting them.

There is nothing invasive about *H. patulum*, a neatly bushy deciduous shrub 3 or 4 feet high and a little more in diameter, but it is sometimes apt to seed itself about freely so that surplus seedlings may have to be removed. The yellow flowers are more saucer-shaped than in most other species and are very freely produced in July and August. There is a variety named *henryi* which has larger flowers and another hypericum, named Hidcote, which is superior in bloom even to this and is usually regarded as a form of *H. patulum* though I think this is open to doubt. It is, in my view, the finest of all shrubby hypericums, making a big more or less evergreen bush 5 or 6 feet high and flowering from July right on into the autumn.

The evergreen *H. moserianum*, a hybrid between *H. patulum* and *H. calycinum*, has the low stature of the latter without its invasive tendencies and there is a very pretty variety of it, named *tricolor*, in which the leaves are variegated with pink and white. *H.* Rowallane Hybrid is also, as its name proclaims, a hybrid but a rather tender one which needs a warm sheltered place if it is not to be killed to ground level each winter. Where it can grow undamaged it makes a graceful shrub up to 8 feet high with large, bowl-shaped flowers of exceptionally rich yellow colour.

All these shrubby hypericums can be raised from cuttings in

August in a propagating frame but the species are even more readily raised from seed. They are not fussy about soil or situation.

ILEX *(Holly)*

The common holly, *Ilex aquifolium*, is an excellent hedge plant but not, perhaps, quite worth planting as a specimen shrub if only because it has so many more interesting forms, some with larger foliage, some with silver or golden variegated leaves, at least two with yellow berries. All these grow just as readily as the common holly in an ordinary soil and sunny or partially shaded position. All are rather difficult to propagate from cuttings, for which reason they are usually grafted on to seedlings of the common holly. And all can be pruned in spring or early autumn if it is desired to keep them to a special shape or size.

A peculiarity of the holly is that generally a plant will produce flowers of one sex only. Only the female flowers can produce berries and then only if fertilized with pollen from male flowers, so that often it is necessary to choose varieties with this important point in mind. *I. a. argentea marginata* which has white margins to its leaves, is a female variety. Golden King, perhaps the best yellow-variegated holly, is also berry-bearing. By contrast Silver Queen and Golden Queen, also white- and yellow-variegated, produce male flowers only. *I. a. aurea-marginata* (Plate 13), is a name covering a group of similar forms all with a golden margin to the leaves. Some, at least, of these are berry-bearing. One yellow-berried holly is named *fructu-luteo*, another, more narrowly erect in habit, *pyramidalis fructu-luteo*. Yet another remarkable variety is *ferox*, called the Hedgehog Holly because it produces spines on the surface as well as along the edges of its leaves. This is a male variety.

There are, in addition, several very large-leaved hollies which are often described as varieties of the common holly but are, in fact, varieties of a hybrid, *I. altaclarensis*, which has the common holly as one of its parents and a more tender, Canary Island species, *I. perado*, as the other. The two best of these handsome forms are known as *camelliaefolia*, which is female and, therefore, berry bearing, and *hodginsii*, a male form.

There are a number of other species of holly, mostly evergreen, though a few, such as *I. laevigata* and *I. macrocarpa*, are deciduous, but none superior to our native hollies as garden trees. *I. pernyi* makes a neat, slow-growing evergreen shrub and *I. platyphylla*, another Canary Island holly has large leaves, is quick-growing and usually berries well.

These exotic hollies need the same treatment as the native holly.

INULA

Hardy herbaceous perennials with large, yellow, daisy-type flowers in summer. Some are rather coarse plants, more suitable for the wild garden than the herbaceous border, but all are showy and easily grown in almost any soil and open or even partially

73

Ilex camelliaefolia

Ilex aquifolium ferox

Inula helenium

Iris kaempferi

shaded positions. The two smallest are *Inula acaulis*, which is quite stemless, and *I. ensifolia* which is about 9 inches tall. At the other extreme is *I. macrocephala* with large flowers carried on 4 to 6 foot stems. Intermediate kinds suitable for the border are *I. oculis-Christi* (Plate 13) and *I. orientalis* (better known as *I. glandulosa*) both 1½ to 2 feet high. *I. helenium* is a native British plant well worth a place in the garden, with silken-hairy leaves and clusters of yellow flowers in July and August. The plant grows about 6 feet high and is popularly known as Elecampane. All inulas can be increased by division in either spring or autumn.

IPHEION

This pretty little blue-flowered perennial, *Ipheion uniflorum* (Plate 13), a favourite with cottage gardeners for edging, has suffered from a superfluity of botanical names. At various times it has been *Brodiaea*, *Milla* and *Triteleia* and the only thing that has not changed is its second, or specific name. It is an easily grown plant in any well-drained soil and sunny position. It grows about 9 inches tall and produces its flowers for many weeks in spring. *Ipheion uniflorum* is not fussy about soil, can be planted in spring or autumn and is readily increased by division, preferably in spring.

IRIS

This is another of those great genera of plants, with so many species and such vast numbers of garden varieties that many books have been devoted exclusively to the subject without exhausting it.

In gardens it is the June-flowering bearded irises that have been most highly developed. These derive in part from *Iris germanica*, the German Iris or Purple Flag, in part from the Austrian *I. pallida*, which has a delightful, pale blue fragrant variety named *dalmatica*, in part also from the yellow and purple *I. variegata*, with other species, no doubt, brought in from time to time by enterprising breeders in search of greater variety. The result is a bewildering list of varieties, in height ranging from 18 inches or so to 5 or 6 feet, in colour covering a vast range of shades from which only true reds and crimsons seem to be now excluded. All flower in May or June, are sun-lovers and like well-drained but not poor soils. Lime or chalk is helpful but not essential. Many are fine, hardy, free flowering plants, but in the search for size, perfection of form and even greater variety of colour, constitution has sometimes been sacrificed and disease occasionally takes more than its fair toll.

Less 'improved' and, perhaps for that very reason, more reliably robust, are the varieties of *I. sibirica*, a more slender and graceful plant than any of the June hybrid irises and one which will succeed just as well in a damp spot or even in a bog garden as under drier conditions. The colour range is white and pale blue to purple. *I laevigata* and *I. kaempferi* are real moisture lovers, the former actually preferring to have its crowns just submerged at the edge of a pool or slow moving stream. The flowers are large, richly coloured and carried in June and July or 3 foot stems.

The so-called Crimean irises are varieties of *I. chamaeiris*, often wrongly described as *I. pumila* which is a different and even shorter-stemmed plant. They look like dwarf June bearded irises but flower in May and have a more restricted colour range.

Also well suited to the rock garden are the early flowering bulbous-rooted irises of which the two most popular are *I. reticulata* and *I. histrioides* (Plate 13). The latter tends to be the earlier of the two and in a mild winter or sheltered spot may be already opening its plump, short-stemmed, light blue flowers in January, so that outdoors it often needs the protection of a pane of glass. It is closely followed by the taller, much deeper violet-purple *I. reticulata*, known as the Violet-scented Iris because of its fragrance. It makes a first-class pot plant for the unheated greenhouse as well as being reliable in well-drained soil and a sunny place outdoors. The yellow-flowered *I. danfordiae* is out at the same time but is not so popular.

Latterly the slender, 18-inch high varieties of *I. douglasiana* have been becoming increasingly popular, and in America a great many varieties of *I. spuria* have been raised in a considerable range of colours, including attractive shades of yellow, bronze and blue. They are hardy and easily grown border plants 2 or 3 feet in height.

The very popular English and Spanish irises are bulbous rooted plants derived from *I. xiphioides* and *I. xiphium*. They must be planted in autumn to flower the following June and are excellent cut flowers in shades of blue and yellow as well as white and various combinations of these.

The Algerian Iris, *I. tingitana*, is very like a Spanish Iris but less hardy and usually grown as a greenhouse plant for winter or early spring cut flower. Also winter-flowering but quite hardy is *I. unguicularis* better known as *I. stylosa*, a lovely plant whose only fault is that it tends to hide its pale blue flowers among its ample foliage. It likes a sunny place.

IXORA

These very handsome plants, usually seen in Britain as greenhouse pot plants, are, in fact, tropical shrubs or small trees. They have evergreen leaves and flattish clusters of starry-looking flowers (a closer inspection will reveal that they are tubular) usually in some vivid shade of orange or red. The most important species from a garden viewpoint is *Ixora coccinea*, with orange-red flowers in summer, but there are also many excellent hybrids and varieties (Plate 13), some of which have finer flowers than the wild kinds. All can be increased by cuttings of firm young shoots inserted in a propagating frame with bottom heat of about 75° to 80° F. Once rooted these cuttings should be potted individually in a rather peaty compost. Being tropical plants they can take all the warmth that may be going in summer, provided they are watered well and syringed frequently, but in

Iris xiphium (Spanish)

Iris unguicularis

Juniperus communis compressa

Juniperus communis fastigiata

autumn and winter the temperature may drop to 50°F. and much less water should be given. No shading will be needed during this resting period, but in summer, shading is desirable to protect the foliage from scorching.

JACOBINIA

Showy plants for the warm greenhouse with short spikes of tubular flowers which in some species are closely clustered into a plume-like head. The genus is very closely allied to Justicia and the two have been much confused by botanists. The two most popular species are *Jacobinia carnea* (Plate 13), with soft salmon-pink flower clusters in early autumn, and *J. coccinea*, with scarlet flowers in late winter. Both can be grown from cuttings of young shoots in spring, rooted in a close propagating frame or box with soil warming or bottom heat. When rooted the cuttings are potted individually in John Innes compost and should be moved on as necessary until they reach the 6-, 7- or 8-inch pots in which they will flower. A temperature of 60°F. will suffice in summer but may rise considerably with sun heat. Temperatures may drop back to 50° to 55°F. in winter. Re-pot when necessary in February or March and pinch out the growing tips occasionally, especially of young plants, to encourage a branching habit. Some shade will be needed from about June to September but not afterwards.

JUNIPERUS *(Juniper)*

Evergreen cone-bearing trees and shrubs all of which do specially well on chalky or limestone soils. They vary greatly in height and habit, some, such as *Juniperus virginiana*, known as Red Cedar, being large trees 50 feet or more in height, some, such as *Juniperus communis compressa*, miniatures no more than a foot or so high and most suitable for the rock garden. This small form of the common juniper is one of the slowest growing of all conifers. It makes a perfect little column of blue-grey foliage and is justly one of the most popular of all rock garden conifers. Very similar in colour and habit, but ten times as large as the Irish Juniper, is *J. communis fastigiata*, which makes a compact and elegant column of growth up to 20 feet in height.

For contrast there are two wide, spreading, almost horizontal junipers. The larger of the two, *J. chinensis pfitzeriana*, grows about 6 feet high and a mature specimen may easily measure 12 or 14 feet across. *J. sabina tamariscifolia* (Plate 13) is no more than 4 feet high, usually less, but may be 8 or 10 feet through.

All junipers can be raised from cuttings of firm young growth in early autumn inserted in sand or sandy soil in a propagating frame or box.

KNIPHOFIA *(Red Hot Poker, Torch Lily)*

These handsome herbaceous plants are all natives of South Africa and so it is not surprising that some are not fully hardy in the British Isles. This, however, is not true of *K. uvaria*, a plant normally about 4 feet high with red and yellow flower

Lycaste
skinneri

Lilium,
Bellingham Hybrid,
'Royal Favourite'

Magnolia
sinensis

Liriodendron
tulipifera

Manettia
inflata

Malus pumila
'John Downie'

Lysichitum
americanum

Odontoglossum
crispum

Narcissus
triandrus

Nigella
damascena

Mimulus
cardinalis

Morina
longifolia

Morus
nigra

Nepenthes
rafflesiana

Narcissus
cyclamineus

Nerium
oleander

Narcissus
bulbocodium

Mentzelia
lindleyi

Miltonia
'Sunrise'

spikes in August, but one which has proved very variable in gardens so that numerous varieties have been raised from it. Some, such as Royal Standard, are dwarfer and more slender than the wild plant, others, such as *nobilis* and *grandis*, are much taller and have larger flower spikes. Forms have been raised, such as *corallina* and Mount Etna, that are wholly scarlet, others, such as Buttercup, are yellow throughout. There is even one remarkable variety, named *erecta*, in which the individual tubular florets start by hanging downwards in the ordinary way but then gradually erect themselves from the bottom upwards so that at the mid-way stage the spike somewhat resembles a rocket. All these are plants for sunny places and good, loamy soils and they all appreciate plenty of moisture during the period at which the flower spikes are developing.

K. galpinii (Plate 13), is a very different plant, much more slender, with grass-like foliage and 2 to 3 feet spikes of orange flowers. It is a very pretty plant, flowering in September and October and, although reasonably hardy, appreciating a sunny, sheltered place.

K. nelsonii and *K. macowanii* are also small species, the former 2 feet high with scarlet and orange flowers, the latter about the same in height with yellow and orange-red spikes. Both are August flowering and need a well-drained soil as they are none too hardy.

Another very distinctive species is *K. caulescens*, which branches from a central stem or 'trunk' rather like a yucca. It flowers earlier than most, in June, and the yellow and red flowers are particularly densely packed in the spike.

A beautiful hybrid of uncertain origin is *K.* Maid of Orleans. It is of average height but the 'pokers' are rather more slender than in *K. uvaria* and are ivory white. It is not one of the hardiest but will succeed in well-drained sheltered places.

All kniphofias can be increased by careful division in spring or autumn. They can also be raised from seed, though seedlings may take two or three years before they flower and, if the seed is taken from garden varieties or hybrids, there is likely to be variation in the seedlings.

KOLKWITZIA

Kolkwitzia amabilis (Plate 14) is a deciduous shrub looking very much like a very elegant, small-flowered weigela. The flowers, which appear in May and June, are pale pink with a touch of yellow. It is a beautiful shrub when well suited by soil and situation, but it likes sun and warmth. I believe there are at least two forms of it about and that one flowers more freely than the other, so that it is wise, when buying plants, to enquire whether they have been raised from a free-flowering parent. Full grown it is about 7 feet high and as much through. It should be planted in a sunny, sheltered position in well drained but reasonably good soil. No pruning is required. Propagation is by cuttings of either half-ripe growth in July or of fully-ripe growth in October.

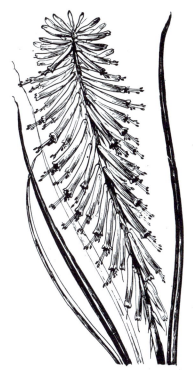

Kniphofia galpinii

Kniphofia caulescens

Lachenalia bulbifera

Laeliocattleya hybrid

LACHENALIA *(Cape Cowslip)*

South African bulbs suitable for cultivation in cool greenhouses. They make elegant spikes of hanging, tubular flowers, a little reminiscent of those of a bluebell or hyacinth, but usually yellow or yellow and red. Two of the best are *Lachenalia aloides nelsonii*, about 12 inches high and yellow, and *L. bulbifera* (better known as *L. pendula*) which is a little shorter and red, yellow and green. There are also a number of hybrids, such as Burnham Gold (Plate 14), which extend the usefulness and variety of the genus as ornamental plants for pots or hanging baskets. Most flower in spring. Bulbs should be potted or placed in baskets in August and thereafter should be grown in a light, airy greenhouse in a temperature between 50° and 60°F. The bulbs should be about 3 inches apart and covered with half-an-inch of soil. John Innes compost is suitable. Lachenalias should be watered fairly freely while in growth but should be gradually dried off after flowering and allowed to be completely dry for several weeks before they are repotted. Propagation is by seed sown in the greenhouse in early spring or by small bulbs removed at potting time.

LAELIOCATTLEYA

These handsome and usually highly coloured orchids are bi-generic hybrids between *Laelia* and *Cattleya*. In general their flowers are rather smaller than those of cattleya but they include many rich and unusual shades of purple. coppery-red, salmon and mauve. Most of the varieties cultivated, and there are a great many of them, have 'fancy' names such as Britannia, Osiris, Pontami, Danae and Cyrano but a few, such as *bella*, *exoniensis* and *veitchiana*, have been given garden names in Latin form. All need the same cultural treatment as cattleyas and most are winter flowering, though there are some, such as *Laeliocattleya callistoglossa*, which flower in late summer or autumn.

LAGERSTROEMIA *(Crape Myrtle)*

Lagerstroemia indica (Plate 14) is a handsome shrub or small tree frequently used for street planting in the Mediterranean countries, but in Britain too tender to be grown outdoors. However it makes an excellent pot plant and flowers freely even when kept far below its natural size. The bright, rose-pink flowers wreath the branches throughout the later summer. The crape myrtle should be grown in John Innes compost and is best potted (or re-potted when necessary) in March. During much of the year it will need no artificial heat, but in winter a temperature of around 45° to 50°F. should be maintained. Water should be given fairly freely in spring and summer, and plants can be syringed daily, but water must be given very sparingly in winter and the atmosphere kept dry then. In February all growth made the previous year can be cut back fairly hard. Propagation is by cuttings of young shoots in March or April, inserted in sand, or very sandy soil, in a close frame or propagating box with soil warming or bottom heat.

LATHYRUS (Pea)

The popular sweet pea is an annual species of this genus, its botanical name being *Lathyrus odoratus*, but it has been so highly developed in gardens, both as to the size and form of its flowers and their colour range, that the garden varieties bear little resemblance to the wild plant which is their forebear. Every year new varieties are raised, new names added to the catalogues, so that the enthusiasm of the sweet pea grower is constantly titillated by the advent of novelty. Greater numbers of flowers have been added to the spike, so that six per stem is now considered nothing remarkable, extra petals have been added to the flowers, increased frilling to the petals and a greater colour range, though as yet no really yellow sweet pea has been raised. All are grown from seed sown in spring or autumn and, though excellent plants can be grown for garden decoration quite naturally on bushy pea sticks, for cutting and exhibition the plants are usually restricted to one stem each and tied to tall bamboo canes. For this purpose seed is usually sown in early October under glass, but for garden display seed is sown outdoors in spring.

Besides this popular plant there are other excellent species of lathyrus worthy of a place in the garden. One of the best of these is *L. latifolius*, the Everlasting Pea, a perennial, herbaceous climber with spikes of rose or white flowers not unlike those of a sweet pea but smaller and scentless. It is very easily grown in almost any soil and sunny position, will climb to a height of about 8 feet and can be easily increased by seed sown in spring. Particularly lovely is the pure white variety known as The Bride, but this will not breed true from seed and must be raised from cuttings of the young shoots in early spring, rooted in a frame.

L. grandiflorus (Plate 14) is an annual climber with very large rose flowers produced in clusters of two or three. It is grown from seed sown in March or April where the plants are to flower.

L. vernus is a dwarf, bushy perennial, no more than 1 foot high, with numerous spikes of small pink or purplish flowers in May. It is a pretty plant for the front of a border or it may be grown in the rock garden. It likes well-drained soil and can be raised from seed sown in a frame or greenhouse in spring.

LAYIA

Only one species, *Layia elegans* (Plate 14), is likely to be seen in British gardens and that is something of a rarity despite the fact that it is a pretty annual, quite hardy and producing showy yellow and white daisy-flowers for several weeks. It makes a bushy plant 12 to 18 inches in height and will grow and flower freely in any reasonable soil and sunny position. Seed should be sown in March or April where the plants are to flower, the seedlings being thinned to 9 inches.

LEONOTIS (Lion's Ear)

Showy shrubs or sub-shrubs which are in general too tender to be grown outdoors in Britain, though the best of them, *Leonotis*

Lathyrus latifolius

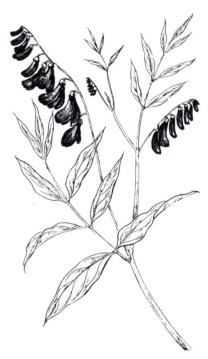

Lathyrus vernus

Lilium formosanum

Lilium auratum

leonurus (Plate 14), sometimes thrives in Devon, Cornwall and other mild places. It is a striking plant, 3 or 4 feet high, occasionally more, with long spikes of bright orange-red flowers produced in whorls in autumn or winter. Outdoors it should be given well-drained soil and a sunny, warm, sheltered position. Under glass it can be grown as a pot plant in John Innes compost and will only need enough artificial heat to keep out frost. Plants can be pruned a little after flowering to keep them from becoming straggly or too big. Potting is best done in March. Propagation is by cuttings of firm young shoots in sandy soil in a close frame.

LEPTOSPERMUM *(Manuka)*

Evergreen shrubs or small trees of which the best for British gardens is *Leptospermum scoparium*. This is hardy in the south and west and may be grown in many other parts of the country if it can be given a sunny but sheltered position. In colder places it must be treated as a cool greenhouse pot plant. It has very small leaves and white flowers clustered along the slender, wiry stems in June, and makes a tall bush up to 15 feet in very favourable places. Better still is the variety named *nichollsii* (Plate 14), in which the flowers are carmine red. There is also a prostrate, pink-flowered variety which is said to be hardier and another with double white flowers named *flore pleno*. All like well-drained soils of the type that suit heathers. They can be raised from seed but the selected forms are better increased by cuttings of half-ripe shoots in July, rooted in sand in a propagating frame, preferably with a little soil warming.

LILIUM *(Lily)*

There are so many lilies, and so many beautiful garden plants among them, that it is impossible to do them justice in a few paragraphs. This is one of those splendidly varied genera that demands a book to itself if any justice is to be done.

Most popular of hardy lilies today are *Lilium candidum*, the white Madonna lily, and *L. regale*, the white gold-flushed Regal Lily. Both are supremely easy to grow in any ordinary soil. The Madonna Lily likes sun, the Regal Lily will succeed equally well in sun or half-shade, and can be raised so readily from seed that seedlings may be flowered in their second year.

Two fine orange-red lilies with large, spreading clusters of hanging flowers are *L. tigrinum*, the Tiger Lily, and *L. henryi*, which has acquired no popular name. Both have dark brown or blackish spots on the flowers and both are fine, vigorous plants, the Tiger Lily usually about 6 feet high, *L. henryi* as much as 8 or 9 feet under favourable conditions.

L. chalcedonicum is known as the Scarlet Turk's-Cap Lily because of the vivid red of its flowers and the way in which the narrow petals are swept back. It is a brilliant lily and not a difficult one to grow.

The Yellow Turk's Cap Lily, *L. pyrenaicum*, suffers from the drawback of a rather unpleasant smell.

The Turk's Cap Lily is *L. martagon*, a variable plant as to

Paeonia ludlowii

Parthenocissus henryana

Pelargonium [Regal form]

Parrotia persica

Onosma tauricum

noopordon anthium

Oncidium varicosum rogersii

Parochetus communis

Othonnopsis cheirifolia

Pelargonium 'Mrs Henry Cox'

Papaver rhoeas [Shirley variety]

Pieris
forrestii

Picea
pungens
glauca

Philodendron
scandens

Phlox drummondii
[garden forms]

Polygala
chamaebuxus

Physalis
franchetii

Polygonum
campanulatum

Portulaca
grandiflora

Potentilla
'Master Floris'

Pleione
pricei

Phytolacca
clavigera

Piptanthus
nepalensis

C. Newsome-Taylor

colour, some forms being old-rose or dulled pink, some wine purple, one pure white. All are easily grown and look particularly lovely planted among low growing shrubs.

L. formosanum, L. sulphureum and *L. longiflorum* all have long trumpet flowers and all are rather tender, *L. longiflorum* so much so that it is usually grown as a pot plant in the greenhouse. It is often gently forced to bring it into bloom at Easter when its elegant, pure white flowers are much in demand for church decoration.

The nodding, recurved *L. speciosum*, white and rose in the common form, but running to several varieties, some nearly wholly white, others with much deeper colouring, is also predominantly a greenhouse plant for summer flowering, but can be grown outdoors in sheltered places. It is rather late flowering.

L. monadelphum is a tall lily with hanging golden-yellow flowers. *L. szovitsianum* is much like it and sometimes listed as a variety of it. *L. pardalinum*, the Leopard Lily, is yet another with pendent flowers much like those of the Turk's Cap lilies in form but deep orange-red heavily spotted with dark purple. Then there are the very numerous Orange Lilies usually grouped under the name *Lilium umbellatum*, though botanists seem to regard *L. hollandicum* or *L. maculatum* as more correct. These vary in height from 1 to 3 feet, produce their flowers in clusters looking up, and are yellow, orange or red. All are immensely showy plants, easily grown in any well-drained soil and fairly sunny, open place. *L. bulbiferum croceum* is similar but may be taller, and *L. maculatum*, better known as *L. thunbergianum*, also has the same style of flowering.

The Bellingham hybrids (Plate 15) are much taller plants, 5 feet at least, often more, with great branching sprays of hanging flowers in various shades of yellow and orange. They are lilies for thin woodland or to be planted among low-growing shrubs that will shade their roots.

L. auratum, the Golden-rayed Lily of Japan, has produced many splendid garden forms as well as some rather difficult hybrids with *L. speciosum*. The garden forms usually have more highly coloured flowers than the type, with flushes or bands of pink or red further to enliven the natural white or yellow, purple-spotted flower. *L. auratum platyphyllum* (Plate 14) differs in having flowers of exceptional size. All like peaty, lime-free soil and a cool root run in the shade of shrubs, such as low-growing azaleas or rhododendrons.

All the garden forms of lily must be propagated by removing offsets (small bulbs) from the larger bulbs or by placing mature bulb scales in boxes filled with sand so that bulbils (tiny bulbs) form on them after a few months. They seldom come true to type from seed. The species, however, can be raised from seed, some being rather slow to flower but others, such as *L. regale* and *L. formosanum*, maturing quite quickly.

Most lilies like deep, cool, leafy or peaty soils. A few, such as *L. candidum* and *L. chalcedonicum*, do not mind lime but most soon fall into ill-health on markedly alkaline soils. All can be

F

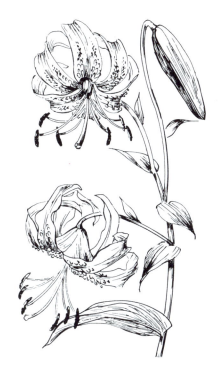

Lilium henryi

Lilium chalcedonicum

Lycaste hera

Lysichitum camtschatcense

planted in autumn, but it is better to move *L. candidum* and its lovely buff-yellow hybrid, *L. testaceum*, earlier, in August or early September. The difficulty is to get delivery of bulbs then. These two kinds are also peculiar in liking their bulbs almost on the surface, whereas most lilies need to be planted about 6 inches deep. There is no need to disturb them annually if doing well.

LIRIODENDRON *(Tulip Tree)*

This remarkable deciduous tree, *Liriodendron tulipifera* (Plate 15), will eventually grow to a great size but is worth growing as a young tree only if there is not room for it to develop fully. It has unusually shaped leaves that look as if the ends had been cut off. These are a rather light green, especially when young, and in autumn they turn bright yellow. As the tree matures it commences to produce its rather curious, cup-shaped, green and orange-yellow flowers, not showy but unusual and interesting. Eventually the tree makes a tall and shapely specimen with a very handsome bole. It will grow in any reasonable soil but likes best a deep, rich loam. It is a little tender when young and, in particular, the young leaves are apt to be cut by a sharp April or May frost, so that it is not wise to plant this tree in frost pockets. It does not transplant well and small, young specimens are best obtained and planted in spring. No pruning is required. Propagation is by seed sown in a greenhouse or frame in spring, but germination is slow and unreliable.

LYCASTE

A genus of tender orchids for moderately heated greenhouse of which by far the most popular and useful is *Lycaste skinneri* (Plate 15). This is a plant of moderate size with white, rose-flushed flowers produced throughout the late winter months. It has a number of varieties differing mainly in the degree of colouring of their flowers. Although the flowers are solitary they are individually quite large and very attractive. *L. skinneri* should be grown in a mixture of three parts of sphagnum moss, two parts of osmunda fibre and one part of leaf mould, and repotted in March or April after flowering. In winter a minimum temperature of 55°F. will suffice, rising with sun heat in summer but never becoming very hot. In summer the plants must be shaded from direct sunlight and ventilated well. They also need a fair amount of water but this should be gradually cut down in autumn so that by winter watering may almost cease. The water should be applied direct to the compost and not splashed all over the plants. *L. deppei*, with green and white flowers spotted with purple and red, blooms at about the same season and requires similar treatment. There are also some attractive hybrids such as the yellow *L. hera*.

LYSICHITUM *(Skunk Cabbage)*

Hardy bog plants with arum-like flowers and large, rather coarse leaves. They are showy plants for the streamside or to grow at the edge of a pool, but they need plenty of room. The two species grown are *Lysichitum americanum* (Plate 15), with butter-yellow flowers (they are really spathes encircling the true flowers borne on a column-shaped spadix) and *L. camtschatcense*, which is white. Both are hardy and easily grown provided they have plenty of moisture. They can be increased by division in spring which is also the best planting season. Seedlings can also be raised, provided they can be given the necessary very wet conditions.

MAGNOLIA *(Cucumber Tree, Yulan, Lily Tree)*

To most people magnolia conjures up a picture of sumptuous white or pink blooms, like thick-petalled tulips, borne with great profusion on bare stems in spring. That is a true enough picture of the Yulan, *Magnolia denudata*, a handsome deciduous tree 20 or 30 feet in height with pure white flowers, or of any of the numerous forms of *M. soulangiana*, which are similar in size and habit and have a colour range from white to purple. But it is a very partial picture of this great genus, which includes evergreen as well as deciduous species, summer as well as spring flowers, and shrubs in addition to trees.

The first to bloom is *M. stellata*, which seldom exceeds 12 feet in height and is often seen as a bush of about 8 or 9 feet high and diameter. The flowers are white or occasionally a very soft pink, and they have much narrower petals than the later spring flowering magnolias.

It is followed closely by *M. denudata*, and then within a week or so come a number of lovely species and varieties including two small-flowered but very beautiful kinds that are not sufficiently seen. These are *M. kobus* and *M. salicifolia*, both slenderly built and graceful trees but *M. kobus* capable of making a much bigger specimen in the long run.

M. soulangiana has a great many varieties, differing mainly in colour but also a little in flowering time. All are trees of fine, spreading habit, ultimately about 20 or 30 feet high and rather more through. The darkest coloured and also the latest in flower is *lennei*, a wonderful wine-purple bloom of great size and substance that continues until the end of May. The variety *rustica rubra* comes near it in colour, *alba* is pure white and the form usually sold as *M. soulangiana* without any additional label is white flushed with purple.

M. liliflora, a purple-flowered species, flowers in late May and makes a link with the true summer-flowering magnolias such as *M. sinensis* (Plate 15), *M. sieboldii*, *M. wilsonii*, *M. watsoni* and *M. highdownensis*. All these are totally different in appearance from the spring-flowering magnolias, the flowers being saucer shaped and pendent, each with a conspicuous central crimson boss of stamens and borne among the leaves, not before them. They are less spectacular than the early magnolias but no less beautiful and delightfully fragrant.

The big Himalayan tree magnolias, of which *M. campbellii* and *M. mollicomata* are the best known examples, are superb but rather impossible for most gardens because of their great

Magnolia stellata

Magnolia salicifolia

Malus lemoinei

Malus baccata

size—they may reach a height of 60 or 70 feet—their comparative tenderness, and their slowness in starting to flower.

More generally useful is the evergreen *M. grandiflora*, a big tree in warm countries, but in Britain more usually grown against a wall when it is capable of covering a considerable area with its large, laurel-like leaves. The flowers, like large white water-lilies, appear in late summer.

All magnolias like good, loamy soils, well supplied with humus. They enjoy being mulched with peat or leaf-mould, hate root disturbance or injury and are best planted while still quite young. Few of them really like lime or chalk but many will grow on moderately alkaline soils, particularly if plenty of humus is added. They can be raised from seed but this is sometimes slow in germinating. They can also be increased by layering in May or June, and by grafting in spring, seedling magnolias being used as stocks.

MALUS *(Apple)*

The ornamental apples are among the most valuable of spring flowering trees and in addition to those kinds grown solely for their flowers, there are also some Crab Apples of which the fruits are at least equally important from a decorative standpoint.

Principal of the flowering apples are *Malus floribunda*, *M. lemoinei*, *M. purpurea*, *M. aldenhamensis* and *M. eleyi*. *M. floribunda* makes quite a small tree, rarely much more than 15 feet high though occasionally 20 feet, with a slightly weeping habit and abundant flowers which are red in the bud but nearly white when fully open. It is one of the loveliest of all flowering trees in April and early May.

M. purpurea has larger, rosy-red flowers and the other three are all wine-purple in colour and are very much alike to the non-expert. *M. eleyi* often follows its flowers with quite a good crop of cherry-like purple fruits but as a cropper it is surpassed by the Siberian Crab, *M. baccata*, a shapely tree 30 feet or thereabouts in height, with white flowers followed by cherry-like red fruits. There is also a yellow-fruited variety.

There are also several fine varieties of our British crab apple, *M. pumila*, of which the best are John Downie (Plate 15) with egg-shaped scarlet and yellow fruits, Dartmouth Crab, with globular, purplish-red fruits and Golden Hornet which is yellow throughout.

All these ornamental apples thrive in any reasonable soil and open position. They can be pruned each winter to keep them in shape and size. Species can be raised from seed but the garden varieties, and kinds such as *M. floribunda* which rarely produce seed, are increased by grafting in spring or budding in summer.

MANETTIA

Slender greenhouse climbing plants, the two most popular of which are *Manettia bicolor* and *M. inflata* (Plate 15). Both are similar in appearance, twining plants with small, tubular flowers which are half red, half yellow. They can be grown as pot plants trained around three or four slender canes, or they can be planted out to grow more extensively on wires strained under the greenhouse rafters. They are spring flowering. Both these manettias need a warm greenhouse (minimum winter temperature 55°F., summer 65°F. upwards) and can be grown in an ordinary John Innes compost. They should be watered fairly freely in spring and summer, moderately in autumn, sparingly in winter. They can be easily increased by cuttings of young shoots in a propagating frame with bottom heat.

MASDEVALLIA

Beautiful orchids for the moderately heated greenhouse. They require very similar conditions to odontoglossums, a compost of chopped osmunda fibre and sphagnum moss in about equal parts, a minimum winter temperature of 50°F., rising to about 60°F. minimum in summer, and plenty of ventilation whenever weather conditions permit. The flowers are remarkable for the long 'tail' which extends sometimes from all three sepals, sometimes, as in the popular crimson-flowered *Masdevallia coccinea*, only from the upper sepal. Repotting should be done just before new growth starts (usually in March). Water should be given in winter as well as summer as there is no season of rest.

MENTZELIA

Mentzelia lindleyi (Plate 15) is a showy hardy annual frequently known in gardens as *Bartonia aurea*. It is grown from seed sown in March or April where it is to flower and seedlings should be thinned to 9 inches. Plants grow about 2 feet in height and produce an abundance of widely opened, almost flat, bright yellow flowers in summer. This mentzelia likes a sunny place and a reasonably well-drained soil, but is not otherwise in the least difficult to grow. It should be more widely planted.

MICHAUXIA

These beautiful but rather temperamental relations of the campanula are mostly biennials, short-lived perennials, or, perhaps more accurately, monocarpic plants, i.e. plants that die after flowering. The best known species, though still somewhat of a rarity, is *Michauxia campanuloides*, a 5 or 6 foot high plant with quite large bell-shaped flowers which are white, more or less suffused with purple. It is grown from seed sown in a greenhouse or frame in spring and the seedlings should be planted out in a warm, sheltered place in very well-drained soil. They will go on growing for a year or so and then bloom, set seed and die.

MILTONIA

Handsome orchids (Plate 16) with sprays of large, often richly coloured, more or less, flat flowers that have a certain resemblance to enormous pansies. Almost all the varieties cultivated are hybrids, though one species, *M. vexillaria*, is also grown considerably and is itself one of the principal parents of the hybrids.

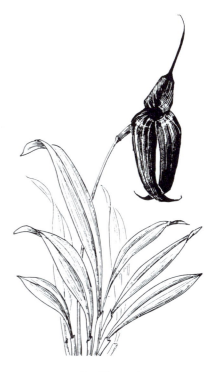

Masdevallia coccinea

Michauxia campanuloides

Mimulus aurantiacus

Trumpet Daffodil 'W. P. Milner'

All miltonias like a winter temperature between 55°F. and 60°F. and this can rise considerably in summer provided there is ample moisture and shading, which should be rather more dense than for most orchids. Most miltonias flower in late spring and early summer. The resting season is in winter but even then sufficient water is needed to keep the compost moist for the plants do not become so completely dormant as some orchids. Repotting is done in September in a compost of about equal parts of chopped osmunda fibre and sphagnum moss, with just a little dried cow dung added.

MIMULUS (*Monkey Flower, Musk*)

There are both annual and perennial species of mimulus and plants for the greenhouse as well as for the open air. Perhaps the most famous, though today very little grown, is the Musk, *Mimulus moschatus*, the prostrate, spreading perennial with the little pale yellow, brown spotted flowers that once had a highly distinctive perfume and then mysteriously lost it, no one knows how or why.

M. luteus is the Monkey Musk, an easily grown perennial for damp places. It will even grow in quite swift-running streams, provided they are sufficiently shallow. Typically it has bright yellow, red-spotted flowers on foot high stems in summer but there are several varieties of it some much more heavily spotted than others.

Lower growing and more highly coloured is *M. cupreus*, the Chilean Musk. This likes cool, leafy soil with plenty of moisture in summer but not the very wet conditions that suit the monkey musk. There are several varieties in various shades of copper-red and scarlet but none better than Whitecroft Scarlet.

M. burnetii is a hybrid between *M. luteus* and *M. cupreus* and it has yellow flowers heavily blotched with bronze-red.

Another brilliant kind is *M. cardinalis* (Plate 16) a slightly taller plant with scarlet flowers carried on foot high stems. It will thrive in ordinary soil and a sunny position.

M. lewisii is similar in stature and has pink flowers and it has produced a hybrid with *M. cardinalis* which is named *M. bartonianus* and is rose-red with a yellow, speckled throat.

M. guttatus is not unlike *M. luteus* but has bigger, more heavily spotted flowers, and with *M. luteus* it has produced a race of large-flowered hybrids known as *M. tigrinus*, usually grown from seed as annuals either for planting out or as summer flowering pot plants in the unheated greenhouse.

The plant now known as *M. aurantiacus* will be more familiar to many gardeners as *Diplacus glutinosus*. It is a perennial shrub, 3 or 4 feet high, with sticky leaves and orange-yellow flowers in summer. It is easily grown in ordinary John Innes compost and, as it is nearly hardy, very little heat will be needed to grow it well. It should be pruned a little each February to prevent it from becoming straggly and it can be increased by cuttings of young growth in spring or summer. All the perennial herbaceous musks can be increased by division in spring.

MORINA

Herbaceous perennials with thistle-like leaves, the best species being *Morina longifolia* (Plate 16). This is an unusual and attractive plant with slender, 2-foot spikes of pink (or sometimes red) and white flowers about midsummer. Sometimes a second crop of flowers appears in the early autumn. The foliage is handsome but must be protected from unskilled garden helpers who may mistake it for a thistle. This morina likes a sunny place and reasonably well-drained soil. It can be grown from seed but is also easily increased by division in the spring.

MORUS *(Mulberry)*

The common or black mulberry, *Morus nigra* (Plate 16), is a wide-spreading tree 20 to 30 feet high and sometimes 40 feet or more in diameter. It is slow-growing and often has a twisted appearance, with rugged bark as it ages. The distinctive, blackberry-like fruits are very freely produced and can be rather a nuisance when they fall. The white mulberry, *M. alba*, is the species grown extensively for feeding silkworms. It lacks the romantic appearance of the common mulberry and is not so good a garden tree. Both kinds like good, well-drained, loamy soils and warm, sheltered situation. They are more suitable for the south and west of Britain than for the north and east. Mulberries can be increased by cuttings in July or by layering at almost any time.

NARCISSUS *(Daffodil, Jonquil, Lent Lily)*

This great genus of spring flowers is rich both in wild species and garden varieties; so rich that fanciers of the narcissus have had to invent an elaborate system of classification for the flower, based partly on flower shape and character, partly upon the species from which the garden forms have been developed. Thus the Trumpet daffodils, with their trumpet-like cups or coronas exceeding the length of the perianth segments, bear obvious resemblance to our own native Lent Lily, *Narcissus pseudo-narcissus*, though they generally have much larger flowers and bloom a little later, in April rather than in March. The Cupped Narcissi show evidence of the influence of *N. incomparabilis*, a species widely distributed in the south of Europe, and the Poet's or Pheasant-eyed Narcissi are closely allied to *N. poeticus* a graceful wild plant with white perianth and small, neatly formed yellow and red cup. The fragrant Jonquil, *N. jonquilla*, has reproduced many of its elegant qualities in garden hybrids and another multi-flowered species, *N. tazetta*, known as the Polyanthus Narcissus, has combined with the Poet's Narcissus to produce a very useful race known as Poetaz Narcissi. These have several flowers on a stem, often with brightly coloured cups as in the orange-red and creamy-white St. Agnes.

These are the big groups but there are others which, though less popular, are none the less delightful. The miniature Cyclamen-flowered Narcissus, *N. cyclamineus* (Plate 16), with narrowly

Narcissus jonquilla

Narcissus recurvus

Narcissus 'Queen Anne's Daffodil'

Narcissus 'Silver Chimes'

tubular corona and perianth segments curled right back, is a charming plant itself for the rock garden or naturalizing beside a woodland path and it has handed on some of its highly individual charm to such larger garden versions as Jenny and February Gold. Another miniature, the white or pale yellow flowered *N. triandrus* (Plate 16), with small hanging clusters of flowers, has given, among other garden hybrids, the equally lovely though larger Silver Chimes.

The very late flowering *N. recurvus* is a variety of *N. poeticus* with the same general characters and colour scheme but perianth segments that curve backwards, though not so sharply as those of *N. cyclamineus*. It is intensely fragrant and as it does not flower until May it is useful to lengthen the narcissus season. It has also produced a beautiful double flowered form, often known as the Gardenia-flowered Narcissus, which has retained both its perfume and its lateness.

Of the familiar wildings only the Hoop-Petticoat Daffodil, *N. bulbocodium* (Plate 16), remains relatively 'unimproved' by hybridization or selection. This is, perhaps, just as well as its combination of widely bell-shaped cup with extremely narrow segments, though delightful in a miniature only a few inches in height, could easily look ungainly in a larger version.

In addition to the double form of *N. poeticus recurvus* there are numerous other double-flowered varieties, variously derived. Some, like the early flowering, rather clumsily formed Phoenix, have obvious affinities with the Trumpet daffodils, others, such as the almost globular Mrs William Copeland, suggest an origin from the Cup Narcicissi. One lovely old variety is Queen Anne's Double Daffodil, a miniature narcissus no more than 6 inches in height. It must not be confused with Queen Anne's Double Jonquil also known as Pencrebar which bears one or two small completely double flowers on a 6-inch stem.

All narcissi like rich, loamy, rather moist soils but can be grown successfully in almost any soil provided it is well cultivated. Many kinds succeed well naturalized in grass but this must not be cut until after midsummer by which time the daffodil foliage will have died down. Even the tiny *N. bulbocodium* naturalizes well in turf that is composed of the finer grasses. All narcissi should be planted 5 or 6 inches deep in late summer or autumn, the earlier the better as they do not improve by being kept out of the soil. There is no need to lift them annually but when bulbs become overcrowded lifting and dividing should be done in July as soon as the foliage dies down. Narcissi can be raised from seed but it is a slow process.

NEPENTHES *(Pitcher Plant)*

Extraordinary tropical plants which produce pitcher-like appendages from the midribs of the leaves. The purpose of these pitchers, some of which rather resemble an old-fashioned meerschaum pipe with a lid, is to trap insects which are then absorbed as food. The pitchers are often large and handsomely coloured purple, crimson, pink or brown, sometimes spotted or veined. There are numerous species such as *Nepenthes hookeriana*, with short green, red-spotted pitchers, *N. maxima*, pitchers green heavily mottled with purple, *N. rafflesiana* (Plate 16) with long rather slender pitchers, *N. sanguinea* with reddish pitchers, and *N. rajah* with the largest pitchers of all. Many garden hybrids have been raised from these and other species but as they have almost all been given Latin names it is difficult to distinguish hybrids from species. A few outstanding hybrids are *N. chelsonii* with yellowish-green, purple-spotted pitchers; *N. intermedia*, bright green and purple; *N. mastersiana*, deep red and purple, and *N. wittei*, green and reddish-purple.

All nepenthes can be grown quite easily, provided a temperature of 65°F. can be maintained in winter, rising to 70°F. or more in summer and with abundant atmospheric moisture at all times. They are grown in wooden baskets or the well-drained pots used for orchids, in compost similar to that used for orchids, consisting of peat fibre and chopped sphagnum moss (2 parts of peat to 1 of sphagnum). Water should be given freely in summer, moderately in winter. Propagation is by seed or by cuttings of year-old growths struck in heat but both methods need some experience and are, perhaps, best left to professionals.

NERIUM *(Oleander, Rose Bay)*

All through the south of France, Italy and other Mediterranean countries the evergreen oleander bushes with their showy clusters of rose-pink flowers are a familiar sight. They are grown as large bushes in gardens and parks or as small trees in the streets and they seem to thrive in any place that is warm and sunny. In Britain *Nerium oleander* (Plate 16) is too tender to be grown outdoors, but it makes a good pot plant for a sunny greenhouse in which a winter minimum temperature of 45°F. can be maintained. It should be given a large pot or small tub and a good rich compost of the John Innes No. 2 type or, alternatively, it can be planted in a border of good, loamy soil in the greenhouse. Water freely in spring and summer, rather sparingly in autumn and winter. After flowering in summer, prune all young growth rather hard to keep plants bushy and neat. Propagation is by cuttings of well-ripened young growth in August or September, rooted in a warm propagating frame or box.

NIGELLA *(Love-in-a-Mist, Devil-in-a-Bush)*

Elegant hardy annuals easily grown from seed sown in March, April or September where the plants are to flower. Seedlings should be thinned to at least 9 inches. All nigellas like a sunny, open situation and reasonably good, well-drained soil. The most popular kind is *Nigella damascena* (Plate 16) which grows about 18 inches high, has ferny foliage and blue flowers which are deeper and richer in colour in the variety Miss Jekyl. A second good plant is *N. hispanica*, rather similar in general appearance to *N. damascena* but with a deep crimson 'eye' of stamens to each blue flower. It is sometimes known as the Fennel Flower because of its very narrow leaves.

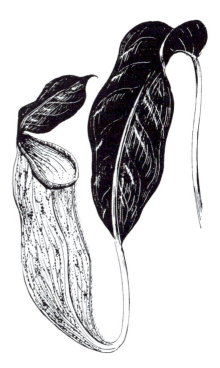

Nepenthes wittei

Nigella hispanica

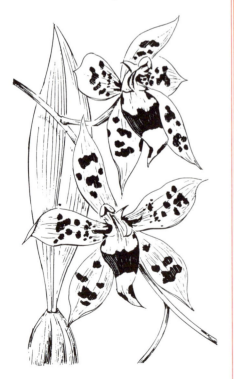

Nomocharis pardanthina

Odontoglossum praevisum

NOMOCHARIS

Beautiful, lily-like plants with bulbous roots and nodding flowers. They like a cool, deep soil consisting largely of leaf-mould or peat and sand, and they also require a shady position, though not where they will have to compete with the roots of trees or large shrubs. A deep, specially prepared bed in thin woodland seems to be the best place for them. All can be raised from seed but it takes several years to get flowering bulbs. Old bulb clusters can be divided in September, the best planting time, and they can also be increased from bulb scales.

The two finest species are *Nomocharis mairei*, with fringed, white, purple-spotted flowers, and *N. pardanthina* with pink, maroon-blotched flowers. Both flower in July, *N. mairei* being about 2 feet high and *N. pardanthina* between $1\frac{1}{2}$ and 3 feet.

ODONTOGLOSSUM

Beautiful and often very graceful orchids which thrive in an equable temperature of around 60°F. winter and summer. It will do them no harm if the winter temperature occasionally falls to 50°F., but more difficulty will be encountered in combating too high temperatures in summer which will encourage thrips and other troubles. In consequence in summer the odontoglossum house should be heavily shaded and freely syringed. It may be necessary to reduce ventilation by day in hot weather to prevent hot, dry air entering the house, and then to open ventilators in the evening to cool the house.

Odontoglossums are grown in a mixture of equal parts of chopped osmunda fibre and sphagnum moss. They are repotted in March and are watered freely in spring and summer, moderately in autumn and winter. Even during the resting season the compost should be kept moist.

The two most popular species are *Odontoglossum crispum* (Plate 16), with arching sprays of white flowers delicately tinted with pink and yellow and with fringed or crimped petals, and *O. grande* with large yellow flowers banded with chestnut. There are also a great many hybrids, many of which have *O. crispum* as one of their parents, or have been raised from other hybrids which can be traced back to *O. crispum*. These hybrids usually have the long, arching flower spikes so typical of *O. crispum* and are often white variously blotched or spotted with purple.

ONCIDIUM

Graceful orchids for the warm greenhouse. Most oncidiums produce large sprays of small flowers, a typical and popular species being *Oncidium varicosum* in which there may be close on 100 yellow and brown flowers in one spray. It is autumn flowering. By contrast the very distinctive *O. papilio* produces only one flower at a time in the inflorescence, though there is a succession of buds which may continue to open most of the year. The flowers are much larger than is normal, with narrow upper sepals and petals a little like the antennae of a butterfly. Hence the popular name Butterfly Orchid.

This is a very large genus and the species differ widely in their cultural requirements. *O. varicosum* likes cool-house treatment with a minimum winter temperature of 50°F. *O. varicosum rogersii* (Plate 17), which has slightly larger flowers, needs similar treatment. *O. papilio* is a tropical plant and likes a minimum of 65°F. even in winter. In general oncidiums do not like heavy shade in summer. They need plenty of water in summer but should have a decided rest in winter when little water is required. February and March are the usual potting months and a compost should be used similar to that recommended for odontoglossums.

ONOPORDON *(Scotch Thistle, Cotton Thistle)*

Striking grey-leaved plants of gaunt, statuesque habit and often 7 or 8 feet in height. The two kinds commonly grown are *O. acanthium* (Plate 17), which is perennial though it may sometimes behave as a biennial, and *O. tauricum* which is biennial and must, therefore, be renewed from seed annually if a succession is to be maintained. Both are grown for the stateliness and rather weird beauty of their growth rather than for their purple, cornflower-like flowers. They like sunny places and well-drained soils. Seed should be sown in spring or early summer in a frame or outdoors, seedlings being pricked out at least 9 inches apart to grow on for final transplanting to their flowering positions in early autumn or, if the soil is heavy, in spring.

ONOSMA *(Golden Drop)*

Small hardy perennials most suitable for the rock garden or a dry wall. They love sun and good drainage and are happiest perched in a crevice on a vertical face, provided they have an ample body of good soil into which to root. The two most generally useful are *Onosma echioides* and *O. tauricum* (Plate 17), both with grey foliage and arching clusters of drooping yellow flowers in summer. There is also *O. albo-roseum* in which the flowers are at first white but later change to pink. It also has the hairy grey foliage of the other two and, like them, flowers in June and July. All can be increased from seed or by cuttings of young growth in summer in a propagating frame or box.

OTHONNOPSIS

Othonnopsis cheirifolia (Plate 17) is a grey-leaved plant with thick, fleshy leaves and sprays of bright yellow daisy-flowers in June. Strictly speaking it is a shrub but as it flops about, never exceeding a foot in height and being far more at home in the rock garden than in the shrub border, it will probably be thought of as a rock plant. It is attractive in foliage and showy in flower but suffers from the drawback of not being reliably hardy in all parts of the British Isles. It is a lover of warm, sunny, even dry places and damp and cold are its enemies. In the south and west it may survive outdoors for years but elsewhere any extra cold spell may kill it in the open. As it can easily be increased by cuttings in summer, inserted in sandy soil in a frame, it is wise to keep a few such cuttings in reserve.

91

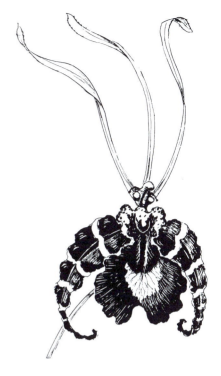

Oncidium papilio

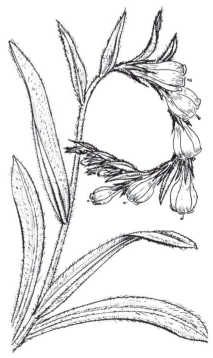

Onosma tauricum

Paeonia lobata

Paeonia suffruticosa 'Constantia

PAEONIA *(Peony)*

These are both herbaceous and shrubby peonies, the latter somewhat misleadingly called Tree Peonies, though no specie or hybrid ever attains anything approaching tree-like proportions.

The old-fashioned herbaceous peony with very double flowers in white, pink, or crimson is *Paeonia officinalis*, a hardy European plant which, although it has been grown in gardens for centuries, has never proved very variable. For variations gardeners had to wait for the introduction of the Chinese Peony, *P. albiflora*, a plant typically white or pink flowered but in gardens running into a great many forms, some single, some semi-double, some fully double, with a colour range from white to crimson and perfume as an additional attraction. There are a great many garden varieties with 'fancy' names such as Duchesse de Nemours, cream, Felix Crousse, crimson, Lady Alexandra Duff, flesh-pink, Monsieur Jules Elie, light rose-pink, Monsieur Martin Cahuzac, deep crimson, Sarah Bernhardt, light pink and Globe of Light, pink and gold.

Other exotic species of herbaceous peonies have been introduced, but none has proved as rich in variety as the Chinese Peony. *P. emodi* is a very lovely plant about 2 feet high with large single white flowers each with a central boss of golden-yellow stamens. The unpronounceable *P. mlokosewitschii* must some day be given an easier name for it is a superb species with big, lemon-yellow flowers on 2½ feet stems in April or May. *P. obovata* has very shapely, single white flowers, *P. tenuifolia* is remarkable for its finely divided, almost fernlike foliage and rich crimson flowers, and *P. peregrina*, often known as *P. lobata*, has flowers of brilliant lobster scarlet.

The Tree Peony is *P. suffruticosa*, often called *P. moutan*. Like *P. albiflora* it came from China and, also like that plant, it has produced a great many varieties. Typically it is a rather sparsely branched shrub 5 or 6 feet high with single white, pink or red flowers. The garden varieties may be single, semi-double or fully double, are usually very large-flowered and the flowers are often blotched with maroon or crimson on a lighter base.

There are other shrubby peonies, though again none has rivalled *P. suffruticosa* in capacity to produce varieties. *P. delavayi* grows about 5 feet high, has very handsome, divided leaves and rather small, blackish-crimson flowers. *P. lutea* is not unlike it in leaf and flower size but the flowers are yellow and *P. ludlowii* (Plate 17), with yellow flowers more prominently displayed, may be no more than a variety of it. There is also a hybrid between *P. delavayi* and *P. lutea*, named *P. lemoinei*, in which the colours of the two parents have been mixed, giving various shades of yellow or orange variously marked or suffused with red.

All herbaceous peonies are easily grown in any fairly rich soil and open position and they can be increased by division in spring or autumn. The tree peonies thrive in similar conditions

92

but the varieties of *P. suffruticosa* appreciate a somewhat sheltered place where they are a little protected from frost. The shrubby species are best increased from seed sown in a greenhouse in spring but the garden varieties of *P. suffruticosa* must be increased by grafting in spring or layering in May or June, preferably the latter as layers behave far more satisfactorily in the garden.

PAPAVER *(Poppy)*

I return to the poppies, already described in *Flowers in Colour* solely to give a picture in colour of what is in some ways the most remarkable and beautiful of all, the annual Shirley poppies (Plate 17) obtained by a process of painstaking selection from our own native scarlet poppy, *Papaver rhoeas*. Considering the absence of variation in this very familiar weed of cornfields, it is an astonishing fact that, without the aid of hybridization, the Rev. W. Wilkes was able, in the early years of the century, to produce all the delicate shades of pink as well as the combinations of pink and white which are to be found in the poppies that bear the name of his place of residence. They are as hardy and easily grown as their parent and can be sown with equal success in spring or early autumn, the only difference being that plants from an autumn sowing will commence to flower in June, those from a spring sowing a month or six weeks later.

PAROCHETUS *(Shamrock Pea)*

A pretty trailing plant with frail stems and clover-like leaves bearing, throughout the summer, pale blue pea-flowers. *Parochetus communis* (Plate 17) likes sun, warmth and plenty of moisture in summer, but it is none too hardy, for which reason it is more commonly seen as a cool greenhouse plant than in the more suitable setting of a rock garden. If it is grown under glass it is best planted in a large, rather shallow pan so that it has plenty of room to ramble. It is easily propagated by detaching rooted pieces at almost any time of the year.

PARROTIA

The species usually grown, *Parrotia persica* (Plate 17), is a tree of moderate size, seldom exceeding 30 feet in height but spreading in habit so that its width may exceed its height, and grown mainly for the vivid autumn colouring of its foliage. The flowers, which appear along the branches in March, are by no means showy but have a character all their own, being small, brush-like clusters of deep red stamens surrounded by brownish bracts. This parrotia is fully hardy and thrives in any reasonable soil and open position. It can be raised from seed sown in a greenhouse or frame in spring.

PARTHENOCISSUS *(Virginia Creeper)*

These popular climbing plants, several of them self-clinging, are often included with the vines under the generic name *Vitis* and are also called *Ampelopsis*, which makes for confusion.

Parochetus communis

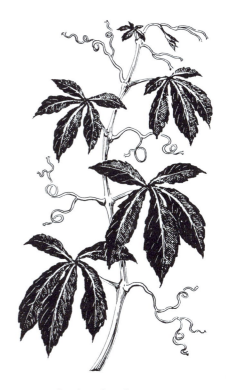

Parthenocissus henryana

Pelargonium 'Lady Plymouth'

Pelargonium fragrans

The very popular small-leaved Virginia Creeper is *Parthenocissus tricuspidata*, also known in gardens as *Vitis inconstans* and *Ampelopsis veitchii*. It is a very variable plant and some of its forms have quite large leaves, but it is the small-leaved varieties such as *lowii* and Beverley Brook that are most sought after. The True Virginia Creeper, *P. quinquefolia*, has leaves composed of five separate leaflets radiating from a common stalk. Very similar is the Common Virginia Creeper, *P. vitacea*, which differs chiefly in not being self-clinging. It needs a pergola or trellis up which it will scramble by means of tendrils like those of a vine. *V. henryana* (Plate 17) is in many ways the most beautiful of all, but on the border-line of hardiness, which means that it should have a warm, sheltered wall. It is self-clinging and has deep velvet-green or purplish-green leaves veined with pink and silver.

All these species will grow in any ordinary soil and can be increased by cuttings in the autumn.

PELARGONIUM *(Geranium)*

This is not only a very big genus but also a complex one, with several big groups of garden hybrids and a great number of species, many of which are only to be found in the collections of specialists.

Broadly the genus may be considered from the garden standpoint in four main groups, the Zonal Pelargoniums, the Ivy-leaved Pelargoniums, the Ornamental-leaved Pelargoniums, the Scented-leaved Pelargoniums and miscellaneous species which come under none of the former headings.

The Zonal Pelargoniums are in part derived from a species named *Pelargonium zonale*, which has a ring of darker colour on the leaves, but their parentage is involved and is reflected in the great variety of garden forms. Many of these, such as the scarlet Gustav Emich and pink King of Denmark, are excellent summer bedding plants but not all are equally successful for this purpose and many beautiful varieties, such as the crimson Elizabeth Cartwright, must be regarded primarily as greenhouse plants. All are readily raised from cuttings which will root in a frame, or even outdoors, in early August or in a greenhouse in March, April or September. They thrive in the John Innes compost, require a winter temperature of 40°F to 50°F. and no artificial heat once danger of frost is past. Normally they are summer flowering, but if flower buds are picked off during summer they will flower in a greenhouse for many weeks in autumn. For bedding out plants must be hardened off for several weeks in a frame before being planted out in late May or early June.

The Ivy-leaved Pelargoniums are derived from *P. peltatum* and are trailing plants which are often trained up canes as 'dot' plants in summer bedding schemes, or may be grown in hanging baskets, window boxes and other places in which they can trail and hang. The most popular variety, Galilee, has double salmon-pink flowers but there are other varieties with a colour range from pale pink to scarlet. Cultivation and propagation are exactly as for the Zonal Pelargoniums.

The Ornamental-leaved Pelargoniums are mostly derived from the Zonal pelargonium though there are also variegated forms of the Ivy-leaved pelargonium. The ornamental varieties have bands of colour, sometimes just green and white or green and yellow, but also in some of the more elaborate varieties with purple or crimson entering in as well. Mrs Henry Cox (Plate 17) is typical of these more highly coloured varieties. All can be used for summer bedding in exactly the same way as the Zonal Pelargoniums.

The Regal Pelargoniums (Plate 17) are purely greenhouse plants flowering in late spring and early summer and making handsome, bushy pot plants. The flowers are much bigger than those of the other popular groups, single or double, with a colour range from pale pink to intense, blackish crimson. Often the flowers are handsomely blotched with crimson, purple or maroon on a lighter ground. They are raised from cuttings in the same way as Zonal Pelargoniums but are not planted outdoors. Instead they may be cut back fairly hard after flowering and then stood outdoors in their pots for a few weeks in July and August, after which they should be returned to the greenhouse.

The Scented-leaved Pelargoniums are extremely variable in both the shape and the perfume of their foliage. *P. tomentosum* has big, softly-hairy leaves smelling of peppermint, whereas *P. crispum* has small, crimped, lemon-scented leaves. The oak-leaved pelargonium, *P. quercifolium*, has deeply divided leaves and a highly distinctive perfume all its own. Others are *P. fragrans*, the nutmeg-scented geranium, *P. exstipulatum* and *P. odoratissimum*. All are good pot plants for a cool greenhouse or a sunny room, are easily increased by cuttings in spring or late summer and are not at all fussy about soil.

PELTIPHYLLUM *(Umbrella-Plant)*

The only species, *Peltiphyllum peltatum*, is generally known in gardens as *Saxifraga peltata*. It is a herbaceous perennial with large leaves carried horizontally, a little like umbrellas, on 2 to 3 feet stems, and long, bare flower stems in spring, before the leaves appear, terminated by flattish heads of pink flowers. It is an unusual plant and rather a handsome one where there is room for it to spread freely, which it will do quickly enough in any good and moist soil. It can be grown in the herbaceous border but is really happier beside a stream or pond. It can be increased by division in spring or autumn.

PHILODENDRON

Tropical plants with large, shining green, leathery leaves. Although many kinds require well-heated greenhouse in which a very moist atmosphere can be maintained, a few are excellent house plants and can be grown for considerable periods in a living room provided it does not become very cold at night. Most popular of all for this purpose is *Philodendron scandens* (Plate 18), a climbing plant which can be trained in many

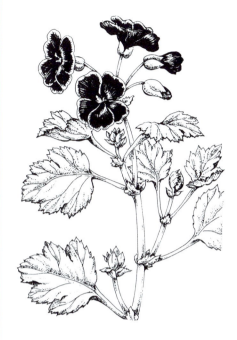

Pelargonium 'Lord Bute'

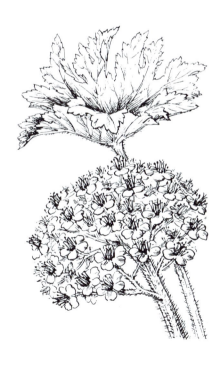

Peltiphyllum peltatum

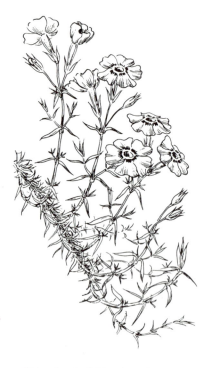

Phlox douglasii 'Boothman's var.'

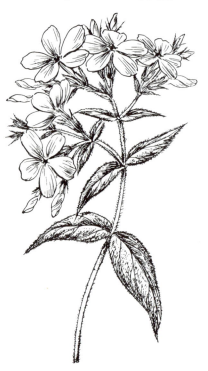

Phlox divaricata laphamii

attractive ways. It should be grown in John Innes compost and be watered freely while in growth, more moderately in winter. It is beneficial to sponge the leaves frequently with water or, if growing in a warm greenhouse, to syringe daily. Propagation is by cuttings of the long stems which often form roots as they grow. The cuttings should be inserted in sand and peat in a propagating frame or box with bottom heat.

PHLOX

The popular herbaceous phlox, flowering in July and August, has been raised from *Phlox paniculata*, a North American plant with light purple or rose flowers. In gardens it has proved rewardingly variable, and has produced a great many varieties ranging in height from foot-high plants, such as the pure white Mia Ruys, to varieties, such as the orange-red Brigadier and rosy-salmon Sir John Falstaff, which are 4 feet or more high. The colour range has also been greatly extended so that deep violet, blue or purple varieties, such as Border Gem and William Kesselring are available; pale mauves and lavenders, such as Caroline van den Berg and Mrs Ethel Prichard; vivid carmines, scarlets and vermilions, such as A. E. Amos and Leo Schlageter; and clear pinks and salmons, such as Sweetheart, Jules Sandeau and Light of Codsall. All like good, rich soil, will grow in sun or partial shade, and can be increased by division in spring or autumn or by root cuttings in winter.

The mat-forming *P. subulata*, a fine plant for a sunny rock garden or dry wall or for edging a border, has also produced some good garden varieties, though not as many as the herbaceous phlox. Two of the best are G. F. Wilson, pale mauve, and Vivid, bright rose-pink. All flower in May and June as does also the more compact *P. douglasii*, which also has several useful varieties including pure white May Snow, pale pink Rose Queen and Lilac Queen, lilac. These alpine phloxes are best increased by cuttings of young growth in a frame in late spring or early summer.

P. divaricata is suitable either for the rock garden or the front of the border; an erect plant 12 to 18 inches high bearing small heads of pale blue flowers in May and June. Its best variety is named *laphamii* and has clear, lavender-blue flowers of superior size. All forms of this phlox can be increased by division.

The brilliant annual *Phlox drummondii* (Plate 18) is much used for summer bedding in parks and other public places, but is scarcely appreciated at its full worth by amateurs. It is a trailing slender plant producing its vividly coloured flowers in small clusters from mid-summer until autumn. The colour range is wide, including many shades of pink, rose, red, carmine, purple, violet and blue as well as white and buff-yellow. This phlox is a half-hardy annual raised from seed sown in a temperature of 60°F to 65°F. in February or March. Seedlings should be pricked off, hardened off and finally planted out in late May or early June where they are to flower. It is a good plan to peg the slender stems to the soil so that a complete ground cover is obtained. The position should be open and sunny.

Rhododendron
williamsianum·

Prunus
campanulatus

Rhazya
orientalis

Rhododendron
campylocarpum

Rhododendron
'Blue Diamond'

Primula
rosea

Punica
granatum

Primula
vialii

Primula auricula
[Alpine form]

Rhododendron
'Lady Chamberlain'

Primula
edgeworthii

Quercus
coccinea

Reevesia
pubescens

Rosa rugosa
'Frau Dagmar Hartopp'

Rosa xanthina spontanea
['Canary Bird']

Rhodohypoxis
baueri

Robinia
hispida

Rosa sericea
pteracantha

Rosa
foliolosa

Rose 'Penelope'
[hybrid musk]

Roscoea
cautleoides

Rosa alb
'Celestia

Rochea
coccinea

Rose 'William Lobb'
[moss]

Rhoeo discolor

PHYSALIS *(Cape Gooseberry)*

The true Cape Gooseberry, with inflated Chinese lantern-like calyces each enclosing one cherry-shaped yellow fruit, is *Physalis peruviana*, a tender perennial that can only be grown outdoors during the summer months. The small berry-like fruit is edible and *P. ixiocarpa*, sometimes known as the Jamberberry, is also cultivated for its edible fruits which are said to make excellent jam. This latter is an annual and is grown just like one of the dwarf bush tomatoes, being raised in a warm greenhouse and planted out in a warm sunny place when danger of frost is past. In America it is known as the Tomatillo.

More popular than either of these are *P. alkekengii* and *P. franchettii* (Plate 18), both hardy perennials and highly ornamental in autumn when the inflated calyces turn bright orange. They can then be cut and used as winter decorations, for which purpose they are usually detached from the stems and wired on to some more decorative foliage. Both are easily grown in any warm, sunny place and reasonably well-drained soil. They differ mainly in size, *P. franchettii* being a little taller and bigger in all its parts than *P. alkekengii*. Both can be increased by division in spring.

PHYTOLACCA *(Red-Ink Plant, Virginian Poke Weed)*

Coarse perennials of which the kind most commonly grown in gardens is *Phytolacca americana*, also sometimes known as *P. decandra*. In good rich soil it will grow 7 or 8 feet high, but more usually is about 5 feet with big, rounded leaves and long narrow spikes of white or occasionally pink flowers followed by dark purple, almost black berries filled with a staining juice. It is a useful plant for the wild garden or for a large border, requiring no particular care as it will thrive in sun or partial shade in almost any soil and is easily raised from seed or by division in spring. Very similar but with soft rose flowers, a rather more compact habit and even darker fruits is *P. clavigera* (Plate 18).

PICEA *(Spruce)*

A big family of evergreen, cone-bearing trees, mostly too large for the garden but one species is very popular because of its neat, Christmas tree shape and beautiful blue-grey foliage. This is the Colorado Spruce, *Picea pungens*, best known in one of its more intensely blue-grey forms such as *glauca* (Plate 18), *kosteriana* or *moerheimii*. Though any will eventually make trees 50 or 60 feet high, they will take a long time in doing so and may be enjoyed for 10 or possibly 20 years as highly ornamental trees of moderate size. More rapid in growth is the Serbian Spruce, *P. omorika*, which makes a narrow but tall spire ultimately 60 or 70 feet high, but often no more than 12 feet through at the base. The foliage is dark green. *P. excelsa* is the common Christmas tree, quick growing and useful as a shelter belt. All will grow in any reasonable soil and open position. The species

G

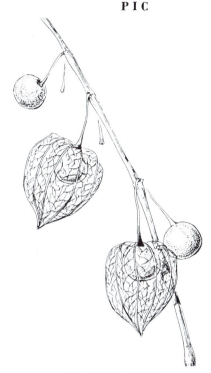

Physalis franchettii

Phytolacca americana (fruits)

Picea omorika

Pieris taiwanensis

can be raised from seed but selected colour forms, such as the very blue forms of the Colorado Spruce, are increased by grafting, usually on to seedlings of the species of which they are varieties.

PIERIS

Evergreen shrubs producing, in spring, clustered sprays of white flowers that are often likened to lily of the valley though, in fact, they are much more like those of a large heather. *P. floribunda* is the smallest of those commonly grown, a broad, rounded bush rarely above 5 feet in height. *P. taiwanensis* is a little bigger, with similar erect sprays of bloom, but in the still larger *P. japonica*, *P. forrestii* (Plate 18) and *P. formosa* the sprays are more arching. *P. forrestii* is remarkable for the vivid rosewood red of its young leaves and shoots in the spring. It is worth planting for this foliage colour alone.

All thrive under the same conditions as rhododendrons, i.e. in a lime-free soil with peat or leaf-mould and with plenty of moisture in summer while they are making their growth. They can be raised from seed sown in a greenhouse or frame in spring or by layering in May.

PIPTANTHUS

Shrubs with yellow, pea-type flowers in late spring. *Piptanthus laburnifolius*, better known as *P. nepalensis* (Plate 18), is the only species much grown, but it has not been widely planted, probably because of a reputation for tenderness. Personally I have found it capable of withstanding quite severe frosts and it has retained its attractive, tripartite leaves even in hard winters, though most authorities say it is deciduous under such conditions. The clusters of yellow flowers look particularly well against the dark leaves and stems. It grows 6 or 8 feet high, sometimes apparently considerably more, is not fussy about soil, likes a sunny position and is very readily raised from seed— in fact self-sown seedlings often appear all round a bush. In cold or exposed gardens it may be trained against a sunny wall or fence.

PLEIONE

A genus of small orchids of which the most useful, both on account of its beauty and its comparative hardiness, is *Pleione pricei* (Plate 18). This is often grown in the alpine house with no more heat than is needed to exclude frost. The hooded flowers stand about 4 inches high, are pale rose and produced in early spring. This pleione looks its best planted freely in a large shallow pan. It will thrive in a mixture of equal parts of loam and osmunda fibre with a small quantity of chopped sphagnum moss, and should be repotted, when necessary, immediately after flowering. Water should be given moderately during the summer, very sparingly in winter when the plant is resting. There are other rather similar species, such as the smaller flowered *P. hookeriana*, *P. praecox* which has several varieties, one white flowered, another a deeper purple, and *P. yunnanensis* which, like *P. praecox*, has the front lobe of the flower fringed.

POLYGALA *(Milkwort)*

The Common Milkwort, *Polygala vulgaris*, can be found growing freely in downland turf in many parts of Britain, a tiny, but pretty blue flower that increases in size and impressiveness if transferred to the rock garden. But the species commonly grown in gardens, *P. chamaebuxus* (Plate 18), is a very different plant, a little spreading shrub about 6 inches high, with neat, box-like leaves and winged flowers which may be either yellow or yellow and purple. It is at its best in June but is seldom without a flower in mild weather. It likes a porous, peaty soil in sun or partial shade and also makes a pleasant pot plant for the alpine house or frame. *P. vayrediae* resembles it in appearance and requirements but is an even smaller plant. Yet another species occasionally grown in sunny rock gardens is *P. calcarea*, a small plant much like *P. vulgaris* and also a native though not a common plant. In good soil it may attain a height of 1 foot but is more usually 6 or 8 inches with slender spikes of blue, pink or white flowers in summer. Both the herbaceous kinds can be increased by division in spring. The shrubby species produce rooted suckers or offshoots that can be dug up in autumn.

POLYGONUM *(Knotweed)*

On the whole this is not a genus to arouse the gardener's affection, but there are good species nevertheless and *Polygonum campanulatum* (Plate 18), *P. vaccinifolium* and *P. baldschuanicum* have strong claims to being the three best.

    P. campanulatum is a hardy herbaceous plant 3 feet high, with clustered sprays of pale pink flowers which have the peculiarity of never seeming to fade or alter from July to October. It creeps about above—not below—ground, likes sun and moisture and is a little variable in colour. *P. vaccinifolium* is an indefatigable creeper or trailer, admirable on dry walls or steep slopes in the rock garden, with slender spikes of pink flowers from August to October. It has no fads. *P. affine* is not unlike it but more compact and with heavier spikes of rose-red flowers.

    P. baldschuanicum is one of the strongest and most rapid growing of all climbing plants. It will soon hide an unsightly shed or cover a dead tree with its clouds of tiny pearl-white or pale pink flowers throughout the late summer. Oddly enough, though it grows so freely, it is rather difficult to propagate—from summer cuttings in a frame with bottom heat.

    Two good herbaceous plants are *P. amplexicaule* and *P. bistorta*, the first 3 feet high with slender rose-red flowers throughout the late summer until September, the second no more than 2 feet high with bright pink flower spikes during the same period. Both plants have white varieties as well as more deeply coloured forms and neither is in the least invasive.

    All these herbaceous knotweeds can be increased by division in spring or autumn.

99

Pleione hookeriana

Polygonum affine

Potentilla fruticosa 'Katherine Dykes'

Primula capitata

PORTULACA

Portulaca grandiflora (Plate 18) is an extremely showy plant with small, fleshy leaves and brightly coloured flowers the size of florins. They may be scarlet, purple or yellow and there are double-flowered as well as single varieties. The whole plant is semi-prostrate and suitable for growing as an edging to a sunny, well-drained border, on top of a dry wall, or on a ledge in the rock garden. It should be treated as a half-hardy annual, seed being sown in a temperature of 60 to 65°F. in February or March, and seedlings pricked-out and hardened-off for planting out in late May or early June.

POTENTILLA *(Cinquefoil)*

The cinquefoils may be considered in three groups as garden plants; shrubs with an unusually long flowering season, herbaceous plants notable for rich and unusual colour combinations, and some very pretty creeping rock plants.

All the important shrubby kinds are varieties or hybrids of *Potentilla fruticosa*, a densely branched shrub usually 3 to 4 feet high, though there are dwarf varieties. All have small yellow or white flowers produced from June to October with a peak period in July. Outstanding garden varieties are Katherine Dykes, with larger and deeper yellow flowers; *vilmoriniana*, which has silvery leaves and pale cream flowers; Farrer's White which is pure white; *farreri*, not to be confused with the last as it is yellow-flowered, more spreading and not so tall; and *nana argentea*, also known as *beesii*, which is the dwarfest of all, not above 18 inches in height, with silvery leaves and bright golden yellow flowers. All these like sunny places and well-drained soils and can be increased by cuttings in late summer. They can be hard pruned each March if large flowers and compact bushes are required or, alternatively, some of the older stems may be cut out to leave more room for the younger growth.

The herbaceous potentillas are mostly hybrids of uncertain parentage, though *P. atrosanguinea*, a crimson flowered Himalayan plant, *P. argyrophylla*, from the same habitat but yellow flowered, and *P. nepalensis*, a rosy-red flowered plant from the Himalaya have played a part. *P. nepalensis* has a lovely carmine-flowered form known as Miss Willmott. As this and the species are no more than 9 inches in height they can be planted in the rock garden if desired. Among the best of the taller hybrids are Gibson's Scarlet, 18 inches and a really brilliant scarlet; Master Floris (Plate 18), orange and red, 2 feet and William Rollison which is about the same in height and has large, double orange flowers. All flower throughout the summer, like sunny places and well-drained soil and are increased by division in spring or autumn.

There are numerous creeping kinds suitable for the rock garden, none more generally useful than *P. aurea*, which has both double and single flowered varieties of lightest golden yellow in early summer; *P. fragiformis*, with strawberry-like

Sedum
kamtschaticum
variegatum

Saxifraga
grisebachii

Rubus
ulmifolius
bellidiflorus

Salvia
farinacea
'Blue Bedder'

Sanguinaria
canadensis plena

Sagittaria
sagittifolia
flore-pleno

Sedum
spathulifolium

Schizostylis
coccinea

Saxifraga
oppositifolia

Sansevieria
trifasciata
laurentii

Scirpus
tabernaemontani
zebrinus

Ruta
chalapensis

Newsome-Taylor

Sorbus
hupehensis

Stephanotis
floribunda

Stewartia
koreana

Senecio speciosus

Stachyurus
praecox

Staphylea
pinnata

Sternbergia
lutea
major

Soldanella alpina

Sparmannia
africana

Sorbaria arborea

leaves and yellow flowers in May and June; *P. nitida*, a lovely little plant with pink flowers and silvery leaves that needs especially gritty soil; and the plant commonly called *P. tonguei*, though its true name is *P. tormentillo-formosa*, a hybrid with soft apricot flowers blotched with crimson. It flowers all the summer. All these can also be increased by division, preferably in spring.

PRIMULA *(Primrose, Polyanthus, Auricula)*

This is one of those vast genera which it is quite impossible to cover adequately in a few paragraphs. In addition to scores of excellent species ranging from bog plants to high mountain types, there are great numbers of hybrids and garden forms, some developed almost out of recognition with the species which were their ancestors, some completely hardy, others requiring greenhouse treatment.

Our native primrose is a primula, its botanical name being *Primula vulgaris*, and it has produced numerous beautiful garden forms, some single flowered, some fully double with a colour range including yellow, pink, red, crimson, lilac, lavender, purple and blue. The polyanthus in all its many rich colours and forms is also derived from the common primrose, probably with the cowslip, *P. veris*, and the oxslip, *P. elatior*, also involved in its ancestry. All these are plants for cool, partially shady places, in rich, rather moist soil. They can be raised from seed sown in a greenhouse or frame in early spring or outdoors in May, or they may be divided in May after flowering.

The auricula is *P. auricula* (Plate 19), a European alpine plant, which in gardens has been so domesticated and pampered that many of the exquisitely coloured 'florist' varieties need a cool greenhouse to bring them to perfection. It is a sun lover and also readily raised from seed or division.

The greenhouse primulas are also garden darlings, highly developed by breeders in search of ever larger flowers and new colours. The three principal groups are *P. obconica*, *P. sinensis* and *P. malacoides*, all winter flowering and all raised from seed each year. *P. obconica* is about a foot high, has 'stellata' forms with more starry flowers in addition to the normal round-flowered type and a colour range mainly in pink, red, mauve, lavender and white.

P. sinensis is a little shorter, with even larger flowers, sometimes beautifully frilled, and a wonderful colour range which leaves out little except yellow.

P. malacoides is the smallest flowered of the trio but makes up in profusion what it lacks in size. Colours are all shades of pink to crimson and white.

All these winter flowering primulas are grown from seed sown in April or May for *P. obconica* and *P. sinensis*, June or July for *P. malacoides*. They do not need any artificial heat in summer and not a lot in winter, *P. malacoides* no more than is necessary to keep out frost. All thrive in the John Innes compost and may be flowered in 4- or 5-inch pots.

Primula malacoides

Primula helodoxa

Primula juliae

Primula florindae

Primula edgeworthii (Plate 19), still sometimes known as *P. winteri*, is a fine example of the mountain primulas. It has leathery, grey-green leaves and blue-lilac flowers in March or April. *P. marginata* is another splendid rock plant, rather like a pale blue auricula with leaves edged with white meal. *P. viali* (Plate 19), another mountaineer, often known as *P. littoniana*, is a highly distinctive plant with close spikes of flowers, rather like some of the hardy orchids, which commence by being lilac and develop to red. It likes a cool fairly rich peaty soil.

The lovely little *P. rosea* (Plate 19), with its clusters of brilliant rose flowers before the leaves appear in spring, is a typical moisture lover, thriving at the edge of a pool or even in a bog garden provided it does not actually get submerged. The same treatment will also suit all the 'candelabra' primulas, plants which bear their flowers in diminishing whorls one above another. *P. helodoxa*, with yellow flowers in May is typical of this group and so are *P. japonica* and *P. pulverulenta*, both magenta flowered in the common forms, but the latter distinguished by the white, mealy covering of leaves and stems. The Bartley strain of *P. pulverulenta* has flowers in many shades of pink. These all flower in May and June. A little later comes the splendid Himalayan cowslip, *Primula florindae* with its great heads of hanging yellow flowers. It needs similar conditions.

P. capitata, with close circular heads of violet-purple flowers, also has this mealy covering and likes cool, leafy or peaty soils, but not wet in winter. *P. denticulata*, called the Drumstick Primrose because of its globular heads of lavender, purple or white flowers, is easier to manage, thriving in the same conditions as the primrose and polyanthus. These conditions also suit the quite prostrate mat-forming *P. juliae* which is sometimes rather shy in producing its wine-purple flowers, and also the many beautiful forms raised by crossing this Himalayan plant with the British primrose. All these are spring flowering.

Most alpine and bog primulas can be raised from seed and some seed themselves freely.

PRUNUS *(Cherry, Bird Cherry, Apricot, Plum, Almond, Peach, Cherry Laurel, Portugal Laurel)*

No genus has enriched our garden with a greater variety of really ornamental trees and shrubs. The cherries alone are sufficiently numerous to fill a book and to them must be added many more excellent species and varieties almost all of which are perfectly hardy and easy to grow.

Most magnificent of all in the size and number of their flowers are the Japanese cherries derived from *Prunus serrulata*. These are all trees, mostly 20 feet or more in height when full grown and flowering in the latter half of April or early May. Beyond that it is impossible to generalize, so much do they vary in habit, type of flower and colour. Some are extremely erect trees, none more so than Amanogawa which has the habit but not the size of a Lombardy poplar. The large double flowers are soft pink. The popular rosy-pink Kanzan, also called Hisakura, is of shuttlecock shape when young but becomes more spreading with age. Fugenzo, which resembles it in colour, is much more spreading throughout its life and the white-flowered Shimidsu Sakura, also known as *longipes*, makes a quite low tree of parasol shape. There are many other lovely kinds such as Tai-haku, with very large single white flowers, Ukon, with double, pale yellow flowers, and *P. yedoensis*, which is really a separate species but closely allied and one of the best because of the freedom and grace with which it produces its single white flowers. *P. campanulata*, from Formosa, has brilliant red flowers but is a little tender. It succeeds in the milder counties.

The Spring Cherry, *P. subhirtella*, has small pale pink flowers and has produced several good varieties including a lovely weeping form named *pendula* and one, named *autumnalis*, which flowers in October and November.

Another splendid kind is *P. sargentii*, a bigger tree than most with single pink flowers in March and wonderful foliage colour in autumn. With *P. subhirtella* it has produced an excellent hybrid named Accolade, with semi-double deep pink flowers.

The native British gean, *P. avium*, is a handsome woodland tree and has a grand garden variety, named *flore plena*, with fully-double white flowers.

The Bird cherries come from a quite different species, *P. padus*, which makes a large, shapely tree. 30 or 40 feet high with short, slender trails of fragrant white flowers in April and May. A superior form is named *watereri*.

The ornamental apricots are not numerous and are a little more exacting but one in particular, *P. mume florepleno*, the Japanese Apricot, is worth a little pains as it is a lovely shrub or small tree with double rosy red flowers in March and April. It needs a warm, sunny situation.

Most important of the ornamental almonds is *P. communis*, also known as *P. amygdalus*. It makes a small shapely tree about 20 feet in height with large single pink flowers in March and early April. *P. triloba flore pleno*, with little rosetted pink flowers clustered all along the stems in March or April, is also an almond but needs a warm sheltered position.

The peaches are all forms of *P. persica* and flower immediately after the almonds. They make small trees 15 to 20 feet high with fine double flowers, deep rose-pink in the popular Clara Meyer, pure white in Iceberg.

Most popular of the ornamental plums is the Purple-leaved Plum, *P. cerasifera atropurpurea*, often known as *P. pissardii*. The small white flowers of this appear in February and March just as the purple leaves are beginning to expand. It makes a tree 20 to 25 feet high. Even more ornamental is the form or hybrid known as *blireana* which has bigger, double, pink flowers.

The Cherry Laurel, *P. lauro-cerasus*, and the Portugal Laurel, *P. lusitanicus*, are so different from the foregoing that it needs some botanical knowledge to appreciate the connexion. These are big evergreen shrubs or trees, the Cherry Laurel with large shining green leaves, the Portugal Laurel with smaller

103

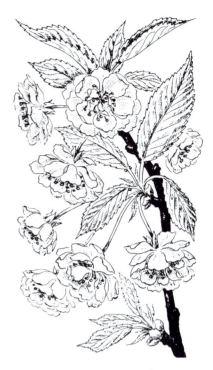

Prunus avium flore plena

Prunus padus watereri

Quercus ilex

Rhaphiolepis delacourii

darker green foliage. Both are much used for making large hedges, but as specimens they exhibit unexpected beauty of flower.

All these species and varieties of prunus can be grown in any reasonable soil and most actually like chalky soil. The species can usually be raised from seed but most of the garden varieties of the cherries, peaches, plums, etc., are increased by budding on to suitable stocks in summer. The Cherry Laurel and Portugal Laurel are increased by cuttings in a frame or outdoors in autumn.

PUNICA *(Pomegranate)*

The only species, *Punica granatum* (Plate 19), is a handsome deciduous shrub or small tree with scarlet flowers, produced successively during most of the summer. It is too tender to succeed right out in the open in Britain, except in the mildest places, but it can often be grown successfully against a sunny wall, though it seldom ripens its large, yellow, many seeded fruits. It likes a good, well-drained soil and as much warmth as possible, and can be raised from seed sown in a warm greenhouse in spring or by half-ripe cuttings in a close frame in July. There are several distinct varieties, including one named *pleniflora*, with double flowers.

QUERCUS *(Oak)*

Though the common oak, *Quercus robur*, is seldom planted in gardens, its variety the Cypress Oak (*fastigiata*), with branches erect and forming a narrow column like those of a Lombardy poplar, is a useful tree where space is limited.

The Scarlet Oak, *Q. coccinea* (Plate 19), makes a fine rounded tree, 50 feet or more high, with leaves much larger than those of the common oak and turning vivid shades of red, crimson and purple before they fall in autumn.

The Holm Oak, *Q. ilex*, is evergreen and was at one time much planted as a hedge plant, especially where a very tall, strong hedge was required. It is not fashionable at the moment but is nevertheless an excellent tree.

All these oaks like good, loamy soils and all except the Cypress Oak, which is grafted on to seedlings of the Common Oak, can be raised from seed (acorns), sown in pans in a frame or outdoors in spring.

RAPHIOLEPIS

These are rather uncommon evergreen shrubs but at least one, *Raphiolepis umbellata*, deserves to be more freely planted in the milder parts of the British Isles because it is a shapely plant making a rounded bush 5 or 6 feet high. The white flowers, which are fragrant, are produced in June in close clusters at the ends of the stems. This shrub likes a sheltered position in good loamy soil and can be increased by cuttings of firm young growth in July, rooted in a propagating frame, preferably with some bottom heat. *R. delacourii* has looser sprays of pink flowers but is more tender.

REEVESIA

These are usually described as greenhouse evergreen shrubs, but one species, *Reevesia pubescens* (Plate 19), grows quite happily outdoors in southern counties, making a neat bush about 4 feet high, with loose sprays of fragrant white flowers in July. Culture is as for rhaphiolepsis.

RHAZYA

Rhazya orientalis (Plate 19) is a pretty little herbaceous plant, about a foot high with sprays of small, forget-me-not blue flowers in July and August. It is a hardy plant but it likes a warm, sunny place in well-drained soil. Though not by any means a plant of outstanding quality it is light and elegant and has the additional merit of novelty as it has been very little planted. It can be increased by division in spring.

RHODODENDRON

This immense genus of flowering shrubs includes all those commonly known by gardeners as azaleas but for the sake of convenience I have kept them apart in this book.

Divorced from azalea all the remaining rhododendrons are evergreen. They range from quite dwarf shrubs such as the yellow flowered *Rhododendron hanceanum nanum*, to trees 30 or 40 feet high such as *R. arboreum*, with red, pink or white flowers, or *R. falconeri* with pale yellow, purple-blotched flowers. The flowering season in mild places starts in early March with such species as white, or blush-pink *R. moupinense*, pale rose *R. praecox*, and soft yellow *R. lutescens* and it finishes about July with white trumpet-flowered *R. auriculatum*, but the real glory of rhododendron time is in May and early June.

The popular conception of a rhododendron is of a shrub with large and very showy, more or less dome-shaped, clusters of bloom and this is a true enough picture of all the so-called hardy hybrids flowering in late May or early June. But there are many other rhododendrons so totally unlike this general picture that many people fail to recognize them as rhododendrons at all. Some have long, tubular, hanging flowers, as in *R. cinnabarinum* which is cinnabar red or yellow flushed with red, and the two beautiful hybrids from it named Lady Chamberlain (Plate 19) and Lady Roseberry. These both have bigger flowers than those of *R. cinnabarinum* and they are variable plants, shades of orange and apricot predominating in Lady Chamberlain, of pink and rose in Lady Roseberry.

Then there are rhododendrons with bell-shaped or cup-shaped flowers, as in the soft yellow *R. campylocarpum* (Plate 19) or the lovely shell pink *R. williamsianum* (Plate 19), the latter a neat shrub with bronze young leaves.

Many rhododendrons have small flowers in little clusters, popular examples of this type being the blue-purple *R. russatum*, which used to have the much prettier name *R. cantabile*, and pink flowered *R. racemosum*. Both are small-leaved shrubs 3 or 4 feet high and may be planted in a large rock garden quite

Rhododendron falconeri

Rhododendron cinnabarinum

Rhododendron decorum

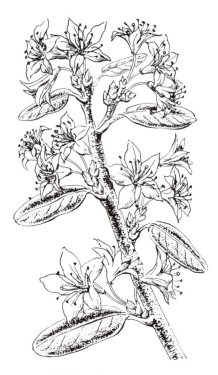

Rhododendron racemosum

as effectively as in a shrub border or thin woodland.

There are many other 'blue' rhododendrons besides *R. russatum*. Perhaps the finest of all is *R. augustinii*, a tall bush with flowers of medium size. It is variable in colour, some forms being no more than amethyst, others a really clear blue quite free of pink. Good hybrids have been raised from it such as Blue Diamond (Plate 19), a more compact shrub with deep lavender-blue flowers.

Species that more nearly approach the popular idea of a rhododendron are *R. decorum* with gleaming white or blush-pink flowers and *R. orbiculare* with deeper rose flowers and almost circular leaves.

There are giant-leaved as well as small-leaved kinds such as *R. falconeri*, already mentioned, *R. macabeanum* with deeper yellow flowers and *R. sino-grande* with leaves that may exceed 2 feet in length and great trusses of creamy flowers.

The species and the first generation hybrids from them have a grace and variety of form not equalled by the more mongrel hardy hybrids but the latter score in ease of culture and general adaptability. All are big, rounded shrubs with good dark green foliage and large, compact flower heads. Colours range from white, palest pink, mauve and silvery lavender to intense crimson and violet purple. All these varieties have garden or 'fancy' names such as Pink Pearl, Cynthia, Britannia, Blue Peter and Mrs G. W. Leak. An effort has been made to introduce yellow which is to be found in such varieties as Dairymaid and Goldsworth Yellow, but this has been achieved only by slight loss of toughness.

Some rhododendrons are extremely fragrant but here again there is generally some lack of hardiness. One of the most generally useful of the very fragrant kinds is *R. loderi*, a magnificent shrub of rather loose habit with very large, widely funnel-shaped flowers which may be white or flushed with pink.

Almost all rhododendrons dislike lime and all appreciate annual mulching with peat or leaf-mould. The less hardy species succeed best in thin woodland and this is true, also, of all the very large-leaved kinds but the hardy hybrids succeed just as well in a sunny as in a partially shaded position provided they do not become very dry in summer.

The wild (species) rhododendrons can be raised from seed sown in a peaty compost in a greenhouse or frame in spring but the hybrids do not breed true from seed and so are either increased by layering in spring or by grafting in spring. Grafting is really a task for the expert and it must be done under glass.

RHODOHYPOXIS

The only species, *Rhodohypoxis baueri* (Plate 20), is a cheerful little rock plant with tufts of narrow leaves and small, starry, rose-red flowers of great brilliance in spring. There are also pink and white varieties. The whole plant only grows about 4 inches high and it must be given a sunny place in the rock garden where it cannot be overrun by more vigorous plants.

Alternatively it may be grown in a pot or pan in the alpine house or frame. It likes a gritty, well-drained soil with enough peat or leaf mould to enable it to hold moisture in summer. It is increased by careful division in spring

RHOEO *(Boat Lily)*

The only species grown, *Rhoeo discolor* (Plate 20), is valued more for its thick sword-shaped leaves, deep green flushed with purple on the undersides, than for the crowded clusters of flowers in their boat-shaped bracts. It is, in fact, a handsome greenhouse foliage plant with leaves a foot long in well-grown specimens. It likes a warm greenhouse and plenty of moisture while it is making its growth in spring and summer. In autumn and winter it should be watered more moderately. Propagation is by division in March or April which are also the best months for repotting.

ROBINIA *(Locust, Acacia)*

The shrubs and trees to which the botanist gives the name acacia are quite dissimilar from those to which the gardener applies the name popularly. These are robinias, belonging to the pea family and with leaves composed of numerous small leaflets. The best known is *Robinia pseudacacia*, the Locust Acacia, a tree eventually 60 feet or so high but often kept much smaller by pruning. It has a mop-headed variety, named *inermis*, which was at one time a favourite for street planting. *R. pseudacacia* is a graceful tree with laburnum-like trails of fragrant white flowers in June.

The Rose Acacia, *R. hispida* (Plate 20), is a shrub not more than 6 feet high with rather large, rose-pink flowers in May and June. Though quite hardy, it has very brittle stems easily damaged by wind, for which reason it is usually grown against a sunny, sheltered wall or fence, rather than fully in the open.

The common acacia can be easily raised from seed and often seeds itself about. The rose acacia is increased by detaching suckers in autumn.

ROCHEA

Succulent plants very closely allied to Crassula and sometimes confused with that genus. The best is *Rochea coccinea* (Plate 20), a plant which produces clusters of vivid scarlet or carmine flowers on 12-inch stems. It makes a fine pot plant for the greenhouse and can be used as a house plant while in flower. It should be grown in a rather gritty compost containing an extra amount of coarse sand or pounded brick. It likes a sunny, airy house with a minimum winter temperature of 45°F. and should be watered rather springly at all times. In summer no artificial heat will be required. Propagation is by cuttings in late spring or summer.

ROSA *(Rose)*

For generations gardeners have bred new roses, intermingling the wild species and their own hybrids to such an extent that it is

Rhododendron praecox

Robinia pseudacacia

107

Rosa spinosissima altaica

Rosa moschata (fruits)

by no means easy to pick a way through them or to devise classifications into which they will fit neatly. Today garden roses are divided into five principal groups: Hybrid Teas, Floribundas, Dwarf Polyanthas, Ramblers and Climbers. To these may be added Hybrid Perpetuals, an old race largely superseded by the Hybrid Teas; Tea roses, beautiful but on the whole a little tender; China roses, with small, shapely flowers a little like some of the Floribundas, Hybrid Musks, shrub-like in character, and a number of old-fashioned roses such as Bourbons, Gallicas, Noisettes, Moss Roses, etc., which at one time were completely neglected but once again have many admirers.

Each of these classes has its own characteristics and uses. The Hybrid Teas are the big, shapely, often very fragrant roses that are everybody's favourite and the popular conception of what a rose really should be. They flower in summer and autumn and need a fair amount of pruning each February or March to keep them in full vigour.

The Floribundas are primarily garden roses; very free flowering but without the size or good shape of the Hybrid Teas. However, these are differences which are gradually being obliterated by cross breeding as many of the newest floribundas can only be distinguished from Hybrid Teas by the greater number and smaller size of their flowers. All need lighter pruning than the Hybrid Teas.

The Dwarf Polyanthas are bush roses with small, rosette flowers in big clusters. In style of flower they resemble the popular Ramblers such as Dorothy Perkins and Excelsa but without their great vigour and capacity to cover considerable areas of fence, trellis, arch or pergola.

The Climbing Roses have larger flowers than the Ramblers, sometimes quite as large as those of the Hybrid Teas, but they are less vigorous than the Ramblers and more suitable for growing on pillars or walls. Mermaid is a climbing rose, but a rather unusual one as it comes of different parentage than most. Its large, single yellow flowers are extremely beautiful and produced throughout the summer and autumn, but it is an intensely thorny rose and one that is rather difficult to increase. All these Climbing Roses need comparatively light pruning.

Light pruning is also the rule for most of the shrub roses and the old-fashioned kinds as well as for the species or unimproved wild roses many of which can be grown as shrubs and are of the greatest beauty. These species range from quite dwarf plants such as *Rosa spinosissima*, the Scotch or Burnet Rose, to giants such as *R. moschata*, the Musk Rose, and *R. multiflora* parent of many of the garden ramblers.

R. spinosissima is itself white, but it has many colour variations and has also produced hybrids of which the much more vigorous Fruhlingsgold, with semi-double creamy-yellow flowers, and Stanwell Perpetual, with double white or flesh pink flowers, are typical. *R. pimpinellifolia* is very similar to *R. spinosissima* and has a lovely pale yellow variety, *altaica*, which makes a first rate garden shrub 8 or 9 feet in height.

Streptosolen
jamesonii

Taxodium
distichum

Tropaeolum
speciosum

Tunica
saxifraga
flore-pleno

Teucrium rosmarinifolium

Tulipa praestans
'Fusilier'

Thuja occidentalis
'Rheingold'

Stokesia
laevis

Ulex europeus
flore-pleno

Thunbergia
alata

Tulipa
kauffmanniana

Tibouchina
semidecandra

Zauschneria
californica

Veratrum album

Vanda caerulea

Vallota
speciosa

Venidio-
Arctotis
hybrids

Zephyranthes
candida

Zygopetalum
mackaii

Ursinia
anethoides

Viburnum
rhytidophyllum

Zenobia
speciosa

The Musk Rose has produced a number of excellent hybrids notable for their late flowering. Penelope (Plate 20), Felicia and Cornelia are typical examples, all big, free-flowering bushes.

R. omeiensis and *R. sericea* have such large thorns that these become a decorative feature which is even more apparent in the form *R. omeiensis pteracantha*, often known as *R. sericea pteracantha* (Plate 20), which is actually grown more for its translucent thorns than for its flowers. *R. rugosa*, much used as a stock for standard roses, makes a good shrub or hedge and has some fine garden varieties such as the pale pink Frau Dagmar Hartopp (Plate 20), double white Blanc Double de Coubert and intense magenta Roseraie de l'Hay.

Canary Bird is another name for *R. xanthina spontanea* (Plate 20), a handsome shrub with arching sprays of single yellow flowers. *R. foliolosa* (Plate 20) is unique in the narrowness of its leaves and it makes a low spreading bush producing its single rose-red flowers for many weeks in summer.

R. alba is so named because of the grey colour of its leaves. It is a useful shrub with many garden varieties of which the lovely semi-double, shell pink Celestial (Plate 20) is probably the best. *R. rubrifolia*, has purplish-grey leaves.

The Moss Roses are so-called because of the moss-like spines with which their stems are covered. A hundred years ago they were among the most popular of garden roses and it is predominantly the old Victorian varieties, such as William Lobb (Plate 20) and Nuits de Young, that must be bought, few new varieties having been raised in our century.

There are roses such as *R. pomifera* and *R. moyesii* that are grown principally for their showy scarlet hips, and the sweet briar, *R. rubiginosa*, is cultivated for the fragrance of its foliage, particularly apparent in warm, damp weather.

All these wild roses and the garden varieties raised from them like good loamy soils, but many of them will put up with more lime in the soil than is tolerable to the hybrid teas. The species can be raised from seed or cuttings, the garden hybrids by cuttings or budding. Budding is the almost invariable method of propagation used for the Hybrid Teas, Floribundas and other highly developed garden races but many of the more vigorous kinds will grow equally well from cuttings and amateurs might well use this method more, both because of its ease and because it overcomes the problem of suckers. October is the best month during which to take cuttings and they can be rooted in a frame or in a sheltered place outdoors.

ROSCOEA

Unusual looking, fleshy-rooted herbaceous plants more suited to the rock garden than to the border. The most popular species, *Roscoea cautleoides* (Plate 20), grows about a foot high and produces short spikes of hooded, primrose-yellow flowers in early summer. *R. purpurea* is similar in height and opens its dull-purple flowers in late summer. Both need a soil rich in humus and porous without being dry.

109

Rosa rubrifolia

Rosa pomifera (fruits)

Rubus illecebrosus

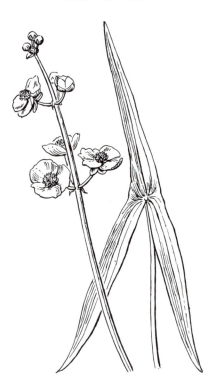

Sagittaria sagittifolia

Plenty of peat or leaf mould and sharp sand should be used in preparing a place for these plants which should be planted with the bulb-like rhizomes about 6 inches below soil level. They are increased by careful division in spring.

RUBUS *(Bramble)*

Gardeners are apt to think of the brambles solely in terms of the blackberry, loganberry and other utilitarian fruits, but there are, in addition, a number of highly ornamental shrubs of easy culture in any reasonable soil and open or even partially shaded position. Some, such as *Rubus biflorus*, *R. cockburnianus* and *R. lasiostylus*, are grown principally for their strong white or blue-white stems and are often referred to as Whitewash Brambles. Others, such as the large white-flowered *R. deliciosus* and double pink-flowered *R. ulmifolius bellidiflorus* (Plate 21), are grown for their flowers, and yet others, such as the Japanese Wineberry, *R. phoenicolasius* and the bushy, semi-herbaceous *R. illecebrosus*, are valued mainly for the decorative quality of their fruits. The last-named species is often known as the Strawberry-Raspberry, but it is a misleading name as, though the large red fruits do look rather like strawberries, the plant is a wild species and is not descended from either the strawberry or the raspberry.

Most brambles can be increased by careful division in autumn and all can be raised from seed.

RUTA *(Rue)*

Though several species of ruta are known in British gardens, only one is at all commonly seen and that is the Common Rue or Herb of Grace, *Ruta graveolens*. A compact, bushy, evergreen shrub, 2 to 3 feet high, it is valued for its rather ferny, aromatic, blue-grey foliage rather than for its sprays of yellow flowers in summer. Some varieties have better foliage colour than others and Jackman's Blue is a particularly good one. Rue thrives in light, well-drained soils and warm, sunny places, but is not really at all fussy. It benefits from an annual trimming with shears or secateurs in April to keep it neat and tidy. It can be increased by cuttings in summer or autumn. Similar in all its needs but nothing like so familiar as *R. chalapensis* (Plate 21). It might easily be mistaken for the Common Rue but has more freely-divided leaves and somewhat larger sprays of yellow flowers.

SAGITTARIA *(Arrow Head)*

Handsome herbaceous plants to be grown in pools or at the margins of slow-moving streams. The most popular is the Common Arrow Head, *Sagittaria sagittifolia*, a British plant and therefore of unquestionable hardiness. It will grow in water up to 18 inches deep, has broadly arrow-shaped, shining green leaves carried well above the water and, in summer, spikes of white and purple flowers which are double in the variety *flore-pleno* (Plate 21). Like other aquatics it is best planted in late spring or early summer. It can be increased by division stiffly erect spikes of small flowers which are greenish white in *Veratrum album* (Plate 24), nearly black in *V. nigrum* and light green in *V. viride*. All three are plants of unusual appearance and, as they are not difficult to grow, it is surprising that they remain so little known. They like good soil well supplied with humus. They can be raised from seed or by division in spring.

VIBURNUM *(Guelder Rose, Snowball Tree, Laurustinus)*

There is great variety in this useful and beautiful genus of shrubs or small trees which includes both deciduous and ever-green kinds. The common Guelder Rose, *Viburnum opulus*, is a familiar British native, a vigorous deciduous shrub 10 or 12 feet in height with flat heads of white flowers mostly small but surrounded by a ring of large flowers. In autumn this shrub produces heavy crops of brilliant scarlet berries, a little like red currants. It is a fine shrub but not much planted in gardens, probably because it is a native. Far more popular with gardeners is the variety known as *sterile* in which the flowers are sterile, and therefore produce no fruits, but make handsome amends for this deficiency by being all of the large type and arranged in a ball-like head for which reason it is called the Snowball Tree.

There is an Asiatic species, *V. tomentosum*, which has this same peculiarity of producing two forms, one with mostly fertile flowers surrounded by a ring of the large white flowers, the other producing nothing but sterile flowers in a globular head. Both are lovely and popular May flowering shrubs but in this instance the fertile form is, if anything, more beautiful then the sterile because of the way in which the flower clusters are produced all along the branches, one practically touching the next. There are two specially fine varieties of this fertile form of *V. tomentosum*, one named *mariesii*, the other Lanarth. The sterile form, popularly known as the Japanese Snowball Tree, is botanically *V. tomentosum plicatum*. All grow to 8 or 9 feet.

Several viburnums flower in winter and are so hardy that they will continue to flower even after quite severe frost. In many ways the most generally useful of these, because of its freedom, is *V. fragrans*, a 9 to 10 foot, rather erect shrub with apple-blossom pink flowers. *V. grandiflorum* is much like it but has larger flowers of a much deeper pink, and there is a good hybrid between the two, named *V. bodnantense*, which is inter-mediate in character. All are very fragrant.

Fragrance is also an outstanding quality of spring flowering *V. carlesii*, a fine shrub 4 or 5 feet high with clusters of white, pink-tinged flowers. It has also produced two good hybrids, *V. carlcephalum* with much larger flower heads and *V. burkwoodii* which is much taller than *V. carlesii* and has evergreen foliage.

Two evergreen viburnums remarkably contrasted for size are *V. davidii* and *V. rhytidophyllum* (Plate 24), the first a spread-ing shrub usually no more than 2 feet high, the second a large and quick growing shrub some 10 feet in height. Both are chiefly valued for their large dark green leaves which in *V. rhytidophyl-*

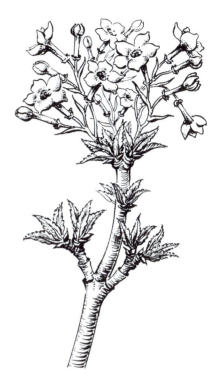

Viburnum fragrans

Viburnum carlesii

INDEX

to popular and catalogue names